LAW ENFORCEMENT CODE

AS A LAW ENFORCEMENT OFFICER, my fundamental duty is to serve mankind; to safeguard lives and property; to protect the innocent against deception, the peaceful against violence or disorder; and to respect the Constitutional rights of all men to liberty, equality and justice.

I WILL keep my private life unsullied as an example to all; maintain courageous calm in the face of danger, scorn, or ridicule; develop self-restraint; and be constantly mindful of the welfare of others. Honest in thought and deed in both my personal and official life, I will be exemplary in obeying the laws of the land and the regulations of my department. Whatever I see or hear of a confidential nature or that is confided to me in my official capacity will be kept ever secret unless revelation is necessary in the performance of my duty.

I WILL never act officiously or permit personal feelings, prejudices, animosities or friendships to influence my decisions. With no compromise for crime and with relentless prosecution of criminals, I will enforce the law courteously and appropriately without fear or favor, malice or ill will, never employing unnecessary force or violence and never accepting gratuities.

I RECOGNIZE the badge of my office as a symbol of public faith, and I accept it as a public trust to be held so long as I am true to the ethics of the police service. I will constantly strive to achieve these objectives and ideals, dedicating myself before God to my chosen profession . . . law enforcement.

FOUNDATIONS OF LAW ENFORCEMENT AND CRIMINAL JUSTICE

Robert G. Caldwell , B.S., M.A., Ph.D., LL.B.

William Nardini , B.A., M.A., Ph.D.

FOUNDATIONS OF LAW ENFORCEMENT AND CRIMINAL JUSTICE

BOBBS-MERRILL EDUCATIONAL PUBLISHING

Indianapolis

To LaMerle and Georgia Ann

The authors wish to thank the Ronald Press Company for permission to quote from the following books: *Criminology* by Robert G. Caldwell, copyright 1965, and *Juvenile Delinquency* by Robert G. Caldwell and James A. Black, copyright 1971.

The Bobbs-Merrill Company, Inc.
4300 West 62nd Street
Indianapolis, Indiana 46268

First Edition
First Printing 1977
Designed by Viki Webb
Library of Congress Cataloging in Publication Data
Caldwell, Robert Graham, 1904-
    Foundations of law enforcement and criminal justice.

    1. Criminal justice, Administration of—United States. 2. Law enforcement—United States. 3. Criminal procedure—United States. I. Nardini, William, 1929-   joint author. II. Title.
KF9223.C33   364'.973   76-46478
ISBN 0-672-61412-X

CONTENTS

132, 205

Preface

Never has education in law enforcement been so important as it is today. Gone are the days when a police recruit might be expected to assume his duties after having been given a gun, a badge, and a uniform and placed under the supervision of an experienced officer for a few weeks while on patrol. The problems of police work have become so difficult that now they can be effectively handled only by officers who have had special education and training.

Industrialization, urbanization, technological improvements, and the mobility and migration of populations have brought a very complex and mass-oriented society to America, generating overwhelming social problems and evoking laws and judicial decisions that are sometimes so involved they confound even the experts. In such a society, the police officer must have broad discretionary powers so that he can act quickly in the protection of life and property, but these powers must be guided by education and training if they are to be used intelligently, competently, and effectively. In fact, education and training are of the very essence of professionalization, the goal of all modern police planning.

In the furtherance of education and training in police work, this text introduces the reader to the nature of law enforcement and criminal justice, their major problems, the principal causes of these problems, and various proposals for their reduction. It includes, therefore, chapters on such matters as police organization and administration, the criminal law, the selection, education, and training of police officers, the operation of the patrol, the functions of criminal investigation, the regulation of traffic, the maintenance of police records, and the importance of planning. In each chapter, however, an effort is made to treat the subject matter from both the practical and academic points of view so that the text can be of use not only to the practitioner, but also to the academician and the general reader.

However, the text sees law enforcement as only one part of the broader system of criminal justice, for criminal justice also includes criminal prosecution and corrections and emphasizes that the functioning of each part of this system affects, and thereby strengthens or weakens, the other parts. So, for example, the police are in a strategic position to detect the causes of crime and delinquency and to prevent such acts. Their vigor and efficiency largely determine society's reaction to violations of the law, and the way in which they handle the offender may greatly affect the possibility of his rehabilitation. On the other hand, the police may be seriously hampered by court decisions that flout the code of morality, engender public distrust, and permit the convicted offender to escape his just deserts.

The text unequivocally takes the stand that the police must be professionalized, that, to this end, they must be administered in accordance with the highest standards, applicable to all under all circumstances, that they must be freed from the unreasonable controls imposed by the courts, so that the exercise of broad discretionary powers in law enforcement is possible, that they must be accepted as equal partners in the operation of the criminal justice system, and that their interests and point of view must be given due consideration if this system is to function effectively. In taking this stand, the text carefully examines the latest research on the causation of crime and delinquency, critically analyzes the operation of the courts and recent United States Supreme Court decisions, and explores some important aspects of the work of correctional agencies and institutions.

The text does not stop here, however. Recognizing that law enforcement agencies do not have the sole responsibility for the prevention of crime and delinquency, but that every part of society—indeed, every citizen—has this responsibility, it stresses the importance of developing an enlightened public opinion that will steadily and vigorously support the efforts of police officials and of encouraging citizen participation in the work of law enforcement. Does this mean that the text favors the establishment of a civilian board with the power to review the activities of the police department? The answer would be no if this board were authorized to interfere in any way with the department's authority over personnel management and discipline. The authors believe that this kind of interference would undermine and destroy the authority of the chief, open the door to the politics of pressure groups, and thus block the progress that is being made in the professionalization of police services. However, this does not mean that they are opposed to the creation of a board of distinguished citizens appointed by the chief or the police commissioner to consider complaints about police work and to make recommendations regarding the improvement of the department.

Thus, because of the range and depth of this text, it can be recommended not only for students intending to enter the fields of law enforcement and corrections and workers already active in these fields, but also for all other persons seeking useful information about the control and prevention of crime and delinquency.

The authors have drawn upon many resources in the preparation of this text, and they have indicated this indebtedness in the footnotes. In addition, they especially thank Professor Edmund W. Grosskopf of the Department of Criminology, Indiana State University, for carefully reading the entire manuscript and offering valuable suggestions for its improvement, and Miss Eula Van Meter and Miss Doris Marie McIntire for their excellent checking and typing of the manuscript.

Terre Haute, Indiana   Robert G. Caldwell
March, 1976   William Nardini

CHAPTER 1

HISTORY OF ANGLO-AMERICAN
LAW ENFORCEMENT

IMPORTANCE OF THE POLICE

No public agency or institution is of greater importance to the community than the police.[1] If this statement seems surprising, one need only consider these facts. The police are charged with the maintenance of order and the enforcement of the law. They must therefore act to regulate and protect the community with respect to public health, comfort, morals, safety, and prosperity. It is not surprising, then, that the police officer is usually the first point of contact between the citizen and the law. Indeed, for many persons, the police are the law, and for this reason their appearance, conduct, and effectiveness do much to destroy or create respect for the law.

Furthermore, the increasing complexity of our society, with its urbanization, industrialization, technological improvement, and mobility, has brought greater need for law and efficient police protection. The police, moreover, are in a strategic position to detect and reduce the causes of crime and delinquency and to prevent these acts.

Finally, if for no other reason, the police are important because they are so numerous and cost so much. In 1967, the President's Commission on Law Enforcement and Administration of Justice stated that about 420,000 people were working for approximately 40,000 separate law enforcement agencies, which were spending more than two-and-a-half billion dollars a year.[2] Burdened with increasing duties, the police forces in the big cities of the country have grown enormously. On October 31, 1975, New York City had 33,401

---

[1]Robert G. Caldwell, *Criminology* (New York: The Ronald Press Co., 1965), pp. 283, 284. The word "police" is used here in its broadest sense to include all law enforcement agencies.

[2]The President's Commission on Law Enforcement and Administration of Justice, *Task Force Report: The Police* (Washington, D.C.: Government Printing Office, 1967). p.1.

full-time employees in its police department, the largest in the nation; Chicago, 14,834; Los Angeles, 10,554; Philadelphia, 9,027; and Detroit, 6,017.[3] Moreover, the number of police and their cost would be even greater if all the communities in the United States were given adequate police service and protection.

COMPOSITION OF THE POLICE

Each political area in the United States may have its own police. Therefore various types of police agencies, having general or specialized functions, exist on all levels of government.

On the federal level, for example, some departments have their own investigative units, each of which is charged with enforcement of the particular laws over which its department has jurisdiction. Among these units we may note the Federal Bureau of Investigation of the Justice Department, the Immigration Border Patrol of the Justice Department, and the Secret Service Division of the Treasury Department. The Army and Navy also may serve as police forces during emergencies.

Some states maintain state police units that have authority to exercise general powers of law enforcement. Other states, although having statewide police organizations, limit their authority to patrolling highways, protecting life and property on them, and enforcing motor vehicle laws. A number of states have also established state bureaus of investigation, which operate as clearing houses for criminal identification, and, upon request, give assistance to local authorities. And in all states various departments have minor investigative units, each of which functions within a limited scope to enforce the particular laws with which its department deals. State militias also may perform police functions during emergencies.

On the local level, almost every political area has some kind of police. The county has a sheriff, who is assisted by as many deputies as he may appoint. Some counties have their own police forces, which either duplicate the sheriff's jurisdiction or virtually displace it. The township has its constable, the village or town its marshal or a very small police force, and the city its municipal police department. Furthermore, on the local level as on the state level, various depart-

---

[3]Federal Bureau of Investigation, *Uniform Crime Reports*, 1975 (Washington, D. C.: Government Printing Office, 1976), 246-54 Table 75.

ments and bureaus maintain minor investigative units which have limited police powers.

In addition to the public law enforcement agencies, there are various kinds of private police who are privately employed, financed, supervised, and controlled, although sometimes they are commissioned as public agents. Private police are used in a variety of ways. Industrial plants, hotels, department stores, railroads, bankers' associations, and insurance companies employ special agents to guard their properties and interests. In many small communities, merchants' associations employ night watchmen to protect their stores and office buildings. Private detective agencies furnish protection for race tracks, conventions, expositions, exhibits, entertainments, and various types of public assemblages.

It is apparent from the foregoing that there is no national police system in the United States and that law enforcement is largely in the hands of local governments. In fact—and this point should not be forgotten—a national police system, including all the police officers of the country, would be completely out of harmony with the principles of the Founding Fathers. With the memory of the despotism of centralized governments in Europe fresh in their minds, they created a federal government with limited, delegated powers and reserved most of the powers to the states and the people.

BASIC OBJECTIVES OF THE POLICE

The following are the basic objectives of the public police agencies that are authorized to exercise general powers of law enforcement:
1.   The prevention of crime and delinquency by helping to modify and change the conditions that produce them, by instilling respect for law and order, and by cooperating with other agencies in the promotion of the public welfare.
2.   The repression of the criminality and delinquency of persons so inclined by patrolling neighborhoods, inspecting premises, and keeping fully informed regarding the affairs of the community.
3.   The apprehension and identification of offenders and the accumulation of evidence against persons charged with crime and delinquency.
4.   The recovery of stolen property so as to reduce the cost of crime and to restrain those who, though not active criminals themselves, might benefit from the gains of crime and delinquency.

5. The regulation of people in their noncriminal activities, for
    example, by the direction of traffic and the enforcement of sanita-
    tion and licensing laws and ordinances[4].

    Let us now turn to an examination of the historical background of
the existing public police agencies in the United States. This will help
us to understand some of the problems involved in achieving the
basic objectives of the police and the differences of opinion regarding
the possible solutions of these problems.

ENGLISH FOUNDATIONS

The foundations of our law enforcement structure were laid in early
England, so that is where we must begin our examination. As far back
as the seventeenth century, France and other continental countries
had professional police forces of a sort. England, however, fearing
that these forces might bring the same kind of oppression to her that
they had so often caused on the continent, did not establish police
organizations, in the modern sense of the term, until the nineteenth
century. In fact, early England did not even have a permanent army of
paid soldiers that might have been used to enforce criminal laws,
because the cost of maintaining such a military organization was
considered too high.

For many years, therefore, in her efforts to enforce the law,
England relied largely on informers and the rewarding of private
citizens for making arrests. This somewhat makeshift method was
introduced during the reign of Alfred the Great (about 871-901). It
encouraged mutual responsibility among local groups of citizens
pledged to maintain law and order. Since every member of the group
was responsible not only for his own actions but also for those of his
neighbors, this method was called the "mutual pledge system." When
a crime was committed, each member was duty-bound to raise the
"hue and cry," collect his neighbors, and pursue the alleged criminal.
As an added incentive for law enforcement, these citizens had to pay a
fine if they did not apprehend the offender.

The groups upon which this mutual responsibility for police
action was placed were called "tithings," and each tithing was composed of ten families. Later, ten tithings were grouped together to

---

[4]Caldwell, pp. 285, 286.

become what was called the "hundred," that is, a group of one hundred families.

During the reign of Edward I (1272-1307), a genuine effort was made to create a more effective police system. The Statute of Winchester, enacted in 1285, preserved and codified the well-tried features of earlier systems and in particular reaffirmed the feature of local responsibility for policing a district. This was the only general public measure of any consequence enacted to regulate the policing of the country between the Norman Conquest in 1066 and the Metropolitan Police Act of 1829. As a result, for nearly six hundred years it laid down the basic principles of English law enforcement.

At this time the hundred was under the command of the constable, whose history can be traced back to the Anglo-Saxon period, which began about the middle of the fifth century. The constable, who was appointed by a local nobleman, was now given the additional duty of supervising the armor and equipment of the men of the hundred, who were responsible not only for the pursuit of law violators but also for military defense. Every township had its constable, and as the men of the hundred devoted themselves more and more to matters of defense, the constable became more and more involved in the pursuit of lawbreakers. Consequently, the ancient custom of "hue and cry" gradually declined and the constable began to emerge as England's first real police officer and the primary law enforcement agent in all the towns of the country. For many years, however, he continued to perform a great variety of duties, ranging all the way from the collection of taxes to the supervision of highways.

While Edward I was still king, another step was taken to strengthen the law enforcement structure of the country. This created the first official police forces in the large towns. Called the "watch and ward," these forces were responsible for protecting property against fire, guarding the gates of the city, and arresting alleged criminals. The "ward" was on duty during the day and the "watch" during the night, and as a result the larger towns were given round-the-clock protection.

After the constable had been put in charge of the hundred, hundreds were grouped to form a "shire," a geographical area equivalent to a county. Each shire, containing several hundreds, was placed under the supervision of a "shire-reeve" or sheriff. The sheriff was appointed by the Crown and was responsible to the local nobleman for the effective enforcement of the law in the shire, while the constable's authority remained limited to his original hundred. However, the sheriff soon moved beyond his supervisory role to participate in the pursuit and apprehension of violators of the law.

Like the office of constable, that of sheriff had roots which extended back into the Anglo-Saxon period. At that time the sheriff was, in the full sense of the word, the king's steward. Within the limits of his jurisdictional area, the shire, he acted with great authority in interpreting and enforcing the king's orders in civil, military, fiscal, and judicial affairs. The Norman Conquest merely tended to strengthen the foundations of the sheriff's office and to systematize its operation, and during the late eleventh and the twelfth century he wielded great power.

However, the development of the powers of the justice of the peace, which were considerably extended during the reign of Edward III (1327-1377), definitely contributed to the decline of the sheriff.[5] The justices of the peace, who were originally noblemen, were appointed by the king to assist the sheriff in policing the county, but they eventually assumed the local judicial functions formerly performed by the sheriff. Meanwhile the constable, who retained his authority over the hundred, became an assistant to the justice of the peace and was held responsible for supervising the night watchmen of the watch and ward, making inquiries into offenses, serving summonses, executing warrants, and taking charge of prisoners. Thus, with the development of the office of the justice of the peace, there began the formal separation between the judge and the police officer.

With the passing of years during the fourteenth century, more and more authority over law enforcement was lodged in the central government, and the justice of the peace, as an appointee of the king, exercised an increasing degree of control over the locally appointed constable. By the end of the century the constable no longer functioned independently as an official of the "mutual pledge system" but instead occupied a position definitely subordinate to that of the justice of the peace and served subject to his command. In this way was established the justice of the peace-constable pattern which tended to endure until the second quarter of the nineteenth century.

In the meantime the mutual pledge system continued to decline. Although citizens were required by law to take their turn at police work, they gradually evaded the service by hiring others to do the work for them. Even the constables employed deputies or substitutes,

---

[5]The growth of the office of coroner also took some work and duties from the sheriff.

but since these were usually ignorant and incompetent they, too, contributed to the undermining of the mutual pledge system.

Confronted with increasing problems during the seventeenth and eighteenth centuries, some cities experimented with various methods of policing, supporting them with assistance from a paid night watch force. Apparently, however, the night watch was not effective. It did little more than patrol the streets, from time to time crying out the hour of the night, the condition of the weather, and the reassuring words, "All is well."

These developments made it obvious that additional steps were needed to strengthen the machinery of law enforcement. Furthermore, the situation was worsening under the increasing impact of the Industrial Revolution, which was sending thousands of families into factory towns and causing unprecedented economic dislocations and social disorders. Responding to this need of better law enforcement, both private organizations and Parliament took action. A number of civic associations, like the Bow Street Horse and Foot Patrol, were formed to police the streets and highways leading out of London, and statutes were enacted creating public offices which later came to be known as police offices. Each of these offices was occupied by three paid justices of the peace, who were authorized to employ paid constables.

By the beginning of the nineteenth century nine police offices had been established within the metropolitan area of London, but apparently little effort was made to coordinate their activities. This breakdown in coordination was reportedly caused by the refusal of one office to communicate with another for fear the other might claim credit for the detection and apprehension of an offender. This weakness was especially damaging to law enforcement in London, where the police seemed powerless to control the activities of highwaymen, bank robbers, thieves, and marauding juveniles. To assist the police, gaslights were placed on the streets of London in the early part of the nineteenth century in the hope that they would discourage thieves and other lawbreakers.

Finally in 1829, at the urging of Sir Robert Peel, Parliament passed an "Act for Improving the Police In and Near the Metropolis," establishing the first organized British metropolitan police force. However, an area in the heart of London, known as the City of London, was not included in the jurisdiction of the metropolitan police, and today the City of London still has a separate police force.

The passage of this Metropolitan Police Act was a milestone in the history of the police in England. Indeed, it may be said that modern policing in England began with this act.

Sir Robert Peel was a man of vision, and the fundamental principles that he espoused in his efforts to reform the police were not only sound and enduring, but little different from those advocated by modern police authorities. For example, he believed that the police must be organized along military lines and placed under government control. He believed that police strength must be deployed in accordance with the requirements of time and area. He believed that the careful selection and training of police personnel are vitally important and that the proper conduct and good appearance of the individual officer are indispensable. He believed also that policemen should be initially employed on a probationary basis, that adequate police records must be maintained, and that police headquarters should be centrally located and made easily accessible to the people.

The metropolitan police, the first English police to wear a definite uniform, were organized like a military unit. The men, who were later called "Bobbies" in honor of Sir Robert, were commanded by two magistrates, who were later known as commissioners. The commissioners were given administrative but not judicial duties, but the ultimate responsibility for equipping, paying, maintaining, and, to a certain degree, supervising the Bobbies was vested in the Home Secretary. The Secretary, in turn, was held accountable to Parliament for his exercise of authority over the new police force. Although at first this force suffered from low salaries, shortage of manpower, and political interference, it proved so effective in suppressing crime and apprehending criminals that within five years the provinces, which were troubled with increasing crime and violent riots, asked London for assistance in policing their areas.

Shortly after the passage of the Metropolitan Police Act, Parliament began to pass a series of police reform bills. One of these, the Municipal Corporations Act of 1835, established police forces in the cities and towns of England. Another, passed in 1839, empowered justices of the peace to create police forces in the counties. A third, the County and Borough Police Act of 1856, made it compulsory for each county to establish paid police forces.

It is generally agreed that Sir Robert Peel made a great contribution to the development of a modern police system in England. It is agreed also that the reforms he initiated provided a model for other countries, including the United States, to use in the improvement of their law enforcement machinery.

As regular police forces developed in England, the justices of the peace voluntarily relinquished their law enforcement duties and limited themselves to making decisions on questions of law. Thus came to an end the justice of the peace-constable system which had served England for so long.[6]

AMERICAN DEVELOPMENTS

When the English colonists came to America during the seventeenth and eighteenth centuries, they brought with them the law enforcement structure of the mother country. The offices of sheriff and constable were easily transplanted to the new soil of the colonies. The constable became responsible for law enforcement in the towns and the sheriff for that in the counties. During the colonial period the Crown-appointed governors gave these offices to large landowners who were loyal to the king. After the Revolution the tendency was to select sheriffs and constables by popular vote.

URBAN POLICE

In many of the colonial cities, the British constable-night watch system was adopted. Thus, as early as 1636, Boston had night watchmen as well as a military guard, and New York and Philadelphia soon developed a similar night watch force. The New York night watchmen became known as the "Rattlewatch" because they carried rattles while on duty to inform citizens of their watchful presence.

As towns in the United States grew in size and population during the first half of the nineteenth century, their constables could not cope with the increasing disorders. Lawlessness spread throughout the country, as it had under the same system in England years before. New York, Philadelphia, Baltimore, and Cincinnati became "crime-ridden," and in some cities roving young rowdies threatened to overwhelm the crude police forces. Efforts were made to improve the situation, but most of them were devoted to relatively unimportant

---

[6]The President's Commission on Law Enforcement and Administration of Justice, pp. 3-5; Bruce Smith, *Police Systems in the United States* (New York: Harper and Brothers, Publishers, 1960), pp. 66-70; Leon Radzinowicz, *A History of English Criminal Law and Its Administration from 1750* (New York: The Macmillan Co., 1957), Vol. II, pp. 33-167, 403, 404; Thomas A. Critchley, *A History of Police in England and Wales, 900-1966* (London: Constable and Company, Ltd., 1967); W. L. Melville Lee, *A History of Police in England* (Montclair, N.J.: Paterson Smith Publishing Corporation, 1971).

matters or wasted on an overcautious approach to questions that demanded vigorous action. Patrols were redistributed and new ways of selecting watchmen were tried. Various methods were used to reduce political interference without arousing popular distrust of armed and disciplined police forces, for it was widely assumed that a strong, professional police department would endanger freedom and democracy.

Eventually, however, many cities, like those in England, began to develop municipal police forces to replace the constable-night watch system. Philadelphia was one of the first to move in this direction in 1833, but its force functioned for only a short time. The ordinance that provided for a day force of twenty-four men and a night watch of one hundred twenty was soon repealed. A few years later, in 1838, Boston organized a day police force to supplement its night watch, and other cities soon took similar action. However, some serious problems developed in the operation of these early "two-force" police systems. Each force was under a separate administration and in the absence of proper coordination misunderstandings, rivalry, and jealousy tended to alienate one force from the other.

In 1844 the New York legislature, recognizing the weaknesses of the "two-force" system, passed a law that authorized the creation of a unified day and night police force. Thus the separate night watch was abolished and the foundation was laid for America's first modern police department. Not long after this Boston consolidated its night watch with the day force, and other cities, following the New York model, soon unified their police forces. By the 1870's the largest cities in the country had unified "full-time" police forces, and by the early 1900's virtually all cities of any importance had adopted this kind of system. Gradually these forces were placed under the control of a chief or commissioner, who was often appointed by the mayor, sometimes with the consent of the city council and sometimes elected by the people.

Despite these moves to strengthen America's law enforcement structure, serious problems continued to plague the police, and many of them still persist. Salaries were too low to attract a sufficient number of well-qualified candidates. Departments were hampered by manpower shortages. Administrative policies were vacillating and indecisive. Methods were crude and inadequate. Political corruption was undermining the vitality of many forces, and police posts were constantly changing hands, with political "fixers" often dictating the price and conditions of each change. As one would expect as a result of these factors, the police were not respected, not progressive, and not notably successful.

In an attempt to reduce these problems, local administrative boards were created to assume the control previously exercised over police affairs by mayors and city councils. Unfortunately, this move, which was designed primarily to take the police out of politics, was unsuccessful, largely because the judges, lawyers, and local businessmen who composed the boards were not expert in handling complex police problems.

As the nineteenth century came to a close, another attempt was made to reform the administrative machinery of the police. Noting that police problems were especially acute in urban areas, the state legislatures, which were controlled by rural representatives, enacted laws creating state boards to administer the operation of local police departments. For several important reasons, this move met with little success. Although it was designed to eliminate politics from law enforcement, it merely substituted state politics for local politics. For example, state control was not uniformly applied but directed primarily at the larger cities in order to insure rural domination in public affairs. Furthermore, it introduced the thorny issue of home rule. The state boards were not responsible to the local citizens who continued to pay for their police service, and when state and city governments were not allied politically, or when the policies of the board were not in harmony with the views of the local populations, the resulting conflicts seriously interfered with the effective operation of police departments. Consequently, the hand of the state was generally withdrawn under pressure for home rule. However, in some cities in a few states (for example, in Missouri, Maryland, Massachusetts, Maine, and New Hampshire) a reminder of this once widespread development is still to be found in the present control of police forces by the state.

Although police departments continued to grow in size and function during the last half of the nineteenth century, little study was made of the significant social changes that were occurring in American society or of the way these social changes were affecting police work. Nevertheless, a few constructive innovations were introduced. In some cities civil service proved helpful in reducing political interference. In some cities merit employment and promotion were adopted, and in the early decades of the twentieth century police training schools were organized in some cities, though on a somewhat modest scale. Even so, it was not until the 1940's and especially the

1950's that the movement to establish recruit training programs made important gains.

Many other important improvements have been made in law enforcement during the past few decades. Some cities, counties, and states have already greatly increased the efficiency of their police through reorganization and the introduction of modern techniques for detecting and apprehending offenders. Many others are now undertaking similar modernization. But in spite of these improvements the professionalization of America's urban police forces is being impeded by a number of perennial problems.[7] Among them are political interference and corruption, the overlapping of responsibilities and the duplication of effort of many independent agencies, an inadequate number of sufficiently qualified personnel, unattractive salaries and working conditions, and insufficient public support.[8]

RURAL AND SUBURBAN POLICE

The offices of sheriff, constable, and town marshal still exist in the United States. Every county has its sheriff, and in all but a few instances he still exercises his ancient police powers, although as a rule, unless a town or city requests his services, he does so only in the unincorporated areas of the county. Nevertheless, serious difficulties interfere with the efficient operation of his office. Since he is usually selected by popular election, he is naturally and inevitably immersed in partisan politics. Never do the formal qualifications for office go beyond such elementary matters as age, residence, and citizenship. Usually the term of office runs for only two or four years, and sometimes the occupant may not succeed himself. Once in office, an inefficient sheriff can feel quite secure, for he can be removed only for moral turpitude or malfeasance, and even then only by the operation of complex legal machinery. Since his term in office may be limited to a few years, the sheriff tends to cling to his private occupation, and so while discharging his public duties he may also, for example, engage in farming or run some small business. He seldom has had any previous experience in police work, and even if he has his many other duties limit the use of it.

Almost everywhere in the United States the sheriff has the re-

---

[7]Police problems will be analyzed in detail in succeeding chapters as the various aspects of police work are examined.

[8]The President's Commission on Law Enforcement and Administration of Justice, pp. 5-7; Smith, pp. 104-106.

sponsibility for the service of civil process and the management of the county jail. Furthermore, in some counties the fee system provides the sheriff with all or part of his compensation and so tends to direct his efforts into his more lucrative tasks and away from his unpleasant police duties. In fact, many sheriffs rely heavily on the fees which they receive for the performance of almost every official act. These fees may sometimes reach unbelievable amounts, making the sheriff the best-paid public official in the county and building his position into the most desirable "political plum" in the state.

Some counties are now trying to overcome the inherent weaknesses of the sheriff's office. Deputies have been employed for regular patrol work, modern means of transportation and communication have been adopted, and training programs have been initiated. In some cases these efforts have been very productive, but in many counties the sheriff system has already collapsed. Untrained personnel, short terms, political domination, public distrust, the increasing complexity of rural life, and the encroachment of organized crime have so handicapped the office of sheriff that it has become increasingly ineffective as a law enforcement agency. In some counties the situation is now so serious that the sheriff has to receive help from urban, state, and federal police.[9]

Where the constable still functions, he is an officer of a town or township. Selected by popular vote or casual appointment, he usually does not have to meet any standards except those of residence and citizenship. Rarely has he had any experience or training that will help him in the performance of his duties. He almost always derives his sole compensation from fees, which he receives for a variety of services, but these fees amount to much less than those received by the sheriff. Consequently, the constable is strictly a part-time officer who must depend on private sources for most of his income. Since he receives no compensation for doing police work, he tends to devote his time to other duties, such as the service of civil process, collecting taxes, and issuing notices of local elections.

It now appears that the constable has outlived his usefulness and that the office might be abolished without doing any harm to the administration of justice. In fact, the office has already disappeared in many sections of the country, where its work has been taken over by regular organized town police.[10]

---

[9]Caldwell, pp. 287, 288.
[10]Ibid., p. 288

The town marshal and the village policeman, who are still serving in some parts of the country, have been subjected to the same
criticisms that have been directed against the constable. As in the case
of the latter, they are almost always untrained, dominated by partisan
politics, poorly paid, and employed on a part-time basis. The result
has been that both offices command little respect, often remain vacant
for long periods, and provide little police protection.[11]

County police forces have been organized in some areas where
the sheriff-constable system has failed. Sometimes these police function as an integral part of the sheriff's office; sometimes they serve
under other public authorities, such as the county board or the county
judge.[12] Nevertheless, the average number of law enforcement officers serving on the county level remains small. In fact, in 1966 only
about 200 counties of the 3,050 in the United States had a sheriff's staff
of more than fifty officers.[13]

STATE POLICE

The states have the primary constitutional power to maintain
order within their own boundaries, and all of them have exercised this
power by enacting broad criminal codes, which have delegated most
of the responsibility for law enforcement to the local governments.
Even so, such conditions as the increasing mobility of population, the
continuing inadequacy of local policing by constables and sheriffs,
and the inability or unwillingness of urban police forces to pursue law
violators beyond their own jurisdictional limits have convinced state
legislatures of the need of statewide police forces.

The Texas Rangers were the earliest form of state police to appear
in the United States. Their history dates from the days of the Texas
Republic. In 1835 three companies of Texas Rangers were authorized
by the provisional government of Texas to engage in military service
on the Mexican border. For many years, however, the Rangers were
used only as a border patrol.

In 1865 Massachusetts appointed a few "state constables" who
were given general police powers to be exercised anywhere in the
state. One might say, therefore, that Massachusetts was the first state
to create a general state police force. During the early years of the

---

[11]Ibid., pp. 288, 289.
[12]Smith, pp. 71-103.
[13]The President's Commission on Law Enforcement and Administration
of Justice, p. 9.

twentieth century Connecticut, Arizona, and New Mexico organized specialized state police forces, but not until 1905, when Pennsylvania created its State Constabulary, did the United States acquire its first modern state police system authorized to enforce all state laws. Although New York and Michigan established state police units in 1917, the movement to create such agencies did not gain much momentum until after World War I. Then, within a few years, West Virginia, New Jersey, and Rhode Island enacted laws for this purpose. Today every state except Hawaii has some form of state police, but most states have not authorized their units to exercise general powers of law enforcement.

State police agencies operate under the leadership of an executive appointed by the governor (sometimes with the consent of the state legislature) and in most states serving at the governor's pleasure. Most state police units are not under civil service, and in some the administrative head has complete authority to select, promote, discipline, and control the rank and file. However, the best organizations require the applicant to pass physical and mental examinations, a character investigation, and an oral interview, and most of them emphasize both recruit and in-service training. In general, therefore, the state police have been better selected and trained than the local police and in no small degree are free from the handicap of "politics."

In the fully developed state police departments, like those of Pennsylvania, Massachusetts, New York, New Jersey, and some other states, uniformed state troopers patrol highways and roads and have authority to enforce all state laws. Usually they may not do so in municipalities unless local authorities request their assistance, but when pursuing offenders they may go anywhere within the state, regardless of city or county boundaries, in order to make arrests. Equipped with modern means of transportation and communication, they can now provide protection for large areas that formerly were comparatively isolated, and when given full authority they become the most important police agency in rural areas and to a great extent supersede the sheriff-constable system.

Nevertheless, the establishment of state police agencies has not been without opposition. Organized labor has condemned the state police as a tool of the employer and a threat to legitimate labor activity. Sheriffs have feared that the state police may crowd out all other law enforcement officers in rural areas. Some citizens' groups have contended that the state police may develop into an instrument of oppression like the Ogpu of Soviet Russia or the Gestapo of Nazi

Germany. Despite this opposition, however, the state police have become an important law enforcement agency throughout the United States, and all signs point to their continued development and expansion.[14]

FEDERAL POLICE

As you have learned, general law enforcement is reserved by the Constitution to the several states and through them to their political subdivisions, the counties, cities, towns, villages, and townships. Furthermore, the Supreme Court has ruled that there are no common law offenses against the federal government, and so the powers of the federal police are limited to the enforcement of federal statutes. The states, therefore, constitute the primary agencies of crime control. Even so, the law enforcement responsibilities of the federal government have continued to grow, although in a sporadic and highly specialized way.

Actually, federal law enforcement began as early as 1789, when the Revenue Cutter Service was established to assist in the prevention of smuggling. Other important steps were taken in 1836, when Congress authorized the Postmaster General to pay salaries to agents charged with investigation of infringements involving postal matters, and later when it passed legislation regarding internal revenue investigation and narcotics control. Then, in 1868, Congress authorized the creation of a force of twenty-five detectives. This force was increased in 1915, and in 1924 J. Edgar Hoover organized the Federal Bureau of Investigation in the Justice Department.

During the twentieth century the passage of an increasing number of federal laws has greatly expanded the law enforcement responsibilities of federal agencies, especially those of the Federal Bureau of Investigation. For example, its work has rapidly grown as a result of the enactment of legislation dealing with such matters as violations of the antitrust laws, bankruptcy frauds, crimes on the high seas, crimes on government reservations, kidnapping, treason, espionage, white slave traffic, drugs, the transportation of stolen motor vehicles from one state to another, gambling, and civil rights.

However, over the years this unsystematic growth of federal agencies has produced a fragmentation of federal police powers, an

---

[14]Caldwell, pp. 300-302; The President's Commission on Law Enforcement and Administration of Justice, pp. 6, 8.

overlapping of jurisdiction, and a confusion and rivalry that have interfered with administrative efficiency. Furthermore, the interlacing of law enforcement activities with others of a varied nature makes it difficult to determine which agencies are primarily of a police character. For example, the Coast Guard, which patrols the ocean and lake shores of the United States, has been given general powers of criminal law enforcement and is a police agency with broad statutory jurisdiction. Yet the Coast Guard is not a civil police agency in the full sense of the term, because its policies, methods, and procedures are closely related to those of the Army and Navy and in the event of war its control is automatically transferred from the Department of Transportation to the Navy. In fact, in emergencies the Army and Navy also may act as police forces, and many other governmental units, such as the Public Health Service and various bureaus of the Departments of Agriculture and Commerce, have certain police characteristics.

However, there are some major federal police agencies of a civil or non-military character which enforce penal statutes of general application throughout the domain of the federal government. These agencies, which do the greater part of the law enforcement work of the federal government, are located in the Treasury and Justice Departments and the United States Postal Service. Those in the Treasury Department include the Bureau of Internal Revenue, the Bureau of Customs, and the Secret Service. Those in the Justice Department are the Drug Enforcement Administration, the Immigration Border Patrol, and the Federal Bureau of Investigation. The Office of Postal Inspection Service is under the direction of the Assistant Postmaster General and is concerned with all violations of the postal laws.

The work of some of these agencies might well be consolidated in one governmental unit, and greater coordination should be introduced throughout the federal law enforcement service. In general, however, the work of the federal police is of a high quality, and its specialists rank among the best in the world.[15]

DECENTRALIZATION OF POLICE POWER

In 1967 there were 40,000 separate law enforcement agencies on federal, state, and local levels of government in the United States.

---

[15]Caldwell, pp. 303-309; The President's Commission on Law Enforcement and Administration of Justice, pp. 6-8. More information regarding the federal police will be presented in Chapter III.

However, these agencies were not evenly distributed over the three levels, for law enforcement is primarily a responsibility of local governments. In fact, there were only fifty of these agencies on the federal level and two hundred on the state level. The remainder were on the local level: 3,050 in counties, 3,700 in cities, and 33,000—the great majority—in boroughs, towns, and villages. A good example of the multiplicity of law enforcement agencies is to be found in DuPage and Cook Counties in Illinois, which encompass much of metropolitan Chicago. In 1967, in addition to the city of Chicago, these two counties contained one hundred nineteen municipalities. Thus, because local autonomy in law enforcement is still firmly established in the United States, the power for maintaining public order and enforcing the law is extremely decentralized, and this is accentuated by the fact that a police officer's authority for law enforcement is usually limited to a single jurisdiction.

As a result, law enforcement in the United States suffers from needless duplication of efforts, overlapping of jurisdiction, lack of coordination in administrative policies, and inadequacies within individual police units. Sincere, competent police administrators face serious difficulties in their battle with the modern motorized criminal, who uses municipal, county, and state borders to serve his own ends. When he strikes, the police in one jurisdiction must frequently rely on the cooperation of police in other jurisdictions to secure his arrest. This is usually given without hesitation, and prearranged roadblocks and sending out general alarms over a wide area by means of modern systems of communication have proved very effective in apprehending criminals.

Even so, cooperation, though essential, is not enough. The lack of a coordinated command and standardized procedures often creates confusion among cooperating police units and renders their efforts fruitless. Consequently, several methods have been developed to achieve coordination. One is the regional police organization, which has been recommended for metropolitan areas. Organizations of this kind, involving the coordination and some consolidation of police agencies, are now functioning in the metropolitan areas of Atlanta, Georgia, and Miami, Florida.

Another method for accomplishing coordination is the interstate compact. Article I, Section 10, of the Constitution provides that states may enter into compacts with the consent of Congress. In pursuance of this provision, Congress, by the Interstate Compact Bill of 1934, gave consent in advance to all states to form pacts in the field of crime prevention and law enforcement. Accordingly, the states have entered into a number of such compacts. One of these is the extradition law, which simplifies the procedure by which a state can secure an offender who has fled to another state. Another is the attendance-of-witnesses law, which improves the method for securing out-of-state witnesses. Still another is the fresh pursuit law, which permits an officer in pursuit of a felon (that is, in fresh pursuit) to cross the boundary line into any state that has passed the law in order to make an arrest.

In addition, some proposals go beyond cooperation and coordination and recommend consolidation of certain police agencies into larger units. These include the following:

1. All county, town, and small municipal forces should be consolidated into a single police agency having county-wide jurisdiction. Some counties have moved in this direction by the creation of county police forces. This kind of consolidation would certainly improve the police services in the counties adopting it. However, the taxpayers in small cities would probably not want to assume the additional financial burden involved, even though it might exist only in the short run, and the police departments in these cities might not like to surrender their separate existences.

2. All county, town, and municipal forces, both large and small, in metropolitan areas should be consolidated in a single metropolitan district police force vested with district-wide jurisdiction. This proposal faces almost insurmountable constitutional obstacles in metropolitan areas where two or more states are involved. However, it is entirely feasible in metropolitan areas that are within the borders of a single state, and some steps toward consolidation have been taken in various ways in a few such areas, as in Atlanta, Georgia, and Miami, Florida.

3. The public police agencies of a state should be consolidated and placed under the control of a centralized state administration. Many rural areas are already receiving most of their police protection and services from state police units. In some states where this is being done, the transition to a consolidated police organization for all rural areas might be feasible. However, many experts in the police field oppose the inclusion of cities and towns in this plan on the ground that it would contribute to an excessive centralization of power on the state level, in disregard of the fact that the fundamental problems of law enforcement call for solutions on the local level.

4. All police agencies of the country should be consolidated into a national police force under centralized federal control. This proposal has little support among police authorities. It involves a complete violation of the principles of our form of constitutional government, which call for the maintenance of a system of checks and balances in a federal union of states. Indeed, the late J. Edgar Hoover, for many years Director of the Federal Bureau of Investigation and a strong advocate of vigorous law enforcement, opposed any further centralization of police power in a state or federal agency and believed that a consolidation of police power in the federal government would be a distinct danger to representative government in America.[16] At present, some police authorities fear that laws recently enacted by Congress which provide for federal grants-in-aid to state and local governments for law enforcement purposes will lead to increased federal control of police agencies throughout the country. Similar legislation, they argue, has already tended to produce this kind of control in the fields of health, education, and welfare.

The future development of American police agencies will probably not follow any one particular pattern but instead will vary from area to area and state to state. In some states, a single police force for all rural areas and operating under centralized state control may eventually be established. On the other hand, the large police departments of the great cities will probably maintain their separate existences, but elsewhere consolidations at the county level can be expected, and in the long run these should bring improved service at a lower cost.[17]

---

[16]John Edgar Hoover, "The Basis of Sound Law Enforcement," *The Annals of the American Academy of Political and Social Science*, CCXCI (Jan., 1954), pp. 39-42.

[17]The President's Commission on Law Enforcement and Administration of Justice, pp. 7-9.

CHAPTER II

THE CAUSATION OF
CRIME AND DELINQUENCY

MAGNITUDE OF THE PROBLEM

During 1975 over eleven million serious crimes[1] were reported to law enforcement agencies in the United States. This represented an increase of ten percent in these crimes since 1974. In other words, 5,282 serious crimes per 100,000 inhabitants were reported during 1975, and thus it appears that the risk of being a victim of these crimes increased thirty-three percent since 1970.

These statistics, drawn from the Uniform Crime Reports,[2] forcibly bring to our attention the enormity of the crime problem in the United States. Although the primary purpose of these reports, as they explain, is to provide a reliable fund of nationwide criminal statistics for administrative and operational use by law enforcement agencies and executives,[3] their "crimes known to the police," in spite of certain limitations,[4] do provide the best available index of crime in the United States.

The *Uniform Crime Reports* may not give us an entirely accurate picture of the crime problem in our country, but whatever the size and nature of the problem may be, there is no question that the best way to

---

[1]The term "serious crimes" includes murder, non-negligent manslaughter, forcible rape, robbery, aggravated assault, burglary, larceny, and auto theft. Murder, non-negligent manslaughter, forcible rape, robbery, and aggravated assault comprised 9 percent of the serious crimes reported to law enforcement agencies during 1975—a 5 percent increase in these crimes since 1974.

[2]Federal Bureau of Investigation, *Uniform Crime Reports*, 1975 (Washington, D.C.: Government Printing Office, 1976), pp. 10, 11

[3]Ibid., p. 2.

[4]The use of the *Uniform Crime Reports* as an index of crime has received considerable criticism. For an analysis of some of this criticism, see Robert G. Caldwell and James A. Black, *Juvenile Delinquency* (New York: The Ronald Press Co., 1971), pp. 52-57.

reduce it is to use the knowledge we have regarding its causation. We shall now turn to a brief examination of this knowledge.

PERSONAL INFLUENCES

HEREDITY

The total of characteristics transmitted from one generation to another through the germ plasm is called "heredity." Although it brings to each generation all the anatomical and physiological materials out of which the human body is made, it does not completely determine man's behavior, for man's original nature is greatly modified by social experience. However, heredity does furnish potentialities and does impose limits, and so it affects man's development.

How much of man comes from heredity and how much comes from environment? This question, unfortunately, cannot be completely answered even by an intensive study of the individual case, for too many obstacles stand in the way of securing an answer. For one thing, the human genetic system is very complex. Further, even during the prenatal period the threads of heredity are already inextricably interwoven with those of the environment. Since much of man's heredity remains latent in recessive genes, a normal person may carry recessive defective genes that may appear in his children. A certain kind of defect, for example feeblemindedness, may be caused by heredity in one person and by the environment in another. Again, some hereditary characteristics appear only gradually through the process of maturation, and their nature is thus obscured by environmental influences.

Thus we must conclude that the influence of heredity in human behavior, whether the latter is law-abiding or criminal, cannot be precisely measured. However, this does not mean that heredity can be disregarded in the study of the causation of crime and delinquency, any more than environmental influences can be disregarded, simply because we cannot measure them precisely. Indeed, in a particular case heredity may be the major influence in an individual's behavior, whether it be criminal or not.

RACE

A race is a group of individuals who have in common certain hereditary characteristics. On the basis of certain physical characteristics, races have been classified into three principal divisions, the Caucasoid, the Mongoloid, and the Negroid.

Does the fact that races have different physical characteristics mean that they have also different innate capacities and abilities? This question has caused a great controversy and as yet has not received a complete answer. However, even if we could conclusively prove that racial inequality does exist, its influence would have to be seen in its interaction with other influences. Like any other single influence, it could not inevitably cause crime and delinquency, although it might be a very important influence in a particular case.

Entirely apart from the question of innate racial differences, the physical characteristics of a race, as measured by cultural values, do affect what it is and can be in any society, and thus indirectly affect the nature and extent of its law violations. In any event, regardless of the influence race may have in the process of causation, this much is certain: The amount of crime and delinquency of the Negro in the United States is clearly out of proportion to his numbers in the population.

SEX AND AGE

More than five times as many males as females were arrested during 1974, even though female arrests increased four percent and male arrests only two percent. While females are arrested for a great variety of crimes, during 1975 about 75 percent of them were arrested for only ten different kinds of offenses: larceny, assault, embezzlement and fraud, prostitution and commercialized vice, violation of narcotic drug laws, driving under the influence of alcohol, violation of liquor laws, drunkenness, disorderly conduct, and being a runaway.

During 1975 persons under 15 years of age constituted nine percent of total police arrests; persons under 18 years of age, 26 percent; and persons under 21 years of age, 42 percent. Furthermore, persons under 18 made up 55 percent of the arrests for auto theft, 53 percent of the arrests for burglary, 49 percent of the arrests for larceny, 34 percent of the arrests for robbery, 18 percent of the arrests for forcible rape, 18 percent of the arrests for aggravated assault, and 10 percent of the arrests for murder and non-negligent manslaughter.[5]

---

[5]Federal Bureau of Investigation, *Uniform Crime Reports*, 1975, p. 188, Table 35; p. 190, Table 37; p. 191, Table 38.

Thus it can be seen that sex and age affect both the amount and the nature of law violations, but they do so in interaction with other influences. There is no reason to believe that the female is inherently "better" and therefore inherently less criminal than the male. The biology of woman, which gives her the function of bearing children and in general makes her physically weaker, operates not alone but in interaction with the traditions and customs of our society to cause the differences between the sexes in law violations. In the United States the female is still more closely supervised and protected than the male and is concerned primarily with domestic affairs. Consequently, she is placed in fewer situations conducive to crime and delinquency, and her peculiar interests are reflected in her infractions of the law.

In the same way age must be seen as it interacts with the cultural influences in a society. Childhood, adolescence, adulthood, and old age have different meanings in different cultures, and the duties, responsibilities, and rights of each vary from society to society. Obviously, certain acts require the agility and daring of youth, whereas others call for the skill and judgment of maturity, and physiological changes involve difficulties of adjustment regardless of the cultures. Nevertheless, whether the act committed is defined as lawful or criminal will depend upon the culture of the society in which the individual seeks adjustment.[6]

ANATOMICAL AND PHYSIOLOGICAL CHARACTERISTICS

Body build, physical defects, abnormalities and disorders, glandular problems, and so on may cause troublesome behavioral problems, but even when they do the result is not necessarily crime or delinquency. For example, the individual reacts to body build in terms of the meaning it has in his life. But when an individual has a body build that is considered unattractive by his culture he does not necessarily seek relief from his tortured feelings by violating the law. On the contrary, he may learn to live with his problem, find relief from his frustrations and bitterness through some lawful adjustment, or even be driven to great heights of ambition and success in some lawful business or profession. And so it may be in the case of any individual who has a physical handicap. Obviously many persons who have handicaps violate the law, but so do many normal, healthy persons. Moreover, we do not know how many of the afflicted persons are

---

[6]Robert G. Caldwell, Criminology (New York: The Ronald Press Co., 1965), pp. 226-28.

either law-abiding or law-violating. Thus, even though a physical defect, abnormality, or disorder may be a contributing or even a major factor in causing an individual to violate the law, we do not have enough knowledge to generalize about the importance of these conditions and their interaction with other factors in the total causation of crime and delinquency.[7]

PERSONALITY

The term "personality" here is defined as the totality of the characteristics of the individual. Thus it may be said to be the unique combination of heredity and environment brought to a focus in the individual. Functioning through the satisfaction of its needs, the personality is developed, nourished, and organized or frustrated, distorted, and disorganized as those needs are satisfied or not. These needs, which are largely organic at birth, become increasingly social as the individual moves more and more into relationships with others, but throughout life personal and environmental obstacles interfere with their satisfaction and cause personality conflicts and pain.

Sometimes the individual handles these conflicts satisfactorily on a factual basis. Sometimes changes in the situation remove conflicts. Many conflicts persist, however, and the individual strives to adjust to them by using such mechanisms as repression, daydreaming, regression, sublimation, rationalization, compensation, and projection. All of these are normal devices and are employed every day by normal persons to reduce tensions and relieve anxiety, although the individual often may be completely or partially unaware that he is doing so. Used excessively, however, such mechanisms may twist the personality and push the individual into some form of mental disease, and although they usually do not lead to crime and delinquency they sometimes do. Nevertheless, even though the mechanisms of adjustment lead the individual into violations of the law, he has not necessarily become mentally ill. In fact—and this is important—usually his mental health is not affected at all.

"But," it may be asked, "does the mere possession of certain personality traits such as anxiety, aggressiveness, and so on necessarily cause crime and delinquency?" The sound view seems to be that personality traits alone do not cause crime and delinquency, that they

---

[7]Caldwell and Black, pp. 87, 88.

132,205

must be seen in their functional relationship with one another and with other influences, and that emotional disturbances and personality traits may largely result from criminal or delinquent behavior as well as help to cause it. Furthermore, as the individual's personality develops he absorbs the values of his culture, and although he inevitably suffers from personality conflicts he tends to become law-abiding. Even so, the personality, like the society in which it functions, is never completely organized but always contains inconsistent and inharmonious elements.

SELF

Many social scientists object to the term "personality needs" because, they claim, it puts too much stress on biological influences. They prefer the concept "self," which emphasizes social and cultural influences and the rationality and purposiveness of human behavior. Self may be defined as that organization of qualities which the person attributes to himself.

According to some sociologists and social psychologists, the self originates and develops in the process of socialization. Through the use of language and gestures, the person comes to see himself as others see him and learns what is expected of him in various situations. Thus, because he tends to fashion this behavior in accordance with the group's expectations, the character and culture of the group largely determine the development of the self, and what a person thinks of himself—his self-conception—becomes the important influence in the causation of his behavior, whether it be law-abiding or law-violating.[8] However, since the self, like the personality, never becomes completely organized but always contains inconsistent and inharmonious elements, the individual seeks to defend his self-image against the personal and environmental conflicts that threaten it. In this defense, he resorts to various mechanisms similar to those used in the functioning of the personality, and the results with respect to law violation and mental health are about the same as those produced in that process.

---

[8]This explanation regarding the nature and development of the self is known as the "symbolic interaction theory." Another theory of the self has been advanced by Carl Rogers, who puts more stress on the individual and his psychology. See Carl Rogers, *Client-Centered Therapy: Its Current Practice, Implications, and Theory* (Boston: Houghton Mifflin Co., 1951). See also Caldwell and Black, pp. 91-93; Melvin H. Marx, ed., *Theories in Contemporary Psychology* (New York: The Macmillan Co., 1963).

Many criticisms have been advanced against this theory of human behavior. For example, critics have argued that it neglects the influence exerted by the unconscious, fails to tell us very much about the learning process and motivation, and provides no effective method for measuring the self and its functioning. They argue further that, overlooking the fact that the individual has a reality apart from the group, the theory strips him of his creative powers and reduces him to a mere shadowy reflection of the group's specifications.

CHARACTER

The concept "character," according to some writers, can provide us with a more complete view of human behavior than either of the concepts "personality" or "self." Here character is defined as the whole of the individual's distinctive qualities expressed and measured in terms of the values of his culture. Heredity, social experience, and culture all interweave in the making of character, but in addition character must be seen as a unique combination of values—the objective values of culture becoming subjective in character. Indeed, morality is of the very essence of character, which accordingly is described as good or bad.

But there is more to the meaning of character than this. Personality and self, contend some critics, readily lend themselves to an interpretation that converts the individual into a mechanical man, the first activating him by psychological forces, the second by social ones. Character, on the other hand, fully recognizes that man has a reality apart from the group, endowing him with creative and self-directing powers. Thus, say these critics, man, never just a creature of his environment, is able to formulate his own standards and rules and use them to initiate, plan, and control, and his adaption to his environment is always creative.

Character, then, pictures man as having the power to weave the environmental and personal influences in his life into a choice and as being responsible for his choice. He does not need to transfer his conscience to an "expert" to find relief from his problems, for he has the capacity to carry his griefs and sorrows and to handle the stigmas and penalties from which he may suffer and to use them as a factual basis for building a better life. Obviously, every society must concern itself with the character development of its members and endeavor to direct it to the support of law and order.[9]

---

[9]Caldwell and Black, p. 94.

MENTAL ABNORMALITIES

Mental deficiency, sometimes called feeblemindedness, may be defined as a state of mental retardation or incomplete development existing from birth or early infancy, as a result of which the person is unable to meet the social expectations of his society. On the basis of mental age and intelligence quotient, mental deficiency has been classified into idiocy, imbecility, and moronity.[10] The idiot and the imbecile are easily recognized, and usually they are under such care and supervision as to prevent them from getting into trouble. The moron, on the other hand, has a normal appearance and blends imperceptibly into the borderline groups. Apparently even he does not constitute a major threat to society, however, for the available evidence indicates that his offenses tend to be minor ones.

However, it is difficult to analyze the relationship between mental deficiency and crime and delinquency. Here are some of the reasons: the various levels of mental deficiency blend into one another; no sharp line divides mental deficiency from normal intelligence; mentally deficient persons may suffer also from some mental disease; and intelligence tests cannot completely separate hereditary influences from those of the environment. Consequently, at present any conclusion regarding mental deficiency must be considered as tentative.

Mental disease, or mental disorder, may be defined as a state of mental unbalance or derangement which prevents a person from assuming responsibility for his support or causes him to be a positive menace to the health and safety of the community. Unlike mental deficiency, it does not imply a lack or incompleteness of mental development. Instead, it refers to a mind that has developed normally, almost always to maturity, and then has become disordered or deranged. However, a mentally deficient person may become mentally diseased, and a mentally diseased person may deteriorate from normal intelligence to moronity.

There are two major types of mental disease, the psychoses and the psychoneuroses, or neuroses. The psychoses, which are the most severe disturbances of the personality, cause the person to lose contact completely or partly with reality and require medical or even

---

[10]Mental age is a person's level of performance as measured by that expected of persons at various chronological ages. The intelligence quotient of a person is derived by dividing his mental age by his chronological age and multiplying it by 100 (to remove decimal places).

special institutional care. They may be divided into two types. One is caused by or associated with an impairment of the brain, such as psychoses with epilepsy, syphilis, cerebral arteriosclerosis, and toxic conditions. The other includes those without clearly defined structural change in the brain, often called "functional psychoses," important among which are schizophrenia, manic-depressive psychosis, and paranoia.

The psychoneuroses, or neuroses, tend to make the person less efficient personally and socially, but usually they do not necessitate special care or institutionalization. Generally believed to be functional, that is, caused by personality conflicts rather than by some organic condition, these mental diseases produce various symptoms, such as exaggerated feelings of fatigue, pronounced sensitiveness to noises, anxieties, morbid fears, obsessions, compulsions, the loss of some faculty, and the paralysis of some muscles.

Serious difficulties confront the investigator in the field of mental disease. There is considerable disagreement among psychiatrists regarding the nature of the mental diseases, their causes and classification, and the methods of diagnosis, and much of the content of psychiatry cannot be scientifically substantiated. It is not surprising, then, that we do not know how many persons are mentally diseased or how many mentally diseased persons are delinquent or criminal.

Nevertheless, we do know that neither mental deficiency nor mental disease inevitably causes crime and delinquency. Some persons with mental abnormalities do violate the law, but many others do not, and the great majority of delinquents and criminals, like the great majority of law-abiding persons, are mentally normal. Of course, a mental abnormality may be an influence in criminal or delinquent behavior—even the major one in a particular case—but, like all the other personal influences, mental abnormalities must be seen in their interaction with all other influences in the causation of human behavior, whether it be law-abiding or law-violating.

ENVIRONMENTAL INFLUENCES

THE HOME AND THE FAMILY

Despite the rapid and widespread social changes that have weakened the foundations of the American family, it continues to exert a deep and persistent influence in the life of the individual. In the intimacy of the family's relationships, the child receives basic physical and emotional satisfactions, as well as protection, guidance, and moral instruction, during his most impressionable years. There, too, he first learns about himself and his physical, social, and cultural surroundings and acquires attitudes, habits, character traits, and a sense of right and wrong that tend to endure throughout his life. Furthermore, so important is the family in the transmission and preservation of culture that it is not only the cradle of personality but also the nursery of all other social institutions. And since it is functionally related to these institutions, it tends to reflect and augment their organization and disorganization.

Every society, if it is to survive, must establish and preserve rules and standards (social norms) for the guidance, protection, and regulation of its members. To the extent that a home departs from what is considered normal, it is a deviant home and a center of deviation pressures and thus may contribute to crime and delinquency. Although a deviant home does not inevitably cause crime and delinquency, it does increase the possibility that they will occur. Deviant homes may be classified into four major types: (1) the broken home, (2) the functionally inadequate home, (3) the socially, morally, or culturally abnormal home, and (4) the economically insecure home.

In the monogamous family, the relatively permanent union of a father and a mother enables both to play important parts in the rearing of children. To this union, the father brings a male, the mother a female, point of view, and thus each supplements and complements the other in the functioning of the family. Therefore, when the home is broken by the loss of one parent through death, divorce, separation, desertion, or commitment to an institution, there is a serious interference with the normal processes of life. Since it is assumed that the presence of both parents is essential to the development of well-balanced and socially adjusted children, broken homes are generally believed to contribute to crime and delinquency. And the majority of court reports and studies tend to support this belief, although the causal process involved is now known to be much more complex than it was once thought to be.

The functionally inadequate home produces a great deal of friction and frustration. It is filled with discord and dissension between the parents, favoritism, parental rejection of children, rivalry between brothers and sisters, emotional insecurity, self-pity, jealousy, domination, pampering, neglect, or any of the other conditions that distort, impoverish, or disorganize the personalities of children. Many studies and clinical experience have shown that the functionally inadequate home also contributes to crime and delinquency. Lack of love and affection and faulty discipline, especially when it is highly permissive, excessively severe, or grossly inconsistent, appear to be particularly detrimental to the sound development of the child, leaving him unprepared to cope with life's problems and disappointments. Indeed, suffering from conflict and frustration, both parents and children may find relief in violations of the law, or, fleeing from a home torn with friction, they may seek comfort in the harmful companionship of persons who are engaged in crime or delinquency.

The *socially, morally, or culturally abnormal home* is one in which there are racial differences, a physically or psychologically abnormal parent, immorality, criminality, or diverse cultural standards. Such factors make it difficult for children to receive a system of values generally accepted in the community and thus interfere with adequate training for successful living. Interracial marriages are not generally favored in the United States, and children born of them are comfortable in neither race and often bitter, resentful, and emotionally insecure. Consequently, they face serious problems in their efforts to find success and happiness.

Similar problems of adjustment confront children who have a parent suffering from a serious disability, like blindness, deafness, paralysis, or mental illness. These children may feel ashamed or apologetic about the condition of their parent and, seeking relief from their tensions, frustrations, feelings of guilt, and conflicts, they may find comfort in undesirable or even delinquent or criminal associations.

Children exposed to lewdness, vulgarity, drunkenness, brutality, immorality, vice, and crime at home tend to accept these conditions as normal and desirable. They fashion themselves after the models so seductively exhibited and slide easily into delinquency and crime.

According to the findings of many studies and investigations, culture conflict is an important cause of crime and delinquency. These findings, however, must be interpreted with care, for the offense rates of American-born children of immigrants are affected not only by culture conflicts but also by poverty, minority status, and the conditions in the areas where many foreign-born families live. Even so, many of the children in the homes of immigrants are torn by culture conflicts. Divided in their loyalties between parents on the one hand and friends, teachers, and neighbors on the other, they are often confused, rebellious, reckless, and even ashamed of their parents. They may break away from parental controls and guidance and find satisfaction for their needs and desires in delinquency and crime.

The *economically insecure home* may contribute directly to crime and delinquency, as when a child steals so that he will not suffer from hunger or cold. Usually, however, its influence is exerted through a complex set of relationships. Poverty may cause the absence from home of working parents and the loss of their restraining influence and guidance. It may also cause the early employment of children and their subjection to great temptations, the association of children with delinquent gangs, the overcrowding of the home and its attendant sacrifice of privacy, and so on. Of course, poverty does not necessarily drive a person into violation of the law, and many law-abiding adults and children come from poor homes, but the fact remains that the great majority of criminals and delinquents come from economically insecure homes. Thus this type of home must be considered a crime and delinquency risk.

Numerous studies and investigations have clearly shown the great importance of the family. They have indicated that whatever in its structure, its internal functioning, or its external relationships reduces its authority and influence in the rearing of children also increases the possibility of crime and delinquency. One can readily understand, therefore, why all students of crime and delinquency believe that a strong, effective, and viable family system continues to be our strongest bulwark against these problems.[11]

THE NEIGHBORHOOD

Although the neighborhood, like the family, has declined as an agency of social control, it still exerts an important influence in our society, especially in the development of the child. Thus, it can supplement and fortify the influence of the home, the church, and the school in the maintenance of law and order, or it can contribute to crime and delinquency by blocking basic personality needs, engendering culture conflicts, and fostering antisocial values.

Crime and delinquency rates vary from neighborhood to neighborhood. They tend to be highest near the central business district and large industrial areas and to decrease from the center of the city to its boundaries. The areas of the city having the highest rates of crime and delinquency have been called "delinquency areas." They are characterized by physical deterioration, congested but de-

---

[11]The President's Commission on Law Enforcement and Administration of Justice, *The Challenge of Crime in a Free Society* (Washington, D.C.: Government Printing Office, 1967), pp. 63-66.

creasing population, economic insecurity, poor housing, low standards of living, family disintegration, high rates of population movement, truancy, infant mortality, and mental disorder, conflicting cultural standards, little concerted action to solve common problems, and other such conditions. All these conditions are symptomatic of the decline of the neighborhood as an agency of social control.

In such an area, crime and delinquency persist not only because of the absence of constructive neighborhood influences, but also because various forms of lawlessness have become traditional and are transmitted through neighborhood groups and institutions. However, we must remember that the neighborhood is functionally related to the organized society of which it is a part, and so, although it generates antisocial forces of its own, it also communicates others which originate elsewhere.[12]

THE PLAY-GROUP AND THE GANG

All children everywhere participate in spontaneous play-groups, and this intimate form of association influences them in amazing ways. It affects their speech and manners, their methods of play, their attitudes toward themselves and others, and their morals and ideals. Through its unsupervised activities, the play-group often preserves and transmits traditions and techniques of delinquency and, indeed, may surpass even the home as an educational agency.

The gang, another form of intimate association, has a more permanent membership and a more definite organization than the spontaneous play-group, from which, however, it frequently emerges. Developing to meet the needs of children and young people where other outlets for their interests and energies fail to do so, the gang supplies its members with excitement and adventure, recognition for skills, prowess, and daring, and security and protection from the interference of parents, teachers, and the police. Even so—and there is a tendency to overlook this—most gangs are rather loosely organized groups with changing memberships. Some members of a gang will move in and out of its activities as they see fit to do so.

Although some gangs include girls and a few contain only girls, most are composed entirely of boys and young men. However, gangs are not necessarily a cause of crime, nor are all gangs criminal. In fact, they have in them the potentialities of both good and evil. When they

[12]Caldwell, pp. 267, 268; Clifford R. Shaw and Henry D. McKay, *Juvenile Delinquency and Urban Areas* (Chicago: University of Chicago Press, 1969).

are properly directed, gangs may become assets to the community, often developing into clubs, fraternities, lodges, and other similar organizations, but if they are neglected or unwisely handled they may come into increasing conflict with the community. They may acquire an antisocial solidarity and engage in demoralizing activities, which may range from truancy, rowdiness, and vandalism to the most outrageous crimes.

The gang appears more frequently, and at its worst, in delinquency areas. There it absorbs a disproportionate amount of its members' interests and energies and operates as a most effective agency of demoralization. There, also, the boy is almost predestined to the life of the gang, for it stands virtually alone in supplying the interests, activities, and satisfactions which he so urgently needs. The possible consequences of this cannot be fully appreciated unless one understands that companionship exerts an important influence in the causation of crime and delinquency. Thus, it is estimated that anywhere from 60 to 90 percent of all delinquent activity occurs in the company of others.

At the same time one should not forget that the gang reflects the adult life and customs of the neighborhood in which it functions and that its activities must be seen with reference to the moral codes and conduct of the adult world. In this connection it should also be observed that adults cannot persistently violate the moral standards they advocate for their children and at the same time expect young people to remain unaffected by their bad examples.

In coming to a conclusion about the influence of the gang, one must admit that it does not necessarily contribute to crime and delinquency. Nevertheless, when a child is born into an unsatisfactory family situation, when he is reared in a delinquency area, and when his play-group is a delinquent gang, the possibilities are great that he will come into conflict with the law.[13]

RELIGION

With its emphasis on reverence for God, the highest spiritual values of man, the worth and dignity of the individual, and respect for his person and property, religion should be expected to exert a powerful influence for social control and law observance in the United States. It may indeed do this, but at present we have no conclusive

---

[13]Caldwell, pp. 268-70.

statistical evidence regarding the effects of religion on crime and delinquency. The studies that have been made have not succeeded in disentangling the influence of religion from the web of relationships into which it is woven along with other influences, such as those of the home, the neighborhood, ethnic background, education, economic status, race, and so on. Consequently, investigators have given us information not about religion itself but about the effects of the interaction of a number of influences, among which religion is included.

Nevertheless, it seems reasonable to assume that social norms, including the law, are greatly strengthened when they are given the support of religion and associated with the regular teaching of religious principles. When this is done, violations of the law are not just crimes but abhorrent acts that are condemned by deep religious convictions. In this way, religion can create a strong resistance to criminal impulses and desires.

EDUCATION

America has great faith not only in religion but also in education. In fact, many of her major national policies are based on the assumption that the more education her people have, the more they will respect and obey the law, the greater happiness and prosperity they will experience, and the stronger and better their government will become. Furthermore, there appears to be evidence that this faith is not entirely misplaced. All the studies and investigations show that offenders include a comparatively large number of persons who have had school behavior problems, truancy problems, and an inadequate amount of education. However, one should not jump to the conclusion that formal education of itself bears an important relationship to crime and delinquency. This is not necessarily true and cannot be shown to be true in general, although it may be true in individual cases.

On the other hand, one should not conclude that formal education is unimportant, but rather that it must be seen in its interaction with other influences, like the home, the child's personality, the play-group, the neighborhood, and so on. Moreover, even if we ascribe importance to formal education, this does not mean that its most essential element is the mere imparting of knowledge. Much more essential is the way in which education directly or indirectly molds the character of the child.

RECREATION

In general, what has been said about formal education applies equally well to supervised recreation. Many studies have shown that children may engage in unguided play without becoming delinquent and that many persons who never violate the law prefer and need such recreation. They have shown also that many offenders take part in organized recreation and remain offenders and that no one has proved that organized recreation of itself prevents crime and delinquency or that its absence alone causes them. Nevertheless, this does not mean that we should not have organized recreation. Indeed, every child should have access to wholesome leisure-time activity, and some children, both delinquents and nondelinquents, need and enjoy supervised recreation and often benefit from it. Thus, although organized recreation, like formal education, is no panacea, when it is judiciously planned and competently administered it can be an important part of a program for the prevention of crime and delinquency.

MASS MEDIA

The term "mass media" is used here to refer to such impersonal means of communication as newspapers, magazines, comic books, radio, television, and motion pictures. Since these media do affect the lives of so many persons, they have been charged with causing crime and delinquency by making crime seem attractive, exciting, glamorous, and profitable, by featuring violence, brutality, and lawlessness, by giving publicity and prestige to crooks, gangsters, gamblers, confidence men, racketeers, and hoodlums, by denigrating and ridiculing the courts and law enforcement agencies, and by other such undesirable practices.

This charge may be true, but thus far studies and investigations have not brought conclusive results and indicate, in fact, that we know little about the effects of these media on human behavior. Nevertheless, we can draw some tentative conclusions from the evidence that we do have. Persons who have already acquired delinquent or criminal tendencies or who have abnormal psychogenic traits may have these tendencies strengthened by motion pictures, comic books, or radio or television programs, but it is doubtful whether persons who do not have such tendencies or traits become criminals or delinquents solely because of the effects of the mass media. We must add, however, that children are more susceptible to the influence of the mass media than adults. Also, there are many highly suggestible, restless, and unstable persons with criminal and delinquent tendencies who can be influenced by the mass media, and the number of these persons is probably growing. Furthermore, we must understand that the mass media are exerting an increasing influence in our complex society and profoundly affecting its culture, and to the extent that these media are creating a cynical indifference to questions of morality and an irresponsible permissiveness, they are producing changes that, in turn, will ultimately contribute to crime and delinquency.

ECONOMIC INFLUENCE

Many studies and investigations have been made to determine the relationship between economic influences and crime and delinquency. In these efforts two important methods have been used: (1) a comparative analysis of the economic status of offenders and nonoffenders, and (2) an examination of the relation of delinquency and crime rates and the business cycle. Neither of these methods has been very fruitful, although they have shown that the relationship between economic conditions and crime and delinquency is not a simple and direct one. Apparently poverty is related to these problems chiefly through such conditions as bad housing, inadequate education and recreation, domestic discord, neglect and improper discipline, early employment of children, immoral neighborhood influences, and so on.

The complexity of the relationship is revealed especially by the fact that many poverty-stricken persons never become offenders, that some wealthy persons do, that both law-violating and law-abiding persons come from the same poor family and from the same blighted neighborhood, and that many persons in slum areas do not become chronically criminal or delinquent at all. Nevertheless, we must conclude that the lower economic classes do have higher rates of crime and delinquency than the upper economic classes in the United States, and that certainly poverty does constitute a crime and delinquency risk; that is, its presence increases the possibility of crime and delinquency.[14]

---

[14]Caldwell and Black, pp. 132-46.

SOME CONCLUDING REMARKS

The brief examination of the personal and environmental influences that we have just completed has shown that there is no simple explanation of crime and delinquency. The nature and extent of these influences and their varying combinations differ greatly from one case to another. The personal influences contribute to crime and delinquency by limiting and decreasing the creative and adjustment potentialities of man. The environmental influences contribute by blocking or interfering with the satisfaction of the personality needs of the individual, or by instilling values that bring him into conflict with the values of organized society, or by both. Human behavior, however, whether law-abiding or law-violating, is the resultant of the interaction of personal and environmental influences. In some cases of crime or delinquency the influences causing deviation may be more personal than environmental, whereas in others the reverse may be true, but never is a person a criminal only because of personality characteristics or only because of the internalization of values that are unacceptable to organized society. There is always a mixture of these influences as they interact in varying proportions.

In our efforts to understand the interweaving and interacting of personal and environmental influences in the individual case, the concept "character," according to some writers, can provide us with a more complete view of human behavior than either of the concepts "personality" or "self." As we have explained, they contend that personality and self readily lend themselves to an interpretation that turns the individual into a mechanical man, the first activating him by psychological forces, the second by social ones. Character, on the contrary, they say, fully recognizes and emphasizes the creative and self-directing powers of man. In its view, he has a reality apart from the group. Never just a creature of his environment, he is able to establish and develop his own standards and rules and to use them to initiate, plan, and control; his adaptation is always creative. Thus the concept "character" pictures man as having the power to weave the personal and environmental influences of his life into a choice and holds him responsible for his choice.

Each of the various disciplines—biology, geography, psychology, psychiatry, sociology, and social psychology—has used its own point of view, concepts, and theories in an effort to explain the causation of crime and delinquency. Most of the scholars in all these disciplines, while stressing the superior virtues of their own discipline, have recognized the contributions of other disciplines and have taken into consideration the importance of both personal and environmental influences.[15] Thus they employ a "multiple-factor" approach to the problem of causation. Emphasizing that criminology deals with very complex problems about which our knowledge is quite meager, they have used a wide frame of reference and have presented loosely drawn conclusions. In fact, many scholars, believing that the search for a general theory of causation is at present unrealistic, now recommend that we seek separate theories of the various types of crime and delinquency in the hope that these will provide us with deeper insights into causation and eventually lay the foundation for a general theory.

This examination of the personal and environmental influences has stressed the complexity of causation and the paucity of our knowledge about it. However, this should not be allowed to obscure the fact that studies have consistently revealed the presence of certain personal and environmental influences, such as serious personality maladjustments, inadequate families, delinquent gangs, and disorganized communities, during the childhood and early adolescence of criminals. It is true that many persons are law-abiding despite these influences, but this should not deter us from reducing or eliminating them so that they will not overwhelm those who do succumb and thus become delinquents and criminals.[16]

---

[15]A few writers, however, have attempted to give a simple and complete explanation of causation, stressing their own theories virtually to the exclusion of all others. For a critical analysis of two of these theories, the psychoanalytic theory originated by Sigmund Freud, a psychiatrist, and the differential association theory of Edwin Sutherland, a sociologist, see Caldwell, Chapter 10.

[16]Caldwell, pp. 277-80.

CHAPTER III

POLICE ORGANIZATION
AND ADMINISTRATION

The study of police service or law enforcement must include an analysis, description, and understanding of the organization (structure) and administration (function) of this important governmental service. As is the case with all types of governmental agencies, police agencies involve people who perform certain duties within an organizational framework prescribed by law and by administrative policies and directives. Therefore, it is of the utmost importance that one comprehend the nature and purpose of public organization and administration in general, and police organization and administration in particular.

Two well-known scholars have defined organization and administration as follows:

> Organization is the structuring of individuals and functions into productive relationships; administration is concerned with decision making and the direction of individuals to achieve ends that have been determined by political leaders.[1]

There are various types of organizations which are usually classified very broadly as either public or private and bureaucratic or voluntary. Obviously, large police agencies are public and bureaucratic organizations. Many years ago Max Weber described a bureaucracy as having: (1) a continuous organization of official functions bound by rules; (2) a specified sphere of influence, that is, the competence, labor, and resources to perform specialized types of functions; (3) an organization of offices which follows the principle of hierarchy, that is, one in which each lower office is under the control and supervision of a higher one; and (4) a formulation of administrative

---

[1] J. M. Pfiffner and R. V. Presthus, *Public Administration* (New York: The Ronald Press Co., 1969), p. 5.

acts, decisions, and rules, which are recorded in writing, even in cases where oral discussion is the rule or is even mandatory.[2]

All public organizations are managed by people who are referred to as "administrators" or "the administration." By public administrators we mean persons who are responsible for the carrying out of public policy as developed by a political government in accordance with law and the directives of the elected executive leaders. Pfiffner and Presthus, in describing administration and its relationship to organization, view organization as structure and administration as process. According to this view, then, the term "administration" refers to the lively interpersonal aspects of public administration, including the making of policy, the coordinating of individual and group effort, and the building of morale.[3]

There are many types of public agencies which have been established by law to perform specific types of governmental services. One can cite such well-known federal governmental departments as Health, Education, and Welfare, Justice, Defense, Labor, Commerce, and so on, and their state government counterparts often referred to as departments of Mental Health, Correction, Education, Welfare, Police, and so on. Regardless of the type of public agency, all possess at least the following basic characteristics:

1. A law mandating the agency's existence and defining its mission in government service.
2. A definite organizational structure, depicted in a chart or table of organization, indicating its relationship to other agencies as well as its own bureaus, divisions, and sections.
3. An administration, or the people who are legally responsible for managing the agency, including their specific duties, responsibilities, and the status and relationship of personnel to one another.
4. A political basis and control, which determines its chief administrators and the kind and amount of its available resources.
5. An informal structure involving the behavior of agency personnel to others of the same or higher rank in a way that may slowly modify the agency's formal structure and increase or decrease its

---

[2]Max Weber, *The Theory of Social and Economic Organization* (New York: The Ronald Press Co., 1969), p. 5.
[3]Pfiffner and Presthus, p. 8.

capabilities to achieve the goals specified for it by law or by rules and regulation.[4]

Thus it can be seen that all public agencies have a structure (organization), or the grouping of various activities into sub-units, and function (administration) specifying the status and function of personnel positions and the operations, or actual activities, carried on by the agency.[5]

Regarding administration, it is important to emphasize the interpersonal or behavioral theory of organizations. According to this theory, public agencies are made up of individuals who interact with one another and form behavioral systems of both a formal and an informal nature. This personnel behavior determines the ability of an organization to achieve its goals adequately, that is, to provide public service.[6]

POLICE ORGANIZATION AND ADMINISTRATION

Police agencies are public service agencies primarily responsible for maintaining order and enforcing laws, but they are also responsible "for the regulation and protection of the community especially with respect to matters affecting public health, comfort, morals, safety, or prosperity."[7]

As such, police agencies possess the same basic characteristics as other public agencies described above. Thus a police department has a structure and an administration. The administration typically inincludes the chief of police, one or more assistant chiefs, inspectors,

---

[4]For a further analysis of the impact of such informal structures the reader is referred to: P. E. Blau, *Bureaucracy in Modern Society* (New York: Random House, 1956); W. H. Whyte, *The Organization Man* (New York: Doubleday, 1957); A. Etzioni, *Modern Organizations* (Englewood Cliffs, N. J.: Prentice-Hall, Inc., 1954); D. R. Creassey, *The Prison* (New York; Holt, Rinehart, and Winston, Inc., 1961).

[5]See Ralph M. Stoghill, "Dimensions of Organizational Theory," in *Approaches to Organizational Design,* edited by James D. Thompson (Pittsburgh: University of Pittsburgh Press, 1966).

[6]Ibid.; Ralph R. Hampton, Charles E. Summer, Ross A. Webber, *Organizational Behavior and the Practice and Management* (Glenview, Ill.: Scott, Foresman & Co., 1968).

[7]Robert G. Caldwell, *Criminology,* 2nd ed. (New York: The Ronald Press Co., 1965), p. 283.

majors, captains, lieutenants, sergeants, officers, investigators, and various staff specialists in the areas of records and communications, planning and research, criminalistics, budget, and personnel. (See Charts I through V in Appendix B for examples of recommended tables of organization for city police departments of various sizes.[8])

In examining Charts I through V, you must keep in mind certain fundamental principles of organization that must be observed if efficiency is to be achieved in the operation of a police department. These organizational principles are summarized as follows:

1. Basic organizational units must be created. Similar activities should be grouped together in divisions and bureaus and each basic unit placed under the control of a single person. Thus all crime prevention activities should be combined in one unit and all traffic work in another.

2. Lines of demarcation between units must be clearly drawn and precisely defined so that confusion about responsibility, duplication of effort, and neglect of duty will be prevented.

3. Channels for the flow of information and the delegation of authority must be established so that the coordination of effort into a unified force can be achieved.

4. The distinction between line and staff activities must be recognized in order to prevent the interruption of the flow of authority. Line activities are those which carry out directly the purposes for which the department was created. Typical line activities are patrol, investigation, and crime prevention. Staff activities are not concerned *directly* with basic objectives but are designed to be of service to personnel engaged in live activities. Typical staff activities are records, personnel, communications, and maintenance.

5. Unity of command must be established. Each individual, unit, and situation should be under the immediate control of only one person in order to avoid the friction that results from the duplication of direction and supervision. This principle must be observed from the top to the bottom of the organization.

6. The span of control must not be excessive. No more units or persons should be placed under a single executive or supervisor than he can effectively supervise.

---

[8]These charts were reproduced with the approval of the International Association of Chiefs of Police and the authors from O. W. Wilson and Roy C. McClaren, *Police Administration* (New York: McGraw-Hill Book Co., 1972), pp. 100-106.

7. Responsibility must be clearly fixed. Each task should be made the unmistakable duty of some particular person.

8. Supervision of each person at the level of his work must be provided at all times and places. Thus the police officer reports to his sergeant, the sergeant to his lieutenant, the lieutenant to his captain, and so on.

9. Responsibility must carry with it commensurate authority. So, each supervisor must have the authority to order his subordinates to perform their designated duties.

10. Persons must be held strictly accountable for the authority delegated to them.[9]

Thus, a police department, like any other formal organization, has a formal structure established to make possible the most efficient performance of police functions, that is, the enforcement of the law, the protection of life and property, and the preservation of the peace. Every individual in the police organization occupies a particular status, or position, and in accordance with this status is expected to perform certain roles; and such is the rule from the chief or superintendent of police down to the officer in the field. This is the formal and official set of relationships shown in the table of organization of any given police department.

INFORMAL ORGANIZATION

In addition to the formal, legal, administrative organization described above, every police department has one or more non-formal, or infor-

---

[9]For a more detailed analysis of police administration and organization, the reader should review the following texts: V. A. Leonard and Harry W. More, Police Organization and Management (New York: The Foundation Press, Inc., 1971); O. W. Wilson and Roy C. McClaren, Police Administration (New York: McGraw-Hill Book Co., 1972); The Institute for Training in Municipal Administration, Municipal Police Administration (Washington, D. C.: International City Management Association, 1971); The President's Commission on Law Enforcement and Administration of Justice, Task Force Report: The Police (Washington, D. C.: Government Printing Office, 1967); National Advisory Commission on Criminal Justice Standards and Goals, Task Force on Police (Washington, D. C.: Government Printing Office, 1973); Paul M. Whisenand and R. Fred Ferguson, The Managing of Police Organizations (Englewood Cliffs, N.J.: Prentice-Hall, Inc., 1973); Donald G. Hanna and William D. Gentel, A Guide to Primary Police Management Concepts (Springfield, Illinois: Charles C. Thomas, Publisher, 1971).

mal, organizations which exert an important influence on the department's ability to achieve its goals in a professional, legal, and effective manner. Informal organizations are small groups of individuals, common to all human associations, which become especially important to individuals in the large and complex bureaucracies or departments in modern industrial and urban society.

In general, the term "informal organization" refers to the intimate association of individuals who may share common values, goals, and interests. Such informal groupings interact regularly with one another and often modify the effectiveness of the formal organization or change its structure and procedures in subtle ways over a period of time. In describing this, Sayles and Strauss state that employees form friendship groups based on their contacts and common interests. In this way they develop a life of their own that is almost completely separate from the work process from which it arises. This life includes a variety of activities, many of which are not specified by the job description—for example, special lunch arrangements, the trading of job duties, fights with those outside the group, and so on. Thus emerges a customary way of doing things—a set of stable characteristics that are hard to change—in fact, an organization in itself.[10]

Informal organization of personnel exists in police agencies and is especially rampant and destructive in those agencies which are large and poorly organized and administered and which fail to solve the important problems facing their personnel. Leonard and More illustrate the impact of informal organization in police departments by noting the rivalry between deputy chiefs, the conflict between specialized units such as patrol and investigations, the tension produced by conflicting goals of officers working in internal affairs or community relations, and the formation of cliques by officers who exercise administrative authority.[11]

Of course, the informal organization of police personnel can also be beneficial, and often is. It assists in informing the personnel about official directives and actions, in putting group pressure on individual officers to be productive and ethical in the execution of their police duties, and in developing an esprit de corps that is essential to the police agency.

Therefore, it is important to know that informal organizations do

---

[10]L. R. Sayles and G. Strauss, *Human Behavior in Organizations* (Englewood Cliffs, N. J.: Prentice-Hall, Inc., 1966), p. 89.
[11]Leonard and More, p. 97.

exist and to understand their nature so that, instead of being allowed to weaken or destroy a department or agency, they can be used to increase its effectiveness. A great deal of research is needed in this area so that we may more fully understand the characteristics and influence of informal organizations. Such knowledge would greatly assist the police administrator in managing the agency.

CONTEMPORARY ORGANIZATIONAL THEORY

The traditional, and still dominant, view of organizations, including police agencies, is almost entirely job-oriented. It sees the individual as a tool of the department who must help achieve the department's goals at all costs, with little interest being given to his opinions or needs. Such a philosophy of organization dictates that there be a rigid chain of command and unquestioning obedience to orders.

On the other hand, a current behavioral theory of organization emphasizes that all organizations exist for people, are controlled by people, and are composed of people who have values, needs, and differing abilities. It also emphasizes that these facts must be recognized and properly dealt with by the organization's administrators if a police department is to be stable and successful in meeting its goals. Simon states that the pressures of organization tend to suppress individuality and that the individual must surrender some aspects of his freedom and conform to the behavioral norms of the organization.[12]

Barnard illustrates the application of the behavioral theory of organization by explaining how the individual (police personnel) and the organization (police administrators) may be brought together into a more harmonious relationship. This can be accomplished, he claims, by the improvement of personnel management and supervision. Thus the organization would help the individual to acquire those skills which would be beneficial to the individual and the agency. Furthermore, supervision would be made more personalized so as to modify the simple, direct, and often rigid "command-centered approach." For example, before taking definitive action, supervisors would first obtain the facts, analyze them, and try to improve the

---

[12]Herbert A. Simon, *Administrative Behavior* (New York: The Macmillan Co., 1959), Chapter 4.

individual who is being supervised. Disciplinary action would be taken only when everything else failed.[13]

What is important to understand is that the application of either of the above organizational theories singly and in radical or pure form will prove inadequate. Rather, and especially in law enforcement where discipline and controls are essential, some aspects of both theories should be carefully integrated and applied. There must be a clearly defined structure which indicates the various functions to be performed and how they are to be grouped into subunits. However, a police department must also establish and encourage communication between superiors and subordinates and recognize the contributions that the nonsupervisory personnel can make in the formulation of policy and in the solution of problems. A police agency which is either too rigidly bureaucratic and authoritarian or too permissive in allowing personnel to carry on as they please will fall victim to organizational confusion and ineffectiveness.

MAJOR ADMINISTRATIVE FUNCTIONS

Various administrative models have been developed by scholars in the field of public administration, but two models are most often discussed and considered as descriptive of the field. These are the political-pluralist model and the integrationist model.[14] These models have been utilized in analyzing the federal administration, but are also applicable at the state and local levels of government.

In brief, the political-pluralist model sees government agencies, including the police, as highly fragmented administratively and the executive branch of government as unintegrated. Each agency is viewed as being responsible to the politicians and the people it serves, and as playing an essentially political role in its attempts to effect a peaceful resolution of conflicts of interests between such groups that is compatible with the disposition of power in our society.[15]

The primary or major administrative model in existence today is the integrationist model. In this model administration is a closed hierarchical system, with the chief executive at the top, surrounded by a staff of loyal subordinates who are committed to his program.

---

[13]C. I. Barnard, *Functions of the Executive* (Cambridge, Mass.: Technology Press, 1947), pp. 56-59.

[14]Pfiffner and Presthus, p. 177.

[15]Ibid., p. 9.

Below, in classical pyramidal form, is a succession of levels, each responsive to the direction of that above it. Decisions flow from the top and are systematically carried out by non-political technicians.[16]

In actuality, no public agency, including the police, conforms wholly to either of the above administrative models. However, police departments essentially embody the characteristics of the integrationist model. With this in mind, we shall proceed to a description of the major administrative, staff, and field services, as well as the personnel positions, of a typical police department.

STAFF FUNCTIONS AND TECHNICAL SERVICES

The chief administrator or executive officer of a city or local police department is the chief of police, who is usually appointed by the mayor. At the county level, the chief law enforcement officer is the sheriff, the only head of law enforcement who is a constitutional officer elected by the voters of his county.

At the state level, the chief law enforcement officer is the superintendent of police, who is appointed by the governor. Finally, at the federal level, some of the important chief law enforcement officers are as follows:

Director of the Federal Bureau of Investigation (FBI), Department of Justice, who is appointed by the President with the advice and consent of the Senate. The FBI is responsible for investigating all violations of federal laws except those which have been assigned by law or otherwise to some other federal agency. The FBI has jurisdiction over more than 180 investigative matters, such as espionage, sabotage, treason, and most of the other violations of the federal criminal code.

Commissioner of the Immigration and Naturalization Service, Department of Justice, who is appointed by the President with the advice and consent of the Senate. This service administers the immigration and naturalization laws relating to the admission, exclusion, and deportation of aliens, and the naturalization of aliens lawfully resident in the United States.

Administrator, Drug Enforcement Administration, Department of Justice, who is appointed by the President with the advice and consent of the Senate. This bureau is charged with all drug enforce-

---

[16]Ibid.

ment responsibilities and was established by the President on March 28, 1973. This *new* drug law enforcement agency within the Department of Justice consolidated the activities of the Bureau of Customs, the Bureau of Narcotics and Dangerous Drugs, the Office for Drug Abuse Law Enforcement, the Office of National Narcotics Intelligence, and the Research and Development efforts for drug enforcement both domestically and internationally.

Commissioner of the Bureau of Customs, Department of the Treasury, who is appointed by the Secretary of the Treasury. The functions of this bureau are to assess and collect duties and taxes on imported merchandise, to control carriers and merchandise imported into or exported from the United States, and to combat smuggling and other violations of the laws regulating imports and exports.

Commissioner of the Internal Revenue Service, Department of the Treasury, who is appointed by the President with the advice and consent of the Senate. This service superintends the assessment and collection of all taxes providing internal revenue, and administers and enforces the laws and regulations related to alcohol, tobacco, and firearms.

Director of the United States Secret Service, Department of the Treasury, who is appointed by the Secretary of the Treasury. This service is authorized to protect the person of the President of the United States, members of his immediate family, the President-elect, the Vice President, or other officer next in succession, as well as to detect and arrest any person committing any offense against the laws of the United States relating to coins, obligations, and securities of the United States and foreign governments.

Other responsibilities of the United States Secret Service include the supervision of the White House Police Force, which is charged with the protection of the executive mansion and grounds, and the Treasury Guard Force, which protects the main treasury buildings and the cash, bonds, and other securities in the treasury vaults.

Assistant Postmaster General, Inspection Service, of the United States Post Office Department, who is appointed by the Postmaster General. His office is concerned with mail losses, wrongful use of the mails, and all other violations of the postal laws.

All the heads of police agencies have a number of staff persons who perform functions essential to the agency. These staff personnel do not ordinarily have direct authority over field activities but perform such services as: (1) planning, research, and statistics; (2) inspection—internal affairs; (3) personnel administration and training; (4) communications; (5) public education and information; (6) budget, purchasing, supply, maintenance, and property control; (7) jail administration; (8) criminalistics; and (9) legal services.

PLANNING, RESEARCH, AND STATISTICS

This important staff service involves the study of current and long-range agency needs and priorities and the establishment of programs and procedures that, in the light of such study, are deemed necessary. There must be a valid, reliable, and continuous method for gathering statistics which will indicate what the police department is doing and how effectively goals and legal obligations are being met.

The management of a police agency in modern society requires able administrators. These administrators should have an expert staff to advise them on such matters as the quantity and quality of personnel, the need for additional personnel and resources, the improved utilization of personnel, and the new and more effective programs, procedures, and methods in the detection and apprehension of offenders and the prevention of crime and delinquency. However, all this in turn is dependent upon the availability of valid, reliable, and adequate records to indicate trends, needs, agency effectiveness, and so on.

INSPECTION—INTERNAL AFFAIRS

All police agencies should have a carefully chosen administrator-inspector and, where necessary, assistants whose primary responsibility is to make certain that all personnel perform satisfactorily and in accordance with the laws, goals, and functions of the agency. Of course, in small agencies inspections are carried out by an employee who performs other related duties. The police inspector reports directly to the chief of police the result of: (1) open inspection of personnel, material, procedures, and police operations; (2) corrective actions taken regarding unsatisfactory conditions; and (3) the appraisal of such matters as public relations, conditions in the community affecting police operations, and the morale of personnel.[17]

However, the obvious and most important function of the inspector is to ensure that the law enforcement agency is functioning most effectively and in accordance with the law.

---

[17]The Institute for Training in Municipal Administration (Chicago, 1961), p. 114.

PERSONNEL ADMINISTRATION AND TRAINING

All organizations, including the police, are structured, staffed, and administered by people. Therefore, the police will be professional and effective in performing their duties only if there are adequate personnel and training policies administered by competent and highly qualified persons. Personnel administration and training include:

1. The analysis and description of every job or position in the police agency.
2. The recruitment and appointment of personnel with specific qualifications to fill specific jobs.
3. The evaluation, promotion, and transfer of police personnel currently in the department.
4. The establishment and administration of wage scales for specific jobs.
5. The training of service personnel to ensure adequate work performance.
6. The overall review of individual cases of suspension or dismissal.

COMMUNICATIONS

All police agencies must have an adequate communications system between police personnel for receiving and quickly transmitting information and complaints from citizens. In order to accomplish this, modern communications systems must include a dispatch center which receives and records calls for police service, determines the authority of the agency to handle them, and quickly transmits them to the proper police personnel or unit for necessary action. In addition, good communications systems allow various police agencies at the local, state, and federal levels to exchange information for the purpose of assisting one another in police functions.

Modern police communications systems include the teletype, the telephone, and the radio, all of which can provide constant voice contact between a police officer and his base station while he is away from his vehicle or on foot patrol. More recent developments include mobile teleprinters, digital communications, and portable radios.

PUBLIC EDUCATION AND INFORMATION

A most important, and often the least developed, function of the police is the prevention of crime and delinquency. This can be partly accomplished by informing the public of precautions they can take to prevent crime and delinquency and to avoid becoming victims of crime.

The police have an obligation to inform the public of the amount and type of criminality taking place in any given locale. They also have an obligation to educate the public regarding the role of the police in crime control and the ways in which citizens themselves can assist the police, and thus themselves, in the prevention of crime and the apprehension of law violators. To accomplish this public education and information function, qualified staff should be assigned to train all police personnel in public relations practices, particularly with respect to policies governing contacts with the mass media, planning special activities, giving speeches, and courteous conduct. They should also establish positive relations with minority groups, businessmen, school children and their parents, and the general public.

BUDGET, PURCHASING, SUPPLY, MAINTENANCE, AND PROPERTY CONTROL

Sound fiscal management, maintenance, and property control are essential for the administration of a police agency. These important staff services include budget planning and execution and the purchase and proper maintenance and control of necessary supplies and equipment.

The budget process should be designed to develop a definite and realistic plan to accomplish the goals of policing. Budgeting must include past, present, and anticipated expenditures by indicating specific functions, activities, and projects to be accomplished. There is no more important staff responsibility than fiscal administration. An adequate and qualified staff must be available to prepare a budget and carry on all the financial functions of the department. Without such a staff, the department will not receive enough money, the money allocated will not be spent properly or effectively, and the department's policing function will be inadequate.

JAIL ADMINISTRATION

There are more than 3,000 county jails and 10,000 city jails in the United States, most of which are under the direct management of sheriffs and city chiefs of police. This highly important and specialized aspect of police administration is often neglected or given low priority in terms of staffing and resources. Local jails exist for (1) holding prisoners for hearings, trial, sentence, and transfer, (2) short sentence confinement, (3) reception and diagnostic procedures, including pre-sentence preparation, and (4) housing work-releasees returned from a prison for pre-release assistance.[18]

Although jail management is essentially a police responsibility, most authorities consider it to be the responsibility of professionally trained correctional personnel. If correctional agencies would administer jails, additional police personnel would be free to enforce the law on the street.

CRIMINALISTICS

In a society as large, complex, and technologically advanced as ours, it is most important that the methods and findings of psychology, chemistry, physics, biology, and other sciences be utilized to solve crimes. The use of such techniques and knowledge in police work is called criminalistics or forensic science.

Criminalistics can be used to help the police establish that a crime has actually been committed and to gather, preserve, analyze, and present evidence in court so that a successful solution of the crime can be realized. All this is accomplished by establishing a crime laboratory within the agency and staffing it with qualified personnel. The laboratory will have three major functions: (1) assisting in the search for evidence at the crime scene; (2) providing an analysis of fingerprints, blood, seminal stains, dusts, soils, fibers, gunpowder, documents, tiremarks, drugs, and other such evidence; and (3) assisting in the preparation and presentation of scientifically tested evidence in court.

When an agency is too small to establish its own crime laboratory, it may cooperate with other police agencies in establishing a regional or multi-departmental laboratory, or it may utilize part-time experts and consultants in chemistry, physics, biology, and other sciences.

LEGAL SERVICES

Another very critical staff function in any law enforcement agency is legal services. Law enforcement is a highly legalistic governmental activity, and recent decisions of the United States Supreme

---

[18]The National Sheriff's Association, *Manual on Jail Administration* (Washington, D. C.: The National Sheriff's Association, 1970), p. 3.

Court make it essential for the police to be provided with legal officers or advisers. The principal duties of the legal officer and his staff are training and continuing education, policy planning, liaison with the legislature and the community, conducting civil suits against individual officers, and handling problems rising out of specific investigations.[19]

FIELD SERVICES

As we have already explained, police agencies are responsible for the regulation and protection of the community in accordance with the law. In assuming this responsibility, they spend most of their time, resources, and personnel in the performance of field, or operational, services. These include patrol, traffic control, criminal investigation, vice control, and juvenile delinquency prevention and control.[20]

PATROL

The major activity of most police departments is patrolling regularly, on foot and in vehicles, the area for which the department is responsible. In the performance of their duties, patrol officers form the first line of contact between the citizen and the law, and much of the effectiveness of law enforcement depends on their being well-trained, alert, courteous, and distributed where needed in the community. In fact, it is the patrol officers who most often prevent crime, enforce the law, protect life and property, preserve the peace, and apprehend criminals.

During their patrolling, police inspect, observe, control public gatherings, and engage in many other miscellaneous field services. For example, they care for the injured and the sick, look after or destroy stray animals, report leaking water mains, defective pavements and sidewalks, inadequate street lighting, and so on. The basic assumption of patrolling is that it increases the threat of apprehension and thus causes the potential offender to believe he has no reasonable opportunity for violating the law successfully.[21]

---

[19]The President's Commission on Law Enforcement and Administration of Justice, *Task Force Report: The Police* (Washington, D. C.: U. S. Government Printing Office, 1967), p. 63.

[20]Wilson, p. 4.

[21]Municipal Police Administration, p. 78.

TRAFFIC CONTROL

The control of traffic involves maintaining order on streets and highways to make them safe and easy to use, enforcing traffic laws and regulations, and investigating accidents. Today traffic control constitutes the greatest of all the regulatory tasks for which the police are responsible, and in some areas its growth has produced a serious drain on the manpower and resources of law enforcement agencies.[22]

CRIMINAL INVESTIGATION

A systematic inquiry aimed at the identification and apprehension of alleged law violators is known as criminal investigation. Therefore the investigative function of police agencies involves all personnel connected with the enforcement function, and especially the line police officer, who often is the first to know of criminal law violations.

Most police agencies except those with purely investigative responsibilities, such as the FBI, have established a separate department unit to handle criminal investigations. These units are often referred to as the detective division and more recently the criminal investigation division. The reason for organizing a special investigative unit is to have persons especially trained and available to follow up on crimes which have been committed but have not resulted in arrest of an alleged offender and to seek the recovery of stolen property. In large metropolitan departments there are many criminal investigators, who often specialize in the investigation of particular crimes, such as burglaries, homicides, larcenies, auto thefts, narcotics, and so on. In smaller departments, investigations are handled entirely by uniformed personnel or by a small number of investigators assisted by uniformed personnel.

VICE CONTROL

Vice control refers to the enforcement of laws relating to prostitution, gambling, narcotics, and the illegal manufacture and sale of liquor. In some agencies vice control is assigned to a specialized unit or to specific personnel within the criminal investigation division. In other departments, vice control, intelligence, and organized crime are the responsibility of a separate unit or division.

---

[22]Ibid., p. 106.

Because citizens willingly participate in vice offenses, prosecution and the elimination of vice are difficult. However, it must be remembered that where vice exists there tends to be an increased amount of criminality, as offenders are attracted to such activities. Finally, most vice is directly or indirectly tied to organized crime, which makes its fortunes from providing such illegal services to the community.

JUVENILE DELINQUENCY PREVENTION AND CONTROL

The purpose of police-juvenile operations is to prevent and control juvenile delinquency. In providing this service in medium to large police departments, carefully selected and specially trained personnel should be assigned to a separate unit for that specific purpose. Such units investigate complaints against juveniles, properly process juveniles who are a danger to the community, prevent and repress delinquent behavior, work closely with the schools and parents of delinquent children, and cooperate with other police personnel in investigating offenses committed by juveniles. It must be remembered, however, that juvenile delinquents are not generally processed as adult criminals and that they must therefore be handled in accordance with the delinquency law. This law stresses the age of the delinquent and the need to act as "substitute" parents in assisting and correcting the child in trouble.

In this chapter we have presented a very basic outline of the organization and administration of the typical law enforcement agencies in the United States. It must be realized, of course, that the police and other administration-of-justice agencies have only recently been provided with some of the necessary and modern means to enable them to perform in a proficient manner. For the first time in the history of this nation, the police are being given adequate funds, and all indications lead one to believe that there will be an upgrading of police agencies and that, as a result, modern technology, research, education, and training will be brought to bear to a greater extent and with more effectiveness upon police problems.

Furthermore, attempts are now being made to reorganize and restructure police agencies so that they will incorporate the latest developments in organizational and administrative principles. Therefore, on the basis of these developments, one may expect that future police organizations will combine many like functions into fewer bureaus, divisions, and subunits. One may also expect them to decentralize many services, with an accompanying delegation of authority to lower-echelon personnel, and to increase the professionalization and education of personnel and thus reduce negative political influences in administration.

PROBLEMS OF SPECIALIZATION

In the above discussion of the line and staff functions of a modern police department, it is apparent that such a department is characterized by specialization. Some personnel are trained and assigned to investigate homicides, bank robberies, sex crimes, and so on. Other personnel are responsible for such highly specialized functions as evidence gathering, communications, records, finances, planning, research, and traffic control. The larger the police department, the greater the amount of specialization—that is, the greater the number of police personnel who will concentrate their efforts in one specialized activity of law enforcement.

Any modern, complex organization is composed of specialists who are essential to ensure that highly technical tasks are adequately performed. The obvious advantages of specialization include (1) the assigning of particular tasks to special units and individuals and holding them responsible for the performance of those tasks, (2) the more adequate training and development of competent personnel to solve crimes properly, and (3) the development of job interest and high morale among personnel.

However, there are also disadvantages of specialization, such as (1) the inability of specialists to perform or solve quickly police problems other than those for which they are specifically responsible, (2) the development of complicated bureaucratic procedures and a division of labor which may obstruct the prompt solution of crime problems, and (3) the inability to coordinate many highly specialized units. This last factor often results in conflict between units where specific functions are related but are assigned to different personnel with independent supervisors.[23]

The important thing to realize is that specialization is essential to

---

[23]Wilson and McClaren, pp. 79-86; National Advisory Commission on Criminal Justice Standards and Goals, *Task Force Report on Police*, pp. 206-220.

any modern police department. However, there should only be as much specialization as is essential to assist the police agency to adequately fulfill its goals. Anything more will result in a complex, static, and unmanageable police department which will be unable to meet its legal responsibilities properly.

CHAPTER IV

PLANNING, RECORDS, RESEARCH AND TECHNOLOGY

TOOLS OF ADMINISTRATION

The management of a police agency in urban America requires able administrators. These administrators in turn must have a staff of experts who can advise them on such matters as (1) the current quality and quantity of personnel, (2) the need for additional personnel and resources, (3) ways to improve the utilization of existing personnel, (4) the establishment of new and more effective programs and procedures to more adequately achieve the agency's goals, and (5) the establishment and supervision of valid and reliable records and an information gathering system for the recording and analysis of data to be used in determining trends, needs, and agency effectiveness. It should be obvious, therefore, that the planning, records, statistics, and research functions of a police agency are of critical importance if the agency is to perform its functions adequately. A police administrator would find it most difficult to decide on new policies and programs, as well as justify requests for additional funds, without the presentation of "hard" data, and such data can be developed only by qualified planners, researchers, statisticians, and other technicians. Let us, therefore, examine these matters in this chapter.

PLANNING

Planning may be defined as "a dynamic process . . . for generating plans that provide an organization with sustained renewal and change in terms of more effective goal accomplishment."[1] It is clear

---

[1]Paul M. Whisenand and R. Fred Ferguson, *The Managing of Police Organizations* (Englewood Cliffs, N.J.: Prentice-Hall, 1973), p. 93. The reader is referred to this excellent and current text on planning and police management for a more thorough and detailed discussion.

from the above definition that planning is a process and an important
function in the management of police agencies. Therefore, police
administrators must have a basic understanding of planning, and they
should have available to them qualified planning and research personnel to assist in the development of short-term and long-term plans.

The planning process is a part of the overall management of the
police department. It involves both simple and complex planning to
achieve the department's goals which include (1) the prevention of
crime and delinquency, (2) the repression of crime and delinquency,
(3) the recovery of stolen property, and (4) the regulation of certain
types of noncriminal behavior. Therefore, the planning process is
established to help achieve the above objectives (1) by analyzing and
identifying the problems facing the police agency, (2) by establishing
specific short-term and long-term goals of the agency, (3) by developing various types of possible actions to achieve these goals, and (4) by
establishing and implementing appropriate procedures to achieve the
desired goals.[2]

Obviously, in order that the planning and research activities of
the police department be adequately administered, professionally
qualified planners and researchers must be appointed, and this
should be done without regard to prior service within a police agency.
The most qualified staff should consist of persons with previous
police experience plus professional education in planning and research methods and procedures. However, given the unavailability of
such personnel, the lateral appointment of college-educated planners
and researchers, who should have course work in criminology and
police science, would be the most desirable. As an example, Indiana
State University has recently developed a Master of Arts degree in
Planning with a specialty in Criminology.[3]

Finally, the research and planning staff should be a separate
administrative unit within the police department, the head of which
should be answerable directly to the Chief of Police. The number of
personnel assigned to such a unit is determined by the size of the
police agency. Small departments may hire only one person and have
available part-time consultants to assist in the planning and research
functions.

---

[2]Ibid., pp. 93.
[3]For further information regarding such a curriculum, the reader should
contact the Center for Urban and Regional Studies, Indiana State University,
Terre Haute, Indiana.

PLANNING AND POLICE ADMINISTRATION

Law enforcement is a very complex, demanding, sensitive, and important governmental service involving the supervision of many personnel, the utilization of expensive equipment, and the management of significant sums of public funds. The public has a right to know how such funds are being expended and to make certain that a police agency administers its services in compliance with the law and sound governmental policy. Therefore, a quality planning, records, and research staff is essential. Such a staff has four main responsibilities: (1) to improve police management and organization; (2) to assist in the design, supervision, and implementation of adequate and essential paper forms and a records system; (3) to generate and analyze valid and reliable data on a regular basis of all aspects of the department's activities; and (4) to establish research projects to determine the need for new policies, procedures, and the utilization of existing police personnel and resources to meet changing needs.

In essence, the purpose of planning is to ensure that the police agency is carefully, professionally, regularly, and logically scrutinizing its entire activities so that it can more adequately achieve its goals. However, effective planning is dependent upon the existence of adequate, valid, and reliable data recorded on carefully established record forms. Without such forms, police planners and administrators would not have the essential information to make appropriate decisions, plans, policies, and so on.

An Example of Planning. Let us assume that a given police department needs a more relevant and comprehensive in-service training program for its personnel. The department has made such a determination because certain factually validated incidences such as the following are increasing: (1) injuries to officers or citizens in rather routine arrest situations; (2) escapes of persons in police custody; (3) failures to comply with legal requirements in arrest, search, and seizure activities; (4) officers who are unable to write adequate investigative or general police reports; (5) charges of police brutality; (6) improper use of interrogation techniques; and (7) unnecessary destruction of crime scene evidence by investigating officers.

On the basis of such incidences, a good police administrator asks his planning and research unit to establish an overall plan to develop a training program that will make certain all personnel are properly informed, through regular and intensive training sessions, on how to perform adequately their duties in the above situations. This, of course, would be done in close consultation with the training personnel and all relevant supervisory staff. The result will be the development of a plan for training that, briefly stated, will appear as follows:

A.   **PROGRAM IDENTIFICATION**
1. Number—A-6-72
2. Title—REFRESHER, IN-SERVICE TRAINING FOR POLICE PERSONNEL

B.   **OBJECTIVES**
This plan is designed to accomplish the following training objectives:
1. To provide in-service and refresher training for all police officers
2. To purchase the necessary training aids as well as to purchase texts and other materials to evaluate the program
3. To provide funds allowing officers to attend training during duty hours, or to pay for off-duty training participation

C.   **IMPLEMENTATION**
Training programs will be developed and implemented to meet the above stated needs of police personnel. The subject matter to be stressed will include:
1. Criminal law
2. Pertinent court decisions
3. Report writing
4. Criminal investigation
5. Community and human relations
6. Handling of juvenile problems
7. Management and supervisory training
8. Personal defense

D.   **EVALUATION COMPONENT**
An evaluation will be conducted to determine the quality of instruction, including the adequacy of the curriculum, classroom environment, tests, and training aids and materials. This evaluation will be directed by staff personnel and independent consultants, and the information to be utilized in the evaluation will cover:
1. Numbers and levels of personnel attending training sessions

2. Number of hours of training and the type of subject matter
3. Opinions from trainees
4. Post-training impact on officers in the field[4]

As indicated in the above illustration, planning is an important management activity of a police agency. However, for planning to be adequate, it is essential that information be adequately and regularly obtained and recorded on well designed and properly administered records.

RECORDS AND STATISTICS

The establishment of records and statistical information concerning all activities of the department, together with the use of modern computer technology, is necessary if a police agency is to carry out its duties in modern urban America. The development of a computer-based records and statistical reporting system (often called an information system) makes possible the collection of such essential data as the following:

1. Number of arrests made and the reasons for the arrests
2. Number of cases cleared by the department
3. Amount of response time to a complaint for police service after a complaint is received by the department
4. Number and types of crimes detected by the police
5. Types of persons arrested
6. Types of evidence gathered by the police and its ultimate use
7. Number of convictions compared with the number of persons arrested
8. Number of cases still pending
9. Amount and type of training department personnel receive
10. Assignment of personnel in terms of shifts, types of cases, patrol areas, and so on
11. Amount and classification of fingerprints and mug shots

Thus, by such a system, these and much more operational and administrative data can be thoroughly analyzed and made easily, quickly, and reliably retrievable to assist in the effective management and

---

[4]Indiana Criminal Justice Planning Agency, *Comprehensive Criminal Justice Plan and Action Grant Application, Fiscal Year, 1972* (Indianapolis: The Agency, 1972), pp. 303-11. (Slightly revised for illustrative purposes.)

operation of a police department. Of course, the size of the department will determine the amount and type of computer technology to be used. A small department will use existing computer equipment in other government agencies, whereas large departments can justify leasing their own equipment.

The Kansas City, Missouri, Police Department in 1968 developed a police computer system referred to as Alert 1.[5] The computers are used to serve the informational needs of the officer in the field and provide information on wanted persons, stolen autos, and persons potentially dangerous to the officer, and to supply information on arrests, offenses, and stolen property. This well-developed system also includes knowledge about arrest, search and seizure warrants, names of victims, and much more operational and management information.

Another example of the development of computer information systems is the Pattern Recognition and Information Correlation (PATRIC) developed by the Los Angeles Police Department personnel with the assistance of the city administration and the System Development Corporation in 1972.[6] The purpose of the PATRIC system is to improve the analysis of crime-related information by correlating a *suspect with his method of operation and stolen property information.*

With this system, information needed by police personnel can be easily available and quickly retrievable for the officer through the computer and can be a considerable saving in time and money that otherwise might be used in manually searching police records. For example, if a detective has an unsolved case, he can have computer personnel search for similar cases by matching the method of committing the crime with a suspect's description, and perhaps a vehicle description, so that possible suspects who have committed similar crimes can be identified. The detective then has specific suspects whom he can investigate further in order to solve a crime.

The above are only two examples of the many uses police departments are making of computer hardware and technically trained

---

[5]The discussion of this system is taken from a paper presented to the 1972 National Symposium on Criminal Justice Systems by Melvin F. Bockelman, Manager, Computer Systems Division, Kansas City, Missouri, Police Department.

[6]See: Los Angeles Police Department and System Development Corporation, *Patric Design Requirements* (Los Angeles: The Corporation, July 17, 1972), I, 1-4; III, 4.

personnel to develop, program, and analyze the mountainous amount of record and statistical information that is being collected and to provide information quickly to police administrators and field officers. Colton made a recent survey of computer use by the police, and some of his conclusions are as follows: (1) 38.8 percent of police departments he surveyed were using a computer; (2) by 1974 almost two-thirds of the responding police departments would be using computers; (3) almost 70 percent of cities over 100,000 were using computers as compared with 23.4 percent of cities under 100,000.

Colton also found that agencies with computers were using them for the following purposes:
1. To help police officers make a rapid inquiry to identify people and stolen property.
2. To provide for automated records of traffic accidents, traffic citations, and parking violations.
3. To keep an accounting of people arrested, released, or released on bail.
4. To provide for assisting in the command and control of police units in the field and thus assist in more rapidly dispatching units to calls.
5. To provide officers investigating crimes with information on crime patterns, offenders' methods of operation, nickname files, and fingerprint matching.
6. To provide police administrators with such management information as personnel records, payrolls, budgets, equipment inventory, and the like.[7]

Clearly, then, for legal and administrative reasons, police agencies must regularly collect and record data on all aspects of their activities, and such information must be reliable and easily retrievable for use. This requires the use of modern technology, the appointment of professionally qualified computer personnel, and the training of existing personnel for the proper collection and recording of data. Of course, critical to any information system is the availability of well-designed and properly completed record forms. The data taken from these forms can be analyzed and used to determine the department's needs, to plan new procedures, to request funds, to conduct special research projects, and most importantly, to prepare a case for prosecution in court.

---

[7]Kent W. Colton, *Use of Computers by Police: Patterns of Success and Failure* (Washington, D. C.: International City Management Association, 1972), pp. 1-4.

What, then, are some of the necessary and basic records of a police department?[8] First, there are records for gathering data regarding daily police activities, which are really case records completed for each complaint or report made to the police. Then there are daily police activities records which include the names of persons wanted, reports by investigating officers, and the daily bulletin, which is a brief log of every case coming to the attention of the police. Finally, there are other important records, such as those relating to persons arrested, fingerprints, accident reports, budget and accounting information, equipment and property maintenance, and so on.

It is obvious from the foregoing that without records there would be no permanent and regularly collected data, or statistics, to be tabulated and stored in the computer and to be available to police administrators when they seek to determine the department's financial needs and effectiveness. However, there is another very important reason for having good records on which to record data validly and reliably. That other purpose is research.

RESEARCH

Research is a process whereby facts are brought together, organized, and interpreted in order to explain some problem or phenomenon. An excellent definition of the purpose of research is ". . . to discover answers to meaningful questions through the application of scientific procedures."[9] The research process includes a statement of the problem to be researched, a description of the design of the research study, the methods to be used in collecting data, and the results of the research, which can then be used to establish new policies, procedures, or the more effective utilization of available resources.

Most research in law enforcement is of an operations or applied type. In other words, its primary purpose is to seek answers to problems facing the police in the carrying out of routine patrol and investigative activities, or in the solving of problems in the management of

---

[8]For an excellent discussion of specific types of police records and the establishment of a records system, the reader is referred to: The Institute for Training in Municipal Administration, Municipal Police Administration (Washington, D.C.: International City Management Association, 1971).

[9]Marie Jahoda, Morton Deutsch, and Stuart W. Cook, Research Methods in Social Relations (New York: The Dryden Press, 1954), p. 2.

a police department.[10] Very little research has been done in the field of law enforcement because of the lack of professionally trained research persons in police agencies and, until recently, the lack of resources to assist in the research process. However, the grave crime and delinquency problems in the United States have led to the granting of large sums of money for upgrading police services. A major result of this has been the need to determine, through research, the nature and purpose of the current police systems so that their problems, needs, and solutions can be established through additional and more continuous and sophisticated research.

RESEARCH IN LAW ENFORCEMENT

Most of the research in police agencies today is restricted almost totally to a few of the larger county, city, and state agencies and to the federal service.[11] Much of the research now being carried out involves the testing of equipment and products used by the police, and very little research is experimental or related to the development of new techniques. However, more research of all types is now in process, and all indications are that research will increase rapidly in the near future. More and more professionally educated researchers and computer experts are being added to police staffs, and sophisticated computer technology is being purchased at an accelerated rate.

Given the need for research, what are some of the problems of law enforcement which need solution or further information? There are many researchable problems. Let us briefly discuss a few.

Patrol.   What, for example, is the most effective way to utilize available patrol personnel to prevent crime and answer complaints? Should the greatest number of patrol personnel be utilized in the highest crime areas? What will be the impact in both the high, medium, and low crime areas under such a practice? Is the use of foot patrolmen more effective in preventing and repressing crime than that of the motorized officer? Is a combination foot and motorized

---

[10]For some excellent references with regard to the research method, the reader is referred to: Julian L. Somon, *Basic Research Methods in Social Science* (New York: Random House, 1969); John T. Doby, *An Introduction to Social Research* (New York: Appleton-Century-Crofts, 1967); Matilda W. Riley, *Sociological Research* (New York: Harcourt, Brace & World, Inc., 1963); The Institute for Defense Analysis, *Task Force Report: Science and Technology* (Washington, D. C.: The President's Commission on Law Enforcement and Administration of Justice, 1967).

[11]Wilson, p. 172.

patrol the most effective? What kinds of factors assist in the apprehension of suspects?

Investigative Operations.   On what basis should personnel be selected as investigators? What qualities are essential to be a successful investigator? Is there any desirable relationship between the types of cases to be investigated and the personal characteristics of a given investigator? What investigative techniques are most effective?

Personnel.   How should prospective police officers be selected, and what traits are related to success or failure in police work? What is the relationship between the height and weight of a police officer and his ability to perform routine police work versus riot or crowd control duties? What specific psychological traits are most essential for police work? Is there any relationship between a recruit's background characteristics and his ability to handle adequately persons from minority groups? What criteria should be used in selecting officers for promotion?

The above questions and many more must be answered through research to assist the police in effectively performing their duties. Several interesting and provocative studies have been completed or planned by various agencies and private foundations in the area of law enforcement, and some of these will now be described.

EXAMPLE OF RESEARCH IN LAW ENFORCEMENT

The Chicago Police Department was awarded a grant in August, 1967, under the provisions of the Law Enforcement Assistance Act, a federal act providing funds through the Law Enforcement Assistance Administration of the Department of Justice. The primary goals of the grant were to (1) demonstrate the applicability of operations research and systems analysis techniques to problems of resource allocation in a major police department; (2) prove the feasibility of conducting operations research studies with an "in-house" scientific group as opposed to the practice of using outside civilian consultants; and (3) familiarize, indoctrinate, and train police officials from Chicago and other cities in approaches, capabilities, and limitations of operations research.[12] Let us look briefly at one of the findings of the Chicago project to exemplify the role of planning, statistics, and research techniques.

---

[12]Operations Research Task Force of the Chicago Police Department, *Allocations of Resources in the Chicago Police Department* (Washington, D.C.: U.S. Department of Justice, March, 1972), p. xii.

The Chicago Police Department research group was interested in improving the quickness of the police response to a request from citizens for service. The objective was to study the current response time to citizen calls and to indicate how the response function can be more effective. The researchers found that patrol cars are dispatched on about 8,000 calls per day, and that about half of such calls occur during the hours of 6:00 p.m. to 2:00 a.m. They further found that only 12-15 percent of all calls for service, to which patrol cars were dispatched, involved crimes.[13] Thus, the many calls received by the police were of a non-emergency nature and so diverted essential police patrol cars from emergency calls, especially in the cases of criminality. One of the many conclusions and recommendations of the research team was that calls coming in for police service should be screened and that non-emergency calls for police service should be deferred. The result was the easing of excessive work loads on police officers, freeing them to answer emergency-type calls more quickly, as well as to free police cars for regular preventive patrols.

Other current examples of research and evaluation of police programs are those financed by a non-profit funding agency called the Police Foundation, which was established in 1970 by the Ford Foundation. With Police Foundation funds the Kansas City Police Department is currently experimenting with a "Proactive-Reactive Patrol Deployment Project."[14] The purpose of this experiment is to provide more efficient and effective police patrol practices in Kansas City, Missouri. The plan is to identify three similar geographical areas and to use a different patrol strategy in each of the areas. In one area, the total emphasis will be placed upon responding to citizens' calls for service as rapidly as possible. In another area, the emphasis will be not only on responding to calls for service, but also on engaging in aggressive patrol techniques known as preventive patrol. In the non-experimental, or regular patrol areas, present and usual operating procedures will be used.[15]

The purpose of this experiment is to determine whether there are any significant differences in the use of various types of patrol tactics in preventing crime and delivering police services. In the words of the project director for the Kansas City Police Department, "The

---

[13]Ibid., p. 32.

[14]George L. Kelling, *Kansas City South Patrol Division: Proactive-Reactive Patrol Deployment Project* (Washington, D.C.: Police Foundation, 1972).

[15]Ibid., pp. 1-2.

proactive-reactive patrol deployment strategy is a vigorous and systematic attempt to test the outcomes of different patrol strategies."[16]

Another study financed by the Police Foundation is being conducted within the Cincinnati Police Department. This study seeks to evaluate the mixing of various types of police services into a Neighborhood Team Policing Program.[17]

The overall purpose of the Community Sector Team Policing (COM-SEC) is to improve the effectiveness of police services to the community by strengthening the relationships between individual officers and the people they serve. In other words, COM-SEC is a method of policing to reduce the crime rate, improve police-community relations, and strengthen citizen cooperation with the police in crime prevention, detection, and apprehension activities.[18] The COM-SEC project is to take place in District One, a representative area, in Cincinnati, and will involve some 83 personnel including 50 patrol units over a 24-hour period. This method of policing attempts to combine the patrol and investigative functions in one team of officers at the community level who will have, under a team supervisor, complete responsibility for solving all law enforcement problems in the community being served.

The above are only some of the many types of research which can be developed to assist in the planning and implementation of new policies and techniques for the police so that they can more effectively accomplish their important goals.

TECHNOLOGY

Throughout this chapter the emphasis has been on the use of the most advanced techniques in managing police agencies, for without adequate planning, records, communications, and research the police department will be utilizing "horse and buggy" methods in a "Cadillac" age. Therefore to properly implement the above management procedures, and to make policing more effective, modern technology must be utilized. Although major advances have been made, a great deal more improvement and modernization must be made in police communications and information systems technology. At the present

---

[16]Ibid., p. 6.

[17]City of Cincinnati, Department of Safety, Division of Police, *Community Sector Team Policing Program* (Cincinnati: Ohio, Division of Police, April, 1972).

[18]Ibid., p. 1.

time, police communications and information technology is some twenty years behind the military and aerospace systems.[19] In the area of communications, the telephone and radio are of critical importance.

THE TELEPHONE SYSTEM

Every police agency should establish a telephone communications system designed to reduce crime through accurate and rapid communication with the public. In an emergency, the public should be able to contact the police immediately by making a single telephone call. Single area-wide emergency numbers, recorded message devices that detail emergency instructions, automatic switching equipment, and well-trained operators are essential.[20] Recording devices should be connected to telephone complaint reception lines so that incidents can be documented, and a police administrator can evaluate the workload and increase the efficiency of the communications system. Such recording devices can also aid in settling public complaints and the just disposition of legal suits arising from deaths, injuries, or property loss alleged to be due to police negligence.

Given the rapid rise in crime, and the growing demand for police services, the single universal emergency number, along with automatic number-identifying equipment, will greatly assist in meeting the public's demand for efficient and speedy police service. The single universal emergency telephone, 911, connects anyone dialing it to an emergency line at the local police agency. Dialing 911 eliminates the time-consuming extra step of having an operator place the emergency call. A complete 911 system should include automatic number identifier (ANI) which will instantaneously inform a police switchboard of the caller's telephone number by means of a visual display device.[21]

RADIO COMMUNICATIONS

Another critical method of communication for effective law enforcement is use of the radio. The National Advisory Commission on Criminal Justice Standards and Goals recommends the following:

---

[19]National Advisory Commission on Criminal Justice Standards and Goals, *Task Force on Police* (Washington, D.C.: U.S. Government Printing Office, 1973), p. 544.

[20]Op. cit., p. 547.

[21]Op. cit., p. 549.

Fig. 4-1: The Chicago Police communications center. (Photo courtesy of the Chicago Police Department)

(1) every state should establish statewide police radio frequencies to be used by state and local police agencies during emergencies; (2) every agency should have a base station, mobile, and portable radio equipment capable of two-way operation on a common statewide police radio frequency; (3) every agency should acquire and operate multichannel mobile and portable radio equipment capable of two-way operation on operational frequencies, and daily car-to-car tactical frequencies; and (4) every police agency should equip every on-duty uniformed officer with a portable radio transceiver capable of providing adequate two-way communications and capable of being carried with reasonable comfort on the person.[22]

An advanced communications system is known as digital com-

---

[22]Op. cit., p. 558.

munications. This is a system by which an officer can send standard messages electronically with the single action of a button on his radio linking him with base stations in a second or two. The officer may also be able to obtain information directly from computer data banks, and he can receive, in visual form in a police vehicle, information via a radioteleprinter.

In addition to utilizing advanced radio and telephonic systems, police agencies must also have the latest technology to establish and use information systems so that crime will be simply and efficiently reported, to assist in criminal investigations, and to provide complete information to other components of the criminal justice system. This will require adequate records and police reports. To accomplish this, The National Advisory Commission on Criminal Justice Standards and Goals recommends that every agency should coordinate its information system with those of other local, regional, state, and Federal law enforcement agencies to facilitate the exchange of information.[23] This would require each agency operating a full-time communications center and employing 15 or more persons to install a basic telecommunications terminal capable of transmitting to and receiving information from other agency information systems. There are a number of such telecommunications networks in operation now, such as the FBI's National Crime Information Center (NCIC), California Law Enforcement Telecommunications System (CLETS), and Automated Want-Warrant System, Los Angeles (AWWS).

In larger municipalities, elaborate communications centers are usually designed and installed. Fig. 4-1, for example, shows the large communications center of the Chicago Police Department.

---

[23]Op. cit., pp. 581-582.

CHAPTER V

SELECTION, TRAINING, AND EDUCATION

THE IMPORTANCE OF QUALIFIED PERSONNEL

A number of police administrators and writers consider police work to be a profession. Certainly there is no reason why it should not be considered a profession or why the police should not be thought of as equal partners in the administration of justice system. However, before true professional status is achieved in law enforcement, certain criteria must be met. These at least include: (1) a common body of knowledge in police science and administration, (2) a viable professional police organization or association, (3) public status and esteem, (4) professionally established selection requirements, (5) a code of ethics, (6) high educational requirements, and (7) a public service orientation. Currently great progress is being made toward the professionalization of police service, but actual professionalism has not been achieved to date. To do so will require the establishment of improved personnel management practices and procedures.[1]

A police agency, like any other government agency, will be able to perform its duties adequately and professionally only if it has a sufficient quantity and quality of personnel. In order to have such personnel, they must be carefully selected, trained, and educated to perform police work. As everyone is aware, police work is very sensitive and demanding. It requires persons who are physically and mentally fit and who can make sound judgments regarding such matters as when to arrest; when physical or deadly force is justified; how to handle family disputes, unruly juveniles, or suspicious persons; how to prevent riots; and how to deal with complex minority-group problems.

---

[1]For an excellent discussion of police professionalism, the reader is referred to Thomas F. Adams, *Law Enforcement* (Englewood Cliffs, N.J.: Prentice-Hall, 1973), pp. 257-263.

Obviously, given the very critical nature of law enforcement and its importance to the community and the entire administration of the justice system, police officers should be carefully selected and adequately trained and educated. Selection and training are two very important aspects of personnel management which include such matters as recruitment, selection criteria, examinations, tests, and training.

Police agencies should also stress that they are equal employment opportunity agencies and should actively seek qualified applicants without regard to race or sex. Under the Extention Act of 1972 (Public Law 92-261), the authority of the Federal Equal Employment Opportunity Commission (EEOC) was extended to cover the employment practices of state and local government agencies. The EEOC *Guidelines on Employee Selection Procedures*, 1970, prohibit the use of any selection procedures that would involve employment discrimination.[2] However, this does not mean that applicants should be appointed as police officers who do not meet appropriate qualifications or who are unable to perform police functions adequately. These matters will now be discussed to impress upon you their importance to police work.

RECRUITMENT

ADVERTISING AND RELATED TECHNIQUES

There is no function more important in the entire employment process than that of recruitment. Recruitment is the procedure whereby qualified applicants are attracted and considered for employment as police officers. After all, a police agency can only select from those who have applied, and it is therefore most imperative that the best possible persons be encouraged to apply. In order to attract the best applicants possible, the police agency must put into effect a vigorous recruitment program designed to reach the best potential pool of police manpower.

There are various recruitment techniques which can be used, and extensive and well-planned advertising methods (such as posters, brochures, newspapers, and TV advertisements) should be utilized. The amount and extent of advertisement will depend upon the need

---

[2]National Advisory Commission on Criminal Justice Standards and Goals, *Task Force on Police* (Washington, D.C.: U.S. Government Printing Office, 1973), pp. 338, 434.

for recruits, but all advertising information should clearly indicate the application requirements, and qualified persons should be encouraged to apply. Written advertisements should be widely circulated, especially at colleges and universities offering degrees in criminology, criminal justice, and law enforcement.

Perhaps the most effective advertising and recruitment program is one conducted on a nationwide basis, preferably by professional advertising firms. There are some 40,000 separate police agencies in the United States, and many of them have poorly planned, financed, and executed recruitment programs which restrict employment to local residents. Such residency requirements should be removed and recruitment carried out on a nationwide basis.

One recruitment method which may be used is to have all departments in a state jointly engage in a statewide recruitment campaign. The reasons for joint or statewide programs include: (1) the availability of more extensive budgets for recruiting at substantially less cost than would be the case with individual departments, (2) the adoption of common application procedures, and (3) the establishment of a vast and excellent manpower pool.[3]

Another effective method for attracting new applicants is the so-called "recruiting-incentive plan," whereby new policemen are recruited through contacts with existing personnel. Various incentives are used to have members of the department act as recruitment officers. For example, if an officer recruits applicants who are subsequently appointed to the department, he will receive a cash bonus or additional vacation days.[4]

A third promising method for recruiting excellent applicants is through the development of formal internship programs with colleges and universities having criminology or law enforcement programs. In this way, students will be assigned to a police agency as a part of their curriculum requirements, and the agency will have an opportunity to attract excellent officers with formal education in the field.

All of the above techniques should clearly indicate the benefits of police work, such as salary and raises, insurance plans, sick leave,

[3]The President's Commission on Law Enforcement and the Administration of Justice, *Task Force Report: The Police* (Washington, D.C.: U.S. Government Printing Office, 1967), pp. 136-37; National Advisory Commission, p. 321.

[4]O. W. Wilson and Roy C. McLaren, *Police Administration*, 3rd ed. (New York: McGraw-Hill Book Co., 1972), p. 253.

retirement benefits, educational opportunities, vacations, and especially the importance of police work to the community.

ELIGIBILITY REQUIREMENTS

A most essential part of the recruitment process is the establishment of eligibility requirements which applicants must satisfy before they can be considered for selection as police officers. Therefore, certain eligibility requirements relevant to police work must be clearly indicated. They must also be nondiscriminatory and contribute toward the professionalization of law enforcement. Obviously, physical and mental requirements must be stringent, and a minimum age is essential. Some of the most frequent eligibility requirements for police service include age, residence, education, and physical requirements. Let us briefly review each of these four factors.

Age Requirements. Most police agencies establish twenty-one as the minimum acceptable age for becoming a policeman, although some agencies require that applicants be up to twenty-five years of age at the time of appointment. However, the trend in the nation is to reduce the age of majority from twenty-one to eighteen, and the result will be the lowering of age requirements for police work. Police service does require vigorous and energetic young persons, and the younger recruit has more potential years of service and will justify the costly investment necessary to recruit and train him. If police departments required all applicants to possess a college degree, then a minimum age of twenty-one would become a reality.

Just as a minimum age requirement is necessary, however, so also must there be a maximum age requirement, and most police departments will reject applicants who are over thirty-five years of age. A noted expert on law enforcement recommends an age limit of twenty-one through twenty-nine, although he does extend the upper limit to a maximum of thirty-five for previous police service on a year-for-year basis.[5] What should be remembered is that the purpose for establishing minimum and maximum age limits is to attract the most vigorous, physically able, and mature applicants, who have reached the legal age of majority, so that they may perform police duties. Given the great and complex responsibilities of policemen, a college degree with a speciality in criminology and law enforcement is desirable, but as long as the police continue to recruit high school graduates, it will be necessary to lower the entrance age requirement

---

[5]Ibid., p. 255.

to eighteen. Regardless of the minimum age requirement, only the mature, stable, and best applicants should be selected for police service.

Residency Requirements. The great majority of departments have residency requirements which vary from six months to several years and require an applicant to be a resident of the state, city, or county in which he is applying. Such a requirement reduces the number of qualified applicants from whom the most promising may be selected. Qualified young persons who are residents of other cities, or small towns and rural areas which lack opportunities in their local police agencies, are often available and interested in police work in other larger communities. It must also be pointed out that a further advantage of appointing an out-of-town applicant is that he has no local friendships or possible feelings of obligation to residents that may influence his official attitude toward them.

The residency requirement can probably be traced back to the depression, when jobs were scarce and local residents were given preference, as well as to the local political structure with its emphasis on local control of government through the appointment of local residents. Many of the larger urban departments are removing the residence requirement, and most police experts support this change. However, citizenship should be required of all candidates, and local residence after appointment is desirable except in communities where such a requirement would work an unnecessary hardship on police officers because of limited housing facilities.

Educational Requirements. As has been stated many times in this text, police work is a complex task in modern urban America, and the proper performance of such a service requires more than physical prowess and common sense. Contemporary police work requires highly educated personnel. However, the majority of police agencies in the United States require, at most, a minimum of a high school education. Thus, various surveys of educational requirements reveal that in 24 percent of the departments surveyed there was no minimum educational prerequisite, while less than 1 percent required any level of college preparation. In the New England states over 72 percent of the departments surveyed did not even require their applicants to have a high school diploma. Finally, a survey of 6,200 officers in 1964 showed that only 30.3 percent had taken one or more college courses and only 7.3 percent had a college degree, while a 1966 survey of 5,700 officers in metropolitan Detroit police agencies revealed that over 75 percent of these officers had not attended college.[6]

The National Advisory Commission on Criminal Justice Standards and Goals indicated in its Task Force Report on Police that every policy agency should establish the following entry-level educational requirements:

1. Immediately require as a condition of initial employment the completion of at least one year of education (30 semester units) at an accredited college or university. If qualified police applicants do not satisfy this requirement but have a high school diploma or its equivalent, they should be employed under a contract requiring completion of the educational requirement within three years of employment.
2. Every police agency should, no later than 1975, require as a condition of initial employment the completion of at least two years of college education.
3. Every police agency should, no later than 1978, require as a condition of initial employment the completion of at least three years of college education.
4. Every police agency should, no later than 1982, require as a condition of initial employment the completion of at least four years of college education.[7]

Given the many difficult decisions that a police officer must make in the course of his work, and the complex knowledge he must possess, it is obvious that relevant higher education is essential. For example, he must be able to read, understand, and apply the many court decisions relating to law enforcement, write clear and substantial reports, and understand the importance of the community structure and human behavior. The fact that this type of knowledge, and much more, is essential today should indicate the importance of requiring a college education for all police, especially those in the metropolitan areas. Certainly a college education should be mandatory for all supervisory personnel, because in most departments administrators are selected from among men of lower rank within the

⁶The President's Commission on Law Enforcement and the Administration of Justice, p. 126.

⁷National Advisory Commission on Criminal Justice Standards and Goals, p. 369.

department. The operation and management of a large police department is as complex as that of any other private or public agency of
comparable size and resources. It can no longer be assumed that a
police agency can be administered effectively by a person whose only
qualification is extensive police experience.

Physical Requirements. It should be obvious that a police officer
must have physical courage and must be in excellent health to perform adequately his most demanding duties. Such qualities may help
to save his own life or the lives of others. However, existing physical
requirements are unnecessarily restrictive in most police departments. Because of this, many otherwise exceptionally qualified applicants are rejected because of height, weight, or vision. For example, a
1962 survey revealed that nearly 85 percent of the police departments
studied had a mandatory height requirement of 5'8" or higher.[8] Certainly, inflexible physical requirements, including height, should be
eliminated. Likewise, there is little reason for requiring near perfect
and uncorrected vision of all applicants, and yet most police agencies
require perfect and uncorrected vision for both eyes, or slightly less
for one eye correctable to 20/20. Many non-police organizations, in
which excellent vision is just as important, have less stringent
standards, for example, professional athletic leagues, the Federal
Aviation Agency, and the United States Army Infantry.

Many police departments are now recognizing that physical requirements are arbitrarily rigid and should be determined on an
individual basis. O. W. Wilson has stated that the physician should
determine height-weight relationship. He has also pointed out that
the majority of officers are on motorized patrol and are trained in
techniques of self-defense which are effective regardless of height or
weight.[9] However, because most police work requires physical
strength and agility, agencies must not establish criteria that will
result in the hiring of officers unable to perform their duties
adequately.[10]

SELECTION

It can be said that there is no more important matter in law enforce-

---

[8]George W. O'Connor, *Survey of Selection Methods* (Washington: International Association of Chiefs of Police, 1962), p. 28.

[9]Wilson and McLaren, p. 257.

[10]National Advisory Commission on Criminal Justice Standards and
Goals, p. 343.

ment than the selection of new police officers. The integrity of a police agency, as well as its ability to carry out its functions, is largely determined by the type of personnel selected as officers. Therefore, it is important to discuss the selection process, which begins after a group of applicants have been found minimally qualified as a result of recruitment procedures.

Only the best applicants should be selected, and a carefully planned procedure must be established to select them. Remember, a police officer must be physically and mentally sound; he must be intelligent and well educated; he must be courageous, impartial, honest, tactful and capable of using sound judgment; finally he must be able to enforce the law sensibly and exercise a great deal of discretionary powers in the protection of life and property. Therefore, the selection process must be structured and administered to select applicants who possess such outstanding attributes. A good selection procedure will include examination and tests, character investigation, oral interview and selection, and a probationary period.

EXAMINATIONS AND TESTS

The purpose of examinations and tests is to assist in the determination of an applicant's intelligence, aptitude, emotional stability, and physical fitness to perform police duties. It is important to remember that except for medical and physical tests and examinations undue dependence on test scores is questionable because of our limited knowledge concerning aptitude, intelligence, and the psychological make-up of man. Such tests are to be used in conjunction with other information about an applicant as determined by a polygraph examination, background investigation, oral interview, and his performance during his probationary period. However, given this caveat, let us review some of the types of examinations and tests that are administered, or should be administered, to all prospective police officers.

In attempting to determine if an applicant has average or above intelligence and is emotionally stable, several well-established tests of mental ability are utilized. These usually include the California Mental Maturity Test, Minnesota Multiphasic Personality Inventory, Army Alpha Test, Army General Classification Test, and the Otis Self-Administering Test of Mental Ability.[11] In addition to these types

---

[11]James W. Osterburg, J. Trubitt, and Richard A. Myren, "Cadet Programs: An Innovative Change," *Journal of Criminal Law, Criminology and Police Science*, LVIII (June, 1967), 112-18.

of tests, some police agencies include a psychiatric examination for all applicants, while others include a psychiatric examination only if there is some question concerning the emotional stability or suitability of a particular applicant. Finally, some police departments are attempting to develop examinations and tests specifically designed to determine if an applicant has the necessary skills to be a police officer. Unfortunately, a fairly recent survey of police agencies indicates that very few departments are evaluating the personalities of applicants, and there is little or no research being done on police selection techniques.[12]

An excellent and extensive review of current selection and promotion techniques utilized by police agencies throughout the country reached the following conclusions:

1. The development of effective unbiased police selection and promotion procedures has limited value, and far more research must be undertaken to develop adequate procedures.
2. There is some evidence supporting the potential value of some written objective tests, situational tests, and personal history data in predicting police officer performance.
3. The specific criteria to be used in selecting or promoting police officers needs far more study, but there is good evidence that a relationship exists between psychological tests of aptitude or intelligence and a recruit's performance in training.[13]

The obvious purpose of physical and medical examinations and tests is to make certain that an applicant is in excellent health, that he possesses the necessary stamina, strength, agility, and general good health to perform police work, and that he will not have an early disability or frequent illness or become a burden to the department and the retirement and pension benefits. A medical examination, preferably by the department physician, will ascertain height and weight requirements, freedom from disabling diseases or physical handicaps, and adequate uncorrected or corrected vision. While

---

[12]J. T. Flynn and M. Peterson, "The Use of Regression in Police Patrolman Selection," *Journal of Criminal Law, Criminology and Police Science*, LXIII (Dec., 1972), 565.

[13]For an excellent review of the recent literature and selection and promotion procedures, the reader is referred to: Deborah Ann Kent and Terry Eisenberg, "The Selection and Review of Recent Literature," *Police Chief* XXXIX (Feb., 1972), 20-29.

physical requirements are critical, they should not be inflexible, and factors such as height should be considered along with the other attributes of the applicant, rather than be automatically disqualifying.

In regard to height, the Attorney General of the United States, Richard G. Kleindienst, on March 9, 1973, issued new guidelines for the Law Enforcement Assistance Administration (LEAA). This division of the United States Department of Justice, which is responsible for allocating anti-crime funds to police agencies, stipulated that police departments receiving such funds are forbidden to establish height requirements that discriminate against minority groups and women. The Attorney General further stated, "The height guideline prohibits the use of minimum height requirements when they tend to disproportionately disqualify persons of certain national origins and races and women from jobs on police forces or other criminal justice agencies, and *are unrelated to the job performance* of law enforcement personnel."[14]

As to strength and agility, departments should establish tests to determine these and particularly to reveal a lack of coordination, strength, and speed necessary for police service.

CHARACTER INVESTIGATION

A properly conducted background investigation is one of the most important checks on an applicant's suitability for police work. Such an investigation requires hours of a trained investigator's time and should be restricted only to those applicants who have successfully passed the medical, physical, psychological, and intelligence tests as well as a polygraph examination. Carefully administered polygraph examinations will greatly reduce the amount of time spent in a background investigation and will result in obtaining critical applicant information not available through normal investigative sources. The character investigation is based upon the candidate's lengthy and detailed personal-history application, and it involves interviewing references and other persons in the applicant's neighborhood and his past and present employers, and a check of his criminal records and fingerprints. The obvious purpose of the character investigation is to determine the applicant's work habits, prior convictions, schooling, prejudices, emotional stability, indebtedness, organizational affiliations, hobbies, and all other relevant informa-

---

[14]Law Enforcement Assistance Administration, *Newsletter*, vol. 3, no. 2, U.S. Department of Justice, p. 2, 1973.

tion regarding his fitness to perform police work. Some departments interview the candidate's immediate family in their homes to ascertain their reaction to police work, and still other agencies require a lie detector test.

Several studies indicate that there is a relationship between certain background characteristics and success in police work. One study of a northeastern city having a population of nearly 200,000 found that that city's police recruit selection criteria indicated an applicant's experience and training represent the best single predictive for subsequent performance in the police training academy.[15] In another study it was found that of one hundred men who had terminated their employment in police work, their former employers characterized them as failures,[16] and that there was a definite relationship between background information and subsequent performance on the job.[17]

It is important to realize that a thorough and systematic character investigation can assist greatly in predicting which applicants are most likely to succeed or fail as police officers. However, it is important that the background investigation be objective and that the same information and methods of gathering data be utilized for each applicant. With the completion of more research on the relationship between precise background factors relating to success or failure in police work, character investigations may necessarily narrow themselves to a careful check of such factors.

ORAL INTERVIEW AND SELECTION

In addition to the above selection procedures, most police agencies use another procedure, the oral interview, to determine the character and fitness of an applicant before his appointment. The oral interview is conducted by a selected group of officers, or a combination of officers and civilian personnel specialists, who interview each applicant to determine his suitability for police work. The advantage of this selection procedure is that it gives the police agency the opportunity to evaluate the demeanor and attitude of the applicant, and through probing questions it can help determine his ability to handle stress situations and to respond appropriately to judgmental

---

[15]Flynn and Peterson, p. 569.

[16]Ruth J. Levy, *Investigation of a Method for Identification of the High Risk Police Applicant* (California: Institute for Local Self Government, 1970).

[17]Gilmore Spencer and Robert Nichols, "A Study of Chicago Police Recruits," *Police Chief*, XXXVIII (1971), 50-55.

questions.[18] Such interviews are necessarily subjective and can result in the introduction of political influence and the bias of individual interviewing officers. Nevertheless, it is an essential part of the selection process, although it should not be given undue weight, and must be considered along with the background investigation and the examinations and tests. Objectivity in the oral interview may be obtained by including members on the board from other police agencies, as well as some citizens. Certainly, no organization would appoint an employee without an oral interview to determine the applicant's fitness for a given position. Once again, however, it should be emphasized that more research is necessary to establish valid and reliable oral interviewing techniques.

PROBATIONARY PERIOD

After the above procedures have been completed successfully, an applicant is finally selected as a police officer. However, there is one final, and most important, element of the selection process to determine the applicant's suitability for police work, and that is the probationary period of appointment.

No matter how carefully a police department has screened and finally selected its personnel, the final, and perhaps most valid, technique for determining an applicant's suitability for police service is actual trial on the job. Police agencies have long recognized that a period of probation is necessary to judge the qualities of a new employee.[19] The desirable probationary period is one year, although most police agencies require a period of only six months.

The probationary period permits the agency to evaluate the recruit's ability to deal adequately with the demands of police work and to note any inadequacies which occur under actual working conditions. Probation should include a careful and consistent evaluation of performance. Such evaluation provides correction of deficiencies in the selection process and may result either in the dismissal of the recruit or in his further guidance and training to assist him in developing those attributes necessary to be a good law enforcement officer. Certainly, the first three to six months of a recruit's employment should be devoted to training in situations where his

[18]For an excellent discussion of the oral interview see: George W. O'Conner, *Survey of Selection Methods* (Washington. D.C.: International Association of Chiefs of Police, 1962).

[19]The President's Commission on Law Enforcement and the Administration of Justice, p. 132.

capabilities can be observed, and his remaining six months to serving in the field as an officer. Probationary officers should be closely supervised, and formal progress reports should be completed on their performance.

The purpose of the probationary period is to assist the officer in becoming an adequate career employee. If this is impossible, that is, if he is unsuitable, the recruit should be dismissed from service. If there are many separations of recruits during the probationary period, the selection procedures are probably inadequate and need substantial revisions and supervision.

It should be obvious from the above discussion that the selection process is essential in appointing quality police recruits. Without a professional and thorough selection procedure, inadequate personnel will be appointed to the department. The result will be citizen complaints and ineffective law enforcement activities. This can quickly lead to corruption, increased crime, and a breakdown of the entire criminal justice system.

After good recruits have been appointed, they must be educated and trained so that they can render satisfactory police service. Police recruits, and existing personnel as well, must be intensively and regularly trained to perform the complex duties of police work in our urban society. Professional education and training is as important for the police officer as it is for the physician, school teacher, lawyer, psychologist, physicist, chemist, or any other professional personnel.

TRAINING

The obvious purpose of education and training is to enable the police to carry out effectively the spirit and letter of the law under which they operate. At the present time, the vast majority of police recruits have had little or no education or training in law enforcement. Therefore, they must receive these within the police agency or in combination with colleges, universities, and police academies. An officer must know the criminal law and its application, understand the ordinances of a given jurisdiction, the rules and regulations of his department, first aid, the use of firearms, self-defense, community relations, and many other matters relevant to police work. He must also be able to read well, write good reports, use technical equipment, and so on. We are primarily concerned here with the training a new recruit must receive upon being selected as a police officer, although we shall also briefly mention continuous training for all personnel already with the department.

RECRUIT TRAINING

This type of training, as its name implies, is the initial in-service training given to all newly appointed police officers. Recruit training of some type is provided by almost all police agencies. It has been found that an average of twelve weeks of such training is provided in the larger city police departments, but the period varies according to the size of a given department. Departments in cities of over 500,000 average 529 hours per year, according to a survey of police agencies by the International Association of Chiefs of Police.[20] For cities from 100,000 to 500,000, recruit training time dropped to 375 hours; in cities of 25,000 to 100,000 population, training time dropped to 240-249 hours; for agencies in cities under 25,000 population, the training time was 210 hours per year.[21] The above survey further indicated that the adequacy of training facilities and staff was most extensive in those cities over 500,000 in population.

Any adequate recruit training program must be at least twelve weeks in length, and should include both classroom and field instruction so that the new officer can relate lecture materials to actual police work in the community. A recruit training program must include specific job skills, but also attitude development, knowledge about the behavioral problems of people, and understanding of the structure and characteristics of the community the officer is to police. Finally, a good recruit training program will include some classroom instruction, followed by actual field training and then a return to the classroom for further instruction and review of the recruit's performance in the field.

A recruit training program should offer classroom and field instruction in at least the following subjects: (1) criminal law; (2) methods of self-defense; (3) the proper use of firearms; (4) the appropriate use of force; (5) local ordinances and agency rules and regulations; (6) specific police tactics and operations; (7) fingerprinting and other criminalistic techniques; (8) investigation; (9) records and communications; (10) press relations; (11) patrol; (12) traffic procedures; (13) report writing; (14) community relations; (15) history and philosophy of law enforcement; (16) the criminal justice system,

---

[20]Wilson and McLaren, p. 305.
[21]Ibid.

including the role of other community agencies; (17) personal appearance, conduct, and attitude; (18) arrest procedures; (19) juvenile procedures; and (20) crowd control.

These basic subjects must be taught effectively, so that the recruit will understand the materials and adequately apply them to police work. To accomplish this, careful attention must be given to the selection of instructors and the methods of instruction. Most training courses are taught almost exclusively by lecture method even though such instruction has limited effectiveness.

A recent computer-assisted instruction technique was demonstrated successfully in the area of police searches, seizures, and the rules of evidence. The Coast Community College District and the Los Angeles Police Department completed a joint project in which computerized case problems were used to reinforce learning, broaden perspectives, and provide simulated field experiences for recruits completing the search and seizure section of training.[22] This experiment was more effective in preparing officers for field work and applying basic rules of evidence to actual criminal investigations than the classroom lecture technique was when used alone.

Other instructional techniques should include the use of films, recordings, TV, and role playing in which each recruit plays the role of criminal, investigator, citizen, supervisor, and so on. What is important is that various instructional methods should be utilized, and the strict lecture method should not be the only training method.

CONTINUOUS TRAINING

After a recruit completes his initial or basic entrance training, he must receive continuous training of a general and specialized nature so that he may keep abreast of new knowledge or be prepared for more specialized work and possible advancement to supervisory positions. Such continuous in-service training usually includes techniques of supervision, recent court decisions and their applicability to police work, criminalistics, techniques of investigation, patrol, management training, and much more. The importance of continuous in-service training is to make certain that all personnel receive the regular and essential instruction so that they may more adequately perform their duties.

---

[22]Richard W. Brightman, *Computer Assisted Instruction Program for Police Training* (Washington, D.C.: U.S. Department of Justice Law Enforcement Assistance Administration, PR 71-5, Dec., 1971).

Aside from training, all new and regular police personnel should be required to attain higher educational degrees. The most desirable situation is to require a relevant college education prior to entrance into police work. Where this is not feasible, every effort should be made to encourage personnel to further their education while on the police force.

EDUCATION AND PROFESSIONALIZATION

If a police force is to become professional, it must require higher educational degrees. That this is essential is evidenced by the development of other professions such as teaching, social work, chemistry, medicine, law, psychology, and many others. The Federal Bureau of Investigation has established a high professional image because of its requirement that all agents possess at least an undergraduate. college degree. There is no reason why similar but more relevant requirements cannot be required of all police personnel. The President's Commission on Law Enforcement and the Administration of Justice recommended, in 1967, that all future personnel should be required to have completed at least two years of college preparation at an accredited institution, and that the ultimate goal should be the requirement that all personnel with general enforcement powers have baccalaureate degrees.[23] At the present time, there are about 515 colleges and universities offering 505 associate degrees, 211 baccalaureate degrees, 41 master's degrees, and nine doctorate degrees in the area of criminology, criminal justice, and police science.[24]

A recent survey, which sought to assess the value trends of police officers in this country by using panels of 52 working police officers and 60 police administrators, law enforcement educators, attorneys, and specialists in social ethics, concluded that the police should become more "professional." Eighty-nine percent of the participants cited continuing education in service and the establishment of

---

[23]President's Commission on Law Enforcement and Administration of Justice, p. 126.

[24]International Association of Chiefs of Police, *1972-73 Directory of Law Enforcement and Criminal Justice Education* (Maryland: International Association of Chiefs of Police, 1972), p. 5.

minimum standards of education and training as essential to "professionalism."[25]

Thus, it appears that the nature of police work and its effect on our society demand that educational requirements for police personnel be raised to the level of a college degree. Certainly, the quality of police service will not significantly improve until steps in this direction have been taken, for "police officers, who, in various unpredictable situations, are required to make difficult judgments, should possess a sound knowledge of society and human behavior."[26]

---

[25]Terry L. Cooper, *The Delphi Project on Police Values* (Los Angeles: Center for Urban Affairs, University of Southern California, March 22, 1973), p. 11.

[26]President's Commission on Law Enforcement and Administration of Justice, p. 126.

CHAPTER VI

PATROL AND
TRAFFIC FUNCTIONS

THE MEANING AND PURPOSE OF PATROL

The largest, most complex, most important, and most indispensable unit of any state or local police agency is the patrol unit. In fact, police agencies were created specifically for the purpose of patrolling the community in order to protect citizens from criminals, and to provide other needed police services. The word "patrol" means to move back and forth in a given geographical area for the purpose of observation and maintaining security. Therefore, the police patrol is the deployment of police officers in a given community to deter criminal activity and to provide day-to-day police services to the community.[1]

Although police work has become complex and includes many specialized activities, the patrol function is its principal activity. All other police services should directly or indirectly assist the patrol force, and only the best personnel should be selected as patrolmen. The patrol force is usually the first point of contact between the citizen, the police, and the entire administration of justice system. It is responsible for the performance of all major police tasks and provides complete coverage of the community at every hour of the day and night.[2] Frequently, the patrolmen in an automobile patrol unit (Fig. 6-1) are the citizen's first contact with a police department.

The personnel of the patrol force generally serve in uniform and are distributed throughout the community in order to perform a variety of essential functions. These functions include patrol and observation, supervising public gatherings, responding to calls for assistance, investigation, collecting and preserving evidence, arrest-

---

[1]National Advisory Commission on Criminal Justice Standards And Goals, *Police* (Washington, D.C.: U.S. Government Printing Office, 1973). p. 189.

[2]O. W. Wilson and Roy C. McLaren, *Police Administration* (New York: McGraw-Hill Book Company, 1972), p. 323.

Fig. 6-1: A typical automobile patrol unit. (Photo courtesy of the Cook County Sheriff's Police Department)

ing offenders, preparing reports, and testifying in court.[3] However, as frequently mentioned in this text, the patrol force performs the above functions because they are essential in fulfilling the police agency's primary objectives, that is, preventing and suppressing crime, arresting offenders, and giving aid and information to all citizens.[4]

---

[3]Institute for Training in Municipal Administration, *Municipal Police Administration* (Washington, D.C.: International City Management Association, 1971), pp. 77-78.

[4]The reader is referred to the following additional texts on the patrol function: National Advisory Commission on Criminal Justice Standards and Goals, *Task Force on Police* (Washington, D.C.: U.S. Government Printing Office, 1973), Chapter 8; N.F. Iannone, *Principles of Police Patrol* (New York: McGraw-Hill Book Company, 1975); Thomas F. Adams, *Police Patrol Tactics and Techniques* (Englewood Cliffs, N.J.: Prentice-Hall, Inc., 1971); Donald T. Shanahan, *Patrol Administration* (Boston: Holbrook Press, Inc., 1975).

In the performance of his legal responsibilities, the patrolman is also a decision-maker. He must decide whether to arrest, make a referral, seek prosecution, or use force, and such decisions have an important effect on the people he serves. In other words, he uses, and must use, a great deal of discretion in enforcing the law, for many laws are ambiguous and he must often make a split-second decision to deal with an incident in an official or unofficial manner. It is the police officer who determines whether to take no action, advise, or warn; he determines whether he must apply physical force, perhaps sufficient to cause death. It is he who must distinguish between a civil and a criminal conflict, between merely unorthodox behavior and a crime, between legitimate dissent and disturbance of the peace.[5] James Q. Wilson, in his excellent study of police behavior, noted that police officers perform a complex task; they work alone or in pairs and are not under continuous supervision. Therefore, the lowest ranking police officer—the patrolman—has the greatest discretion and his behavior is of the greatest concern to the public, the police administrator, and the officer himself.[6]

In the execution of his duties, the patrolman must respond immediately to serious incidents. FBI studies indicate that the clearance rate of crime goes up as the response time of patrol units is reduced. The figures show that police solve two-thirds of the crimes they respond to in less than 2 minutes, but only one out of five when response time is 5 minutes or longer.[7] Therefore, unsolved crime is reduced when agencies insure that patrol officers are available and respond immediately to serious incidents. Thus the proper utilization of diverse types of patrols is essential to good law enforcement.

TYPES OF PATROL

There are many different types and methods of patrol utilized by police agencies in this country. These include (1) automobile patrol, (2) foot patrol, (3) motorcycle and bicycle patrol, (4) aircraft and helicopter patrol, (5) marine patrol, (6) horse patrol, and (7) canine

---

[5]National Advisory Commission on Criminal Justice Standards And Goals, p. 192.

[6]James Q. Wilson, *Varieties of Police Behavior* (New York: Atheneum, 1973), pp. 7-8.

[7]National Advisory Commission on Criminal Justice Standards And Goals, p. 193.

patrol. The particular type of patrol utilized is dependent upon the characteristics and requirements of a given community, but the most common and best known type of uniformed patrol in the United States today is the motorized patrol.

AUTOMOBILE PATROL

The primary method the police use for patrolling American communities is the automobile patrol. This is the use of clearly marked and identified police vehicles by uniformed police personnel. Automobile patrol became the predominant method of patrol because it increased the officer's mobility and his ability to cover a large area and respond more quickly to calls for police service, as well as to give the impression that the police are available and visible at all times. For example, the Indianapolis Police Department in 1969 established a policy of assigning marked patrol cars to individual officers on a twenty-four hour basis. The result is that there are more marked police vehicles on the street at all times, for the Indianapolis officers are allowed to use the cars during off-duty hours. This resulted in more cars being available for emergencies, and since patrolmen were urged to keep their radios on while in the car, it also increased their availability for service.

The use of the automobile shelters the officer from the inclement weather, protects him in a gun battle, shields him from objects dropped from buildings or thrown at him, and allows him to transport several officers or prisoners at one time. Finally the automobile puts him on an equal basis with a law violater who is using an automobile to violate the law.

Of course, there is a major disadvantage in the use of auto patrol in that it causes a loss of personal contact between the officer and the citizen. As a result of this, the officer will not be so well informed about the potential, or actual, commission of crime in his patrol area, and there will be a general decline of mutual understanding and good public relations.

Another important issue in the use of the automobile patrol is whether one or two officers should be assigned to a car. The advantages of the one-man motorized unit follow:

1. Patrol coverage can be twice as extensive as when two men are assigned to a single vehicle.
2. Patrol areas can be reduced in size, thus allowing for quicker response and a more extensive coverage.

3.   A single auto patrol officer is more likely to be observant and alert than when he is accompanied by another officer.
4.   The one-man motorized patrol is less expensive because there is only one salaried officer per car on patrol duty.

On the other hand, there are some arguments in favor of two-man auto patrols, including the following:

1.   One-man cars may be more dangerous because there is no assistance immediately available to the officer in difficulty.
2.   A two-man car doubles the manpower and show of authority.
3.   A lone officer will not assume the necessary risks without additional help.
4.   One man in a patrol car cannot drive and observe effectively matters requiring police action.

For the most part, police agencies utilize one-man auto patrols, and this is especially so in communities with a population of from 10,000 to 100,000 residents.[8] Obviously, the question of whether to have one-man or two-man patrol cars must be considered in the light of circumstances in a given community or section of that community. For example, in many urban communities there has been an increase in serious crimes and attacks on police officers. Since greater protection of the police is therefore required, two-man patrol cars should be used in these areas. Where such conditions do not exist, the one-man patrol is the most efficient auto-patrol method, given modern communications equipment, training, and planning.

FOOT PATROL

The oldest and most commonly known type of patrol is the foot patrol, or the patrolling of communities by walking policemen. Although most of the larger city police departments assign some personnel to foot patrol (a 1966 study of thirty-seven American cities having populations between 300,000 and one million showed that all but four cities had some personnel assigned to walking beats) with rare exceptions only a small percentage of the patrol force was so utilized.[9] A major, and very important, advantage of the foot patrol is

---

[8]Ibid., p. 85.
[9]Police Department of Kansas City, Missouri, *1966 Survey of Municipal Police Departments* (Kansas City, Mo.: Police Department, 1966), p. 22.

that it provides for closer personal relations between the police and the citizen and enables the officer to observe and know a given "beat" area more adequately. This ability is invaluable in the prevention and suppression of crime, and especially in the development of positive police-community relations. However, the use of foot patrols restricts the area to be covered, requires far more personnel, and thus greatly increases the cost of the patrol operation.

The generally accepted point of view is that a decision to use foot patrols should be made only after careful analysis, since it is a highly expensive form of coverage and can be wasteful of manpower. Nevertheless, it is also agreed that some officers should be assigned to foot patrols in commercial and high-crime areas where the need can be justified. In all other areas, officers should be assigned to cars, but should be trained as motorized foot patrolmen; that is, they should leave their cars from time to time so that they can more carefully observe an area, maintain better citizen contact, and provide greater public service. Such a practice will still allow an officer to maintain contact with headquarters by way of portable radio sets, and he can inform his superiors by radio prior to leaving his car on a foot patrol. An officer who spends all of his time on foot covers a small area, engages in much idle gossip, is less mobile, and has no transportation available to him. On the other hand, a completely motorized patrolman can remain hidden in his car when he should be patrolling, is in poorer physical condition because of little or no walking, and will not make on-the-spot inspections or contacts with citizens. Therefore, except where only foot patrols can be justified, the use of officers assigned to cars as foot patrolmen from time to time achieves the best of both the foot- and auto-patrolling methods.

MOTORCYCLE AND BICYCLE PATROL

A number of American police agencies continue to use two-wheel and three-wheel motorcycles, especially for traffic control and special occasions, such as parades and escort duty. In general, however, the use of the two-wheeled motorcycle patrol has decreased in recent years for several important reasons. Departments that have used solo, or two-wheel, motorcycles, have found them to be costly to operate, hazardous to the driver, and inoperative during inclement weather when the police should be most active in the enforcement of traffic regulations or readily available for special escort duties. Additionally, the solo motorcycle is tiring for the driver and has no capacity to transport prisoners, other personnel, or equipment. However, the three-wheel motorcycle can be operated regardless of road conditions and is far less hazardous, less tiring to drive, and has transportation capabilities. In essence, the three-wheel motorcycle has most of the advantages of the solo motorcycle plus greater maneuverability in dense traffic than the automobile. Because of this, most authorities feel that where motorcycles are necessary, the three-wheel motorcycle is to be used. On the other hand, some police agencies are abandoning motorcycles entirely in favor of compact cars for patrolling in dense traffic or highly congested commercial centers, because they have all of the advantages of automobiles, discussed above, and yet they are small and highly maneuverable.

Bicycle patrols are still used in many European countries to a much greater extent than in the United States. However, Baltimore, Maryland, has utilized bicycle patrols since 1915, and is currently using them in dealing with residential burglaries.[10] Prior to the production of automobiles, bicycles were widely used by patrolmen. The bicycle patrol officer is able to patrol a larger area with less fatigue than the foot patrolman, while still maintaining close contact with the citizenry. Furthermore, a bicycle is silent and can be easily concealed or parked, thus allowing the officer to patrol on foot. It is also inexpensive and especially useful in such areas as parks, playgrounds, shopping centers, ocean front resorts, and narrow alleyways and streets. The possibility of the increased use of foot-bicycle patrolling is significantly greater given the development of large and highly dense population centers and the availability of portable police radio equipment.

AIRCRAFT AND HELICOPTER PATROL

One of the most recent developments in police patrolling involves the use of fixed-wing aircraft and the helicopter. See Fig. 6-2. Consider today's extensive use of airplane travel by many people, including those involved in illegal activities. If the police are to perform effectively in modern society, they must utilize aircraft in the performance of both routine and specialized patrol activities. As early as 1925, the Los Angeles County Sheriff's Department formed an all volunteer Reserve Aero Squadron, and a full-time Aero detail is still an official unit of that department.

---

[10]Donald T. Shanahan, pp. 62-63.

Fig. 6-2: Police helicopters are used for traffic control, search, rescue, and air surveillance for officers on the ground. (Photo courtesy of the Chicago Police Department)

The New York Police Department began using aircraft prior to 1929, and the New York Port Authority began using helicopters in 1947 for surveillance, transportation, and rescue.[11] Other cities and state agencies employ helicopters, usually during the daylight hours, and in 1968, California developed an experimental program using helicopters for police patrolling known as Sky Knight.

The Dade County, Florida, Public Safety Department utilized the aerial patrol concept during the latter part of 1959, and at present it effectively utilizes fixed-wing aircraft and helicopters in regular pa-

[11]Law Enforcement Assistance Administration, *Dade County Public Safety Department—STOL* (Washington, D.C.: U.S. Government Printing Office, 1971), p. 16.

trols to prevent crime and to apprehend offenders or engage in surveillance activities. A study conducted by the Dade County Public Safety Department in 1971 established the justification for the effective use of short takeoff and landing aircraft in police patrolling.[12]

The obvious advantages of using aircraft in police work include: (1) a much reduced response time for police service as compared with the automobile; (2) the ability to observe and assist regular police personnel on the ground; (3) the possibility of rooftop surveillance and, in the case of the helicopter, landing almost anywhere; (4) effective routine searches of extensive coastlines or water ways; (5) finding and rescuing lost children and missing persons; and (6) its use as a "backup" to individual officers involved in hazardous or potentially hazardous investigations or control situations. The major limitations of the aerial patrol include inclement weather resulting in the grounding of aircraft and the expense of purchasing and maintaining aircraft and training pilots.

The fixed-winged aircraft is best suited for police areas with lengthy coastlines and inland lakes and mountainous terrain. However, it is the helicopter that is increasingly being used by police agencies across the country, because of its ability to take off and land almost anywhere. The helicopter will become a regular part of many police agencies, and this is justified if it is properly used as equipment to assist in the overall goals of good police work.

MARINE PATROL

Communities with large bodies of water and those along ocean or lake shores must use some marine craft to patrol such areas. Fig. 6-3 illustrates one such patrol boat. Police patrols are also invaluable in patrolling dock and marine areas, beaches, and large recreational water areas. However, extensive police marine patrols are not essential, because the fixed-wing aircraft or helicopter can handle most types of patrol over water; and if significant numbers of marine craft are needed, the services of private boat owners or the Navy or Coast Guard are available.

HORSE PATROL

At the present time, in American police service, horses are rarely used except for special duties in some large cities. An example of such

---

[12]Ibid., pp. 138-43.

Fig. 6-3: Police boats may be used for search, rescue, or enforcement. (Photo courtesy of the Chicago Police Department)

duty is the mounted horse patrol shown in a Chicago park in Fig. 6-4 above.

The almost total elimination of the horse in police patrol is due to the introduction of the automobile, as well as the expense of keeping horses and training personnel to ride them. During the few occasions when horses are needed, such as for crowd control or for leading parades, they may be obtained from private stables for a fee.

CANINE PATROL

Dogs have been used from time to time in police patrol since 1900, but they are now extensively employed by police agencies in the United States. In April, 1957, Baltimore was the only American police force that used trained dog-handler teams on patrol. As of

Fig. 6-4: Mounted police horse patrol in a city park. (Photo courtesy of the Chicago Police Department)

April, 1968, about 200 police agencies used a total of 500 man-dog teams in police patrol work.[13]

Police dogs are especially useful in high-crime areas, in dangerous search situations, in dealing with street gangs, in dispersing a crowd, in taking fleeing suspects into custody, in guarding suspects, in searching alleys, parks, schools, and other large buildings. A most recent use of police dogs is in the search and detection of drugs in packages or on suspects.

A canine corps is essential for most medium-size and large police departments, but careful planning and research must first be completed to determine the specific number and need for police dogs.

[13]Institute for Training in Municipal Administration, p. 94.

Dogs must be housed, transported, trained, and their handlers must be carefully selected and trained.

In view of all that has been said above, you can readily understand why the police patrol is the major function of the police in the performance of their law enforcement duties. Various types of patrol techniques must be used, but today the most dominant one is the automobile patrol, followed by the foot patrol. However, important as the type of patrol is, the method of patrol allocation and distribution is equally essential.

ALLOCATION AND DISTRIBUTION OF PATROLS

It is of the utmost importance that enough personnel be allocated to patrol the community and that they be distributed and scheduled according to the times and places where crime is most likely to occur. The patrol force should be distributed in accordance with the need for their services, and not on the basis of the equal distribution of patrols on all shifts and on all patrol beats of equal size.[14] This is commonly referred to as the proportional distribution of patrol, which was established very early in this century by former Chief August Vollmer of the Berkeley, California, Police Department.[15] Vollmer laid out his patrol beats in two twelve-hour shifts, according to requests for police service in each part of the city. Therefore, some patrolmen would work very large beats, and others smaller beats depending upon the extent of crime. It is important for a police agency to distribute its police patrols on the basis of carefully planned, established, and often revised "need-for-patrol formulas."

In order to determine adequately the allocation and distribution of the patrol force, it is essential to assess carefully and continuously patrol workloads and deployment. Wilson and McLaren developed a detailed manpower distribution procedure which is applicable regardless of the size of the community to be policed. In essence, it involves the regular collection and analysis of data regarding such matters as (1) the number of patrolmen available for patrol duty, (2) the size of the area and the amount of inspectional services to be performed, and (3) an analysis of the number of incidents reported in

---

[14]National Advisory Commission on Criminal Justice Standards and Goals, pp. 199-204.

[15]The President's Commission on Law Enforcement and the Administration of Justice, *Task Force Report: The Police* (Washington, D.C.: U.S. Government Printing Office. 1967), p. 52.

each district, the hour reported, and the hour of occurrence.[16] This kind of data, and much more, is carefully reviewed daily, if necessary, and patrol beats and allocation of personnel are determined on the basis of this review. No longer is an equal number of patrolmen assigned to patrol areas of equal geographical size. Rather, the need of police services determines the size of the patrol beat and the number of personnel assigned.

The International Association of Chiefs of Police has developed a similar but simpler method for the allocation and distribution of patrol manpower, which determines the total number of personnel to be allocated to the patrol function, the number assigned to each shift, the optimum shift hours, the structure of the patrol beats, and other relevant information.[17] These allocation and distribution procedures have been greatly strengthened through the use of computer technology and the use of mathematical models. All of the complex factors relevant to the allocation and distribution of patrol forces are computer-analyzed so that patrol personnel are assigned at the times and to those areas where they are most needed, and their response time to calls for service is minimized.[18]

Larson developed highly sophisticated quantitative models for determining police patrols, taking into account the response time to calls for service, allocation of patrol personnel, and, most importantly, the implementation of a simulation model that allows police administrators to predict patrol procedures without having to disrupt existing police operations. Through his analysis, Larson was able to predict validly and reliably that relatively more units should be allocated to a core city area during busy weekend evenings, and that a fourth shift should be established from 6:00 p.m. to 2.00 a.m. to meet the demand for police services.[19]

Regardless of the ultimate method used to determine the allocation and the distribution of the patrol force, the objective is to use the police where and when they are needed most. Furthermore, each

---

[16]Wilson and McLaren, pp. 666-88. See also Roy C. McLaren, *Law Enforcement Science and Technology* (Washington, D.C.: Thompson Book Co., 1968), p. 599.

[17]Ibid., pp. 689-704.

[18]Phillip S. Mitchell, "Optimal Selection of Police Patrol Beats," *Journal of Criminal Law, Criminology and Police Science*, LXIII, no. 4 (December, 1972), 577-84, See also: Richard C. Larson, *Urban Police Patrol Analysis* (Cambridge, Mass.: The MIT Press, 1972); and Samuel G. Chapmen, *Police Patrol Readings* (Springfield, Ill.: Charles C. Thomas, 1964).

[19]Larson, pp. 166-69.

geographical area patrolled must vary in size according to the need of police services. Therefore, high crime areas will have smaller patrol beats and the largest number of patrolmen will be assigned to them. Likewise, the hours that some personnel will work will be determined by the need for police service, so that more men will work during the periods of high demand. This allows for more patrolmen to be available at peak crime times.

Finally, the police should patrol in a random and unpredictable manner so that potential violators cannot predict when or where they will be. While the officer is patrolling his beat, he should continually make inquiries regarding the affairs of the neighborhood and give the impression that he is alert and well-informed at all times.

TEAM POLICING AND THE TACTICAL UNIT

In recent years innovative policing techniques have been developed to meet the new problems of crime in urban America and to lessen the isolation of the police from the community. Two methods which are currently being utilized by police agencies in the United States are referred to as Team Policing and Tactical Units.

TEAM POLICING

A modern police attempt to reduce isolation and involve community support in law enforcement is the assigning, to a team of police officers, the responsibility for all law enforcement duties in a given area. This method of policing combines the patrol and investigation personnel into a single unit and emphasizes the importance of public cooperation. Such police teams often have the authority to develop programs and procedures according to the needs of the area being policed, and the responsibility for decision-making is placed at the lowest possible organizational level. In many instances, first-line supervisors and patrolmen are required to make final decisions and in essence act as mini-chiefs of police responsible for most administrative and operational activities within the team's responsibility.[20]

The city of Syracuse, New York, in July, 1968, was the first police agency to combine the patrol and investigation function into a police

---

[20]National Advisory Commission on Criminal Justice Standards and Goals, pp. 154-161.

team. The police team consisted of a team leader, deputy leader, and eight policemen. The team was relieved of many routine and non-criminal duties and given responsibility for controlling serious crime, apprehending offenders, and conducting investigations in a small area of the city. The team leader was a lieutenant who was given considerable discretion in directing the activities and operations of the team. Furthermore, the program was decentralized and operated independently of the rest of the agency.[21] Similar policing techniques have been developed in Los Angeles, California, Detroit, Michigan, New York City, Dayton, Ohio, St. Louis, Missouri, Cincinnati, Ohio, and numerous other cities. Certainly team policing must be understood by all police personnel and they must support this type of program if it is to be successful.

TACTICAL UNIT

The tactical unit is a specialized form of police patrol which usually includes a small force of selected officers from within a given agency, and the numbers of officers and the ranks of its supervisors are determined by the size of the unit. Tactical units may vary from a few men on a small force to 200 or more on large forces. New York City's Police Department has 690 carefully chosen and well-trained personnel in its unit; the units of the District of Columbia and Los Angeles number over 200 men.[22] Tactical units are used extensively in many police agencies throughout the country. For example, the Los Angeles Police Department developed the Metropolitan Division in 1930, the Chicago Police Department established the Special Operations Group in 1956, the Detroit Police Department the Tactical Mobile Unit and the Stop the Robberies Enjoy Safe Streets (STRESS) operations, and the Kansas City, Missouri, Police Department uses a tactical force known as the Metro Squad.

Regardless of the name of the above units, tactical units were established to augment the regular patrol force and to deal with special and serious crime problems. It is important that such units be carefully organized and properly supervised if they are to be effective techniques in law enforcement.

---

[21]Op. Cit., p. 157.
[22]Op. Cit., p. 239.

TRAFFIC CONTROL

The police responsibility for the supervision and control of vehicular traffic is a major regulatory function. O. W. Wilson, an expert in the police field, has emphasized the magnitude of this task. He points out that more people are injured and killed in automobile accidents than as a result of the combined totals of all other acts under police control; that the economic loss from these accidents is greater than all other such losses which the police are charged with preventing; that more people are disgruntled with traffic control than with any other police activity, and that traffic control causes the police more annoyance and subjects them to pressure from more sources than the handling of any other problem.[23]

The magnitude of the traffic problem increases annually. Contrary to the opinion of some experts, vehicle registrations have not leveled off but continue to increase at an average annual rate of three percent.[24] With the increase in the number of automobiles, there is an increase in the number of deaths, injuries, and a shortage of adequate parking spaces and highways. The result is a major problem of traffic control and supervision, especially in the large cities. The burden for regulating traffic is again the responsibility of the police. It is a major responsibility, and the police who bear it will find the task impossible without the important contributions of engineering, education, and driver licensing standards.

TRAFFIC ENGINEERING

Traffic engineering as defined by the Institute of Traffic Engineers is "that phase of engineering which deals with the planning and geometric design of streets, highways, and abutting lands, and with traffic operation thereon, as their use is related to the safe, convenient, and economic transportation of persons and goods."[25] The traffic engineer develops general plans for a community-wide transportation system and assists in the redesign of intersections, the installation of traffic signals, signs, pavement markings, traffic flow, and so on. The primary purpose of traffic engineering is to lessen

---

[23]Wilson and McLaren, p. 443.

[24]Institute for Training in Municipal Administration, p. 104.

[25]International Association of Chiefs of Police, *Training Key Volume Four* (Washington, D.C.: International Association of Chiefs of Police, 1971), p. 139.

traffic accidents and congestion and to facilitate the safe and rapid movement of traffic. Therefore, the ability and ease with which the police can accomplish their traffic function depends greatly on the implementation of sound traffic-engineering principles in a given community.

Many of the improvements made through traffic-engineering studies and programs are initially based upon reports made by the police regarding accidents. From these reports the engineer can determine where, when, and under what conditions most accidents occur. Then, from the facts in these reports, he may initiate various solutions to traffic safety, such as installing traffic signals rather than four-way stop signs, removing obstructions at the corners or rounding off the curbs for turns, or requesting the building of non-access highways and streets. Regardless of the problem, the role of the traffic engineer is basic to its solution. However, there is another very critical element relating to traffic control and safety, and that is public education.

EDUCATION

Citizens have to be educated in matters of traffic safety as they affect drivers, pedestrians, and school children. They must also be taught to understand police traffic problems and to support the programs, policies, and methods employed in their solution. One of the most important factors in traffic safety is the human factor. People drive cars, and much depends upon their attitude and knowledge regarding driving and their general conduct on the streets and highways, especially in congested traffic situations. Therefore, a massive and continuous public education program is essential to inform people of traffic problems and to obtain their support of programs, policies, and methods used in their solution. Such educational programs specifically serve the following purposes:

1. They explain the reason for police traffic controls and practices.
2. They show the need for traffic laws and regulations, including their enforcement by the police.
3. They demonstrate the need for engineering improvements.
4. They instruct motorists and pedestrians to move safely by improving their driving skill and walking practices, as well as by increasing the citizen's knowledge of traffic rules and regulations.

Certainly, well-informed and properly trained drivers will play a key role in the reduction of traffic accidents and in general control problems. However, in spite of good traffic engineering and effective public education programs, some persons respond only to the pressure of law enforcement, and the police and the courts must take definite action against them to protect the general public.[26]

DRIVER LICENSING

A major factor in traffic accidents is the driver. Therefore improving driver performance will greatly reduce accidents. The most important purpose of driver licensing is to establish minimum driver performance ability through the initial and continuous testing of driver's license applicants. To make certain that there are uniform statewide driver licensing standards, every state should assume complete responsibility for licensing all drivers. In addition to driver examination and licensing, state agencies should also assume the responsibility for annual vehicle registration and inspection. Carefully defined license suspension and revocation policies should be strictly enforced against violators. "License suspension is a strong deterrent against unsafe driving practices. License revocation should result when a driver has been convicted of manslaughter, of using a vehicle in the commission of a felony, of perjury under motor vehicles laws, or for leaving the scene of an accident."[27]

TRAFFIC ENFORCEMENT

The basic police traffic functions generally include accident investigation, directing traffic, and enforcement. We are here primarily concerned with the enforcement function, which is the police effort directed to obtain compliance with traffic regulations.[28] Police traffic enforcement has several major objectives similar to those that relate to the enforcement of the criminal laws. These include (1) preventing traffic law violations, (2) observing motorists through routine patrols and traffic directing, and (3) investigating traffic violations and making arrests where justified. All of these major police traffic enforcement objectives are implemented through the use of various policing

[26]Wilson and McLaren, pp. 457-58.

[27]National Advisory Commission on Criminal Justice Standards and Goals, p. 229.

[28]International Association of Chiefs of Police, *Training Key Volume Four* (Washington, D.C.: International Association of Chiefs of Police, 1971), p. 139.

techniques. The detection of traffic violations is achieved by an alert and active patrol force which will vary the method of patrol so that officers will be present at the times and places where most violations occur or are likely to occur. To achieve the detection capabilities of the traffic patrol, the timing and routing of patrols, the employment of "at rest" techniques at carefully selected times and places, and the utilization of both "visible" and "non-visible" patrol methods are essential.[29] Such patrol techniques involve the use of maximum observation, the recognition of the signs of potential violators, and the choice of the best positions on streets and highways for patrol effectiveness.

The police will greatly assist in the prevention of traffic violations by establishing a highly visible, aggressive, and "no-nonsense" reputation in traffic enforcement. When the citizenry learn of such an enforcement policy, the deterrent effect on potential violators is significant. Furthermore, when violators are detected, they should be apprehended forthwith, and no preference should be shown regardless of the violator's social status or acquaintance with the "powers-that-be." Wilson and McClaren indicated that enforcement involves not only arrests and fines, but also such nonpunitive techniques as warnings and attendance at traffic-violator schools.[30] Punitive methods are justified when all other methods fail, or where serious violations have occurred.

---

[29]Institute for Training in Municipal Administration, p. 112.
[30]Wilson and McClaren, pp. 457-58.

CHAPTER VII

CRIMINAL INVESTIGATION AND CRIMINALISTICS

THE NATURE AND MEANING OF CRIMINAL INVESTIGATION

"Criminal investigation is police activity directed toward the identification and apprehension of alleged criminals and the accumulation, preservation, and presentation of evidence regarding their alleged crimes."[1]

As can be noted from the above definition, the investigative function of police agencies is a very important one that involves most sworn police personnel, and especially the line officer who is often the first to know of a crime. In view of this, it is essential that all such personnel have a basic understanding of criminal investigation. The patrol officer as the first person with official authority to arrive at the crime scene must care for the injured, conduct a preliminary investigation, protect the crime scene and all physical evidence, and apprehend the offender if he is present or in immediate flight.

However, in many cases of crime, the offender is unknown. Thus, a continuous and intensive but systematic inquiry or investigation must be made by police personnel who are free to spend their full time and efforts in apprehending offenders and recovering stolen property. Such personnel are referred to as detectives or investigators and are trained and experienced in investigative techniques. The use of full-time investigators will free the patrolman so that he may continue his patrolling of a given geographical area in order to prevent other crimes, or be available to answer other citizen complaints or calls for service. However, it is important to emphasize that there must be adequate coordination between the various phases of the investigative process, i.e., the initial and continuing investigation. The success of investigations is greatly increased by the active participation of the patrol force, which should also serve as the eyes and ears of the

---

[1]Robert G. Caldwell, *Criminology*, 2nd ed. (New York: The Ronald Press Co., 1965), p. 317.

detective division. If the patrol and investigative forces operate separately and do not adequately communicate with each other, the solving of criminal cases will be difficult if not impossible.

The mission of some police agencies is entirely investigative in nature, and therefore all of its personnel will devote their entire efforts to investigating crimes or other matters. Examples of such agencies are the Federal Bureau of Investigation and State Bureaus of Investigation. Most other police departments at the state and local level (except for those which are very small) establish special investigative divisions or units to conduct detailed investigations of unsolved crimes. In larger departments, investigators may specialize in the solution of particular types of crimes such as burglaries, homicides, auto thefts, narcotics, robberies, and so forth.

Thus criminal investigation is a specialized aspect of police work which is the responsibility of both the uniformed patrolman and the investigator. In the investigation of crimes, evidence technicians and other highly trained persons, known as criminalists or forensic scientists, assist in the collection, preservation, analysis, and presentation of physical evidence found at the crime scene. Criminalistics and its role in the investigative process will be discussed in a subsequent section of this chapter. The objective in the investigation of a crime is to determine who the criminal is and to develop and present legally acceptable evidence to a court of law so that a conviction is assured and a crime solved. Of course, where property was stolen, it must be recovered and returned to its rightful owner.

TYPES OF INVESTIGATION

There are different types of investigations performed by police agencies depending upon the nature of the case and the legal and administrative responsibilities of a given department. Not all investigations are of a criminal nature. Some investigations involve an inquiry into the background of a person who has made an application for a position with the government. For example, the Federal Bureau of Investigation spends a great deal of investigative time inquiring into the background of applicants for positions of trust in the government. However, our concern here is only with investigations of crimes.

Generally, the criminal investigative process includes the preliminary (or initial) investigation and the follow-up (or continuing) investigation.

PRELIMINARY INVESTIGATION

The preliminary investigation is the initial or beginning phase of a systematic inquiry into an alleged crime. As earlier discussed, the patrolman should always carry out, or participate in, the preliminary investigation except in those cases where the crime was discovered long after it was committed. In such instances the investigator could be the one who conducts both the initial and continuing investigation.[2] This initial, or preliminary, investigation consists of immediate investigative activities to: (1) determine that an offense has actually been committed; (2) locate, identify and interview witnesses, suspects, and the victim; (3) arrange for the preservation, collection and analysis of evidence found at the crime site; (4) record adequately and accurately the crime and note all of the conditions regarding it, that is, report completely in writing what has happened.

Of course, the first responsibility of the officer arriving at the crime scene is essentially noninvestigative in nature and includes care for the injured, the arrest or pursuit of a suspect, and the protection of the entire site of the crime so that physical evidence will not be destroyed or modified. It is after this has been done that the preliminary investigation begins.

Thus, the preliminary investigation is the first inquiry made when a crime has been committed. It is carried out at the crime site to establish facts, and to reconstruct what has occurred. In minor crimes, the entire investigation is usually conducted by the patrolman. Where serious crimes have occurred, the preliminary investigation is completed by the patrolman or the investigator or by both working as a team. However, the role of the patrolman in the initial investigation begins at the time when he arrives at the place of the crime, and it comes to an end when he has done all that he can at this particular stage. It is from this point on that the non-uniformed specialist, the investigator, assumes responsibility in the case and conducts a continuing or follow-up investigation.

FOLLOW-UP INVESTIGATION

The follow-up or continuing investigation is necessary to bring a

---

[2]See: O.W. Wilson, *Police Administration* (New York: McGraw-Hill Book Co., 1963), pp. 281-88; International Association of Chiefs of Police, *Criminal Investigation* (2nd ed.; Gaithersburg, Md., 1975), pp. 7-11; International City Management Association, *Municipal Police Administration*, 7th ed. (Washington, D.C., 1971), Chapter 7.

case to a successful conclusion, or to close an unsolved case if all leads have been exhausted without success. It must also be remembered that all cases must be prepared for presentation in court. This requires the special skills and full time of the investigator, because the patrolman must continue his patrol activities and make himself available to answer other calls for police service.

When the preliminary investigation results in the arrest of the alleged offender, the investigator will concentrate his efforts in collecting the necessary evidence, recovering stolen property, interviewing witnesses, and, most importantly, compiling a comprehensive and properly written report of the investigation for presentation in court. If the offender has not been apprehended, finding him is an additional responsibility of the investigator with the assistance of the patrol officer.

At this point, the follow-up investigation is an extension, or continuation, of the preliminary investigation. The continuing investigation is always necessary in major crimes, but often is not essential in minor crimes where the offender is usually arrested and a report is written by the patrol officer.

In summary, the follow-up investigation includes: (1) the continuation of the initial or preliminary investigation; (2) the determining if available information and evidence is legally admissible in court; (3) the finding, interviewing, and re-interviewing of witnesses to a crime; (4) the discussion with the criminalist of the results of his analysis with regard to physical evidence collected at the scene of the crime; (5) the surveillance and interrogation of suspects; (6) the identification and apprehension of the offender; and (7) the preparation of the entire case for prosecution.[3]

The ultimate objective of a criminal investigation is to present to a court both the suspect and the physical evidence. To accomplish this, the uniformed officer must conduct an adequate initial investigation in order to obtain as much information as quickly as possible concerning a crime.

The follow-up (continuing) investigation is then the extension

---

[3]For an excellent discussion of the preliminary and follow-up investigation, the reader is referred to the following texts: John G. Nelson, *Preliminary Investigation and Police Reporting* (Beverly Hills, Cal.: Glencoe Press, 1970), pp. 3-5; Wilson, pp. 281-85; Paul B. Weston and Kenneth M. Wells, *Criminal Investigation* (Englewood Cliffs, N.J.: Prentice Hall, Inc., 1970), Chapter 2; International Association of Chiefs of Police, Chapter 2; International City Management Association, Chapter 7.

of the initial (preliminary) investigation. Much rests upon the proper coordination and interlocking of these phases of the investigation. A poor initial investigation will often prevent a good "continuing" investigation regardless of the talents of the investigator. Additionally, a good initial investigation is often of little use, if for some reason a proper continuing investigation cannot be completed.

BASIC INVESTIGATIVE PROCEDURE

In carrying out the preliminary and follow-up investigation, certain basic procedures are utilized in order to obtain and evaluate information necessary to solve a crime. A complete investigation includes identifying and apprehending a suspect, and, most importantly, obtaining sufficient evidence to support a criminal charge in court. Therefore, the criminal investigator proceeds by obtaining information and evidence by interrogating a suspect or suspects, and, finally, by assisting in the preparation of the case for prosecution.

OBTAINING INFORMATION

The initial stage of the investigation involves the gathering of information. Information includes tips, rumors, and other relevant data obtained from complainants, witnesses, informants, suspects, and the victim, or from non-human matter or objects used in the commission of a crime or left at the crime scene by the perpetrator. Non-human objects or matter can be anything from a weapon to a trace of blood (Fig. 7-1), hair, clothing fiber, paint, fingerprints, glass, drugs, paint, or any other matter. In some states, and in large police departments, evidence technicians will gather all physical evidence at the crime scene and make it available to the investigator. The investigator will then talk to the victim and witnesses in order to obtain information regarding the identity and description of the offender or suspect, the whereabouts of the offender, the method by which he committed the crime, the motives of the suspect, the description of the objects taken, the statements and actions of the suspect, the order in which events leading to the crime occurred, and the way in which the crime scene has been altered.[4] The investigation will also include asking the victim many questions, such as: Did he

---

[4]O'Hara, pp. 85-101.

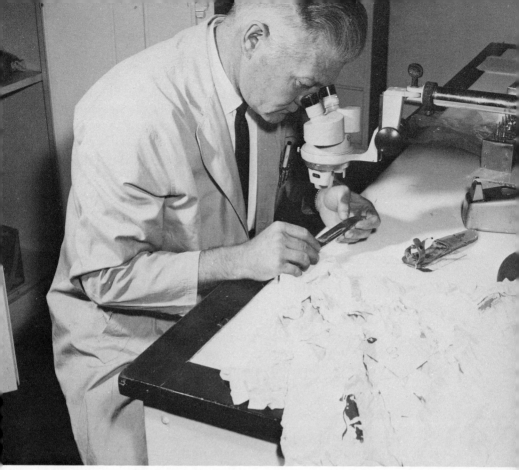

Fig. 7-1: An FBI laboratory expert examining evidence for presence of blood in the serology unit, FBI Laboratory, Washington, D.C. (Photo courtesy of the FBI)

know the suspect? Does he suspect anyone in particular and why? Did the suspect have a weapon? Is there a relationship between the victim and the suspect?[5]

The suspect himself is also a source of information, and through careful interviewing, the investigator will determine if his statements are the same as those obtained from the victim and other witnesses. He will also note the suspect's alibi, motive, whereabouts during the crime, whom he was with, and what he was doing.

Finally, a careful investigation of the crime scene will obtain information from non-human objects. These include fingerprints, tire

[5]Weston and Wells, p. 91.

marks, clothing, weapons, tool marks, and any other physical evidence found at the place of the crime. For example, physical injury to the victim may be caused by a weapon or chemicals which may result in the loss of blood, skin, and hair, or windows, locks, doors, headlights, or other things may have been broken, or furniture may have been moved. Figure 7.1 shows an F.B.I. laboratory expert examining evidence for traces of blood.

All of the information obtained at the crime scene is carefully recorded in a notebook carried by the investigator. Notes will include a careful sketch of the crime scene, and the names of the victim and witnesses and the information they have given, as well as a description of any non-human or physical evidence found where the crime was committed. The information recorded in the investigator's notebook will assist him in making out a formal report, refresh his memory when called to testify in court, and generally help him in reconstructing the events that occurred in a given crime. Such information will also serve as a record of names and places the investigator must later investigate. Finally, the investigator will require that the crime scene be carefully photographed and that all physical evidence be collected and evaluated by trained evidence and laboratory technicians.[6]

After the crime scene has been thoroughly searched and all possible information obtained, the investigation will continue away from the place of the crime and will involve interviewing people and analyzing records and documents to obtain further information. For example, citizens from all walks of life may be contacted about events that occurred at the time and place of the crime, and police records may be examined to see if there is an offender who has committed the same type of crime in the same manner as the one under investigation. The department of motor vehicles provides information regarding operators' licenses, titles of ownership, license plate numbers, serial numbers, and the like, which may identify a vehicle and person present at the crime scene. These and many other sources of information can prove invaluable to a successful investigation.[7]

One of the most effective methods for clearing up an unsolved

---

[6]For an excellent and comprehensive text on the role of the physical evidence technician, the reader is referred to: Clarence H. A. Romig, *The Physical Evidence Technician* (Champaign, Ill.: University of Illinois, June, 1975).

[7]International Association of Chiefs of Police, pp. 96-101.

crime is obtaining critical information from informants, or people who will give information to the investigator. Informants include people from all walks of life, but especially those in particular occupations who may have relevant information, such as barbers, deliverymen, gunsmiths, bartenders, locksmiths, newspaper reporters, prostitutes, waiters and waitresses, neighbors, hotel managers and employees.

In essence, the investigator will use all sources of information at his disposal, and will trace every lead that may assist in the solution of a crime and the arrest of the suspect. At times, investigators will conduct surveillances to develop further leads or information. A survelliance is nothing more than keeping close watch over a person, group, or place in a secretive manner. Its purpose is to detect criminal activities, discover the identity of persons who frequent a particular establishment, obtain evidence of a crime, prevent the commission of a crime, or provide a basis for obtaining a search warrant.[8] There are various types of surveillance, such as visual surveillance, audio surveillance, and contact surveillance.[9]

A *visual surveillance* is keeping watch on a suspect, vehicle, or place visually, often utilizing binoculars, telescopes, and photographic equipment. Such surveillances can be fixed, such as a stakeout or plant, located within a building, vehicle, or on a rooftop. A moving surveillance may be on foot or in a vehicle. An *audio surveillance* makes use of wiretapping and electronic eavesdropping equipment. It involves the interception of telephone communication by tapping wires or the surreptitious placing of miniature microphones, in rooms or on people, to record conversations. *Contact surveillance* techniques use certain fluorescent preparations to stain a person's hands or clothing upon contact, and thus offer observable proof of a connection between the stained person and the object under surveillance.[10] The reader is referred to Chapter 11 for the legal requirements to conduct surveillances.

In addition to the above surveillance techniques, the police will often use personnel as undercover agents. That is, police personnel go under anonymous cover to penetrate criminal groups for the purpose of obtaining information and evidence.

All of the above techniques have been very effective, particu-

---

[8]O'Hara, p. 177.
[9]Weston and Wells, pp. 166-174.
[10]Ibid., p. 171.

larly in the investigation of drug traffic, organized crime, and foreign conspiratorial groups.

When a specific individual is determined to be a criminal suspect, or has important information regarding a crime, he is then interrogated by the investigator.

INTERROGATION

Interrogation is questioning a person in a formal and systematic way and is most often used to question criminal suspects to determine their probable guilt or innocence. Thus, it is a formal method of obtaining information or evidence from a suspect regarding a particular crime. Most of the critical information necessary to solve a crime is currently obtained through interrogation. Authorities make a distinction between interrogation and interviewing. The latter is a less formal and systematic technique for obtaining information from victims and witnesses which is then used to interrogate suspects or prisoners. The purpose of the interrogation is to obtain admissions or a confession of guilt. The reader is referred to the chapters on the criminal law regarding important legal standards to which an investigator must adhere during the interrogation of a suspect.

A well-known authority on criminal investigation has stated that before the policeman interrogates a suspect in police custody he should: (1) identify himself as a police officer, (2) explain to the suspect the nature of the offense under investigation, (3) inform the suspect of his desire to question him regarding the offense under investigation, and (4) inform the suspect of his legal rights.[11]

' The investigator (interrogator in this instance) must possess many important traits if he is to be successful. He must be able to talk with and relate to the person being questioned. He must have a great deal of general knowledge about human behavior and human affairs. He must be alert and have a logical mind so that he may quickly analyze information and the person under interrogation. He must be honest and not make promises to the suspect which he cannot keep, and he must be patient and be able to control his temper.[12]

A very important part of the interrogation will take place in a special interrogation room of the police department. Such a room should be private and free from interruptions. It should also be soundproof and have no windows, telephones, or any other distrac-

---

[11]Ibid., p. 102.
[12]Ibid., pp. 107-10.

tions that will prevent the concentration of both the interrogator and the subject on the matter under questioning.[13] Furthermore, it should have facilities to allow other officers outside the room to observe and hear the suspect during the questioning and to be able to record what has been said.

All the investigator's skills will be brought into play during the interrogation and he will be greatly assisted by any prior information he has obtained about the crime and the suspect, as well as by the use of modern technology such as recording devices, two-way mirrors, listening devices, and so on. However, in the final analysis, the successful interrogator is one who knows what questions to ask and when, and who is able to note the physical and psychological reactions of the person being interrogated. When the interrogation is completed, all information obtained from the suspect and from other sources, together with any physical evidence found at the crime scene, is prepared for prosecution.

CASE PREPARATION

The successful prosecution of criminals depends to a great extent upon the skill and efficiency of the investigator. He must make certain that evidence is preserved and that it is put into such form that it can be used most effectively by the prosecutor. Moreover, the investigator is a key witness for the state. His testimony, his general conduct in court, and his ability to answer questions and supply information may easily make the difference between a conviction and an acquittal.

Good case preparation is good organization. The investigator must bring together in an organized and logical manner all evidence collected during the investigation and present it to the prosecutor. He will prepare a complete case file, including the names of eyewitnesses, evidence, and a confession by the perpetrator. The investigator must be able to demonstrate to the prosecutor and the court that a specific crime was committed at a specified time, date, and place, and that the person named in his report committed the crime.[14] This is commonly referred to as the corpus delicti, or the substance of the crime. Finally, and most importantly, the investigator must testify as a witness, under oath, in court. He should, therefore, know his case well, he should tell the truth, he should be courteous, and he should give direct answers and generally make a good appearance. A suc-

---

[13]Ibid., pp. 111-13.
[14]Ibid., p. 270.

cessful investigation is one in which a crime has been solved and the case closed.

However, police agencies in the United States can no longer rely upon the interrogation or upon archaic, inadequate, and unscientific methods in their efforts to detect and solve crimes. Modern America is a large, complex, industrial, and technological society in which law violators use sophisticated methods and technology in the commission of crime. Furthermore, recent court decisions have imposed formidable restrictions upon police investigative and enforcement practices; police workloads in criminal and noncriminal matters have markedly increased; and the development of police agencies has not kept pace with the alarming growth of crime and the increasing mobility of criminals. Add to this situation these possibilities: the alleged crime may not have been witnessed, witnesses may not be located or may refuse to testify, or important evidence may be inadvertently destroyed or overlooked. Under these circumstances, the investigator, in his search for evidence, must often look beyond whatever he can gain from such sources as the informer and the interrogation. To an increasing extent, the investigator is finding much needed help from the rapidly developing field of criminalistics in the solution of crimes.

CRIMINALISTICS

Criminalistics is generally defined as the application of scientific knowledge and techniques to the detection of crime and the apprehension of criminals. The term "criminalistics" was coined by Hans Gross (1847-1915), an Austrian lawyer who is credited with being one of its principal founders. In its operation, criminalistics draws upon physics, chemistry, biology, psychology, criminology, and other sciences, and requires the services and collaboration of various experts. A brief examination of some of the important methods that have been developed in criminalistics will help you to understand the nature and extent of this field.

The *Bertillon system* was developed by Alphonse Bertillon (1853-1914), head of the Criminal Identification Department of Paris, who introduced this system into France in 1883. In essence, this system uses numerous measurements of the human anatomy, such as height, length of the head, and the span of the arms, and is based upon the assumption that no two persons have the same body meas-

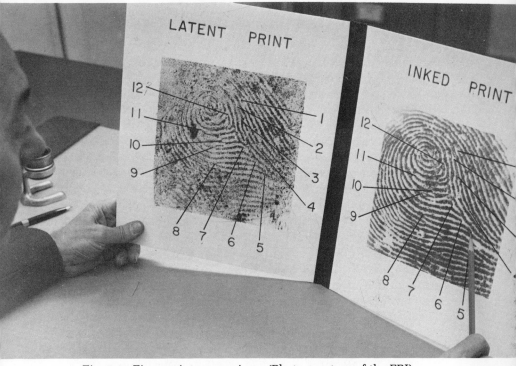

Fig. 7-2: Fingerprint comparison. (Photo courtesy of the FBI)

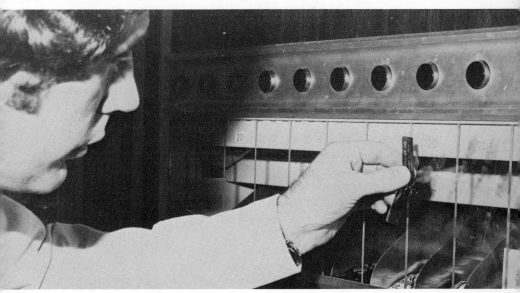

Fig. 7-3: Using fingerprint brush and powder to "lift" a latent fingerprint left at a crime scene. (Photo courtesy of the Cook County Sheriff's Police Department)

urements, and that certain of the measurements do not change after a person reaches maturity. Photographs also were a part of the Bertillon system, as were records of the person's hair and eye color, complexion, scars, tattoo marks, and other distinguishing characteristics. Bertillon's method of identifying criminals is considered to be the first scientific system of identification to be utilized by the police.[15]

The *portrait parle* also was introduced by Bertillon to assist the police in visually identifying offenders from photographs, since obviously it is not possible to stop suspects and take measurements of their bodies to determine their identity. The *portrait parle* is a technique whereby available photographs of wanted persons or known offenders are used and supplemented by a detailed description of the criminal's age, sex, height, weight, complexion, eye and hair color, body build, address, nationality, and any other relevant distinguishing characteristic. The result was a "spoken picture," or *portrait parle*, drawn to include all of the above identifying characteristics, which could be used by the police to arrest a suspect in a given case. The Bertillon system has been largely replaced by the fingerprint system, which is far more valid and reliable and simpler to use. The *portrait parle* is still used in a limited way in some of the larger police agencies to determine the identity of a suspect known only to a witness or a victim, but it has been largely replaced by use of the Identi-Kit. This kit enables an officer or witness to establish the face of a suspect by use of transparencies.

The *Fingerprinting System of Identification (Datyloscopy)* is the most effective method known for the positive identification of law violators. It consists of the impressions left by the patterns of ridges and depressions on the surface of the finger tips. It is believed that there are no two identical fingerprints; at least none have been found since fingerprinting began. Fig. 7-2 shows a fingerprint comparison being made in an FBI fingerprint laboratory.

Sir Francis Galton (1822-1911) made the first study of fingerprints and established a method for classifying them. In 1892, Galton wrote a book entitled *Finger Prints*, in which he describes this method of identification and thus established the beginnings of our present fingerprint system.[16] Galton was an English anthropologist who studied medicine in London.

The apparatus that is required for making fingerprints a matter of

---

[15]Ibid., p. 13.

[16]Francis Galton, *Finger Prints* (London: Macmillan & Co., Ltd., 1892).

record is simple and inexpensive. Printer's ink, or ink of a similar type, is usually employed for making the impressions. It is rolled on a metal or glass sheet or block, a rubber-covered roller being used for spreading the ink. Then the fingers are inked and impressions are made on a blank fingerprint card.

Two types of impressions are taken in fingerprinting. One is called the plain impression, and the other the rolled impression. When the plain impression is made, the fingers are inked with a thin coat of printer's ink and placed flat on a fingerprint blank. When the rolled impression is made, each of the ten fingers is rolled separately on the inked slab from one side to the other and then in the same manner on the fingerprint blank. The rolled impression is made in order to reveal the whole fingerprint pattern so that it can be properly classified. The plain impressions are taken in order to check the rolled impressions, and thus to ascertain whether the latter have been recorded in their proper sequence. If the sequence is not correct, the fingerprints cannot be properly classified.

Since fingerprints must be classified, or put into categories, for the purpose of identification, a method of classification is important. The one most widely used is the Henry or universal system. This method of classifying fingerprints was developed by Sir Edward Henry, who became the commissioner of the metropolitan police force of London in 1903. It was introduced into England in 1901 and is now used in the United States. However, this system is based on the prints of all ten fingers and therefore has definite limitations. Since all ten prints are rarely found at the scene of the crime, its principal uses have been to identify repeaters who have been previously fingerprinted and are again in custody, and to compare prints left at the scene of the crime with those of known suspects whose prints are on file.

Many of the fingerprints found on various surfaces are called *latent* fingerprints because they are not clearly visible. Such prints are clarified by the application of special powders, liquids, and other developing agents as is being done in Fig. 7-3. They are then photographed to convert them into a permanent record. Currently, it is possible to identify a suspect from a single print found at the crime scene by searching through large fingerprint collections. This is known as the *single fingerprint* system of classification. The best known is the Battley system, which was published in 1930 by Harry Battley when he was in charge of the fingerprint bureau of New Scotland Yard, London.

Fig. 7-4: In the FBI laboratory, Washington, D.C., an auto-loading pistol is microscopically examined for distinguishing marks. (Photo courtesy of the FBI)

Ballistics is an American contribution to the science of criminal investigation. The term ballistics technically refers to the science of the motion of projectiles, but has come to mean firearms identification.[17] This is a specialized aspect of criminalistics which involves the identification of firearms and ammunition used in the commission of a crime. In Fig. 7-4, an FBI laboratory technician uses a microscope to carefully examine a firearm.

The person most associated with the science of ballistics is Colonel Calvin Goddard (1891-1955), formerly of the United States Army and a physician by training. For many years, Goddard served as an expert in the identification of firearms in the United States.

[17]Richard H. Ward, *Introduction to Criminal Investigation* (Reading, Massachusetts: Addison-Wesley Publishing Co., 1975), p. 87.

The principal purpose of ballistics is to establish whether or not the weapon and bullet or bullets found at the scene of the crime are the same as the sample bullets fired from the suspect's weapon. The objective is to determine whether a given bullet was used in a particular weapon. If the suspect is found to own the weapon, criminal responsibility may be established. Therefore, this specialized aspect of criminalistics includes: (1) the identification of a firearm used in a crime; (2) a description of the firearm, that is, its model, caliber, type, and serial number; (3) the identification of bullets or cartridge cases found at the scene of the crime to determine the kind of weapon used; (4) a determination or approximation of the distance from which a shot was fired; and (5) the examination of a suspect's body, especially his hands, to determine if he had recently fired a gun.

The Polygraph (lie detector) was developed in 1921 by John A Larson, a former police officer and psychiatrist, and is of great assistance in criminal investigation. "It is designed to record on chart paper certain physiological information put into it by the person taking the test. A qualified examiner must interpret the marks left on the paper, and it is this interpretation that helps the examiner form an opinion of truth or untruth."[18]

When the polygraph is used, several attachments are connected to the suspect, Fig. 7-5. He is then questioned, and the physiological effects of this questioning are mechanically recorded. In essence, the polygraph records various physiological changes a person goes through while being questioned, and it can thus quite accurately determine if a person is telling the truth. The attachments of a polygraph record changes in respiration, blood pressure, and pulse rate. Two other polygraph attachments record the changes in the activity of the sweat pores in a person's hands, and his muscular movements and pressures.[19]

The polygraph is considered to be extremely accurate if used by a highly trained operator and proper test conditions. There are those who claim that they can "beat" the polygraph and thus render it ineffective. Experts have proved the absurdity of such claims.[20] How-

[18]Carl S. Klump, "So You Want To Beat the Polygraph" in *Internal Theft: Investigation and Control*, Sheryl Leininger, Editor (Los Angeles: Security World Publishing Co., Inc., 1975), p. 181.

[19]Fred E. Inbau, Andre A. Moenssens, and Louis R. Vitullo, *Scientific Police Investigation* (New York: Chilton Book Co., 1972), pp. 156, 157.

[20]Klump, pp. 181-191.

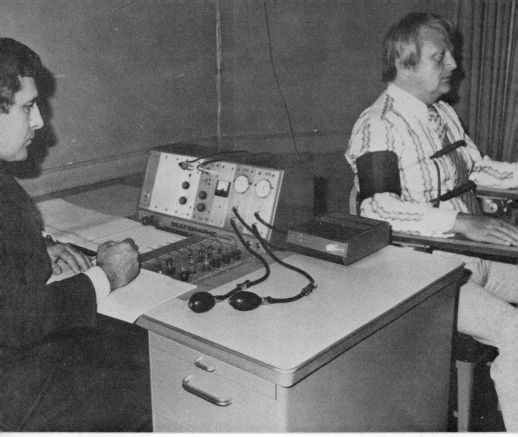

Fig. 7-5: The polygraph in operation. Observe the pheumograph tubes around the subject's chest and upper abdomen, the blood pressure-pulse cuff around the right arm. Electrodes are attached to two fingers of the left hand. (Photo courtesy of the Chicago Professional Polygraph Center, Inc.)

ever, it is important to remember that the polygraph does not detect lies, but only the symptoms of lying which can be discovered and interpreted only by an expert.

The polygraph is very useful in criminal investigations, particularly if there is doubt about a suspect's guilt or if there is a question concerning a victim's story. The polygraph is used extensively to determine which persons are likely suspects, especially during the early part of the preliminary investigation. However, the polygraph method depends heavily upon the ability and integrity of the operator. Therefore, it is critical that a polygraph operator be well trained and certified. Such training usually requires some six months to a year and includes an internship under the supervision of a competent and experienced operator and the academic requirement of a degree in criminology, police science, or other relevant fields. There is every reason to believe that, with the establishment of high and professional polygraph examiner requirements and licensing, the results of the polygraph test will be admissible as evidence in court.

The examination of *questioned documents* can often provide valuable evidence in a case. Albert S. Osborn (1856-1946) is given most of the credit for the establishment of a legally acceptable and scientific method for accomplishing this. In the use of this method the examiner determines the authenticity or genuineness of handwriting and of documents such as letters, checks, telegrams, ledger entries, drivers' licenses, wills, birth certificates, and so forth. The examiner may be called in to study writing or printing on any surface, and his primary function is to determine whether, for example, certain handwriting, forgery, or typewriting has been made by a suspected individual. The examiner may also be asked to study additions, deletions, and erasures on documents, as well as to analyze writing made by fluid or ball-point pens, pencil or rubber stamp, marks, and seal impressions.

Forensic Medicine is the application of medical knowledge to the solution of crime. It is of great assistance in providing evidence regarding such matters as the cause of death, the time of death, the existence of drug addiction, and the presence of poisons. Whenever a crime has been committed, the crime scene should be searched for biological evidence, especially in cases involving homicide and sex offenses. Biological evidence includes blood, semen, saliva, vomitus, perspiration, and fecal matter. A great deal can be established by a careful study of biological evidence at the crime scene. To illustrate:

1. Blood analysis can identify human or animal blood, determine the blood grouping, whether it is from the victim or suspect, and detect alcohol in the blood.
2. An investigation of saliva on a piece of cloth may be used to identify a particular person.
3. The detection of sweat left on an article of clothing at the scene of the crime may assist in tracing a criminal.
4. Hair may be found on the offender, the victim, or the weapon or at the crime scene, and through a study of this evidence a suspect may be linked to the crime.

Voice Identification is one of the most recent techniques that have been developed in criminalistics. This is a method of identifying individuals by the sounds of their voices, as contrasted with visual or fingerprint identification. Thus voiceprinting is based upon the concept of individual uniqueness of speech. Voiceprinting is a graphical print of a person's voice obtained by recording it and feeding the recording into a specially designed sound spectrograph, which reacts to the voice sounds and produces a voiceprint much as the electrocardiogram produces a print of the heart action.

This technique of voice recognition was developed by Lawrence G. Kersta, formerly with the acoustics and speech research laboratory of the Bell Telephone Laboratories. Kersta has since founded his own company, Voiceprint Laboratories.[21]

At the present time voiceprinting is in an experimental stage of development, but in some large police departments personnel have been trained to operate what is known as a voice spectrograph. Voiceprinting is used now only as an investigative aid in identifying criminals who use the phone to make obscene calls, to threaten the bombing of public buildings, or to make extortion threats or ransom demands. It is claimed that no two persons have the same speech pattern (voiceprint), and that attempts to disguise the voice or to imitate another voice can be detected. Of course, the recorded voiceprint must be compared with the voiceprint of the suspect.

OTHER SCIENTIFIC TECHNIQUES

A number of other scientific techniques are being used in criminal investigations. Photography is used to provide pictures of arrested persons or suspects, to obtain pictures of the scenes of crimes and automobile accidents, bodies and wounds, suspected written documents and murder weapons, and practically any other evidence or materials found at the crime scene. Modern photographic equipment permits photographing small details the human eye could not distinguish. Because photography is widely used and understood by the public, it will be quickly understood and appreciated as evidence in court.

Another method for recording the appearance of physical evidence at the crime scene is the making of casts and molds. For example, casts or molds may be made of foot prints, tire marks, teeth, tools, and weapons. From such molds or casts, a scientific comparison can be made with the object suspected of having made the impression. See Fig. 7-6. The value of impressions made by a shoe, hand, tool, or other article is based on the theory that no two physical objects are

---

[21]Inbau, Moenssons, and Vitullo, p. 136.

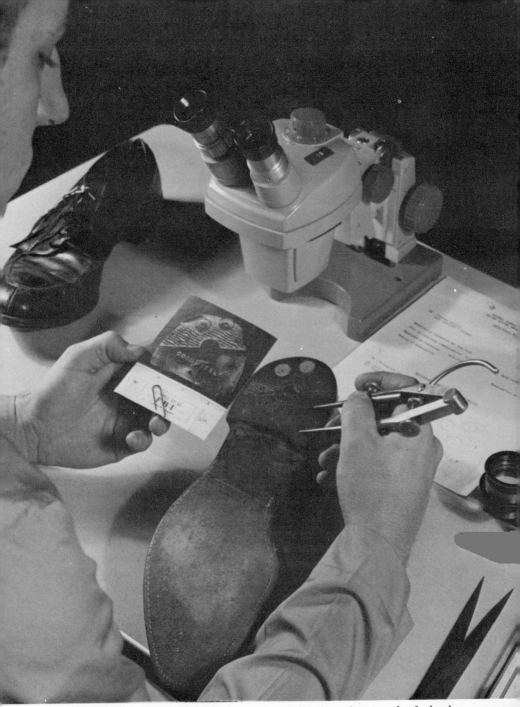
Fig. 7-6: An FBI laboratory examiner compares a photograph of a heel-print with the heel on a suspect's shoe. (Photo courtesy of the FBI)

exactly alike, and if the impressions left at the scene of a crime can be linked to a particular suspect, a crime may be solved.[22]

Other techniques used include the chemical analysis of a questioned substance found at the place of the crime to determine its composition. To illustrate, slight traces of a lipstick, a stained garment, a fragment of glass, or a smear of paint may be found at the crime scene. Chemists can analyze such traces through the use of a spectroscope and, for example, can determine if the bits of paint found on a hit-and-run victim are identical to those found on the auto driven by the suspect.[23]

An analysis of hair and fibers found at the crime scene may assist the criminal investigator in solving a crime. Hair may be found in the immediate area of the crime, or on the body of the victim. Through the use of a microscope, a specimen is verified as being human hair, and an approximate determination can be made as to the sex, age, race, and part of the body from which the specimen came. In some instances, substances found in the hair sample may indicate the occupation of its owner, or, if arsenic is found, that a person was poisoned. Finally, the clothing of persons involved in crimes of violence may adhere to the person of the victim. In hit-and-run cases, fibers from the victim's clothing may be found on the radiator, bumper, grille, or tires of the vehicle.[24] Therefore, through a careful and scientific analysis of fibers found at the crime site, invaluable clues can be obtained to help in the solution of the crime. Types of fibers include wool, silk, fur, cotton, linen, hemp, asbestos, rayon, nylon, orlon, and dacron. Through a comparison of known standards of hair and fibers found on a victim with those of an accused, along with other facts and evidence known to the investigator, guilt or innocence can be determined.

In summary, it can be seen how important the techniques of criminalistics are in the investigation of crimes and the establishment of evidence in accordance with the law. It is in the application of science to criminal investigation that the investigator can become more effective in linking the criminal to a crime in a valid, reliable, and legally permissible manner. The criminalist and the investigator work closely together, beginning with the initial crime scene investigation and then proceeding to the collection, preservation, analysis, and finally the presentation of evidence in court. The goal is to solve

---

[22]Inbau, Moenssens, and Vitullo, pp. 1-20.
[23]O'Hara, pp. 650-64.
[24]Ibid., pp. 709-11.

crimes by legally and skillfully linking the physical evidence found at the crime site to the offender. In this way, the guilty will be punished and the innocent protected.[25]

---

[25]For an excellent review of the techniques of criminalistics the reader is referred to the following texts: Fred E. Inbau, Andre A. Moenssens, and Louis R. Vitullo, *Scientific Police Investigation* (New York: Chilton Book Co., 1972); Charles E. O'Hara, *Fundamentals of Criminal Investigation*, 2d ed. (Springfield, Ill.: Charles C. Thomas, 1971); James W. Osterberg, *The Crime Laboratory* (Bloomington, Ind.: Indiana University Press, 1963); Clarence H. A. Romig, *The Physical Evidence Technician* (Champaign, Ill.: University of Illinois, June, 1975); Richard H. Fox and Carl L. Cunningham, *Crime Scene Search and Physical Evidence Handbook* (Washington, D.C.: U.S. Department of Justice, Law Enforcement Assistance Administration, October, 1973).

CHAPTER VIII

CONTROLLING VICE AND ORGANIZED CRIME

THE NATURE AND EXTENT OF ORGANIZED CRIME

Most people are familiar with the traditional essentially individualistic or unorganized types of crimes, such as murder, robbery, rape, larceny, burglary, and so forth. However, there is another type of crime often referred to as "crime of morality" because it most directly affects the health and morals of the community. Offenses of this type are known as vice offenses and include prostitution, obscenity, use and sale of illegal liquor, illegal gambling, the sale of pornography, and the illegal use and sale of narcotics. Finally, there is a particular kind of criminal activity that is highly organized, "businesslike," and professional. It may include the usual types of criminal activity, but it is especially related to vice crimes. That is, "organized crime" is involved directly and indirectly in many vice crimes. Organized crime and vice are especially unique, complex, and difficult enforcement problems for the police, and for this reason it is important to analyze this type of crime.

Generally speaking, criminal activity may involve the cooperation of different persons or groups, or it may be committed by a single individual. However, organized crime, as the term is used here, has certain characteristics that distinguish it from other more traditional types of crime. For example, it is more than the mere association of a few criminals for the purpose of working as a team (which may be called a mob, gang, or outfit) in the commission of such crimes as confidence games, robbery, burglary, and extortion. Organized crime is, as its name implies, a highly cohesive and well-integrated and structured form of criminal behavior that has the following characteristics:

1. An association of a group of criminals for the purpose of committing crimes for profit. In some cases, this association is relatively permanent, lasting over a period of decades.

132

2. The centralization of authority in the hands of one or a few members of a group.
3. The establishment of a fund of money to be used as capital for the group's criminal enterprises.
4. The organization of the group, involving a division of labor, delegation of duties and responsibilities, and specialization of functions. Some groups specialize in one type, or a few types of crime, but others, especially the more powerful ones, are multipurpose in character, engaging in any activity in which a "fast buck" can be made.
5. The tendency to expand and monopolize. These criminals seek to extend their activities beyond the borders of the area in which they have their headquarters and often secure a monopoly in their criminal enterprises throughout the area. They do not hesitate to use murder, bombing, or any other form of violence to eliminate competition, silence informers, persuade potential victims, or enforce their edicts. Often the larger gangs import gunmen from other areas to do this work for them in order to make detection of their crimes more difficult.
6. Adoption of measures to protect the group and to guard against the interruption of its activities. These include the maintenance of arrangements with some doctors, lawyers, politicians, judges, policemen, and other influential persons, and bribery and other forms of corruption to secure political favors and to avoid arrest and punishment.
7. The establishment of policies of administration, rules of conduct, and methods of operation. The elaborate operations of organized crime require discipline, efficiency, obedience, loyalty, and mutual confidence. Rules, therefore, are strictly enforced and severe penalties are imposed upon their violators.
8. Careful planning to minimize risks and to insure the greatest possible success in the group's criminal enterprises.[1]

It will be noted that organized crime has many characteristics in common with modern business enterprises in the United States. Organization, division of labor, specialization of methods, careful planning, insurance against risks—all these have been successfully utilized and developed by both. This is not surprising, for both are products of the same society and both should be expected to bear

---

[1]Robert G. Caldwell, *Criminology* (New York: The Ronald Press, 1965), pp. 150-151.

marks of that culture. However, all similarities cease at that point, for organized criminals initially use illegal means and activities to achieve financial success. The rewards of such success may then be reinvested in legal businesses to create even greater financial rewards. Organized criminals depend upon the use or threat of force, violence, and bribery and make their fortunes in such criminal activities as prostitution, gambling, illegal liquor, narcotics, pornography, and illegal loans. They profit from the last by forcing the recipient to pay a higher rate of interest than is permitted by law.

There are various types of organized crime in America, but the most common are organized gang criminality, racketeering, and syndicated crime. The first type is the simplest and most poorly structured form and is essentially local in nature. Organized gang criminality was most noticeable during the earlier years of the twentieth century when highly violent crimes were committed, such as robbery, kidnapping, murder, hijacking, and so forth. The Federal Bureau of Investigation played a key role in shattering such gangs by the end of World War II. However, as gang-type criminality decreased, a more subtle, vicious, and indirect type of organized crime developed and became known as racketeering and syndicated crime. Racketeering is the extortion from legitimate or illegitimate business through intimidation or force by an organized criminal gang.[2] Racketeers, unlike the earlier gang types, succeed by collecting tributes, profiting by the industry of others, giving nothing in return, and maintaining their hold by intimidation, force, and terrorism. Illegitimate businesses such as prostitution, gambling, and narcotics, are especially subjected to control by racketeers.

Syndicated crime is the most entrenched, best organized, and most difficult form of organized crime to deal with in America today. It is a highly cohesive national group of professional criminals who are organized in a business-like manner for the purpose of making money through illegal activities. Syndicated criminals are making billions of tax-free dollars annually in such activities as gambling, usurious loans, narcotics, prostitution, and pornography. Syndicated crime is considered to be an "unofficial corporate enterprise" that is America's principal supplier of illegal goods and services—one that does not compete on an equal basis in a free economy. Syndicated crime has some 5,000 powerful leaders at the top of the organizational structure and thousands of middle-management gangsters and

---

[2]Ibid., p. 155.

henchmen who carry out the demands of its leaders. Finally, at the bottom of the structure are many persons marginally associated with organized crime who deal directly with the public.[3] Syndicated crime is often referred to as the "mafia," "La Cosa Nostra," "the syndicate," and "the mob."

What is the extent of organized crime in the United States? Organized crime affects the lives of millions of Americans, but because it operates quietly and through others, its impact is not fully recognized by many citizens. It has been estimated that organized crime is a nationwide syndicate that controls many rackets in most major cities, especially vice activities. A survey of 71 cities indicated that organized criminal groups exist in 80 percent of the cities with over one million residents, in 20 percent of the cities with a population of between one-half million and a million, in 20 percent of the cities with a population of between 250,000 and 500,000, and in over 50 percent of the cities with a population of between 100,000 and 250,000.[4] Organized crime does exist in small cities, but it is more difficult to detect because "local" persons operate as "syndicate men" and deal indirectly with the syndicate leaders in larger cities within the immediate area. The core of organized crime today consists of 24 groups operating a nationwide criminal enterprise, with thousands of offenders working for them.

The greatest source of revenue for organized crime is gambling, followed by usurious loans, narcotics, and prostitution. The best estimates available indicate the annual take from gambling is between 7 and 50 billion dollars, and a billion or more from narcotics.[5] Therefore, organized crime is a serious and major type of crime in America, and most of its success comes from providing illegal services to a

---

[3]The President's Commission on Law Enforcement and Administration of Justice, *Task Force Report: Organized Crime* (Washington, D.C.: U.S. Government Printing Office, 1967), pp. 6-11. The reader is also referred to the following excellent publications on organized crime; Donald R. Cressey, *Theft of the Nation* (New York: Harper & Row, Publishers, 1969); John L. McClellan, *Crime Without Punishment* (New York: Duell, Sloan & Pearce, 1962); Gus Tyler, *Organized Crime in America* (Ann Arbor, Michigan: The University of Michigan Press, 1967); Francis A. J. Ianni, *A Family Business* (New York: Russell Sage Foundation, 1972); Ralph Salerno and John S. Tompkins, *The Crime Federation* (New York: Doubleday & Co., Inc., 1969); Virgil W. Peterson, *Barbarians in Our Midst* (Boston: Little Brown & Co., 1952).

[4]The President's Commission on Law Enforcement and Administration of Justice, pp. 5-6.

[5]Ibid., pp. 3-5

cooperative public in the form of narcotics, prostitution, gambling, and illegal liquor.

THE NATURE AND EXTENT OF VICE

Vice includes individual or group conduct or activity which has been declared by law to be harmful to the public welfare. Vice is usually considered to include illegal gambling, prostitution, the illegal use and sale of narcotics, pornography, and the illegal use and sale of alcoholic beverages. The law stipulates that vice is a crime, and therefore the enforcement of such laws is a police responsibility known as vice control.

The enforcement of vice laws is a very demanding and complex police responsibility, largely because the public condones or participates in such activity and because it is an extensive problem in most cities, often involving members of the local power structure. For example, Chambliss made a study of a city of a million population which he called Rainfall West.[6] He found this city to be typical of most cities in America. That is, most of the population were middle class who believed in the worth of their city and were not aware of the extent of vice operating primarily in the center of the city. However, Chambliss correctly concluded that there are a number of persons who are secretly united to distribute profits, discuss problems, and generally do what is necessary to maintain a profitable and trouble-free vice operation.[7] This cabal includes some important businessmen, law enforcement officers, political leaders, and a major union representative. In essence, Chambliss concluded what most experts already know, that vice is present and active in most American cities, even though it is illegal, and that it is interrelated with a segment of the local political and economic power structure.

Vice flourishes in the lower class or commercial areas of the city and some major political, economic, and law enforcement officials cooperate in allowing such activities even though they are clearly illegal. Chambliss noted that such vice activity is often locally operated, but assistance is received nationally through a distribution system controlled by the syndicate. Furthermore, smooth-running vice operations benefit the ruling elite socially and economically. The

---

[6]William J. Chambliss, "Vice, Corruption, Bureaucracy, and Power," *Wisconsin Law Review* no. 4 (Volume 1971).
[7]Ibid., pp. 1151-52.

general public is satisfied when the control of the vices "gives an appearance of respectability, but a reality of availability."[8]

In many cities, viewing pornographic films, and participation in prostitution and gambling involve some middle- and upper middle-class professionals, such as doctors, lawyers, dentists, and businessmen, as well as blue-collar workers and the impoverished. Gambling includes bookmaking carried on at most locations in the center city, poker games, bingo parlors, off-track betting, casino and roulette, and dice games. Betting ranges from one to five dollars, in the more public games, to unlimited betting in the more private gambling most often frequented by some of the wealthier and "respectable" members of the community.

Prostitution is found in houses supervised by a madam, and in some cities it involves open solicitation of customers, street prostitution arranged through a male go-between known as a pimp, and activities in apartment buildings and especially motels, where "call girls" are discretely available. Pornographic or obscene films are often shown in the back rooms of restaurants, taverns, game rooms, and "adult" book stores as well as in some well-known private clubs.

It is obvious that vice is a major law enforcement problem because it is often supported by some local political leaders, businessmen, law enforcement officials, and most importantly, by some citizens who desire to engage in such activities. Therefore, vice control tends to corrupt law enforcement officials and often encourages other criminal elements to associate with vice activities and to use them to blackmail husbands photographed with prostitutes or to lend money at exorbitant interest rates to enable persons without funds to gamble.

Vice organizations often use the skills of other criminals, or they may depend upon these criminals to dispose of illegal goods. Vice operations and establishments are the scenes of murders, assaults, and robberies. They often encourage individuals victimized by vice to turn to other criminal acts, such as embezzling funds, writing false checks, robbery and larceny to "pay" for their participation in vice. The result is a lowering of community morality, increased venereal disease rates and the expenditures in gambling of huge sums of money that is often needed by the gamblers to support their families and to meet their normal financial obligations. More importantly, vice compromises the integrity of the police, who are sworn to uphold the

---

[8]Ibid., pp. 1157-58.

law, and the business and political structure of a community. Finally, although illegal gambling, prostitution, narcotics, and liquor may be locally "controlled" to some degree, the nationwide distribution of such "services" is provided by organized crime.

THE INTERRELATIONSHIP OF ORGANIZED CRIME AND VICE

Evidence of the interrelationship between organized crime and vice has been noted by a number of authorities. During 1950 and 1951, the Kefauver Committee (the Senate Special Committee to Investigate Organized Crime in Interstate Commerce) and the McClellan Committees established in 1957 (the Senate Permanent Subcommittee on Investigations and the Senate Select Committee on Improper Activities in the Labor or Management Field) conducted the most extensive inquiry into organized crime that had ever been undertaken in the United States.[9] These committees concluded, after a careful investigation, that profits from gambling, amounting to billions of dollars each year, are the principal income for organized crime. The President's Commission on Law Enforcement and Administration of Justice, *Task Report: Organized Crime*, stated in 1967 that organized crime had established an illegal importing business, both wholesaling and retailing, for the distribution of narcotics, and that the large amounts of cash and the international connections necessary for narcotics supplies can be provided only by organized crime.[10] These studies, and many more, also conclude that organized crime and vice cannot exist without the cooperation, "bribing," of *some* law enforcement officials and other public officials, who know of the existence of vice but rarely make an arrest or allow the successful prosecution of cases. It is therefore essential that police agencies carefully select and train their personnel for organized crime and vice control.

---

[9]U.S. Senate Special Committee to Investigate Organized Crime in Interstate Commerce, *Second and Third Interim and Final Reports* (Washington, D.C.: Government Printing Office 1951); U.S. Senate Select Committee on Improper Activities in the Labor or Management Field, *Final Report* (Washington, D.C.: Government Printing Office, 1960). See also John L. McClellan, *Crime Without Punishment* (New York: Duell, Sloan, & Pearce, 1962).

[10]The President's Commission on Law Enforcement and Administration of Justice, *Task Force Report: Organized Crime* (Washington, D.C.: U.S. Government Printing Office, 1967), pp. 3-4.

POLICE FUNCTIONS

The enforcement of laws relating to vice and organized crime is one of the important legal responsibilities of the police. The police are responsible for maintaining order, enforcing the law, preventing crime, and protecting the community with respect to matters affecting the public health, comfort, morals, and safety. These police functions are equally applicable to organized crime and vice control. Since organized crime is far more subtle than the usual crimes against persons or property, its solution requires the use of highly trained and honest police personnel. Unfortunately, until very recently, many police agencies had no effective plan to investigate, prevent, and suppress organized crime and vice. However, note again that vice laws deal with morals of a more personal nature; because of this, the police encounter resistance in enforcement efforts from some of the public and from some governmental officials. This therefore makes organized crime and vice control efforts more difficult. Nevertheless, organized crime and vice are illegal, and our society feels the "strong must help the weak by protecting them from their own folly (participation in vice)."[11]

ORGANIZATION FOR ORGANIZED CRIME AND VICE CONTROL

In order to deal effectively with this complex law enforcement problem, the police must establish a separate unit made up of carefully selected officers in civilian clothes who are trained to investigate and suppress this type of crime. The head of this unit should report directly to the chief of police, and his duties should include the inspection of the efforts of uniformed officers in the policing of vice and organized crime.

The regular beat officer is responsible for the suppression of vice in his area, but he shares this responsibility with the central unit. He can make arrests where obvious law violations occur and can transmit important information he has obtained to the special unit on organized crime and vice control. The special unit, in turn, provides a number of important functions with the assistance of the uniformed patrol force. These include:

---

[11]O.W. Wilson and Roy C. McLaren, *Police Administration* (New York: McGraw-Hill Book Co., 1972), p. 390.

1. The supervision, from the staff level, of the agency's total effort toward the prevention and suppression of organized crime and vice.
2. The giving of advice and manpower to the patrol force in dealing with this type of illegal activity.
3. The taking of necessary actions against vice and organized crime not detected by the patrol force.
4. The gathering of intelligence, that is, information regarding vice and organized crimes.
5. The placing of specific responsibility in one unit for the enforcement of this type of crime.[12]

In essence, the establishment of an administrative unit to investigate and suppress organized crime and vice helps to make certain that specific personnel are concentrating their efforts in this area and this assists the patrolman in suppressing vice on his beat. The patrolman should be trained in and responsible for recognizing and suppressing vice, but he cannot deal effectively with such crimes alone. It is important that he forward to the special unit all information he develops, including information concerning arrests he makes which may be directly or indirectly related to organized crime and vice. This will allow the special unit, with the assistance of the patrol personnel, to develop a well-coordinated, comprehensive, and effective attack on this most difficult type of criminality.

ROTATION OF PERSONNEL, HOURS OF WORK, AND TRAINING

Personnel of the organized crime and vice unit should be transferred to other units when necessary. Such rotation serves as a method for training as many personnel as possible in this type of investigation, prevents long tours of duty in a most difficult type of police work, and provides for new personnel to do undercover work who are not known to the criminal element.[13]

Members assigned to investigate organized crime and vice must be specifically trained to gather intelligence information, to recognize the characteristics of this type of crime, to understand the methods of operation of prostitution, gambling, and illegal narcotics and liquor

---

[12]Ibid., p. 400.

[13]Institute for Training in Municipal Administration, *Municipal Police Administration* (Washington, D.C.: International City Management Association, 1971), pp. 161-62.

sales, and to investigate such crimes by using reliable informants or engaging in undercover operations. In addition, they must receive continuous and intensive training. A number of Federal agencies, for example the Drug Enforcement Agency of the U.S. Department of Justice (formerly the Bureau of Narcotics and Dangerous Drugs), will assist in the training of these officers.

Finally, the organized crime and vice unit personnel should be assigned as a team, and their hours of work should be flexible; that is, they should vary according to the times when they are needed most. The hours of work should also vary from day to day to prevent vice operators from knowing specifically when and where vice officers may be working.[14]

ENFORCEMENT TECHNIQUES

Any effective control of organized crime and vice will require (1) the cooperation of police agencies at the federal, state, and local levels, (2) the recognition and reporting of organized crime and vice by all police personnel, and (3) the employment of specific investigative and other law enforcement techniques to effectuate arrests and convictions.

INTERDEPARTMENTAL COOPERATION AND COORDINATION

Police departments at all governmental levels must exchange information regarding organized crime and vice and regularly meet together to discuss the nature and possible coordinated area-wide efforts to deal with such criminality. In many instances, police agencies refuse to recognize the existence of such crime in their communities, are preoccupied with more local and isolated criminal matters, or feel so strongly about the local control of policing that they allow organized criminals to operate freely across city, county, or state lines. Fortunately, in recent years greater interdepartmental cooperation is taking place.

In 1956, a voluntary organization of law enforcement agencies, the Law Enforcement Intelligence Unit (LEIU), was organized to work for the increased sharing of intelligence information on organized crime and vice.[15] The LEIU encourages personal contact between

---

[14]Ibid.

[15]The President's Commission on Law Enforcement and Administration of Justice, p. 79.

different police agencies and has established a clearing house for criminal intelligence information in the California Bureau of Criminal Identification and Investigation (CII) to which all members contribute and from which they receive information. The New England State Police Compact, also, has been established for much the same purpose, with the important additional function of permitting the sharing of personnel from different police departments in long-term surveillance and investigative work.[16] There is also the Law Enforcement Committee of the New York Metropolitan Council's subcommittee on organized crime, and the New York State Identification and Intelligence System (NYSIIS).

In order to deal adequately with organized crime and vice, all police agencies must cooperate with each other in pooling not only information, but other resources as well. Files of information should be made available to other police agencies, and personnel should be exchanged between agencies for more effective police action.

RECOGNIZING AND REPORTING
ORGANIZED CRIME AND VICE

Before organized crime and vice can be legally dealt with, a great deal of valid and reliable information must be gathered. This type of data is obtained through the use of electronic surveillance techniques, special undercover investigators, informants, and the information obtained by the patrolman during his regular tour of duty. Therefore, all patrol officers should be trained to recognize the possible presence of vice. Each patrolman is a part of a vast, front-line intelligence network that funnels information back up the line to be evaluated.[17] Therefore he must know his patrol area well and establish good relations with the people who live there. The officer should observe the following as possible signs of organized crime:

1. A brisk business regularly occuring at a candy store, grocery store, drug store, or other retail establishment with many customers coming and going, which could indicate the presence of a policy operation or a bookmaker's man.

---

[16]Ibid.

[17]Law Enforcement Assistance Administration, *Police Guide on Organized Crime, U.S. Department of Justice, Technical Assistance Division* (Washington, D.C.: U.S. Government Printing Office, 1972), p. 10.

2. A package being delivered at the same time each day to an establishment, with the package being picked up by another individual, which could indicate a policy drop, or a place where the policy writer sends his slips or day's receipts.

3. A number put on street lamp poles in various locations, which could indicate the winning number for the day's policy play.

4. A beating in a bar or other location near a factory on or near a payday, which could indicate a person's failure to pay his illegal loan to a loan shark.

5. The presence of several organized crime figures at a table in a business establishment and many parked cars outside, which could indicate a meeting of underworld figures or their ownership of the establishment.

6. The arrest of burglars, which could indicate stealing to buy narcotics or pay off illegal loans.

7. A brisk business in a cheap hotel, with many patrons coming or going with little or no baggage, which could be a sign of a call-girl operation at the hotel.

8. The presence of a group which begins to congregate at a certain street location at certain times during each day, which could indicate the gathering of addicts, or users, waiting for a pusher to bring narcotics.[18]

INVESTIGATIVE TECHNIQUES

The investigation of vice and organized crime is often far more difficult than investigation of burglary, murder, larceny, manslaughter, assault and battery, arson, and other such crimes. In these individual or unorganized crimes, there is usually a victim who calls the police and gives them information regarding the criminal act committed. This is not so in organized crime and vice. Victims of vice or organized crime are afraid to inform law enforcement officials, and the people who gamble illegally are willing participants in the violation of the law. The police may be able to develop informants to obtain information about organized crime, but such informants will not testify publicly for fear of their lives. Therefore, the police must develop special techniques to obtain legally admissible evidence to prosecute such criminals. Two major and effective methods of inves-

---

[18]Ibid., pp. 31-39.

tigation include the overt and covert collection of essential information and evidence.[19]

The Overt Collection of Information. This method for gathering information about organized crime and vice involves the use of data developed by other investigators as well as general reports from the uniformed patrolmen. This type of available data can be obtained also from the prosecutor's office, other police agencies, crime commissions, newspapers, public trial records, and congressional and legislative hearings. Furthermore, an effective investigative staff will encourage the public to write letters indicating activities that are illegal or suggesting the corruption of public officials.[20] After all existing information is gathered, it should be carefully analyzed by the investigator to determine the existence of organized crime and vice. After a careful analysis of available information, the investigator must then begin the difficult task of obtaining evidence to make an arrest and bring about a successful prosecution in court. In order to accomplish this, more covert methods of investigation are usually essential.

The Covert Collection of Evidence. This method of investigation involves the acquisition of information about a suspect without his knowledge. One of the most effective means for obtaining valid and reliable information is through the use of electronic surveillance, that is, wiretapping, eavesdropping, or the use of recorders placed on a person. Wiretapping involves the tapping of telephone lines to intercept communications between two parties. Eavesdropping is the placing of miniature microphones within a room to transmit conversations taking place therein or by the placing of a recorder on a person that will allow him to record conversations with others at any time and place. (Refer to Chapter 11 for a detailed discussion of the law with regard to electronic surveillance.) Some states do not permit any electronic surveillance; other states and the federal government will allow it only under specified conditions and often only with prior court approval.

The reason electronic surveillance is so effective in organized crime and vice enforcement is that primary and reliable evidence linking a subject with a criminal act can be obtained with little or no

---

[19]E. Drexel Godfrey and D. R. Harris, *Basic Elements of Intelligence, Law Enforcement Assistance Administration, U.S. Department of Justice* (Washington, D.C.: U.S. Government Printing Office, November, 1971), pp. 14-22.
    [20]Ibid., p. 14.

danger to the investigator. Additionally, it is factual information that does not require fearful victims or informants to testify in open court. This type of information speaks for itself, and it is often effective in bringing about a successful arrest and prosecution. Finally, electronic devices may be placed almost anywhere without the knowledge or detection of persons. Microphones can be very small and hidden in draperies, door frames, molding, floors, ceilings, window casements, bookcases, light fixtures, furniture, behind wallpaper, and in many other places.

Another covert investigative method involves the use of informers. An informer is a person who is not a police officer but who knows of certain criminal activities which he will anonymously report to the police. Obviously, informers are essential to police work, as an investigator cannot be aware of many criminal activities. Informants must be dependable, and their key role is providing information which can be carefully checked by the investigator and which often leads to the detection of criminal activity. A good police agency must have informers, or its ability to cope with crime will be seriously limited.

A third type of covert investigative activity is the undercover agent, or a law enforcement officer who operates in a clandestine fashion to obtain essential information. The covert police operator may work as a cab driver, bellboy, telephone repair man, gambler, or any other person. The primary purpose of the police undercover agent is to locate and identify operations and to secure evidence for presentation.

Control of organized crime and vice is a complex and demanding enforcement problem. However, the policing of this type of criminality is essential. A distinguished law enforcement authority has stated, "Vice if not controlled becomes a nuisance, . . . the health of a participant may be jeopardized. The dissipation of money, the damage to conjugal relationships, the injury to the family, and other social evils that results from vices further justify morals legislation."[21]

---

[21]Wilson and McLaren, p. 390.

CHAPTER IX

THE CRIMINAL LAW

MEANING AND SOURCES OF THE CRIMINAL LAW

The law has two main branches: the civil law and the criminal law. The civil law deals with contracts, wills, marriage, divorce, inheritance, private injuries called torts, and other such subjects. The criminal law, on the other hand, has to do with crimes and punishments. In general, it may be defined as a body of rules regarding human conduct which are prescribed by governmental authority and enforced by penalties imposed by the state.[1] As we shall see, included within the scope of this definition are matters like the definition and classification of crimes, the criminal act, the criminal intent, the capacity to commit crime, exemptions from criminal liability, the parties involved in the commission of a crime, the penalties for crimes, the rules of procedure by which the criminal law is administered, and so on.

The criminal law, in turn, may be classified into two major divisions: the substantive law and the procedural law. The substantive law defines the crime and prescribes the penalties, whereas procedural law—sometimes called adjectival law—consists of rules according to which the substantive law is applied in the apprehension, prosecution, and disposition of persons accused of crime. We shall return to an examination of procedural law in succeeding chapters.

Various theories have been advanced to explain the origin of the criminal law, but no one really knows how or when it began. The studies of known primitive societies show that behavior in them is regulated largely by custom, and that in most cases wrongs are redressed through action taken by the injured party himself. However, even in these societies, certain kinds of behavior, such as acts tending

---

[1]Robert G. Caldwell, *Criminology* (New York: The Ronald Press Co., 1965), p. 45. The word "state" in this definition is used in its generic sense to refer to all levels of political authority, including the local, state, and federal governments.

to anger the gods or endanger the food supply, are deemed so detrimental to the welfare of the group that they are forbidden under threat of penalties imposed by established authority. Thus, as far back as research goes, the criminal law, although admittedly in a crude form, is already at work helping to regulate man's relationships.

When the English colonists came to America, they brought with them legal rules, doctrines, and principles, which they incorporated into their own statutes and case law, expanding and adapting them to fit the conditions of the new country. At present, the criminal law of the United States is administered through the courts, the judge exercising his judgment as he presides in each case. In doing this, however, he is limited by certain well-defined rules, which are designed not only to prevent the abuse of judicial authority, but also to insure consistency in the handling of criminal cases in each jurisdiction. These rules are derived from two sources: the statutory law, which is enacted by legislative bodies and which defines certain acts as crimes and prescribes the penalties to be inflicted upon those convicted of these crimes,[2] and the law of precedent, which originated in England during the twelfth century.

At that time, the local baronial courts there were being replaced by tribunals presided over by the king's judges. These judges traveled about the country and sought precedents for decisions in the customs that were common throughout the realm, using the same principles in their deliberations regardless of where the court was held. As judicial decisions based on such common customs accumulated, they became known as the common law, although they were also called the unwritten law to distinguish this judicially compiled law from the law enacted by legislative bodies. Furthermore, the common law continues to develop as judges deal with new problems, interpret new statutes, and weave into their decisions such influences as ethics, expert opinions, and hitherto unrecognized customs. Since the common law became a guide for judges in the rendering of their decisions, one can see why it is now referred to as the law of precedent. Moreover, it is also a guide for legislators in the preparation and enactment of statutes, and thus the two sources of criminal law interact to form a well-integrated system of legal principles.[3]

---

[2]In the United States, however, the crime of treason is defined in the Federal Constitution, and similar definitions are contained in the state constitutions. Judges, furthermore, must be guided by whatever other constitutional provisions are controlling in the field of criminal law.

[3]Caldwell, pp. 46-48.

The adherence to precedent in the law is known as the doctrine of *stare decisis*, which is Latin for "to adhere to decided cases."[4] This doctrine rests upon the principle that the law should be fixed, definite, and known so that people can rely upon it in the conduct of their business and personal affairs. Consequently, when the law is interpreted to have a certain meaning by the highest court in a jurisdiction, such as one of our states, this becomes the law in that jurisdiction and must be followed in similar cases by all its courts until the interpretation is modified or reversed by competent authority, for example, by a state legislature or supreme court or by the United States Supreme Court.

As the foregoing analysis indicates, the term "common law" has various meanings. Since this is an important term, a summarization of its meanings will be helpful. The term "common law" may mean any of the following:

1. The whole body of laws observed by English-speaking nations as distinguished from the Roman or civil law in effect in Continental Europe.
2. The judicially compiled law of early England, often called the "unwritten law" to contrast it with the statutory law—the "written law"—enacted by Parliament and other legislative bodies.
3. The remedies and methods of procedure administered by the earliest English courts of justice as distinguished from those adopted by other tribunals, such as courts of equity, courts of admiralty, courts of probate, and military courts.
4. The English laws recognized in this country before the Revolution as distinguished from the laws enacted since then by the individual states.
5. The law of precedent, that is, all the authoritative materials used to guide and direct courts and legislative bodies in the performance of their duties but which are not in statutes or constitutions.

Although the common law, or the law of precedent as we are calling it here, is constantly being incorporated into statutes and constitutions and thus becoming "written law," this process is never completed, for, as we have explained, the law of precedent continues to grow through the decisions handed down in our courts. Con-

---

[4]See *Black's Law Dictionary* (St. Paul, Minn.: West Publishing Co., 1933), pp. 1651, 1652.

sequently, the terms "law of precedent" and "unwritten law" are often used synonymously.[5]

This varied use of the term "common law" may at first be confusing but if one remembers its different meanings, he will soon be able to perceive from the context of the term which of them is intended.

THE PURPOSE OF THE CRIMINAL LAW

The purpose of the criminal law is not the punishment of offenders, although, of course, this becomes necessary when the criminal law is violated. Rather its purpose is to define what conduct is "socially intolerable," as measured by the dominant values of the group in which the law functions, and to hold conduct within limits which are reasonably compatible with such values.[6]

In the accomplishment of its purpose, the criminal law not only restrains but also facilitates our social relationships. In the simple, slowly changing life of primitive societies, most conduct is regulated by custom, which, in general, provides a stable, reliable, and effective guide for the affairs of the community. In such societies only a rudimentary criminal law is needed. However, in our rapidly changing, complex society, large numbers of persons, coming from many different backgrounds and often having diverse and conflicting sets of values and highly specialized interests and occupations, commingle and interact in an intense competition for wealth, privileges, and power. Under these conditions, custom is too diluted and uncertain and public opinion too uninformed and fluctuating to provide adequate guidance and control in many areas of social relationships. An already overburdened criminal law, therefore, has been called upon to set up more and more rules and standards so that we can know what we may or may not do in peace and safety and thus avoid ruthless exploitation and destructive conflict.

Even so, the criminal law, in accordance with what is known as the principle of legality, also protects us from the abuse of authority by public officials. This it accomplishes through the prescription and application of specific rules which impose limitations upon the exercise of this authority. Here are a few examples which will show how

---

[5]William C. Robinson, *Elementary Law* (Boston: Little, Brown, and Co., 1910), p. 5; Rollin M. Perkins, *Criminal Law* (Mineola, N.Y.: The Foundation Press, Inc., 1969), p. 25.

[6]See Perkins, p. 4.

this is done. In our jurisprudence no conduct is criminal unless it is so described by the law. Specific charges as stipulated in the law, therefore, must be brought against the accused, and he is then in a position to prepare an adequate defense. Furthermore, no punishment may be inflicted on a person except that which is prescribed by law, and all provisions of the law must be strictly interpreted and not modified to suit the views of the judge. Moreover, retroactive, or *ex post facto*, legislation is forbidden.[7] This prevents a person from being punished as a criminal for an act which was not a crime when it was committed, from receiving more severe punishment than was prescribed at the time of the act, and from being tried under rules of evidence that have been so changed as to make it easier for the state to convict him than it would have been when his act was committed.

The criminal law, therefore, performs valuable functions, but in serving its purpose it necessarily gives more attention to some matters than to others. Thus, the criminal law is primarily concerned with whether a certain individual intended to act in some prohibited way, and with the establishment of a well-integrated system of rules, doctrines, and principles and the rendering of consistent decisions so that the community can have a stable and reliable guide for the conduct of its affairs. Consequently, the criminal law tends to emphasize the crime rather than the criminal, the individual rather than his social relationships, the rational rather than the nonrational, the entity of the law rather than its cultural relationships, and the static rather than the dynamic. This does not mean that the law should necessarily do otherwise or that something else should be substituted for it. It does mean, however, that we must see the law from a broader point of view if we are to have a deeper understanding of its nature and problems.[8] One way to do this is to examine the law as a social institution.

THE LAW AS A SOCIAL INSTITUTION

Men in their interaction with one another and the world of nature have created an artificial environment consisting of material objects and patterns of behavior or social norms. This man-made environ-

---

[7]The Consititution of the United States expressly forbids Congress or any state to enact this type of legislation, and the constitutions of most states contain similar provisions.

[8]Caldwell, pp. 51-53.

ment, which is transmitted from one generation to another, is called "culture," and it provides controls, regulations, and restraints for the behavior of men, as well as the means whereby their needs and desires are satisfied.

Some of the social norms, known as *folkways*, like sleeping in a bed or eating with a knife and a fork, are not considered very important, and their violation brings only mild expressions of disapproval. Others, however, called *mores*, are definitely related to group welfare and thought of in terms of right and wrong, and their infraction provokes moral indignation. Enforced by public opinion, the mores greatly influence our attitudes toward sex, property, and the persons of others and thus give essential support to the criminal law. Still other social norms are judged so important to group welfare, as measured by the dominant values of the group, that certain individuals are given the responsibility of preserving and enforcing them. When social norms in a culture are thus enforced by authority and not just by public opinion, they have become, like the law and the family, *social* institutions.

Thus, the law must be seen as only one of a number of sets of social norms, that is, rules and standards for the guidance and regulation of human behavior, which every society must establish and preserve if it is to survive. These norms, varying in rationality, complexity, and compulsiveness, and tending to express the dominant values of the group, are woven into a system of social control. Part of this system, including the law, is highly formalized and carries with it the weight of institutionalized authority, but much of it is informal, consisting of such influences as public opinion, gossip, the praise and condemnation of the community, and the respect and ridicule of friends and acquaintances. However, because of the law's definition of crimes and prescription of penalties by legislative and judicial action, its general applicability to all members of the group, and its enforcement by political agencies with the full support of the authority of the state, it has a specificity, universality, and officiality not possessed by other parts of the system of social control.[9]

The criminal law, then, is not an entity, aloof and apart from the life of man, but, on the contrary, is intimately related to it, being affected by, as well as affecting, man's familial, economic, religious, educational, and recreational activities. If it is to remain vital and effective, therefore, its rules, doctrines, and principles must not di-

---

[9]*Ibid.*, p. 49.

verge too far from the dominant values of the society in which it functions.[10]

THE LEGAL MEANING OF CRIME

Crime may be defined as any act or omission which the law forbids and for which it prescribes punishment to be administered by the state through a proceeding in its own name.[11] In effect, then, the law says that there are certain kinds of conduct which are considered so detrimental to society, as judged by the dominant values, that action regarding them must be taken by organized society in a regular, definite way and not entrusted to private initiative. Moreover, since society in its corporate capacity enacts the criminal laws, any violation of them, regardless of what form it may take—whether, for example, it be treason, murder, burglary, prostitution, or sodomy—is an act against the state, and even if an individual takes no action, opposes official action, or tries to conceal the crime, the state can and may press charges against the alleged criminal or criminals. In other words, in every crime the state is always the primary victim regardless of the nature of the criminal act or the circumstances in which it is committed. Some writers, disregarding this important aspect of the criminal law, have referred to certain crimes as "crimes without victims," because, they explain, the parties involved in the act of such crimes willingly cooperate in its commission.[12] Although in support of this the claim has been made that it helps to call attention to the need of some reform in the criminal law, it has contributed to superficial understanding and confusion regarding the nature and purpose of the criminal law.

The same criticism can be made of those writers who, seeking to "decriminalize" certain acts, such as prostitution, homosexuality, and so on, contend that we should not try to "legislate morality." It is a mistake to assume that there is anything basically unsound in the

---

[10]Ibid., p. 69.

[11]Justin Miller, Handbook of Criminal Law (St. Paul, Minn.: West Publishing Co., 1934), p. 16; Perkins, p. 9.

[12]See, for example, Edwin M. Schur, Crimes Without Victims (Englewood Cliffs, N.J.: Prentice-Hall, Inc., 1965). More will be said about the nature and purpose of the criminal law in the discussion of punishment in Chapter XII.

legislation of morality, for all substantive criminal law involves this, although the morality incorporated into a particular criminal law may not be that of some, or even of most, of the members of a society. The real question is not whether we should legislate morality, but rather what morality we should legislate.

Crime, however, as we all know, is only one of several kinds of behavior which are called wrongs in our society. For example, sins, vices, and torts, also, are known as wrongs, although only crimes and torts are defined as such by the law. A sin is a transgression, such as blasphemy, which violates divine authority, whereas a vice is an immoral act, such as gluttony, which is directed chiefly against the offender, debasing his character and often injuring his health. A tort is a civil or private wrong, other than a breach of contract, for which the court will provide a remedy in the form of an action for damages.[13] In the case of a tort, private initiative in a civil suit is relied upon to redress the wrong, since the state usually has no power to interfere, and unlike the case of crime, contributory negligence on the part of the injured party may be a complete defense.

Even so, it must be understood that these wrongs overlap in such a way that the distinctions explained above frequently become quite blurred. Thus, a tort, which is called a private wrong, may, as in an automobile accident, affect many people and involve the giving of public relief to the victims and their dependents. Furthermore, what is a crime may also be a sin and a tort, as in the case of the seduction of a woman by a married man. In fact, most legal wrongs, such as assault and battery and criminal libel, are both criminal and tortious, thus not only enabling the state to prosecute, but also providing the individual victim with an opportunity to sue for damages.

In addition, the criminal law changes from time to time and varies from state to state. Consequently, some wrongs that at one time were not criminal are now criminal, whereas others that were criminal are now not criminal and what is a crime in one state may not be one in another. Moreover, as has been explained, the criminal law tends to reflect the dominant values of our society. Although most of the acts and omissions that are made criminal in our society are judged dangerous in terms of the values of most people, others may be considered unimportant or even desirable by some people. Thus, not all provisions of our criminal law enjoy the support of all the people,

---

[13]William L. Prosser, *Handbook of the Law of Torts* (St. Paul. Minn.: West Publishing Co., 1955), pp. 1-12.

and if certain provisions adversely affect the interests of enough people, agitation against them will develop and public opinion may force the repeal or modification of the objectionable provisions. In fact, if repeal or modification cannot be accomplished in an orderly way, the agitation may break out into violent action and open disregard of these provisions and may even contribute to the disrespect of all law.

Of course, what we have said here does not prove that the distinctions made about wrongs serve no purpose, for they do help us to have a deeper understanding of the meaning of crime. It does show, however, that we need to exercise great wisdom and skill in the enactment, administration, and enforcement of the criminal law.

ELEMENTS OF A CRIME

A crime may have two elements: the criminal act or omission and the mental or internal element commonly called the *mens rea* (literally, "guilty mind"), which includes criminal intent and criminal negligence or recklessness. All common law crimes must have both these elements, there being no crime if either is lacking; but in some offenses that did not originate in the common law, for example, the sale of adulterated food, the prohibited act alone, regardless of the intent involved, may constitute the crime. Thus, according to the common law, if a person genuinely believes that a car belongs to him, he does not commit larceny when he takes it. To commit this crime, he must intend to steal another's car. But why does he have the intent to steal the car? Here we must distinguish intent from motive. Intent is the purpose a person has in committing an act, whereas motive is the desire which stimulates him to have the purpose. So, a person may intend to steal a car because he wants to take a trip in it, to sell it, to use it in a robbery, and so on. Motive, furthermore, except in a few offenses like criminal libel, is not an essential element in a crime, and proof of motive is never necessary to secure a conviction if guilt can otherwise be established. Evidence of motive, however, is usually admissible to establish the identity of the perpetrator of the crime, the degree of the crime, and the intent with which it was committed.

In some crimes, the intent of the accused may be inferred from his conduct and the general circumstances of the case. So, if a person shoots another and kills him, the evidence showing this is enough to prove his intent to kill unless there are facts in evidence to the contrary. This type of intent is referred to as "general intent." In some other crimes, however, the evidence necessary to prove intent must be more specific. Thus, if a person is charged with the larceny of a book, the prosecution must prove not only that the accused intended to take the book, but also, more specifically, that he intended to steal it, because the taking of the book might have been only a borrowing of it. This type of intent is called a "specific intent."

Furthermore, a person may be guilty of a crime which is not the one he intended to commit. Thus, where a person engaged in the crime of robbery kills the person being robbed, he is guilty of a criminal homicide. Here the law considers the first act, the robbery, so fraught with danger to the person robbed that it transfers the intent to the second act, the killing, and thus completes the crime of murder. Since in this way the law transfers the intent, it is known as "transferred intent."

In certain other crimes, moreover, the mens rea consists simply of the state of mind that necessarily accompanies a failure to observe proper care. In other words, although the perpetrator does not intend to harm a particular person, he does intend to increase the possibility of such harm, and this is negligence so aggravated as to be called "criminal negligence" or "recklessness" in the law. However, in a case where recklessness is relied upon as the mental element, there must be a legal duty, and not just a moral duty, to act with due care under the circumstances. Thus, if a lifeguard does not do all that he can within reason to save a drowning man, he may be judged to be criminally negligent, whereas a mere passerby may turn his back with impunity on the unfortunate person.

When a crime must have both a mens rea and an act, the two elements must concur in the causation of the crime. Consequently, if a person forms an intent to kill another, then changes his mind but later accidentally kills the other, there is no concurrence of act and intent and so no crime. Furthermore, in some cases, a crime is deemed to exist even if the act committed does not amount to the complete commission of the crime intended. Thus, the crime of attempt is committed when an act is done with specific intent to commit a particular crime and moving toward, but falling short of, its commission; the crime of solicitation exists when one person solicits another to commit a felony even though the person solicited refuses to commit it; and two or more persons are guilty of conspiracy if they combine to commit an unlawful act even though nothing is done to achieve the objectives of the combination. A person who enters a conspiracy,

unless he effectively withdraws, is criminally liable for all the consequences that result from efforts to accomplish the purpose of the
conspiracy and for the acts of all who participate with him in the
commission of the crime. These three crimes show how our society
reaches out its arm of authority and punishes those who may merely
threaten important values which are given protection by the criminal
law.[14]

CLASSIFICATION OF CRIMES

Crimes may be classified in various ways. According to the common
law, crimes are divided into treason, felonies, and misdemeanors, but
modern American law includes treason in the category of felonies. In
the United States, treason is expressly defined by the federal Constitution, which states: "Treason against the United States, shall consist
only in levying war against them, or in adhering to their enemies,
giving them aid and comfort. No person shall be convicted of treason
unless on the testimony of two witnesses to the same overt act, or on
confession in open court."[15] Provisions similar to this are in the
constitutions or statutes of many states. Today, in the United States,
the more serious crimes are called felonies and usually are punishable
by death or by imprisonment in a state or federal prison or reformatory, whereas the less serious offenses are called misdemeanors and
usually are punishable by confinement in a jail or by a fine.[16] In many
American jurisdictions, however, infractions of municipal ordinances, such as those which regulate traffic in our cities, are not
stigmatized as crimes but instead are termed "violations"[17] and are
punishable by a fine.

---

[14]See Perkins, Chapters 6 and 7.

[15]*Constitution of the United States,* Art. III, Sec. 3.

[16]Since the laws of most states do not provide for imprisonment in a state
institution unless the term is at least one year, usually a crime is not a felony
unless the penalty is at least one year's imprisonment. Under the common
law, a felon was compelled to forfeit his lands and goods, and in addition, he
might be subjected to capital or other punishment. Today, some federal felons
in the United States are not even committed to prisons or reformatories but
instead are sent to other kinds of correctional institutions.

[17]The legal distinction between felonies and misdemeanors has not been
clearly preserved in American criminal law. For example, an offense that is a
felony in one state may be a misdemeanor in another. Nevertheless, the
distinction is still an important one in our jurisprudence.

The criminal law also makes a distinction between crimes *mala in se*, or wrongful because of their nature, and crimes *mala prohibita*, or wrongful merely because they are prohibited by law, such as violations of statutes and ordinances designed to secure better management of the affairs of the community. All felonies are *mala in se*, but some misdemeanors are *mala prohibita*. This distinction, however, is open to serious question, for one may ask whether any act serious enough to be defined as a crime is wrongful merely because of such definition, and, indeed, whether any act which is not wrongful because of its nature should be defined as a crime.[18] A more accurate interpretation of the law is that crimes differ only in the degree and not in the kind of wrongfulness, that they constitute a continuum that ranges from the least to the most serious violations of moral standards, and that the positions of crimes in the continuum change as social conditions and the attitudes of the people change.

A third classification of crimes divides them into those that are infamous and those that are non-infamous. Under the common law, an infamous crime is one which, because of its nature, makes the convicted person incompetent as a witness. Included in this category, according to the common law, are treason, felony, and any offense founded in fraud, or the *crimen falsi*. In our federal courts today, a crime is infamous, not because of its nature, but because of the nature of the penalty. Thus, in these courts a crime is infamous if it carries the penalty of imprisonment in a penitentiary or of any imprisonment at hard labor. Some states follow the federal rule in this classification; others, however, follow the common law, using the nature of the offense as the basis for determining whether it is infamous.[19]

Still another classification of crimes is based on the kind of social harm caused by the crime. By this classification, which is used in standard textbooks and criminal codes, crimes are placed under such headings as: offenses against the person; offenses against the habita-

---

[18]See Caldwell, p. 39.

[19]As a result of modern legislation, testimonial disqualification because of infamy has tended to disappear, and the term "infamous crime" would be of no more than historical interest, were it not included in the Fifth Amendment of the United States Constitution and in some state constitutions and statutes. The Fifth Amendment of the federal Constitution provides: "No person shall be held to answer for a capital, or otherwise infamous crime, unless on a presentment or indictment of a grand jury, except in cases arising in the land or naval forces, or in the militia, when in actual service in time of war or public danger, . . ."

tion; offenses against property; offenses against public health, safety, comfort, and morals; offenses against public justice and authority; offenses against public peace; and offenses against the existence of government.

ESSENTIAL CHARACTERISTICS OF SOME CRIMES

Under our federal form of government, each state has reserved for itself all the powers not delegated to the federal government. These powers include the power to enact and enforce its own criminal laws in whatever way it desires, as long as the exercise of this power does not violate any of the principles of the United States Constitution. Each state, therefore, may retain its common law crimes and add statutory crimes to them or abolish the common law crimes and use only statutory crimes. However, if a state retains its common law crimes, any act that was criminal under the common law[20] remains criminal even if it is not made so by statute, whereas if a state abolishes its common law crimes, no act is criminal unless it is defined as such by statute. At present, about half the states in the United States have retained their common law crimes. Consequently, although even in these states most crimes are also covered by statutes, their courts may still consult the common law to determine whether certain acts not specifically defined as crimes by statute are criminal. It is true that this rarely happens today because of the wide range of crimes included in the state criminal laws, but it does give the courts some discretionary power to control certain undesirable situations, for example, those involving acts intended to corrupt the morals of the people.

The federal government, on the other hand, since it is given only certain enumerated powers by our Constitution, cannot make the choice between common law crimes and statutory crimes. If an act is to be made a federal crime, the Congress, within the limits imposed

---

[20]The common law system had its roots in the common customs of the people of England. There, as we have explained, the courts, using these customs as a guide, raised them to the level of law through the development of a system of legal precedents. In contradistinction to this, the civil law, which developed in Continental Europe, had its roots largely in the will of the rulers, who sought to impose their ideas on the people. These two systems, of course, have influenced each other—and this can be seen in the development of the law of the United States—but each has still retained many of its fundamental characteristics.

upon it by the Constitution, must specifically make it a crime by statute. Nevertheless, in the federal jurisdiction, as well as in those state jurisdictions that have not retained their common law crimes, the courts look to the common law when this is necessary to clarify or interpret statutory provisions. This may happen, for example, when a statute names a crime but does not define it.

Unfortunately, the limitations of space in this kind of book make it impossible to do more than to examine briefly the essential characteristics of some of the most common crimes. Even this, however, should give some insight into their nature, but for a more adequate understanding, the reader is urged to consult textbooks on the criminal law and the statutes and decisions of his state government and the federal government.[21]

Homicide is the killing of one human being by another, and it may be either criminal or non-criminal. The death, however, must occur within a year and a day after the act or omission which is alleged to have been the cause of death or the law conclusively presumes that death resulted from some other cause.[22] Criminal homicide may be either murder or manslaughter. Murder is the unlawful killing of one human being by another with malice aforethought. Malice aforethought is said to be present when the perpetrator intends to kill or inflict great bodily injury, or when he willfully acts under such circumstances that there is obviously a plain and strong likelihood that death or great bodily injury may result, or when he intends to commit a dangerous felony—that is, one like arson, rape, robbery, and burglary, in which there is a substantial human risk. Under common law there are no degrees of murder, but in a number of states the crime is divided by statute into two or more degrees according to the heinousness of the deed.

Suicide is murder at common law if done deliberately by one who has the mental capacity to commit a crime. It is still a crime in some states in the United States, and when it is so defined, one who aids another to commit suicide is guilty of murder. Voluntary manslaughter is intentional killing without malice aforethought. It occurs when the killing is committed in the heat of passion induced by great provocation and there has been no reasonable opportunity for the passion to cool. So, if a husband finds his wife engaged in sex rela-

---

[21]In general, the definitions given here have been drawn from the common law wherever this has been possible. For a more detailed treatment of the crimes, see Miller and Perkins.

[22]This rule has been abrogated in some states.

tions with another and he immediately kills her lover, he may be guilty of voluntary manslaughter. Involuntary manslaughter is criminal homicide unintentionally caused and without malice aforethought. It may result from the commission of an unlawful act not amounting to a dangerous felony or from criminal negligence. A person who drives his car while he is intoxicated and kills another is guilty of involuntary manslaughter.

Rape is unlawful sexual intercourse with a woman without her consent. Statutes in most states specify that a female cannot legally consent to sexual intercourse when she is below a certain age, and that sex relations with a female under that age is rape regardless of whether she consents or not.

An assault is either an attempt to commit a battery or an unlawful act which causes another to have reasonable apprehension of receiving an immediate battery. Usually, an assault must consist of more than mere words. If a person raises his fist or a club at another in a threatening manner and thus creates an apprehension that he will strike, or if he does strike at another and misses him, this may be an assault. A battery is the unlawful application of force to the person of another. So, if a person strikes another or angrily pushes him aside, this may be a battery. Although the words "assault and battery" are usually employed together, they are two separate crimes. An assault may not result in a battery, but a battery of necessity includes an assault.

At common law, burglary is the breaking and entering of the dwelling house of another in the nighttime, with an intent to commit a felony. Entry through an opening in the wall or roof is not burglary, although entry through the chimney is, for the chimney is as closed as the nature of things will permit. However, burglary may be committed if there is the slightest movement of any part of the house so as to permit the entry. Although breaking without entry is not burglary, any entry, however slight, is sufficient, as, for example, where a head, a hand, or even a finger is thrust into the house. Usually burglary is committed with intent to steal, but as the definition states, it may occur when the person has an intent to commit any kind of felony. However, burglary has been considerably changed by statutes in most states in order to include such acts as breaking into buildings other than dwelling houses, entering without breaking, and breaking and entering in the daytime as well as at night.

Arson, according to the common law, is the malicious burning of the dwelling house of another. However, like burglary, it has had its meaning changed by statutes in most states. Now, under such statutes, it may be arson to burn not only dwelling houses but also other buildings, for example, warehouses and shops, and other kinds of property, like lumber and hay. Furthermore, in some states, if one burns his own house to secure the insurance, he is guilty of arson.

By the common law, larceny is defined as the trespassory taking and carrying away of the personal property of another from his possession and with intent to steal the property. However, larceny, too, has been modified by statute in the United States and therefore varies from state to state, but in general it now includes the theft of real property, such as growing trees, fruits, and vegetables, as well as personal property and may be either petty larceny, a misdemeanor, or grand larceny, a felony, depending on the value of the property stolen. Even so, the line between petty and grand larceny is fixed at different values, and so what is petty larceny in one state is grand larceny in another.

Robbery is larceny from the person or presence of another by violence or intimidation and against the will of the other. Since some violence or intimidation must be present, or the crime is only larceny, pocket-picking by stealth is not robbery.

Embezzlement, which was not a crime at common law, is the fraudulent appropriation of personal property by one to whom it has been entrusted. The gist of the crime is a breach of trust. Thus, if goods are delivered by the owner to another for transportation and the latter fraudulently appropriates them for his own use, he is guilty of embezzlement.

Obtaining property by false pretense, unless it was a common law cheat, was not a crime under the early common law, but it is now a crime by statute. It is defined as knowingly and designedly obtaining the property of another by means of untrue representations of fact with intent to defraud. Although so-called "puffing statements" or mere exaggerations to induce another to buy an article are not false pretense, specific statements about the nature of a product may be. For example, if the seller calls a car "the best car on the road," he has not committed the crime of false pretense, but if he states that a set of silverware is "sterling" when it is not, he has committed it.

Forgery, a misdemeanor at common law but now almost universally made a felony by statute, may be defined as the fraudulent making of a false writing which has apparent legal significance. To have legal significance, a writing must have some value or purpose other than its own existence, as, for example, in a negotiable instrument, which is a substitute for money, or in a deed to real estate, which passes title from one person to another. Consequently, a writing which exists for itself alone is not subject to forgery. So, if a person, with intent to defraud, copies a famous painting, including the signature of the real artist, and sells it as the original, he is guilty of false pretense but not forgery. Usually a writing is made false by the unauthorized using of the name of another or by making a material alteration of an instrument executed by another. When a person, with intent to defraud, offers as genuine an instrument which he knows to be false, he is guilty of the crime of uttering a forged instrument. For this crime to be committed, it is not necessary that the instrument be actually passed or otherwise used.

Extortion, as a common-law crime, is one form of misconduct in office. In this sense, it is the corrupt collection of an unlawful fee by an officer under pretext of discharging his duties. For example, it is committed when a constable obtains money for discharging a void search warrant. In some states, however, the crime has been enlarged to include the taking of property from another, with his consent, by the wrongful use of force or fear, under circumstances which do not amount to robbery. In its statutory form, extortion is usually a felony and is called "blackmail."

Bigamy is committed when a person who is already legally married marries another during the life of his wife or her husband. Adultery was not a common-law crime in England, but was regarded as an offense against the ecclesiastical law only, and it was therefore punished exclusively in the ecclesiastical courts. In the United States the definition of this crime varies from state to state, but all states agree that in order for the crime to exist, at least one of the parties must be lawfully married to another. Fornication, like adultery, is not a common-law crime, but it has been made a crime in some states. Although it, too, varies from state to state, it may be defined as voluntary sexual intercourse under circumstances not constituting adultery or lawful cohabitation between husband and wife, in short, voluntary sexual intercourse between two unmarried persons.

Compounding crime is the acceptance of anything of value under an unlawful agreement not to prosecute a known offender or to limit or handicap his prosecution. What is accepted need not be money or any object, but may be any advantage accruing to the person forbearing from the alleged offender. Thus, where the owner of stolen goods agrees not to prosecute the thief in return for his giving back the property, the owner is guilty of compounding crime.

Perjury at common law exists when a person who is under oath, or obligated by some legal substitute for an oath, willfully and corruptly gives false testimony, which is considered material to the question under inquiry, during a judicial proceeding or course of justice. A person who induces another to commit perjury is guilty of subornation of perjury.

PROXIMATE CAUSE

In a philosphical sense, one may say that the causes of an act go back to the beginnings of time and that its consequences go forward to eternity. The law, however, cannot use such a broad concept of causation as a standard for measuring human responsibility, for this would impose infinite liability for all wrongful acts, generate boundless conflicts in the community, and crowd the courts with endless litigation. Instead, the law, in its determination of causation, narrows its view by application of a social policy known as "justice," which tends to be an expression of the dominant values of society. But even if a person's act is thus determined to be the "proximate cause," that is, the "legally recognized cause," of the consequences in question, he is not necessarily criminally responsible, because what he did might have been an accident, for example, or he might have been acting in self-defense. In order for the person whose act is the proximate cause to be held criminally responsible, the consequences must be defined as a crime, the requisite mens rea must be present, and he must be without an adequate defense. Thus proximate cause and criminal responsibility are not always identical.

Under our system of criminal law, the general rule is that no one is held to be the proximate cause of harm unless his act was in fact[23] a cause of it. However, in a few instances, a proximate cause may be said to exist even where there is no factual cause. Thus, the law may regard the failure to perform a legal duty as the equivalent of a positive act, and the act of a person may be imputed by law to another member of a conspiracy. On the other hand, not all factual causes are proximate causes. So, an act may be too trivial to be given consideration by the

---

[23]The law analyzes the problems of factual causation in terms of the sine qua non, or the so-called "but for" or "had not" test. In other words, the law asks, "Would the result have occurred, had not the defendant committed the act?"

law, or the chain of causation may be broken by a more immediate independent intervening force, as, for example, when A, who mortally wounded B, is held not to be the proximate cause of B's death because C instantly killed B before B would have died of the wound inflicted by A. If, however, as Perkins explains, an act is a substantial factor and produces the result directly or with the aid of a dependent intervening[24] force other than an extraordinary response of a human being or an animal, the act is the proximate cause of the harm even if the harm was neither foreseeable nor intended. So, if A wounded B who would not have died had he gone to a doctor for treatment, A is the proximate cause of B's death. In this example, the wound inflicted by A is a substantial factor, and since negligence is too common in human behavior to be considered extraordinary, B's failure to go to a doctor is a dependent intervening force that does not break the chain of causation and cooperates with the wound inflicted by A to produce B's death. Even so, regardless of the circumstances, if an act which is substantial produces an intended or reasonably foreseeable result, it is always a proximate cause.[25] So, if A, intending to kill B, ties B to a tree in a woods where there are many wild animals and the animals kill B, A's act is a proximate cause of B's death.

An act, however, may be a proximate cause even though it is only a contributory one, as in the case of concurrent acts of two persons with a common design, or in some instances where the acts are concurrent or successive but independent of each other. Thus, if each of two persons, acting with a common design, inflicts a fatal wound, each is a proximate cause of the death, or if two persons, each acting independently of the other, concurrently or successively inflict wounds which cooperate in producing the death of a third person, each is a proximate cause of the death.

PARTIES TO CRIME

There may be four parties to a crime: the accessory before the fact, the principal in the first degree, the principal in the second degree, and the accessory after the fact. A person who actually commits the crime either by his own hand or through an innocent agent is a principal in

---

[24]A dependent cause is one that is produced by the first cause. An intervening cause is one which comes between an antecedent cause and a consequence.

[25]Perkins, pp. 737, 738.

the first degree. If, although present at the time the crime is committed, a person merely abets another in the commission of the crime, he is a *principal in the second degree.* One who is not present when the act is committed, but who procures, counsels, commands, or abets the principal is an *accessory before the fact.* On the other hand, one who relieves, comforts, or assists another in the effort to hinder the operation of the law and who knows that the other has committed a crime is an *accessory after the fact.* [26] However, this classification of parties is not applied in cases of treason or misdemeanor. In treason all parties are principals, and in misdemeanors, all parties except accessories after the fact, who are not liable in any way, are principals. The term "accomplice" may be used to refer to either a principal or an accessory.

In the United States and England, the common law regarding parties to crime has been greatly modified, and in many parts of our country the distinctions between principals and accessories before the fact have become obsolete. Nevertheless, the term "accessory after the fact" has been generally retained in the United States and is often used to refer to a crime of a lesser degree, exposing the convicted person to a lighter penalty than that given to others involved in the commission of a crime.

A person who acts as an agent in the commission of a crime and who is mentally competent and knowingly executes the commands of another person usually, together with the other person, incurs responsibility for the crime. However, an agent who is sincerely unaware of the nature of his act and has no reason to suspect any wrongdoing is not criminally responsible for his act. According to the common-law rule, a person who has not previously authorized or assented to the criminal acts of his agent is not liable for them even if they are committed during the course of the agent's employment. [27]

CAPACITY TO COMMIT CRIME

IMMATURITY

At common law, a child under the age of seven has no criminal capacity; that is, there is a conclusive presumption of his innocence.

---

[26] The present trend is to exclude from this type of guilt those who are intimately related to the principal.

[27] Perkins, pp. 636-85, 812-15.

In cases of children between the ages of seven and fourteen, there is a rebuttable presumption of criminal incapacity, and thus the child can be convicted of crime only upon the clear proof that he was sufficiently precocious to understand the wrongfulness of his act. This rebuttable presumption of innocence is very stong at the age of seven and gradually decreases until it completely disappears at the age of fourteen. However, by a special rule of the common law, no boy under the age of fourteen can be convicted of rape; that is, there is a conclusive presumption that his *physical immaturity* makes it impossible for him to commit this crime. Some states in the United States follow this rule, but others do not. The child who has reached the age of fourteen has the same criminal capacity as an adult; that is, he is fully responsible for violations of the law. He must, therefore, prove incapacity on some basis other than immaturity—for example, on the basis of insanity. Under the common law, in all cases involving the question of immaturity, the child's criminal capacity or incapacity is determined by his age at the time of the alleged offense and not by his age at the time of the indictment or the trial.

In the United States there has been a tendency to raise the age below which there is complete criminal incapacity. Furthermore, all states have enacted juvenile court laws,[28] which provide that the cases of children charged with having violated the criminal law (usually with some exceptions) shall be handled by juvenile courts and not by criminal courts. If the children are adjudged guilty, they are called "juvenile delinquents" and not "criminals." The effect of this is to relieve children of criminal responsibility if they come under the jurisdiction of the juvenile court. State laws, however, vary with respect to the age of the children over whom this court has jurisdiction. If fact, most of then do not specify any lower age limit and merely state that children under a stipulated age, usually eighteen, are subject to the jurisdiction of the juvenile court.[29]

INTOXICATION

In general, *voluntary intoxication*, whether resulting from alcohol or drugs, does not affect a person's capacity to commit crime and, therefore, does not free him from criminal responsibility for acts committed while he was in that condition. There are, however, some exceptions to the general rule. Thus, if at the time a person commits an

---

[28] See Chapter XIII for the origin and development of the juvenile court.
[29] Perkins, pp. 837-49; Caldwell, Chapter XVI.

act he is so voluntarily intoxicated that he is incapable of forming the specific or special statutory intent required by law, as, for example, that required in the case of larceny, robbery, burglary, and receiving stolen property, he is not criminally responsible. Furthermore, although voluntary intoxication will not free a person completely from the charge of criminal homicide, it may be taken into consideration in determining whether he was in a sudden heat of passion at the time of his act and so may help to reduce the charge from murder to manslaughter. Under no circumstances, however, will voluntary intoxication free a person from criminal responsibility for his act if he formed the intent to commit a crime before he was in that condition.

On the other hand, *involuntary intoxication*, for example, intoxication caused by the coercion, fraud, or stratagem of another, may incapacitate a person to commit a crime. For this to happen, however, the person must have been so intoxicated at the time of his act that he did not have criminal capacity as determined by the rule of insanity in effect in the state where he is tried.[30]

INSANITY

Insanity is any defect or disease of the mind which renders a person incapable of entertaining criminal intent. Therefore, if a person is insane at the time he commits an act, he is not criminally liable. Every person, however, is presumed to be sane and to possess a sufficient degree of reason to be responsible for his acts unless the contrary can be proved by the defense.

Various tests are used by the law to determine whether the accused was insane at the time he committed the alleged crime. One of these is the M'Naghten Rule, or "right and wrong" test, which is used in many states. According to this test, a person is insane if, at the time he committed the act, he did not know the difference between right and wrong with respect to that act.

Critics of the M'Naghten Rule argue that it tests only the rational powers of man and disregards his emotional strains. Since they have stressed the theory that man has irresistible impulses, a few courts have incorporated this theory into the "irresistible impulse" test and use it to supplement the "right and wrong" test. This test states that a man is insane when mental disease or defect renders him incapable of restraining himself, although he understands what he is doing and knows that it is wrong and so would be held sane by the "right and

---

[30]Perkins, pp. 888-909.

wrong" test. Critics of the "irresistible impulse" test contend that it provides the law with no basis for distinguishing an irresistible impulse from a resistible but unresisted impulse and so can be used as a subterfuge to avoid criminal responsibility.

In 1954, the Court of Appeals of the District of Columbia adopted the "product" rule as a test for insanity in a case in which Durham was the defendant. It is, therefore, often called the Durham Rule, but is essentially the same as the test adopted by New Hampshire nearly a century before. According to the Durham Rule, the accused is not criminally responsible if his act was the product of mental disease or mental defect. However, as soon as some evidence of mental abnormality is introduced by the defense, the prosecution has the burden of proving beyond a reasonable doubt that the act was not the product of this abnormality. The "product" test has been adopted by only a few jurisdictions in the United States, for it not only fails to provide criteria for the guidance of the jury, but also requires the prosecutor to accomplish what our present knowledge cannot enable him to do, that is, disprove a causal relation between a mental abnormality and a particular act. In fact, the very court that formulated the "product" rule—the Court of Appeals of the District of Columbia—abandoned it in June, 1972, in the case of *United States v. Brawner,* noting that a principal reason for doing so was that the rule allowed testifying experts to exert undue dominance in the trial.

The American Law Institute, also, has rejected the Durham Rule and, in its Model Penal Code, has proposed still another test for insanity. This test provides that a person should not be held criminally responsible for his act if as a result of mental disease or defect he lacked substantial capacity either to appreciate the criminality of his conduct or to conform his conduct to the requirements of the law. This proposal, which has been called the "substantial capacity" test, has been adopted by some states in the United States. However, it, too, has been severely attacked by critics. They have alleged, for example, that it does not give lay jurors a simple, helpful guide in their efforts to decide whether the accused was insane at the time of his act, and that the second alternative in the test (that is, the part that reads "or to conform his conduct to the requirements of law") permits the defendant to find refuge in what is the equivalent of the "irresistible impulse" test.

As we have indicated, no existing test of insanity is entirely satisfactory, although many students of the law believe that the "right and wrong" test should be retained and amended through interpretation (as it has been in the past) to include modern knowledge regarding the emotional and volitional aspects of human nature. Actually, of course, the real difficulty in devising a test for insanity arises not from the law's indifference to science, but from the lack of medical and psychiatric knowledge of mental abnormalities.[31]

JUSTIFIABLE ACTS AND EXEMPTIONS

In some situations, acts that otherwise would constitute crimes are not criminal because the law, on the ground of public policy, authorizes or commands their commission. Important among these acts, which are said to be justifiable, are those done in the performance of public justice, such as executing criminals, making arrests, preventing escapes, preserving peace, quelling riots, and preventing crimes. In addition, a person who is free from fault is justified in using self-defense if he reasonably believes that he is in imminent danger of battery and that he cannot avoid the threatened harm without using defensive force or giving up some right or privilege. However, his defensive force must not be unreasonable.

In some other situations, the law exempts persons from criminal responsibility. These persons may not be entirely blameless, but because of circumstances beyond their control, they are deemed not sufficiently blameworthy to deserve punishment. Reference to a few of these situations will help you to understand the position of the law on this point.

As a general rule, reasonable ignorance or mistake of fact exempts a person from criminal responsibility if his act would be lawful were the facts as he honestly believes them to be .[32] Thus, a person is not guilty of crime if, on reasonable grounds, he honestly mistakes another for a burglar and kills him. Ignorance of the law, however, is no excuse. If the accused in every case were permitted to plead ignorance of the law as a defense, the machinery of justice would soon come to a halt. Moreover, to recognize ignorance of the law would contradict the very values upon which the law is based. Wise public policy, therefore, calls for the exclusion of this defense, and the courts ad-

---

[31]Caldwell, pp. 360-65; Perkins, pp. 850-88.

[32]If a specific intent or other special mental element is required for guilt of the offense involved, even an unreasonable but honest ignorance or mistake of fact which negatives such intent will exempt the person from criminal responsibility.

judicate each case as if the defendant knew the law. Even so, there are some exceptions to the maxim *ignorantia legis neminem excusat* ("ignorance of the law excuses no man"). For example, the maxim is held not to apply when specific intent is essential to a crime and ignorance of the law negatives the existence of such intent. Hence, where a person takes an automobile which, because of his ignorance of the law, he sincerely believes belongs to him but which belongs to another, he is not guilty of larceny.

Exemption from criminal responsibility is granted also to a person who unintentionally causes harm quite by accident while he is not engaged in any unlawful conduct and is not criminally negligent. Furthermore, compulsion, if sufficiently extreme, will exempt a person not otherwise at fault from criminal responsibility for almost any harm not involving the intentional taking, or attempting to take, the life of an innocent person. And of course, one incurs no criminal liability if he is prevented from performing his legal duty by a storm, flood, or some other act of God. Moreover, the law permits a person, under ordinary circumstances, to use reasonable, nondeadly force to protect his property, and he may, with impunity, go beyond this and use even deadly force to protect his home against a malicious attack made for the purpose of destroying it.[33]

---

[33]Caldwell, pp. 44, 45; Perkins, pp. 806-926.

CHAPTER X

THE LAW ON ARREST
AND SEARCH AND SEIZURE

THE LAW ON ARREST

The authority of both peace officers and private citizens to make arrests is deeply imbedded in the common law of England. When the English colonists came to America, they brought with them the police practices already developed in the mother country and made them a part of our legal tradition. Although the passage of time has modified these practices, the common-law principles upon which they are based have remained largely unchanged and are embodied in our state and federal constitutions and statutes.

The Fourth Amendment of the Federal Constitution contains this provision: "The right of the people to be secure in their persons, houses, papers, and effects, against unreasonable searches and seizures, shall not be violated, and no Warrants shall issue, but upon probable cause, supported by Oath or affirmation, and particularly describing the place to be searched, and the persons or things to be seized."

This is usually cited as the "search-and-seizure amendment," but the inclusion of the word "persons" shows that it also protects individuals from illegal arrests. All doubt about this was dispelled by the Supreme Court in 1959, when, in handing down its decision in the Henry case,[1] it declared that the Fourth Amendment requires warrants for either searches or *arrests* to be issued only upon probable cause.[2] This ruling, however, applied only to *federal* arrests and the states continued to use their own standards until the Supreme Court in 1963, in Ker v. California,[3] applied the Fourth Amendment also to state and local arrests. Consequently, to be valid, such arrests must be

---

[1] *Henry v. United States*, 361 U.S. 98, S.Ct. 168 (1959).

[2] John C. Klotter and Jacqueline H. Kanovitz, *Constitutional Law for Police* (Cincinnati, Oh.: W.H. Anderson Co., 1968), pp. 53, 54.

[3] *Ker v. California*, 374 U.S. 23, 83 S.Ct. 1623 (1963).

made in conformity not only with state constitutions and statutes but also with the Fourth Amendment. According to the United States Supreme Court, probable cause to arrest exists where the facts and circumstances within the knowledge of the arrester and of which he has reasonably trustworthy information are sufficient to justify a man of reasonable caution in the belief that an offense has been committed and that the person to be arrested has committed it.[4] However, courts have recognized that a trained officer, who is an expert in law enforcement, may find "probable cause" to arrest in a situation where an untrained layman would fine none.[5]

An arrest may be defined as the taking of another into custody for the actual or purported purpose of bringing him before a court or official, or of otherwise securing the administration of the law. It is not essential to "lay hands" upon another to consummate an arrest, but there can be no arrest without either a physical touching or a submission to the authority of the person making the arrest. Prompt notice of the purpose of the arrest should be given by the arrester unless he reasonably believes that it is necessary to withhold this in order to protect himself or others or to complete the arrest. An arrest may be made with or without a warrant, by a police officer or by a private person, and for either an alleged felony or an alleged misdemeanor.

A police officer keeps his official authority at all times, regardless of whether he is on or off duty, but he can function as an officer only within the jurisdiction of the political unit which appointed him. Elsewhere he has only the authority of a private person. However, a number of states have laws which provide that an officer of another state, "in fresh pursuit"[6] of a person believed to have committed a felony in that state, may cross their boundaries and function within their territories with the same authority to arrest the fugitive and hold him in custody as local officers have in the case of one alleged to have committed a local felony.[7]

---

[4]*Draper v. United States,* 358 U.S. 307, 79 S.Ct. 329 (1959).

[5]Louis B. Schwartz and Stephen R. Goldstein, *Law Enforcement Handbook for Police* (St. Paul, Minn.: West Publishing Co., 1970), p. 126.

[6]Fresh pursuit may be defined as pursuit without unreasonable interruption or the immediate pursuit of a person who is trying to avoid arrest. See Klotter and Kanovitz, p. 78.

[7]Robert G. Caldwell, *Criminology* (New York: The Ronald Press Co., 1965), pp. 327, 331; Rollin M. Perkins, *Elements of Police Science* (Chicago: The Foundation Press, Inc., 1942), pp. 223, 224, 227; Wayne R. LaFave, *Arrest: The Decision to Take a Suspect into Custody* (Boston: Little, Brown and Company, 1965), pp. 3-7.

ARRESTS WITH A WARRANT

A warrant for arrest is "a written order issued by some competent authority in the name of the state to some authorized officer or individual directing him to arrest an alleged offender and to bring the arrestee before some proper person to be dealt with according to the law."[8] Such a warrant can be issued only by a judge or some other authorized official who is a neutral or impartial person and, therefore, not a police officer or prosecutor. The usual procedure for securing the issuance of the warrant involves the preparation of a written complaint or information which alleges under oath or affirmation[9] certain facts from which the individual issuing the warrant can reasonably assume that a particular person is probably guilty of a specific crime. The complaint need not be based on the direct personal observations of the affiant but instead may be supported by only hearsay information. When hearsay information is offered, however, the magistrate must be apprised of the "underlying circumstances" which led the informant to his conclusion and caused the affiant to believe that his informant was a credible person and that the information was reliable.[10]

In all warrants, the name of the person to be arrested or, if his name is not known, a description which identifies him to a reasonable certainty must be stated. If his name is not known, the warrant may refer to him as "John Doe," and it is then called a "John Doe warrant." To be valid, however, such a warrant must also contain an adequate description of the person to be arrested. The name "John Doe," therefore, may not be placed on a warrant for the purpose of having it refer to some unknown person to be selected for arrest at a later time.

An arrest warrant must not only refer to a specific person but must also state the nature of the offense with which the person to be arrested is charged. Furthermore, only the person or one of the class of persons authorized by the warrant to make the arrest may lawfully execute it. Although under the common law either a law enforcement officer or a private person may be authorized by a warrant to make an arrest, modern statutes often make no provision for the execution of warrants by private persons. However, even under such statutes, an

---

[8]Caldwell, p. 327.

[9]An affirmation may be used by those who object to the taking of an oath. In other words, these persons affirm that they are telling the truth. See also *Coolidge v. New Hampshire*, 91 S.Ct. 2022 (1971).

[10]*Aguilar v. Texas*, 378 U.S. 108, 84 S.Ct. 1509 (1964).

officer may still deputize a private person to execute a particular warrant. When the warrant appears to be valid, that is, fair on its face, and the officer does not abuse his authority in making the arrest or is not aware that the warrant was issued by an unauthorized person, he is protected against liability for false arrest or false imprisonment, even though it is later ascertained that the arrest was not justified.

Unless there is some statutory provision to the contrary, an arrest under a warrant may be made only in the city, town, county, district, state, or other territory within which the official, court, or body issuing the warrant has the authority to order an arrest. Most modern statutes, however, provide that an arrest warrant issued in one county in a state may be executed in any county of that state, and some states have passed statutes conferring validity on out-of-state warrants. An arrest warrant usually remains valid until it is executed. When this is accomplished, the arresting officer, as soon as he can reasonably do so, should show the warrant to the arrestee or advise him of its issuance and inform him of the charges.[11]

ARRESTS WITHOUT A WARRANT

The common law early recognized that it was impractical, if not impossible, to obtain an arrest warrant under some circumstances, and therefore it allowed certain arrests to be made without a warrant. Although the United States Constitution and the constitutions of the various states do not expressly refer to arrest without a warrant, both federal and state laws authorize this type of arrest when certain conditions exist. Recent Supreme Court decisions, however, indicate that the standard for judging "probable cause" in cases where an arrest is made with a warrant is less exacting than that used for measuring the evidence necessary for making an arrest without a warrant. In this way, the Supreme Court has shown its preference for arrests with a warrant.[12]

Under both common and statutory law, a police officer may arrest without a warrant when a felony is committed in his presence. Furthermore, in the great majority of the states, an officer may arrest without a warrant when any type of misdemeanor is committed in his presence. An offense is committed in the presence of the person

---

[11]Caldwell, p. 328; Klotter and Kanovitz, pp. 58-65; Perkins, pp. 231-48; Raymond A. Dahl and Howard H. Boyle, Jr., *Procedure and the Law of Arrest, Search and Seizure* (Milwaukee: Hammersmith-Kortmeyer Co., 1961), pp. 40-56.

[12]Klotter and Kanovitz, pp. 60, 65.

making the arrest if he becomes aware of it through any of his senses. When a felony is not committed in the presence of an officer, the general rule permits him to make an arrest without a warrant if he has reasonable grounds to believe both that a felony has been committed and that the arrestee has committed it. On the other hand, most states do not permit an officer to make an arrest without a warrant for a misdemeanor *not* committed in his presence.

A private person also may make an arrest without a warrant. Like an officer, under both common and statutory law, he may arrest without a warrant when a felony is committed in his presence. When a misdemeanor is committed in his presence, his authority to arrest without a warrant differs from state to state, but in nearly half of the states he has this authority when *any* misdemeanor is committed in his presence. Statutory provisions differ also with respect to the authority of a private person to make an arrest without a warrant for a felony not committed in his presence, but in the great majority of states, he may do this when a felony has actually been committed and he has reasonable grounds to believe that the arrestee is the felon. When, however, a misdemeanor is not committed in the presence of a private person, he may not lawfully arrest without a warrant.[13]

The term "reasonable grounds," which has been used in this section, is now considered to have the same meaning as "probable cause." Although it requires more than mere suspicion, it amounts to less than what is necessary to convict. What constitutes "reasonable grounds" cannot be stated in a simple rule, since whether or not these grounds exist depends upon the circumstances of each case. Nevertheless, in general, "reasonable grounds" may be said to exist if the circumstances of the case are such as to induce an ordinarily prudent and intelligent man to believe that the arrestee is guilty of the crime for which the arrest is made, or to cause him to believe that there is a likelihood of such guilt. Therefore, the arrester may arrest two or more persons if he has reasonable grounds to believe that any one or all of them have committed the crime. Any unlawful arrest, however, exposes the arrester to a suit for damage and perhaps to criminal prosecution.

"POSSE COMITATUS"

When a police officer is making an arrest, he has the authority to call upon private persons for help. Furthermore, the private person

---

[13]Caldwell, pp. 328, 329.

must comply with a reasonable request for such help or be charged with a misdemeanor and may not delay so as to determine what authority the officer has in the particular case. Consequently, such private person not only acquires the authority of the officer but also protection against legal action if the officer is exceeding his authority, provided the private person does not know this fact or has no reason to know it. The person or persons who assist an officer in this way constitute a posse, which is short for *posse comitatus*, meaning the body of inhabitants in a county liable to be summoned by the sherriff to assist in preserving the public peace. The posse differs from the deputy in that the latter serves with both the authority *and* the full responsibility of the officer.

USE OF FORCE

According to the general rule, a police officer or a private person may not use more than reasonable force to make a lawful arrest. Reasonable force means that force which an ordinarily prudent and intelligent person, with the knowledge and in the situation of the arrester, would have deemed reasonable, that is, in accord with reason. However, if the arrestee resists or flees, the arrester (either an officer or a private person) may use even deadly force—that is, force intended or likely to cause death—to effect a lawful arrest on a charge of felony,[14] but not on a charge of misdemeanor, if such force is reasonably necessary.[15] The arrester, moreover, must take and maintain the initiative and is never required to abandon his attempt to make an arrest in order to avoid the use of deadly force in self-defense. In fact, he may always use deadly force if this is necessary, or reasonably appears necessary, to protect himself from death or great

---

[14]The American Law Institute contends that the arrester should be privileged to use deadly force in case of resistance or flight only when the arrestee is sought for a "dangerous" felony; that is, a felony such as arson, burglary, felonious assault, kidnapping, manslaughter, mayhem, murder, rape, and robbery. Some jurisdiction in the United States have adopted this view.

[15]Under the common law, a private person attempting to arrest without a warrant was never privileged to use deadly force merely to arrest another if that person was in fact innocent. According to Perkins, this appears to be true also in the United States, where statutes usually require a warrant of arrest to be executed by a peace officer and the authority of a private person to make an arrest without a warrant is seldom exercised, although this authority is very broad. See Rollin M. Perkins, *Criminal Law* (Mineola, N.Y.: The Foundation Press, Inc., 1969), p. 982.

bodily harm, regardless of whether the arrestee is charged with a felony or only a misdemeanor.

ARREST AND THE FIRST AMENDMENT

Some very difficult problems confront the police officer who is trying to perform his duties in situations involving the First Amendment, the provisions of which guarantee freedom of religion, speech, press, and assembly. These freedoms are highly prized and greatly cherished in our country, but they have never been considered to be absolute by the courts. As in the case of all rights, they must be coupled with responsibilities; that is, they can be exercised only if they are limited by respect for the rights of others.

The United States Supreme Court has recognized the importance of this limitation, and in its decisions on First Amendment cases, it has sought to find a balance between the interests of the individual and those of the community. This broad philosophical approach, however, has left the police very uncertain as to how the law should be applied in many concrete situations. Nevertheless, some guidelines for the formulation of state and local law enforcement policies can be obtained by an examination of the cases.

In its deliberations on First Amendment cases, the Supreme Court has given primary consideration to "the mode of expression, the content of the speech, the time and place of the utterance, and its effect on the social order."[16] The highest degree of constitutional protection has been given to written forms of expression, whereas states and local communities have been allowed to regulate other forms of activity, such as public assemblies, parades, and picketing, to a much greater extent. The Court has made this distinction on the ground that the latter forms of activity are much more likely to inconvenience the community or to endanger its safety and welfare. A municipality, for example, may require those who wish to parade, demonstrate, or picket to obtain a permit or license, specifying the type, time, place, and duration of the activity.[17]

On the other hand, efforts to control the content of speech have been approved by the United States Supreme Court in only a limited

---

[16]Klotter and Kanovitz, pp. 28-52.

[17]See, for example, *United States v. O'Brien*, 391 U.S. 367, 88 S.Ct. 1673 (1968); *Talley v. California*, 362 U.S. 60, 80 S.Ct. 536 (1960); *Cox v. Louisiana*, 379 U.S. 536, 85 S.Ct. 453 (1965); *Cox v. New Hampshire* 312 U.S. 569, 61 S.Ct. 762 (1941).

number of cases, principally in those involving obscenity, insulting and libelous words ("fighting words"), incitement to violence, and "commercially oriented speech." Political and religious speeches have been given the strongest protection by the Court, which has permitted their regulation only when they have constituted a clear and present danger to the health, welfare, morals, or safety of the community.[18]

On the basis of such decisions of the Supreme Court, a few conclusions can be drawn regarding the work of the police as it affects the freedoms guaranteed by the First Amendment. Whenever public gatherings are held, sufficient police power should be present to provide adequate protection for the speakers and to prevent or quell disturbances. Persons who unlawfully interfere with the speaker should be removed from the area. Where there are violations of a permit or license to parade, demonstrate, or picket, arrests should be made on the basis of a warrant so that hasty and unreasonable police action will be avoided. Arrests for failure to obey an order to move on or disperse should be made with extreme caution, since the laws upon which such arrests are based are probably unconstitutionally vague. In general, if a person is where he has a right to be and is not violating any law, he should not be subjected to an arrest merely because he refuses to obey an order to desist. It seems, however, that arrests may be made when valid local traffic regulations are being violated, when there is incitement to riot or to commit some other crime, or when the speaker is uttering insults or "fighting words" that tend to provoke immediate acts of physical retaliation. Even so, in most situations, the better policy calls for the employment of requests, persuasions, and argument before the police finally resort to the making of arrests. If a crowd seems to be getting out of control, the police should seek the voluntary cooperation of the demonstrators in bringing their activities to an end, even if they have not been violating the law. If this is not successful and all reasonable efforts to placate the crowd fail, then in order to prevent bloodshed and damage to property, the police may

---

[18]See, for example, Roth v. United States, 354 U.S. 476, 77 S.Ct. 1304 (1957); Ginsberg v. New York, 390 U.S. 629, 88 S.Ct. 1274 (1968); Chaplinsky v. New Hampshire, 315 U.S. 568, 62 S.Ct. 766 (1942); Gregory v. Chicago, 394 U.S. 111, 89 S.Ct. 946 (1969); Martin v. Struthers, 319 U.S. 141, 63 S.Ct. 862 (1943); Schenck v. United States, 249 U.S. 47, 39 S.Ct. 247 (1919); Dennis v. United States, 341 U.S. 494, 71 S.Ct. 857 (1951); Brandenburg v. Ohio, 395 U.S. 444, 89 S.Ct. 1827 (1969); Adderley v. Florida, 385 U.S. 39, 87 S.Ct. 242 (1967); Cameron v. Johnson, 390 U.S. 611, 88 S.Ct. 1335 (1968).

take demonstrators into "protective custody" without bringing any charges against them.

There are practical advantages to be gained by taking photographs of demonstrations in which controversial views are being expressed. By this means, photographic identification of chronic troublemakers can be made and subsequent police action against them may be indicated by a check of their criminal records, useful information for riot control and the pacification of crowds may be obtained, and the presence of the photographer's camera may be a deterrent to acts of violence. At present, the majority of the authorities passing upon the question have held that on-the-scene picture-taking is constitutional if the photographers remain at a reasonable distance from the demonstrators and do not actively interfere with their peaceful protests.

It is quite clear that police officers are in great need of better guidelines to assist them in handling situations that fall within the scope of the First Amendment. Help should come as soon as possible from the United States Supreme Court, whose decisions have too often only aggravated an already troublesome problem, as well as from state legislatures and local authorities.[19]

DISPOSITION OF THE PRISONER

Since the purpose of lawful arrest is to take the prisoner before a magistrate, judge, or other authorized official for the administration of the law, this disposition of the prisoner should be made with reasonable promptness.[20] In fact, if this is not done, the detention of the prisoner will become unlawful even if the arrest was lawful. The prisoner, however, before being taken to the committing official, may be locked up temporarily for a reasonable time if the circumstances of the case make it necessary. For example, this may be done because the normal facilities for handling the prisoner are not open at the time of his arrest, or because delay in taking him before the committing official may protect lives, preserve important evidence, or expedite the arrest of dangerous persons.[21]

---

[19]Klotter and Kanovitz, pp. 52-63; Ibid., *1975 Supplement to Constitutional Law for Police,* pp. 20-23.

[20]The Federal Rules of Criminal Procedure require an arrested person to be taken "without unnecessary delay" before the nearest available committing official.

[21]Caldwell, p. 332.

DETENTION FOR QUESTIONING, INVESTIGATION, OR INSPECTION

No person who is not subject to lawful arrest may be locked up in jail or prison just for the purpose of questioning or investigation, nor may wholesale arrests of innocent persons be made in the hope of discovering among them some person who is wanted for an alleged crime. However, if a person will not agree to appear and testify in a criminal case, he may be imprisoned as a material witness to guarantee his availability, and persons found at the scene of a crime may be required to remain for a reasonable time, in what is called "technical confinement," so that they may be questioned.

Although it is common police practice to stop and question suspects, both motorists and pedestrians, under circumstances where no lawful arrest can be made, the courts are not uniformly in favor of this practice. Police, however, strongly defend it and argue that it not only prevents crime, but also protects innocent persons, who otherwise might be arrested, from unnecessary embarrassment. A person who is stopped for questioning, however, may refuse to remain with the officer or give any answers and may not thereupon be arrested or searched for his failure to cooperate. On the other hand, in virtually all states, the officer has the authority to stop motor vehicles and demand inspection of drivers' licenses or automobile registrations.[22]

THE LAW ON SEARCH AND SEIZURE

The Fourth Amendment to the Constitution of the United States provides protection against unreasonable searches and seizures and requires that warrants be based upon "probable cause." Originally, this amendment applied only to the federal government, but the Supreme Court has extended its limitations to the states through the "due process clause" of the Fourteenth Amendment. In addition, all state constitutions have a "due process clause" and provisions similar to those of the Fourth Amendment. What is "reasonable" is affected by the circumstances of each case, but in general, as in an arrest, it is measured by what an ordinarily prudent and intelligent man would believe under the same or similar circumstances.

---

[22]Klotter and Kanovitz, pp. 87-91.

KINDS OF LEGAL SEARCH AND SEIZURE

More specifically, such search and seizure is legally "reasonable" (1) when it is properly made under a valid search warrant, (2) when it is an incident to a lawful arrest, (3) when in an emergency situation and for "probable cause" it involves an automobile or other vehicle, and (4) when it is made with valid consent. Thus, a search and seizure is clearly "unreasonable when it is merely *exploratory* and made *solely* in the hope of finding evidence. It must be remembered, however, that neither the federal nor state constitutional restrictions apply to searches and seizures made by private persons who are not acting in a law enforcement capacity. Consequently, evidence which would not be admissible if it were obtained by a law enforcement officer is admissible when it is obtained by a private citizen. But this does not mean that a law enforcement agency may authorize or indirectly employ private citizens to secure evidence of this kind for the state.

Search and Seizure with a Warrant   A search warrant is a written order, issued in the name of the state, signed by a magistrate or other official having the authority to issue it, and directing a peace officer to search for certain property and to bring it before the magistrate or other issuing official. To be valid, a search warrant must be based upon a showing of "probable cause," supported by oath or affirmation, and must describe with particularity the place to be searched and the things to be seized. Like an arrest warrant, a search warrant may be based on hearsay evidence, provided the officer applying for the warrant relates the "underlying circumstances" which led the informant to his conclusion and caused the officer to believe that the evidence was reliable and the informant, credible.[23] In fact, recent judicial decisions, especially those handed down by the United States Supreme Court, clearly show that a warrant may issue on evidence which would not be admissible at a trial.[24] In all applications for a search warrant, however, it is the official who issues the warrant, and not the complainant, who determines whether there is

---

[23]See *Jones v. United States,* 362 U.S. 257, 80 S.Ct. 725 (1960); *Aguilar v. Texas,* 378 U.S. 108, 84 S.Ct. 1509 (1964); *United States v. Ventresca,* 380 U.S. 102, 85 S.Ct. 741 (1965). As in the case of an arrest warrant, only a neutral or impartial person should issue a search warrant, and therefore a police officer or a prosecutor should not do so.

[24]Klotter and Kanovitz, p. 108.

"probable cause," that is, reasonable grounds for the issuance of the warrant.

The home is given special protection under the law in the United States, and it is firmly established that a person's home may not be lawfully searched without a warrant, except as an incident to a lawful arrest therein.[25] Furthermore, the search warrant may be issued only for those objects which may be seized according to the law, but the trend has been to expand the statutory provisions to include all objects that may constitute evidence of the offense in connection with which the warrant is issued.

The United States Supreme Court has supported this trend. In the case of *Warden, Maryland Penitentiary v. Hayden*,[26] the majority of the Court, in reversing previous decisions, rejected the proposition that the Constitution limited searches and seizures to fruits of the crime, weapons by which escape of the person arrested might be effected, and property the possession of which is a crime. By this decision, the Court made it constitutional to seize what is called "mere evidence," that is, any evidence, of the alleged offense by a search warrant. Nevertheless, since the warrant must point to a definitely ascertainable place, the issuance of one for a general search is unlawful, and one thing may not be seized under a warrant that describes another. However, evidence seen during a search under a warrant not specifically describing it may be seized on the basis of what is called the "plain view" doctrine. According to this doctrine, such evidence may be seized if it can be seen by the person making the search from a spot where he has a legal right to be. The reasoning in support of this doctrine is that since no search is required to find such evidence, the constitutional guarantees of the Fourth Amendment do not apply.

---

[25]In 1959, the United States Supreme Court ruled in a five-to-four decision that the city code of Baltimore which authorized a health inspector without a warrant to enter any premises where he suspected there was a public nuisance did not violate the provisions of the Fourth Amendment. See *Frank v. State of Maryland*, 359 U.S. 360, 79 S.Ct. 804 (1959). A few year later, however, the Supreme Court reversed this ruling and held that the administrative inspection of homes, such as that by health or safety officers, should not be made an exception to the requirements of the Fourth Amendment, and that, therefore, an inspector without a warrant should not have the authority to demand admission to a home. *Camara v. Municipal Court of San Francisco*, 387 U.S. 523, 87 S.Ct. 1727 (1967). See also *See v. City of Seattle*, 387 U.S. 541, 87 S.Ct. 1737 (1967).

[26]*Warden, Maryland Penitentiary v. Hayden*, 87 S.Ct. 1642 (1967).

A search warrant must be executed by the person designated by name or class within a reasonable time or within the time specified by statute. After the expiration of this time, an unexecuted warrant becomes void. In general, if the warrant is valid on its face, the officer who executes it is protected from civil and criminal liability unless he abuses his authority in making the arrest or is aware that the warrant was issued by an unauthorized person. Only necessary force may be used in executing a warrant, but this general rule is broad enough to authorize the person conducting the search to break both outer and inner doors if he cannot gain admittance in any other way. In all cases, however, when a warrant is executed, the occupant of the premises should be informed of the intended search and the contents of the warrant, unless this might result in the loss of life or the destruction of the evidence sought. All objects seized under a warrant should be taken to the proper authority without unnecessary delay and a complete inventory of them filed and signed under oath by the person who executed the warrant.[27]

Search Incident to a Lawful Arrest.   Although no specific provision authorizing a search without a warrant is contained in the United States Constitution or the constitutions of the various states, the legality of a search incident to a lawful arrest is solidly established in Anglo-American jurisprudence. Its justification is based on the need to prevent the destruction of evidence and to facilitate the seizure of weapons and other things that might be used to effect an escape or endanger the arrester. Indeed, more searches are made as incidents to arrests than in any other way. Nevertheless, contending that the warrant helps to check the power of the police, the courts prefer that a search be made under a warrant, and the United States Supreme Court has made it quite clear that a search under a warrant may be upheld in a case where a search without one would not. The arrester, furthermore, is better protected against possible legal action by the arrestee when a search warrant is issued.

A search incident to arrest must be reasonable and based upon a

---

[27]Klotter and Kanovitz, pp. 110-12. According to a federal law passed in 1970, agents of the Federal Drug Enforcement Administration, acting under certain defined conditions, may use "no knock" warrants to enter premises without first knocking and announcing authority or purpose. However, the judge or magistrate issuing the "no knock" warrant must be satisfied that it is needed to protect the agent or the evidence sought. In 1974, because law enforcement officers had abused their "no knock" authority, Congress amended the law so as to restrict this type of entry.

lawful arrest. If the arrest in unlawful, the search incident to it is unlawful. Some courts have held that if the search incident to a lawful arrest comes before the arrest, the search is unlawful for this reason alone. The better view is that the contrary is true, for such a search involves no greater invasion of the person's security and privacy than one made after the arrest. Furthermore, if the prior search is not productive, the person may not be subjected to any arrest. In this type of search, the arrester may search the *person* of the arrestee for weapons or evidence and the surrounding area under the *immediate control* of the arrestee, that is, the area into which the arrestee may reach to obtain a weapon or to destroy evidence.[28] If during the search, contraband unrelated to the alleged offense is discovered or observed in "plain view," this, too, may be seized and used to support additional charges against the arrestee. However, the force used by the arrester must be reasonable and not be such as to shock our sense of decency.[29]

In *Terry v. Ohio,* decided on June 10, 1968, the Supreme Court upheld the right of a police officer to stop and frisk persons who, he reasonably suspects, have committed or are about to commit a crime, in order to discover weapons that might be used against the officer. If the frisk, which is a "patting down," an external feeling of the clothing of a person, indicates the presence of weapons, the officer may seize them, and these weapons may then be properly introduced in evidence against the suspect.[30] But suppose a stop-and-frisk does not reveal any weapon but does produce other evidence, such as drugs,

---

[28]*Chimel v. California,* 395 U.S. 752, 89 S.Ct. 2034 (1969). In the *Chimel* case, the Supreme Court definitely restricted the area that might be searched as an incident to arrest and thus reversed *Harris v. United States,* 331 U.S. 145, 67 S.Ct. 1098 (1947), which had been a controlling case up until then. In the *Harris* case, the Supreme Court, by a majority of five-to-four, held that an incidental search might extend to an entire four-room apartment, even though the defendent was arrested in the living room. See also *United States v. Robinson,* 414 U.S. 218, 94 S.Ct. 467 (1973).

[29]The Supreme Court has ruled that if unreasonable force is used in extracting something from the body of a person, this violates due process of law and the evidence is inadmissible in state and federal courts. See *Rochin v. California,* 342 U.S. 165 (1952).

[30]*Terry v. Ohio,* 392 U.S. 1, 88 S.Ct. 1868 (1968). The Supreme Court, furthermore, has ruled that information obtained from an informant may justify a stop-and-frisk, that a weapon discovered in this way may afford reasonable ground for further search incident to the ensuing arrest, and that other evidence found during the search incident to the lawful arrest is admissible. See *Adams v. Williams,* 407 U.S. 143 (1972).

burglar's tools, or some incriminating statement. Is this kind of evidence admissible? Presumably it is, but the Supreme Court has not yet specifically ruled on the point, and the case law regarding it is still in the process of development.

Search Based on "Probable Cause."   When an officer has reasonable grounds for believing that an automobile or other vehicle is being used to carry contraband, he may conduct a search of the vehicle without obtaining a warrant.[31] This kind of search has been held to be legal upon the utilitarian grounds that the vehicle may move away before the officer can secure a warrant. But an emergency must exist; that is, there must be not only "probable cause" but also a *real* danger of the vehicle's being moved. Nevertheless, this kind of search has a definite advantage over search as an incident to arrest, for whereas the latter must be confined to the area of the car under the "immediate control" of the arrestee, a search for "probable cause" may cover the entire car. In some cases, the circumstances are such that the officer must decide which of these two kinds of search is advisable.

In all cases where a vehicle has been legally impounded by the police, they have the duty, either by law or regulation, to make an inventory search and a list of the contents. This is necessary for the protection of both police and the arrestee. If evidence is discovered during this inventory search, it is admissible in court to support a criminal prosecution.[32] But it is advisable to have the inventory search made by someone other than the officer who brought the vehicle to the station—preferably by the person whose routine duty it is to do this kind of work. This will guard against the charge that the impounding was a mere subterfuge on the part of the police to gain access to the vehicle and, therefore, not a legal basis for a search.

Search Made with Valid Consent.   An individual may waive his constitutional rights regarding search and seizure and consent to a search. This consent must be positive and voluntary and given by one who has adequate knowledge of his constitutional rights and the legal capacity to consent. However, a police officer need not warn a person of his right to refuse to consent to a search as a prerequisite for securing a valid consent, at least in cases where the consenting person is not in custody. Consequently, valid consent has not been given

---

[31]*Carroll v. United States,* 267 U.S. 132 (1925). See also *Cardwell v. Lewis,* 417 U.S. 583, 94 S.Ct. 2464 (1974).
[32]Klotter and Kanovitz, pp. 137, 138.

when a person merely submits to the authority of the officer, when a landlord consents to the search of a leased premises, or when a child consents to the search of the premises of a parent.[33]

THE EXCLUSIONARY RULE

Under our law, anyone who makes an unlawful search and seizure is subject to a suit for damages and perhaps to criminal prosecution, but according to the common law, the admissibility of evidence is not affected by the illegality of the means by which it is obtained. For many years the courts in the United States followed the common-law rule and admitted evidence even though it was obtained by an illegal search and seizure. In 1914, however, in Weeks v. United States,[34] the United States Supreme Court held that the admission of illegally seized evidence was violative of the Fourth Amendment, and that, therefore, such evidence should be excluded from federal courts, although this ruling did not affect the police activities of state and local officers. Consequently, the Weeks case put into operation an "exclusionary rule" applicable only to federal officers. Six years later, in Silverthorne Lumber Co. v. United States,[35] the Court tightened the restrictions on federal officers and the admissibility of evidence by declaring that not only was the evidence illegally obtained inadmissible in federal courts but also the leads and other information derived from it. Thus the "fruit-of-the-poisonous-tree doctrine" was established.

Then, in 1949, in Wolf v. Colorado,[36] the Court went a step further and ruled that unreasonable searches and seizures by state law enforcement officers violated the "due-process clause" of the Fourteenth Amendment, but that the states were still not required to exclude illegally secured evidence. In 1956, however, the exclusionary rule was extended against federal officers when the Supreme Court ruled that they might not turn over to state authorities for use in state prosecutions any evidence previously held inadmissible in a federal court because it had been illegally seized by them.[37]

Even so, federal officers continued to get evidence from state

---

[33]Ibid., pp. 126-29; Schneckloth v. Bustamonte, 412 U.S. 218, 93 S.Ct. 2041 (1973).

[34]Weeks v. United States, 232 U.S. 383 (1914).

[35]Silverthorne Lumber Co. v. United States, 251 U.S. 385 (1920).

[36]Wolf v. Colorado, 338 U.S. 25 (1949).

[37]Rea v. United States, 350 U.S. 214 (1956).

officers, and this was admissible in federal courts, provided that there was nothing illegal in the way it was handed over, even if the state officers had illegally obtained the evidence. It was said, therefore, that state officers were handing over evidence to federal officers on a "silver platter." But the Supreme Court ended this practice in 1960, when it ruled, in Elkins v. United States,[38] that evidence obtained by a state officer was inadmissible in a federal court if it had been secured in a way that would have been illegal for a federal officer. Finally, in 1961, a divided Supreme Court in the Mapp case overruled the Wolf case. As a result, evidence obtained by an unlawful search and seizure is now inadmissible in both state and federal courts,[39] and so the "exclusionary rule" is applicable to all law enforcement officers.

---

[38]Elkins v. United States, 364 U.S. 206 (1960).
[39]Mapp v. Ohio, 367 U.S. 643, 81 S. Ct. 1684 (1961).

CHAPTER XI

ADDITIONAL LAW ON THE ACQUISITION OF EVIDENCE

WIRE TAPPING, EAVESDROPPING, AND SURVEILLANCE

The question of the constitutionality of wire tapping came before the Supreme Court for the first time in 1928, in the important case of *Olmstead v. United States*.[1] In this case, the court, in a five-to-four decision, ruled that wire tapping did not violate the Fourth Amendment. A few years later, Congress, exercising its power to regulate interstate and foreign commerce, passed the Federal Communications Act of 1934. Section 605 of this act provided that "no person not being authorized by the sender shall intercept any communication and divulge or publish the existence, contents, substance, purport, effect or meaning of such intercepted communication to any person."[2]

This section of the Act of 1934 did not provide for the exclusion of evidence secured in the violation of the act, but the Supreme Court in 1937, in the first *Nardone* case, ruled that such evidence should not be admissible in *federal* courts, explaining that to admit it would be tantamount to sanctioning a federal crime in a federal court.[3] This decision was fortified by that of the second *Nardone* case, which held that leads and other derivative evidence obtained by a violation of the Act of 1934 also were inadmissible in a *federal* court.[4] In thus prohibiting the indirect use of such evidence, the Court applied what is known as the "fruit-of-the-poisonous-tree doctrine."

In *Schwartz v. Texas*, the Supreme Court ruled that state and local peace officers, as well as federal officers, were prohibited from wire tapping by the Act of 1934, but that even so, the state courts

---

[1]*Olmstead v. United States,* 277 U.S. 438 (1928).
[2]47 U.S.C., Section 605 (1946).
[3]*Nardone v. United States,* 302 U.S. 379 (1937).
[4]*Nardone v. United States,* 308 U.S. 338, 60 S. Ct. 266 (1939).

might continue to admit the illegal wiretap evidence.[5] Then, in *Benanti v. United States*, the Supreme Court tightened its restrictions on wire tapping by holding that wire-tap evidence regardless of its source, that is, whether obtained by federal or state officers, was inadmissible in *federal* courts.[6]

The Federal Communications Act of 1934 applied only to the interception of telephone, telegraph, and radiotelegraph conversations. Protection against other forms of eavesdropping, such as that by microphones and detectaphones, was available if the aggrieved person could show that there had been an unreasonable search and seizure, that is, a *physical invasion or trespass* in violation of the Fourth Amendment. Thus, in *Goldman v. United States*, the Supreme Court ruled that there had been no unreasonable search and seizure when federal officers placed a detectaphone *against* the wall of a private office and so, since there had been no physical invasion of the office, the evidence secured was admissible.[7]

However, in 1967, the Supreme Court, by its decision in *Katz v. United States*, overturned its rulings in both the *Olmstead* and *Goldman* cases. In the *Katz* case, the Court held that the protection of the Fourth Amendment applies to an individual's reasonable expectations of privacy in his communications and conversations with others as well as to his person, house, papers, and effects. By this decision the Court rejected the contention that surveillance without any trespass and without the seizure of any material object is constitutional and emphasized that the Fourth Amendment protects people in their reasonable expectation of privacy, not places.[8] The following year, by its decision in *Lee v. Florida*, the Supreme Court reversed its ruling in *Schwartz v. Texas* and declared that evidence obtained in contravention of Section 605 of the Federal Communications Act of 1934 would no longer be admissible in *state* courts.[9]

The *Katz* case, by applying the Fourth Amendment to electronic investigations and making them subject to the warrant system, prepared the way for federal legislation which would permit wire tap-

---

[5]*Schwartz v. Texas*, 344 U.S. 199, 73 S.Ct. 232 (1952).

[6]*Benanti v. United States*, 355 U.S. 96, 78 S.Ct. 155 (1957).

[7]*Goldman v. United States*, 316 U.S. 129, 62 S.Ct. 993 (1942). See also *On Lee v. United States*, 343 U.S. 747, 72 S.Ct. 967 (1952); *Silverman v. United States*, 365 U.S. 505, 81 S.Ct. 679 (1961).

[8]*Katz v. United States*, 389 U.S. 347, 88 S.Ct. 507 (1967).

[9]*Lee v. Florida*, 88 S.Ct. 2096 (1968).

ping and eavesdropping by court order.[10] Congress took the necessary action and included Title III, which supersedes Section 605 of the Federal Communications Act of 1934, in the Omnibus Crime Control and Safe Streets Act of 1968 (sometimes called the Crime Control Act of 1968). The new federal law prohibits all surreptitious listening, whether of wire (wire tapping) or of oral communications (eavesdropping), by federal, state, or local agencies unless such listening is authorized in accordance with the law's provisions.[11] Law enforcement officers may tap wires or eavesdrop only when authorized to do so by order of the appropriate federal or state judge in certain types of serious crimes.[12] The application for the judicial order must be in writing, based on oath or affirmation, and must show "probable cause" to believe that the serious offense is being, or about to be, committed, that messages regarding it will be obtained through the interception, and that normal investigative procedures have been tried and failed or are too dangerous or unlikely to succeed. The listening order may not remain in effect any longer than thirty days. In emergencies which involve organized crime or threats to the national security, messages may be intercepted without prior judicial order, but afterwards application for the order must be made to the judge within forty-eight hours. However, state and local officers may tap wires and eavesdrop only if the state has a statute containing provisions similar to those of the federal law. On the other hand, the

---

[10]John C. Klotter and Jacqueline R. Kanovitz, *1970 Supplement to Constitutional Law for Police* (Cincinnati: The W.H. Anderson Company, 1969), p. 20.

[11]Unauthorized wire tapping or eavesdropping is a federal felony punishable by a fine of not more than $10,000 or imprisonment for not more than five years, or both.

[12]The law covers such serious crimes as murder, kidnapping, robbery, narcotics offenses, bribery, and so on, and, in addition, on the federal level, counterfeiting and threats to the national security or the life of the President. On June 19, 1972, in a case in which the United States Attorney General stated that he had approved warrantless wiretaps to protect the national security, the Supreme Court, in a unanimous ruling, declared such eavesdropping unconstitutional if it is not conducted under a warrant issued by a federal court. This decision applied only to attempts against national security coming from *domestic* sources and left unanswered questions regarding warrantless wiretaps in cases involving *foreign* powers or their agents. See *United States v. United States District Court*, 407 U.S. 297 (1972). See also *Gelbard v. United States* 408 U.S. 41 (1972); *United States v. Calandra*, 414 U.S. 338, 94 S.Ct. 613 (1974); *United States v. Giordano*, 416 U.S. 505, 94 S.Ct 1820 (1974); *United States v. Chavez*, 416 U.S. 562, 94 S.Ct. 1849 (1974).

federal law does not force the states to legalize wire tapping if they do not wish to do so.

Title III of the Crime Control Act of 1968 also specifically provides that all illegally obtained evidence, both direct and indirect (leads and other derivative evidence) is inadmissible in *both* state and federal courts. Thus, the "fruit-of-the-poisonous-tree doctrine" of the second *Nardone* decision is expressly incorporated into the new federal law.[13]

Eavesdropping is defined by Title III as listening by means of any electronic, mechanical, or other device to anything said by a person in a situation where he is justified in reasonably believing that he has privacy. Consequently, the provisions of the federal law do not apply in situations where the speaker is conversing in a voice loud enough to be heard by the unaided human ear, or apparently where listening occurs by picking up the receiver of a person's own telephone, or apparently where the conversation is recorded or transmitted by a device concealed on an agent or informant to whom the suspect is speaking, since the device merely preserves an accurate record of what the suspect freely discloses to the listener. In these situations the person whose conversation is overheard or recorded does not have a reasonable expectation of privacy. Furthermore, an interception[14] of a wire or oral communication by a person who is a party to the communication or with the consent of one of the parties to the communication does not have to conform to the requirements of Title III.

In summary, then, these points regarding wire tapping and eavesdropping should be emphasized:

1. The search-and-seizure provisions of the Fourth Amendment protect the individual's reasonable expectations of privacy in his oral and wire communications from surreptitious listening by state and federal agencies unless this is done through the warrant system.
2. Title III of the Crime Control Act of 1968, which supersedes Section 605 of the Federal Communications Act of 1934, provides

---

[13]The motion to suppress evidence obtained by illegal wire tapping or eavesdropping may be raised by an "aggrieved person," who is defined as a person who was a party to any intercepted wire or oral communication or a person against whom the interception was directed.

[14]The federal Crime Control Act of 1968 defines "interception" as the aural acquisition of the contents of any wire or oral communication through the use of any electronic, mechanical, or other device.

the procedure by which state and federal agencies can engage in legal wire tapping and eavesdropping through the issuance of court orders.

3. All evidence, both direct or indirect, illegally obtained by wire tapping or eavesdropping by either state or federal agencies is inadmissible in both state and federal courts.

Surveillance is subject to about the same constitutional limitations as surreptitious listening. Anything that can be observed in a public place or that is visible to the public at large is not protected by the Fourth Amendment even if the surveillance is surreptitious. Furthermore, the use of such visual tools as flashlights, searchlights, field glasses, or telescopic lenses to facilitate surveillance is permissible in any situation where viewing without such tools would be legal. Thus, one does not need a warrant to examine the interior of a house or an automobile through a window, but spying through a keyhole or a peephole carries one into a zone protected by the Constitution.[15]

Surreptitious listening and viewing by law enforcement officers have provoked an intensive controversy in the United States. Opponents contend that these techniques are dangerous and unnecessary invasions of the individual rights. Many police and public officials, on the other hand, insist that they are essential to effective law enforcement, and that they can be regulated in such a way as to protect the rights of innocent persons. However, regardless of the controversy, the great threat to our national security by organized crime and foreign conspiracies makes it unwise to prohibit the use of these techniques by law enforcement agencies. What is needed is a procedure which permits their use under certain conditions. Such a procedure now exists as a result of recent decisions by the Supreme Court and the enactment of the Federal Crime Control Act of 1968, which have placed these techniques within the control of our conventional warrant system.

INFORMERS AND ENTRAPMENT

Informers have always been important in the work of law-enforcement agencies, especially in the investigation of vice and organized crime, and the courts, in order to protect such persons from

---

[15]John C. Klotter and Jacqueline R. Kanovitz, *Constitutional Law for Police* (Cincinnati: The W.H. Anderson Co., 1968), pp. 172-75.

reprisals and to support their cooperation with the police, have developed the "informer's privilege." This means that the state will do all that it can to preserve the anonymity of the informer. Warrants may be based on evidence supplied by an informer, and although he must be shown to be a credible person and his information reliable, he does not have to be identified or produced before the official issuing of the warrant.[16] Furthermore, under the rule announced in *Scher v. United States,*[17] public policy forbids the disclosure of an informer's identity during a criminal prosecution unless this is essential to the defense, and this rule has been reaffirmed since the decision was handed down in that case.[18]

Law enforcement officers must also employ misrepresentation, deception, and artifice in their efforts to prevent crime and to apprehend alleged criminals. In the use of such tactics, officers may provide an opportunity for an offender to commit a crime which he has already planned, but they must not plant the idea to commit the crime in his mind. If they do, the crime is the product of their creative activity, and the defense of illegal entrapment is available to the accused.[19]

CONFESSIONS

A confession is a statement or acknowledgment of guilt made by a person accused of a crime.[20] However, it is admissible in evidence against the accused only if it is freely and voluntarily given. This rule, known as the "free-and-voluntary rule," is based upon the belief that only a confession given without coercion can be relied on as trustworthy. Its application requires an examination of the "totality of

---

[16]*Aguilar v. Texas,* 378 U.S. 108, 84 S.Ct. 1509 (1964).

[17]*Scher v. United States,* 305 U.S. 251, 59 S.Ct. 174 (1938).

[18]See *McCray v. Illinois,* 386 U.S. 300, 87 S.Ct. 1056 (1967).

[19]See *Sorrells v. United States,* 287 U.S. 435, 53 S.Ct. 210 (1932); *Sherman v. United States,* 356 U.S. 369, 78 S.Ct. 819 (1958). See also *United States v. Russell,* 411 U.S. 423 (1973).

[20]Whereas a confession is a complete acknowledgment of guilt of a crime, an admission is an act or statement which only partly incriminates the accused. For example, an admission is made when the accused says that he was at the scene of the crime. In order to be admissible as evidence in court, an admission must meet the same requirements as a confession. Gilbert B. Stuckey, *Evidence for the Law Enforcement Officer* (New York: McGraw-Hill Book Company, 1968), pp. 133, 169.

circumstances" surrounding each confession in order to determine whether the confession was freely and voluntarily given. Although this rule, which is deeply rooted in Anglo-American jurisprudence, had been recognized for a long time in all the states, in 1936 the Supreme Court, in *Brown v. Mississippi*,[21] by using the "due-process clause" of the Fourteenth Amendment, established its authority to review all state cases in which the highest court of a state upholds a confession as having been freely and voluntarily given. This means that the Supreme Court can reverse a decision based upon a confession if the state standard of what is free and voluntary does not conform to its standard.

Prior to this, in 1897, the Supreme Court, in *Bram v. United States*,[22] had applied the "self-incrimination clause" of the Fifth Amendment to the question of the admissibility of a confession as evidence in a *federal* court. Then, after the passage of many years, the Supreme Court, in June, 1964, in *Malloy v. Hogan*,[23] extended the application of the self-incrimination provision of the Fifth Amendment to the states by way of the Fourteenth Amendment. Consequently, at present, when evidence against the accused is obtained through compulsory self-incrimination, it is inadmissible in a criminal case in either a state or federal court. However, in order to understand fully the meaning of this rule, we must now turn our attention to what constitutes "compulsion" and "self-incrimination."

WHAT IS "COMPULSION"?

The most extreme form of compulsion exists when physical brutality, such as beating or kicking, is used to get information about an alleged crime.[24] But compulsion consists not only of actual physical mistreatment, which is rarely used today, but also of any discomfort suffered by the person during his interrogation. Such discomfort may be felt by the accused during a lengthy interrogation when he is not permitted to sit, to rest, or to go to the toilet. Furthermore, as the courts have repeatedly emphasized, even psychological pressure, or mental stress, may be considered compulsion. Such pressure may be pro-

---

[21]*Brown v. Mississippi*, 297 U.S. 278 (1936).

[22]*Bram v. United States*, 168 U.S. 532 (1897).

[23]*Malloy v. Hogan*, 378 U.S. 1, 84 S.Ct. 1489 (1964).

[24]The infliction of suffering, mental or physical, upon a person in order to get evidence about an alleged crime is usually referred to as the "third degree."

duced in a variety of ways, as, for example, by a threat of violence, by a gesture indicating that violence will occur, by the mere suggestion that the accused will have an "easier time of it" if he confesses, by interrogation in the presence of a large number of officers, by the promise of immunity or leniency, by the offer to help the family of the accused, by the threat to take action against his wife, or by insinuations designed to convince the accused that his guilt has already been established.[25]

However, neither the fact that a person is under arrest nor the fact that his interrogation extended over a period of time is of itself sufficient to render a confession or admission inadmissible. Even so, in all cases the prosecution must be able to prove that every consideration was given to the person and that nothing was done to interfere with his mental freedom during the period when he was questioned and his confession or admission was given.[26]

WHAT IS "SELF-INCRIMINATION"?

There has been considerable controversy in the courts and elsewhere over the meaning of the term "self-incrimination." Nevertheless, the weight of authority clearly supports the view that there is *no* self-incrimination when a person is compelled to do any of the following:

1. Give up his shoes so that they may be compared with tracks at the scene of the crime, or to put his shoes or feet into prints for such a comparison.
2. Submit to an examination of his body for wounds, marks, and identifying scars.
3. Change his clothing for the purpose of helping witnesses to a crime to identify the perpetrator.
4. Shave, get a hair cut, take off spectacles, or remove any disguise to facilitate identification.
5. Stand up in court or place himself within full view of witnesses and the jury.
6. Submit to a police "lineup" or "show-up" so that he can be viewed alongside other persons by witnesses to the crime.[27]

---

[25]See, for example, *Chambers v. Florida,* 309 U.S. 227 (1940); *Ashcraft v. Tennessee,* 322 U.S. 143 (1944); *Spano v. New York,* 360 U.S. 315 (1959); *Rogers v. Richmond,* 365 U.S. 534 (1961).

[26]Stuckey, p. 140.

7. Submit to fingerprinting so that his prints can be compared with those found at the scene of the crime.

8. Have his photograph taken.

9. Give a specimen of his handwriting for purposes of comparison with that of a document.

10. Speak so that his voice may be compared with that of the perpetrator of a crime.

11. Submit to the removal of foreign objects of evidentiary value either from the surface of the body (as in the removal of scrapings from underneath the fingernails so as to determine the presence of bits of skin or blood) or from within the body (as in the removal of the contents of the stomach so as to determine the presence of marihuana.

12. Submit to the removal of specimens of his body fluids, such as blood and urine, or of his breath in order to examine them for alcoholic contents.[28]

In each of these instances, the list of which is suggestive rather than

---

[27]The Supreme Court has left no doubt that there is no violation of the "self-incrimination clause" of the Fifth Amendment when a person is compelled to stand in a police "line-up." However, it has also declared that a person must be represented by counsel when he is placed in a police "line-up" because this, said the Court, is a *critical* stage in a criminal proceeding. *United States v. Wade*, 87 S.Ct. 1926 (1967). Later, on June 7, 1972, the Supreme Court qualified its decision in the *Wade* case when, by a vote of five to four, it ruled that a "line-up" after arrest, but before the initiating of any adversary criminal proceeding (whether by way of formal charge, preliminary hearing, indictment, information, or arraignment), unlike the postindictment confrontation involved in the *Wade* case, is not a criminal prosecution at which the accused, as a matter of absolute right, is entitled to counsel. See *Kirby v. Illinois*, 406 U.S. 682 (1972). Therefore, the accused does not have the right to counsel at a victim-suspect confrontation on the street or at a police-station showup if these take place before any adversary proceeding has been initiated against him.

[28]In *Schmerber v. California*, 384 U.S. 757, 86 S.Ct. 1826 (1966), the Supreme Court ruled that when a person is compelled to submit to the removal of a blood sample, there is no violation of the "self-incrimination clause" of the Fifth Amendment. However, the Court cautioned that the blood sample should be taken by medical personnel. See also *Breithaupt v. Abram*, 352 U.S. 432, 77 S.Ct. 408 (1957). On the other hand, the Supreme Court has declared that if unreasonable force is used in extracting something from the body of the person, this violates due process of law, and the evidence is inadmissible in state and federal courts. See *Rochin v. California*, 342 U.S. 165 (1952).

exhaustive, since there is no self-incrimination, the use of compulsion does not of itself render the evidence inadmissible.[29]

It should now be explained that the ultimate test regarding compulsory self-incrimination is this: Has evidence of a *testimonial* nature been secured by compulsion? In other words, if an *incriminating oral* or *written statement* is extracted from the accused by compulsion, it is inadmissible as evidence. In view of this, legal authority is clearly of the opinion that evidence obtained by compelling a person to take lie-detector or truth-serum tests is inadmissible in court.

ADDITIONAL RULES

Until about the middle of the twentieth century, the admissibility of confessions depended entirely upon whether they were freely and voluntarily given.[30] Then in 1943, the Supreme Court, with its decision in *McNabb v. United States,*[31] began to establish additional rules governing the admissibility of confessions. In this case, the Court formulated the rule that even if they are freely and voluntarily given, confessions are inadmissible if they are obtained during an unnecessary delay in arraignment. However, if the delay occurs after the confession, it alone will not make the confession inadmissible. Since the Court vigorously reaffirmed this rule in *Mallory v. United States,*[32] it is usually referred to as the "McNabb-Mallory rule." It was based entirely on the ground that evidence obtained in disregard of procedures set up by Congress should not be admissible. At first, this rule was applicable only to federal courts, but later, by the Supreme Court's decision in *Miranda v. Arizona,*[33] its application was extended to state courts.

In the case of *Escobedo v. Illinois,*[34] the Supreme Court established the rule that a confession is inadmissible in both state and federal courts, if it is obtained from a person·in police custody whose

---

[29]Robert G. Caldwell, *Criminology* (New York: The Ronald Press Co., 1965), pp. 343, 344.

[30]Stuckey, p. 134.

[31]*McNabb v. United States,* 318 U.S. 332, 63 S.Ct. 608 (1943).

[32]*Mallory v. United States,* 354 U.S. 449, 77 S.Ct. 1356 (1957).

[33]*Miranda v. Arizona,* 384 U.S. 436, 86 S.Ct. 1602 (1966).

[34]*Escobedo v. Illinois,* 378 U.S. 478, 84 S.Ct. 1758 (1964). According to the decision in this case, when the criminal process shifts from investigatory to accusatory, focuses on the accused, and seeks to elicit a confession, the adversary system begins to operate and he must be permitted to consult with counsel.

request for counsel has been denied. Several years later, this rule was supplemented and strengthened by the "Miranda rule," which was laid down in Miranda v. Arizona. This rule requires that if a person is taken into custody or otherwise deprived of his freedom of action in any significant way, he must be given the following warnings before he is questioned by law enforcement officials:

"You have the right to remain silent and say nothing.

"If you do make a statement, anything you say can and will be used against you in court.

"You have the right to have an attorney present or to consult with an attorney.

"If you cannot afford an attorney, one will be appointed for you prior to any questioning if you so desire."

The person must have the opportunity to exercise his rights throughout the questioning, and if he indicates at any time that he does not wish to be interrogated or that he desires to consult with an attorney, the questioning must stop. The person may waive his rights, but he must do this with a positive statement made voluntarily, knowingly, and intelligently. The "Miranda rule" must be followed or a confession obtained from a person who was in custody and subjected to interrogation will not be admissible as evidence in either state or federal courts. However, statements made freely by persons not in custody, or apparently even in custody but not being interrogated, are in no way affected by this rule.

If the suspect does not waive his rights and has legal counsel, he will probably not make any statement or confession, for undoubtedly his lawyer will tell him not to say anything to the police under any circumstances. Furthermore, under the "Miranda rule", no threats, promises, deception, or trickery may be used to induce the suspect to waive his rights. But suppose the waiver of his rights has been properly obtained, and he has submitted to interrogation. May threats, promises, deception, or trickery be used to induce the suspect to make a confession or statement without endangering its admissibility? As we have seen, it has been well established for a long time that the use of threats renders a confession or statement inadmissible in all courts. "But what about promises, deception, or trickery?" it may be asked. With respect to promises, the general rule has been this: The promise should not be such as is likely to cause the suspect to make a statement or confession. Thus, a statement or confession extracted by a promise of immunity or leniency has been inadmissible. Trickery or deception of itself, however, has not caused a statement or confession to be inadmissible. For example, if, in order to obtain a confession, officers told a suspect that his fingerprints had been found at the scene of the crime or that his accomplice had confessed, when in fact this had not happened, and they thereby induced him to confess, the confession has still been admissible. The rule, as applied by state courts, has been that deception or trickery may be employed unless it is calculated to prompt the suspect to confess falsely or to make a false statement. What, then, may we conclude regarding the use of promises, deception, or trickery after the suspect has properly waived his rights? The *Miranda* decision does not specifically cover this question, but its far-reaching implications indicate that even in this situation, the interrogator should avoid all such inducements.

Furthermore, the Supreme Court has applied the "fruit-of-the-poisonous-tree doctrine" to confessions. Consequently, a confession given as a direct result of an unlawful arrest has been ruled inadmissible, since it was the "fruit" of illegal police action.[35] By the same reasoning, any evidence indirectly secured through an inadmissible confession will be considered the "fruit" of that "poisonous" confession and thus also inadmissible. Moreover, once a confession is unlawfully obtained, there is a presumption that a subsequent confession of the same crime is affected by the same influences and that, therefore, it, too, is inadmissible, although this presumption can be overcome by clear and convincing evidence.[36] In fact, the Court has set itself so strongly against the admissibility of illegally obtained confessions that it has ruled that when such a confession is used in evidence in a criminal trial, the conviction must be reversed even if the other evidence is sufficient to convict the accused. This, argued the Court, must be done because it is impossible to determine what

---

[35]*Wong Sun v. United States*, 371 U.S. 471 (1963). See also *Traub v. Connecticut*, 374 U.S. 493 (1963).

In June, 1975, the United States Supreme Court held that the *Miranda* warnings alone cannot preserve the admissibility of a voluntary confession following an illegal arrest. See *Brown v. Illinois*, 95 S.Ct. 2254, 45 L.Ed. 2d. 416 (1975).

[36]See, for example, *Payne v. State*, 332 S.W. (2d) 233 (1960).

influence the confession had in securing the conviction.[37] Thus, as an examination of these rules indicates, it is not enough that a confession be freely and voluntarily given. In addition, it must be obtained in accordance with strict procedural rules or it will not be admissible as evidence in either state or federal courts.

THE OMNIBUS CRIME CONTROL AND SAFE STREETS ACT OF 1968.

The Supreme Court in its exclusion of confessions has gone far beyond the "free and voluntary rule." To an increasing extent, by holding that confessions are inadmissible, it has sought to discipline the law enforcement officer. In effect, it has said to the officer, "If you do not obtain evidence in accordance with our instructions, it will be inadmissible even if it is true." This attempt to impose what has been called unreasonable restrictions on police activities has aroused widespread opposition, which finally moved Congress to include certain counteracting provisions in the Omnibus Crime Control and Safe Streets Act of 1968.

This act made voluntariness the sole criterion of the admissibility of confessions in *federal* courts. In effect, therefore, this means that confessions would not be inadmissible in *federal* courts simply because the confession was obtained during an unnecessary delay in arraignment or simply because the *"Miranda* rule" was not followed. Furthermore, it would make eyewitness testimony as to the identity of the accused admissible at the trial even though counsel was not present at the lineup or other confrontation. Thus the Crime Control Act of 1968 seeks to make the Supreme Court's rulings in the *McNabb-Mallory, Miranda*, and *Wade* decisions inoperative in federal cases. And if the Supreme Court upholds the provisions of the Crime Control Act of 1968, the *state* courts, also, will probably be

---

[37]*Payne v. Arkansas*, 356 U.S. 560 (1958). But see also *Schneble v. Florida*, 92 S.Ct. 1056 (1972); and *Michigan v. Tucker*, 417 U.S. 433, 94 S.Ct. 2357 (1974). In the *Tucker* case, the United States Supreme Court, in refusing to hold evidence inadmissible because the *Miranda* rule had not been strictly applied, stated that "we must consider whether the sanction serves a valid and useful purpose." However, the full meaning of the *Tucker* decision remains unclear.

freed from the rulings in these cases, for it is highly unlikely that the state courts will be subjected to greater restrictions than the federal courts. However, until the Supreme Court rules on the Crime Control Act of 1968, it is advisable for law enforcement officials to continue to act in accordance with these decisions.

CHAPTER XII

CRIMINAL COURTS AND PROCEDURE

ORGANIZATION OF COURTS

In the United States, justice is administered through a dual court system, that is, through the federal and state judicial systems, which are designed to be independent of each other. Persons accused of violating state criminal laws are tried in state courts, whereas the jurisdiction of the federal courts is restricted to matters arising under the United States Constitution and the federal laws and treaties. As it has been definitely established that there are no federal common law crimes, all federal crimes must be created by acts of the Congress. However, since an act may be defined as a crime by both state and federal governments, an offender may be tried and punished for the same act by both a state court and a federal court.[1]

In the federal judicial system, the principal courts are the United States Supreme Court, the courts of appeals (until 1948, known as the "Circuit Courts of Appeals"), and the district courts. Only the Supreme Court was established by the Constitution; the other federal courts were created by laws enacted by Congress. The Supreme Court, composed of a chief justice and eight associate justices, has limited original jurisdiction; that is, it has authority over a few cases at their inception, the most important of which are suits between two states. In practice, however, it is essentially an appellate court, receiving most of its cases from the lower federal courts. Moreover, the appellate jurisdiction of the Supreme Court is largely discretionary, which

---

[1]Robert G. Caldwell, *Criminology* (New York: The Ronald Press Co., 1965), pp. 345-47; Hazel B. Kerper, *Introduction to the Criminal Justice System* (St. Paul, Minn.: West Publishing Co., 1972), pp. 208-16. See also The President's Commission on Law Enforcement and Administration of Justice, *The Challenge of Crime in a Free Society* (Washington, D.C.: Government Printing Office, 1967), pp. 125-57; *ibid., Task Force Report: The Courts* (Washington, D.C.: Government Printing Office, 1967).

means that it is obligated to hear on appeal only a few kinds of cases, and its right to review the decisions of state criminal courts is limited to those cases in which the accused has successfully raised a substantial "federal question," that is, a question involving a federal statute or the United States Constitution.[2]

In 1975, there were eleven federal courts of appeals, including that of the District of Columbia. These courts have no original jurisdiction, and like the Supreme Court, they function without a jury. Each of them normally has three judges (although this number may be increased to as many as nine), who review cases appealed from the federal district courts, which are the principal courts of original jurisdiction in the federal judicial system.

The district courts, each of which is usually presided over by a single judge, are the courts in which the great majority of federal cases are begun, either before a judge or before a judge and jury, and at least one of these courts is located in every state in the United States. All federal judges are appointed by the President and confirmed by the Senate and can be removed from office only by impeachment.

In each federal judicial district, there is at least one federal magistrate. Formerly called a commissioner, he is appointed for a term of four years by the federal district court and is supervised by it. Performing duties similar to those of a magistrate in the state judicial system, he issues warrants, arraigns defendants, fixes bail, holds preliminary hearings, and tries minor offenders. Another officer, called a United States marshal, who is appointed for a term of four years by the President and confirmed by the Senate, is attached to each district court. He has duties similar to those of a sheriff. In addition, each federal judicial district has a United States district attorney, who is appointed for a term of four years by the President and confirmed by the Senate and is under the supervision of the Attorney General. He prosecutes all persons accused of federal crimes and handles civil actions in which the United States is a party. At the head of the United States Justice Department is the Attorney General. Appointed by the President, confirmed by the Senate, and a member of the cabinet, he

---

[2] A person who has been convicted of a crime in a state trial court and on appeal has been denied a hearing by the highest appellate court of the state may petition the Supreme Court for a *writ of certiorari* if a "federal question" has been raised in his case. This is a writ by which the Supreme Court commands a lower court to send up the record of a case for its review. The Supreme Court may, at its discretion, grant or deny the petition for a *writ of certiorari*.

represents the federal government in cases before the United States Supreme Court and gives legal advice upon questions submitted to him.

The state judicial system for the disposition of criminal cases usually consists of a supreme court, a number of trial courts of general jurisdiction, and a larger number of inferior courts. Thus, as in the federal judicial system, most states have three levels of courts. In some states, however, intermediate courts of appeal have been established to relieve the pressure on the supreme court, and the volume and complexity of cases have forced some large cities to create such special courts as traffic courts and family courts.

The state supreme courts, like the United States Supreme Court, are essentially appellate courts with limited original jurisdiction. The number of justices serving on the state supreme court varies from state to state, but usually they are elected to office.

The state trial courts of general jurisdiction have different names in different states, bearing such titles as superior courts, courts of oyer and terminer, courts of quarter sessions, circuit courts, district courts, and criminal courts.[3] Usually these courts serve a district composed of more than one county or have general trial jurisdiction in a large metropolitan area. In many states they handle both civil and criminal cases. Having wide original jurisdiction, they are served by both a judge and a jury, although cases may be tried in them without a jury. Most of the serious litigation originates in the trial courts, and they dispose of the great bulk of the major cases throughout the country, for relatively few cases tried in them are appealed. In addition, the trial courts have the power to review cases appealed to them from the inferior courts. In most states, the trial court judges are selected by popular vote.

On the lowest level of each state's judicial system are a large number of inferior courts that handle minor cases with as little formality as possible. Known by such names as justice of the peace courts, magistrate's courts, police courts, mayor's courts, and municipal courts, the inferior courts usually try cases without a jury, and appeals from them may be taken to the trial courts. The inferior court performs two functions in the administration of criminal justice: (1) it holds

---

[3] The title that the trial court has indicates some aspect or function which it has or originally had. Thus, "oyer and terminer" means to hear and determine; the term "circuit" refers to the fact that the judge travels from one court to another; and the term "quarter sessions" indicates that the court has four sessions each year.

preliminary hearings of cases involving serious offenses, which are later adjudicated in the trial court; and (2) it conducts trials of minor offenses, in the disposition of which it may impose fines or short terms of imprisonment. In most states, the official who presides in the inferior court is chosen by popular vote.

In each state, county or district attorneys prepare the formal charges, marshal the evidence, and conduct the criminal prosecutions. The chief law officer of the state is the attorney general, who serves as the head of its legal department. All these law officers are usually selected by popular vote.

Another county official who may play an important part in a criminal case is the coroner. Usually he is an elected official and is not required to be a licensed physician. His principal duty is to hold inquisitions in cases when it appears that a person has died in some violent or unlawful manner. A coroner's jury assists him in the performance of this duty and renders a verdict or opinion regarding the cause of the death. If the jury decides that a crime has been committed, their report, which is only advisory and not binding on the prosecuting attorney, may become the basis of an indictment and a warrant for the arrest of the alleged offender. There is, however, increasing dissatisfaction with the office of the coroner, and a growing agitation is calling for its elimination and the division of its duties between the county or district attorney and a medical examiner. In fact, this has already been accomplished in some states.

THE ADVERSARY SYSTEM

The process by which guilt or innocence of the accused is determined has taken various forms in legal history. At an earlier time, the fate of the accused was decided by ordeal—ordeal by fire, water, or combat. If he was not burned, drowned, or defeated, he was declared to be innocent. In combat, both the accused and the state might be represented by champions. Today, under our law, an adversary system is used to establish the guilt or innocence of the accused. This means that the opposing parties—the defense and the prosecution—in accordance with certain prescribed rules, engage in a contest over which a judge presides, directing the proceeding and enforcing the rules. The adversary system is based on the assumption that the truth will be most effectively and completely revealed when "contentious opposing advocates" vigorously present evidence and press theories of law in support of their cases.[4]

However, the adversary system is not used in most countries. For example, on the continent of Europe, what has been called the "inquisitorial system" is employed. Under this system, the state seeks to establish the guilt of the accused before it places him on trial. Consequently, when he is brought to court, he is presumed to be guilty—not innocent—and he is then given the burden of proving his innocence. Furthermore, in his efforts to do this, he is judged not by a jury of his peers, but by one or more judges who are appointed by the state.[5]

It should not be assumed that the opposing parties under the adversary system are as sharply divided and as antagonistic as the term "adversary" seems to indicate. For example, the magistrate is supposed to represent both the state and the accused and to protect and balance the interests of all concerned. Furthermore, although the prosecuting attorney is responsible for as vigorous a prosecution as the law permits, he is also obligated to protect the defendant against persecution and the violation of his legal rights. And the judge of a trial court does not have to be a "mere umpire" of a contest, as some of his critics have argued. He has broad powers which enable him to act in a positive and constructive way in protecting the interests of both the state and the defendant and in directing the trial toward a just conclusion. For example, he may pass on the fitness of jurors to serve, limit the admissibility of evidence, protect witnesses during cross-examination, even summon witnesses and interrogate them, discontinue a trial for lack of evidence, hold persons in contempt of court, order an acquittal, set aside a verdict of conviction and order a new trial, and so on.

Moreover, under the adversary system the defendant has certain guarantees and protections which help to offset the great power which the state can exercise against him. Thus, at the very beginning he is presumed to be innocent until proved guilty, and the state is required to prove his guilt, not by a mere preponderance of the evidence but beyond a reasonable doubt. In addition, as we shall see, he has other strongly secured rights, which further fortify his position, such as the right to be notified of the charges, to be represented

---

[4]Ronald L. Carlson, *Criminal Justice Procedure for Police* (Cincinnati; The W. H. Anderson Company, 1970), p. 209.

[5]Kerper, p. 182.

by counsel, to be given a public and impartial trial before a jury of his peers, and so on. In fact, many students of the law believe that the "scales of justice" have now been tipped too far in favor of the defendant under the adversary system.

JURISDICTION OF THE CRIMINAL COURT

The jurisdiction of the criminal court means its authority to hear a case, to determine the guilt or innocence of the accused, and to punish the convicted. It includes authority over the person of the accused and over the offense with which he is charged. No court, however, has unlimited jurisdiction, all being limited by constitutional and statutory provisions.

Jurisdiction over the person of the accused is obtained by his arrest or by his consent to the jurisdiction without an arrest. Jurisdiction over the offense is regulated in terms of such matters as the locality of the offense, the nature of the offense, the nature of the punishment, and the nature of the proceeding. Thus, a court in the county or the district of a state or in the federal district in which the offense was committed has jurisdiction over the offense. Furthermore, trial courts have jurisdiction over felonies and offenses punishable by imprisonment in a state or federal penitentiary or reformatory; magistrate's or other inferior courts usually have jurisdiction over misdemeanors and offenses punishable by fines or imprisonment in a jail or other local institution; and juvenile courts have jurisdiction over acts of delinquency. Finally, if a criminal case has not been tried before, it is handled by a court of original jurisdiction, such as a magistrate's court or a trial court. On the other hand, if a case is being appealed, it goes to a court of appellate jurisdiction, which has the authority to review cases coming up from lower courts. So, if we combine all these possibilities in one example, we can say that if an adult commits a state felony in the first judicial district of a state, he will be tried in the trial court of that district, from the verdict of which he may then appeal.

If only one court has authority to hear a case, that court is said to have exclusive jurisdiction over the case. However, if two or more courts have authority to hear a case, the courts have concurrent jurisdiction, and the court which first obtains jurisdiction over the person has the initial right to try him. So, if A, by a single act, violates both a state and a federal law, thus causing his offense to come under the concurrent jurisdiction of a state court and a federal court, and later a federal officer arrests him, a federal court has the initial right to try his case.

THE CRIMINAL PROSECUTION

ARREST OR SUMMONS

The criminal prosecution of an alleged offender, as shown in Chart No.6 in Appendix B, follows the same essential steps in both the state and federal judicial systems.[6] The basis for it is formed by either an arrest or a summons. A summons is an official notice order-ing a person to appear in court at a certain time to answer a complaint that has been made against him. It is used most often in cases involv-ing minor offenses, such as traffic violations. When an arrest is made, the prisoner is taken to a police station or a sheriff's office, "booked," and then confined until a hearing of his case can be held. "Booking" is the making of the official record of the arrest on the police "blotter" or arrest book. It usually includes the entry of the suspect's name, the time of the arrest, the offenses charged, and the name of the arresting officer. Sometimes, however, "booking" is used to refer to everything that goes on in the station house between the arrest and the appear-ance before the magistrate,[7] including such procedures as searching the suspect, fingerprinting him, and so on. In some jurisdictions, the suspect may be given a brief hearing before a police official prior to his being taken to the magistrate. In general, an alleged criminal who "turns state's evidence," that is, testifies against his confederates, is given immunity from prosecution. However, promises of immunity from further prosecution, given by law enforcement officials in order to induce a suspect to plead guilty to a crime, are not sanctioned by the law and do not bar prosecution.

---

[6]Caldwell, pp. 347-58; Clarence N. Callender, *American Courts* (New York: McGraw-Hill Book Co., Inc., 1927), pp. 17-20, 22-48b, 79-125, 165-98; Lester Bernhardt Orfield, *Criminal Procedure from Arrest to Appeal* (New York: New York University Press, 1947), pp. 194-592; Ernst W. Puttkammer, *Administration of Criminal Law* (Chicago: University of Chicago Press, 1953), pp. 125-53, 164-238; John N. Ferdico, *Criminal Procedure for the Law Enforcement Officer* (St. Paul, Minn.: West Publishing Co., 1975), pp. 314-27.

[7]For simplification, the term "magistrate" will be used in the discussion of criminal prosecution whenever reference is made to the judge of an inferior court.

RIGHTS OF THE ACCUSED

The accused has many valuable rights guaranteed by constitutional and statutory provisions. He has the right (1) to be protected against unreasonable searches and seizures, (2) to be informed of his constitutional rights, (3) to be released on bail except in certain cases involving serious crimes, (4) to have free access to counsel (but he may waive this right if he does so "knowingly and intelligently," that is, if he makes this choice deliberately and with a full understanding of what it means to have the assistance of counsel), (5) to have a copy of the charges against him, (6) to confront the witnesses for the prosecution and to cross-examine them in person or by counsel, (7) to have the use of the court's process for subpoenaing witnesses, (8) to have a fair, speedy, and public trial, (9) to refuse to testify in his own behalf so as to avoid self-incrimination, (10) to have a trial by jury for all except petty offenses, (11) to have protection against prejudicial, irrelevant, and hearsay testimony, (12) to have proof of guilt beyond a reasonable doubt, (13) to be protected against double jeopardy, or being tried twice for the same offense, and (14) to have access to a higher court for the purpose of appeal.

During the last few years, the Supreme Court has applied many of the provisions of the Bill of Rights to the states. The only ones which relate directly to criminal prosecution that have not thus far been so applied are the prohibition against excessive bail (which, however, is contained in all state constitutions) and the requirement of prosecution of infamous crimes by grand jury indictment.

TRIAL BY MAGISTRATE

Federal and state laws require that the arrested person be taken promptly before a magistrate, who will then establish the identity of the accused, inform him of the nature of the charges and his constitutional rights, and, in most cases, fix his bail or release him on his own recognizance. If the accused is charged with a petty crime,[8] his case will be disposed of by trial before the magistrate, during which the

---

[8]According to federal practice, a petty offense is one for which the penalty does not exceed imprisonment for six months or a fine of not more than $500. The distinction between a petty crime and a major one varies from state to state, but the great bulk of the misdemeanors in all states carry a maximum penalty of only 30 days in jail and so are everywhere well within the category of a petty offense. Ronald L. Carlson, *Criminal Justice Procedure for Police* (Cincinnati: The W.H. Anderson Company, 1970), pp. 185, 186.

accused has the right to counsel. In fact, the United States Supreme Court has ruled that an indigent defendent has the right to have free counsel if the petty offense with which he is charged involves the possibility of a jail sentence, regardless of how short it may be.[9] Even so, many trials before a magistrate are conducted without a jury, a prosecutor, or a defense attorney, and in these, the magistrate decides both questions of law and questions of fact. If as a result of the trial, the accused is found guilty, the magistrate imposes a fine or a jail sentence or both. Most states permit the defendent to appeal from a conviction in a magistrate's court; sometimes the state, also, has the right to appeal.

PRELIMINARY HEARING

When a person is accused of a major crime, he may be given a preliminary hearing, or examination, before the magistrate, ordinarily within a few hours after his arrest; but usually this hearing is not used if the grand jury is, because both have about the same function. In fact, in most states where both these steps in the prosecution are made available, the preliminary hearing may be waived by the accused. The purpose of the preliminary hearing is to determine whether there is sufficient evidence to justify holding the accused for further proceedings by the grand jury or the trial court.

A defendant may have his counsel at a preliminary hearing, and although most states do not appoint counsel for an indigent defendant while he is deciding whether to proceed with such a hearing, many states do provide him with one after he has decided to have the hearing. This is in response to recent Supreme Court cases[10] which emphasize that the preliminary hearing may be a critical stage in the

---

[9]See *Argersinger v. Hamlin,* 407 U.S. 25 (1972).

The National Advisory Commission on Criminal Justice Standards and Goals recommends that the arrestee should be presented before a judicial officer within six hours after his arrest. The commission recommends also that the importance of "screening" should be openly recognized, and that the accused should be "screened out" of the criminal justice system if the admissible evidence against him appears insufficient to obtain a conviction and sustain it on appeal, or if the costs of prosecution will outweigh its benefits. See National Advisory Commission on Criminal Justice Standards and Goals, *Task Force Report on Courts* (Washington, D.C.; U.S. Government Printing Office, 1973). pp. 17-23, 77.

[10]See *White v. Maryland,* 373 U.S. 59, 83 S. Ct. 1050 (1963); *Coleman v. Alabama,* 399 U.S. 1, 90 S.Ct. 1999 (1970).

criminal prosecution.[11] If the accused is discharged after the preliminary hearing, this usually concludes the prosecution of the case, but he may be rearrested on the same charge if for any reason it later appears that he may be more successfully prosecuted. If, on the other hand, he is held for trial, he may be released on bail or detained in the local jail.

BAIL

Bail is security furnished to the court in order to ensure the appearance of the defendant whenever his presence is needed. When bail is granted, the defendant is released under conditions imposed by the court. In certain cases, usually those of a minor nature, the prisoner may secure a release on his own recognizance or promise to return for the hearing. The constitutions of most states provide that all persons shall be bailable by sufficient sureties, except when they are charged with capital crimes and the proof is evident or the presumption of guilt is great. When the prisoner is entitled to bail, the court must grant it to him. State and federal constitutions (Eighth Amendment of the United States Constitution) provide that excessive bail shall not be exacted, and, therefore, it must be set at an amount which is judged reasonably necessary to guarantee the subsequent appearance of the defendant. Bail may be secured at various stages of the prosecution, usually up to the time of final conviction and sometimes after this if an appeal is carried to a higher court. However, the general constitutional guarantees of bail are applicable only before the conviction of the accused. Usually the power to grant bail after conviction is entrusted to the trial court. If bail is defaulted, the accused is subject to arrest and imprisonment until final disposition of his case is reached.

One of the criticisms of the American bail system has been that it gives "dangerous criminals" an opportunity to continue their depredations while they are free on bond. To prevent this, a proposal has been made that these criminals should not be granted bail but instead should be kept in preventive pretrial detention. However, this propo-

---

[11]For example, as in the *White* case, if the defendant, without the presence or advice of counsel, enters a plea of guilty at the preliminary hearing, this plea may later be introduced as evidence against him in the trial court. The Supreme Court in that case held that only the advice of counsel could enable the accused to know all the defenses that are available to him and thus be in a position to plead intelligently.

sal has met with the argument that it is unconstitutional and fails to provide adequate criteria for identifying "dangerous criminals." Apparently, the question of pretrial detention will have to be settled by the courts.[12]

WRIT OF HABEAS CORPUS

The right to the writ of habeas corpus is guaranteed by provisions in the constitutions of the states and the federal government. This writ is so called because it is directed to a person who detains another in custody and orders him to produce or, according to the meaning of the Latin words, "habeas corpus," have the body of the confined person before the court for a specified purpose. This is the proper remedy for anyone who is being illegally detained. The application for the writ of habeas corpus is made in a petition to the court by the detained person or by his attorney. After this has been done, the detained person is brought before the judge, who investigates the case. If the judge decides that detention is illegal, he discharges the person, releases him on bail, or disposes of the case in some other way, but if the judge finds that the detention is lawful, he recommits the prisoner to his custodian.

THE INDICTMENT

If, after a preliminary hearing, the magistrate finds that further action should be taken in the case, or if the case is to be taken directly to a grand jury without a preliminary hearing, the district or county attorney proceeds with the preparation of an indictment, which is a formal written statement charging the person named therein with an offense. The indictment is submitted to the grand jury, which must determine whether there is sufficient evidence to continue the prosecution; that is, whether the evidence before it, if not contradicted or rebutted, is sufficient to convict the accused of a crime. If

---

[12]The District of Columbia Court Reform and Criminal Procedure Act of 1970 provides for preventive detention. However, "the chief finding of the first ten months of observation has been the virtual non-use of the preventive detention law. The law was invoked with respect to only 20 of a total of more than 6,000 felony defendants who entered the D.C. Criminal Justice system during the period." See Nan C. Bases and William F. McDonald, *Preventive Detention in the District of Columbia: The First Ten Months* (Washington, D.C.: Georgetown Institute of Criminal Law and Procedure, March, 1972), p. 69.

the grand jury by a majority vote so decides, it endorses the indictment as a "true bill," and the accused is held for action by the trial court.[13] If the grand jury during its investigations discovers definite evidence that a crime has been committed by someone against whom no indictment has been prepared, it has the authority to make a "presentment" against that person. It thus instructs the prosecuting attorney to prepare the necessary indictment against the person, which it then approves.

INFORMATION

Instead of an indictment by a grand jury, an information prepared by the prosecuting attorney and filed with the court may be used to bring the accused to trial. In some states, the information is available only in cases of misdemeanors, but in others it may be used for both felonies and misdemeanors. In the federal jurisdiction, indictment by a grand jury is required in felony cases and in some serious misdemeanors, but the information is proper in minor cases and is frequently used in them. Although the prosecuting attorney in some states may employ the information to initiate a criminal prosecution when he receives affidavits of witnesses that a crime has been committed, usually it is based upon the findings of a preliminary hearing by a magistrate.

ARRAIGNMENT AND PLEAS

After the defendent has been indicted or an information has been prepared in his case, he is then taken before the court to answer the charges against him. This is called the "arraignment." If the defendant is in custody, he is brought before the court, but if he has been released on bail, he and his sureties are notifies to be in court at a certain time. If he fails to appear, the court issues a warrant for his arrest. In cases where the defendant who is on bail cannot be found,

---

[13]The defendant's constitutional right to representation by counsel, either retained or appointed, does not extend to the proceedings of the grand jury. These proceedings are protected by rules of secrecy, and the defendant has no right to participate in them or even to be kept informed about them. Furthermore, the United States Supreme Court has held that the Fourth Amendment does not require suppression of unlawfully seized evidence from grand jury proceedings, and that, therefore, a witness cannot refuse to testify before the grand jury on the grounds that the inquiry was derived from evidence obtained during an unlawful search and seizure. See *United States v. Calandra*, 414 U.S. 338, 94 S.Ct. 613 (1974).

and there is no satisfactory explanation for his absence, the judge orders the surety to pay the amount of the bail to the county.

The defendant has the right to have counsel at the arraignment, and since the Supreme Court has ruled that the arraignment may be a critical stage of the criminal prosecution,[14] the trend has been to appoint free counsel to represent an indigent person at this proceeding. During the arraignment, the defendant has the opportunity to object to the indictment, alleging, for example, that it does not set forth the offense as defined by law, or that the facts recited in it do not constitute the offense charged. The objection to the indictment may be by demurrer or by a motion to quash or to dismiss, but in either case a petition is prepared which states the reasons for the action and calls upon the court to set aside the indictment and discharge the defendant. If the indictment contains a fundamental defect which cannot be amended by the court, the judge will sustain the demurrer or motion and discharge the defendant. However, if no such defect is found in the indictment, the judge will order any necessary amendment of it or overrule the objection to it. The defendant must then enter a plea of "guilty" or "not guilty."[15]

The plea of "guilty" admits the correctness of the charge, and the court then has the authority to impose sentence; but if the defendant pleads "not guilty," the case goes to trial.[16] Usually a plea of "not guilty" is entered for a defendant who stands mute or refuses to plead, but a plea once made may be changed at the discretion of the court.

Under certain circumstances, however, several other pleas may be entered by the accused during the arraignment. In general, these pleas are subject to the discretion of the court, but if the court rules against them, redress may be sought through an appeal. Among these pleas are the following:

---

[14]The Supreme Court has held that the assistance of counsel is mandatory if crucial decisions must be made at the arraignment, for in such a case valuable rights of the defendant can be lost by failure to make a timely assertion at that time. See *Hamilton v. Alabama*, 368 U.S. 52, 82 S.Ct. 157 (1961).

[15]Some jurisdictions permit the defendant to enter the plea of *nolo contendere* (the Latin for "I do not wish to contend"). This plea is an implied admission of guilt and permits the court to impose sentence, but unlike the plea of "guilty," it has no effect beyond the particular case and so afterward cannot be taken advantage of by any private interested party. Usually, it is accepted only in cases involving minor offenses.

[16]For leading cases on guilty pleas, see *McCarthy v. United States*, 394 U.S. 459, 89 S.Ct. 1166 (1969); *Boykin v. Alabama*, 395 U.S. 238 (1969).

A Plea to the Jurisdiction of the Court.   This plea questions the authority of the court to try the case, either because the offense was not committed within the territorial jurisdiction of the court or because the court has no jurisdiction over the person of the defendant or his alleged offense.

A Plea for a Change of Venue[17].   This plea asks that the trial be held in a different county or district, complaining that the defendant cannot secure a fair trial in the place where he is being prosecuted.

Pleas in Abatement.   By these pleas the defendant raises such questions as the insufficiency of a preliminary hearing or the defects in the organization of the grand jury. These are called "dilatory pleas" because they merely delay the trial until the formal errors have been corrected.

Special Pleas in Bar of the Prosecution.   One important special plea in bar is the plea of limitations, which declares that so much time has elapsed since the alleged offense was committed that the statute of limitations no longer permits a prosecution. The period within which a criminal action must be initiated depends upon the crime and varies from state to state, but no limitations are imposed on prosecutions for murder.

A second special plea in bar is the plea of "double jeopardy." This plea declares that the defendant has previously been acquitted or convicted of the offense charged, or that he was at some prior time placed in jeopardy for the same offense. In 1969, the Supreme Court[18] applied the double jeopardy provision of the Fifth Amendment to the states, so no person may now be put in double jeopardy in any court, federal or state, in the United States. Jeopardy is said to attach when the jury has been sworn if the accused is tried by jury or when the court begins to hear evidence if he is tried by the court without a jury. However, if a mistrial occurs under certain conditions or the jury disagrees, another trial is not thereby barred. Furthermore, if an act is an offense against two states or against both a state and the United States, the offender may be prosecuted and punished by both jurisdictions, and a plea of former jeopardy in one will not bar a prosecution in the other, unless this is specifically provided for by statute.[19]

---

[17]From the French meaning "neighborhood."

[18]*Benton v. Maryland,*395 U.S. 784, 89 S.Ct. 2056 (1969).

[19]In *Waller v. Florida,* 397 U.S. 387, 90 S.Ct. 1184 (1970), the Supreme Court ruled that a state and municipalities in it are not separate sovereigns, and that, therefore, a defendant cannot be prosecuted twice for the same offense by them.

Sometimes insanity is alleged in a special plea, but usually it is urged as a matter of defense under the plea of "not guilty." If any special plea in bar of the prosecution is sustained by the court, it constitutes a bar to further prosecution.

"NOLLE PROSEQUI"

Sometimes, because witnesses are not available or certain evidence is lacking, or because of some similar reason, the prosecuting attorney is not in a position to continue the prosecution of a case. He may then enter on the record a "nolle prosequi" (Latin for "to be unwilling to prosecute") or "nolpros." This means that he does not intend to prosecute the case further on the existing bill of indictment. If this is done before the jury has been sworn or before any evidence has been heard in a trial by a judge without a jury, it is not a bar to a subsequent prosecution, and, therefore, the accused may be arrested, indicted, and tried again for the same offense. In some states, however, the prosecuting attorney must secure the approval of the court before he can enter a "nolle prosequi."

PRETRIAL HEARINGS AND CONFERENCES

Hearings and conferences held before the trial usually deal with the defense discovery of evidence and the suppression of confessions and seized evidence. The defense attorney often makes motions asking the judge to require the prosecution to turn over certain records, documents, and other evidence which will help him in the preparation of his case for trial. Since the defense makes the motion for discovery, it has the burden of proving that the request is a reasonable one, and that the evidence is material to the preparation of the case. Prosecutors, however, tend to resist these motions on the grounds that they may lead to the fabrication of counteracting evidence or the intimidation of witnesses. Although some states deny any discovery of evidence by the defense, the trend is definitely in favor of it.[20]

---

[20]Carlson, pp. 57-67.

The National Advisory Commission on Criminal Justice Standards and Goals recommends that an offender be diverted into noncriminal programs before formal trial or conviction when there is a substantial likelihood that conviction could be obtained and that the benefits to society derived from this diversion would outweigh any harm done to society by abandoning criminal prosecution. See National Advisory Commission on Criminal Justice Standards and Goals, pp. 32-41.

THE TRIAL

The defendant has the right to trial by jury if his allege offense carries a punishment of more than six months in prison. [21] However, except in a few states, the defendant may waive a jury trial and elect trial by the judge alone. The methods used in selecting the jurors differ in various states, but usually the choices are made more or less at random from tax lists or lists of voters. In this way, the court is provided with a panel of about thirty or forty jurors, and from this panel, the required number of jurors is chosen by lot. This number is almost always twelve, but in certain cases, some states permit the use of a smaller number, such as six.

During the selection of the jury, both the prosecution and the defense have the right to challenge jurors. The challenge may be an objection to the entire jury, stating, for example, that the jury was selected in an irregular manner, or an objection to an individual juror. The challenge of the individual juror may be either a "challenge for cause" or a "peremptory challenge." A challenge for cause cites the reason for the objection. For example, it may state that the juror is not a citizen or that he is related to the defendant. A peremptory challenge, on the other hand, gives no reason for the objection. Although an unlimited number of challenges for cause may be used, the number of peremptory challenges is regulated by statute. Usually only a few peremptory challenges are permitted in cases involving minor crimes, but as many as twenty or thirty may be permitted to each side in felonies. If a challenge is overruled by the court, the objecting party may later use this as the basis of an appeal.

After the selection of the jury has been completed, the jurors are sworn in and the case is ready to proceed. The defendant has the right to be represented by counsel in all federal and state prosecutions. If he is too poor to employ his own counsel, the court must provide him

---

[21]In *Duncan v. Louisiana*, 391 U.S. 145, 88 S.Ct. 1444 (1968), the Supreme Court extended the Federal Constitution's guarantee of trial by jury to the states. In *Baldwin v. New York*, 90 S.Ct. 1886 (1970), the Supreme Court ruled that the defendant has a right to trial by jury if the crime with which he is charged carries a punishment of more than six months in prison. In another decision, the Supreme Court held that trial by a six-man jury satisfies the Sixth Amendment requirement of trial by jury. *Williams v. Florida*, 397 U.S. 902, 90 S.Ct. 1893 (1970). This last decision, therefore, upheld the laws of a number of states which provide that certain criminal cases may be tried before juries consisting of less than twelve members.

with free counsel,[22] but the defendant may waive his right to counsel. However, in all cases where he has counsel, he is entitled to full and free communication with him. Furthermore, the defendant has the right to a public trial when this right can be exercised without danger to the order and decorum of the court.

The prosecution has the burden of proof, and, therefore, the prosecuting attorney makes the opening speech to the jury, stating briefly the charges contained in the bill of indictment and outlining the evidence to be offered in support of it. When the prosecution has finished, the defense has the opportunity to give its opening statement, although it may postpone its remarks until after the state's evidence has been introduced, or it may decide to omit its opening statement entirely. The prosecution then calls the witnesses for the state and conducts the direct examinations, and, after the cross-examination by the defense, it may conduct a redirect examination. No leading questions, or questions which directly suggest the desired answers, may be asked the witness during the direct examination unless he is hostile to the examiner and in no other way can be compelled to disclose the truth, but such questions are permissible during the cross-examination. When all the witnesses for the state have been examined and all its other evidence has been introduced, the prosecuting attorney advises the court that the prosecution rests its case.

The defense then proceeds to introduce its evidence unless it can induce the judge to sustain a motion for the dismissal of the case on the ground that the evidence submitted by the state is not legally sufficient to justify a conviction. When the witnesses for the defense are called to the stand, the attorney for the defense conducts the direct and redirect examinations and the prosecution cross-examines. The defendant has the constitutional right to refuse to testify. He may take the stand *voluntarily,* but not under compulsion. Furthermore, the prosecuting attorney may not comment unfavorably upon the failure

---

[22]In *Gideon v. Wainwright,* 372 U.S. 335, 83 S.Ct. 792 (1963), the Supreme Court held that the right to counsel guaranteed by the Sixth Amendment was applicable to the states through the due process clause of the Fourteenth Amendment. Since the *Gideon* case, the Supreme Court has extended the right to counsel, including the indigent's right to appointed counsel, to all "critical stages" in the process of criminal justice. Consequently, it is possible that the accused will be represented by counsel from the time of arrest throughout the trial and even to the conclusion of an appeal.

of the defendant to testify,[23] nor may the judge in his instructions to the jury or the jury in their deliberations give unfavorable interpretation to the defendant's silence. To permit otherwise, it is claimed, would amount to forcing the accused to testify under the threat that to refuse might be interpreted as an admission of guilt. If, however, the defendant does testify, he may be cross-examined as any other witness. Each side may object to questions from time to time, and the judge either sustains or denies the objections. In some states the attorney for the defense must take exceptions to the rulings of the court so as to lay the basis for an appeal if this becomes necessary. At the conclusion of the defense, the prosecution has the opportunity to rebut the evidence presented by the defense, and, in turn, the defense has the opportunity to introduce evidence in the rejoinder to refute the rebuttal.

After all the evidence has been brought before the court, the case is ready for the arguments to the jury. As a rule, the first speech is made by the prosecution, which may make only a brief statement or an elaborate argument, assembling all the points brought out in the testimony and concluding with an eloquent plea for conviction. The kind of speech that the prosecution delivers will depend largely on the importance of the case. The attorney for the defense, however, usually takes full advantage of the opportunity to address the jury, often resorting to every device to appeal to the emotions of the jury. The prosecution is entitled to the last word, and it is allowed another chance to answer arguments raised by the defense.

After arguments of the prosecution and the defense have been presented, the judge delivers his charge to the jury. The purpose of the

---

[23]*Griffin v. California*, 380 U.S. 609, 85 S.Ct. 1229 (1965). In 1972, however, the Supreme Court voted five to two to uphold a federal law and a state statute that granted limited immunity to a witness. The Court ruled that the United States or a state under such a law can compel testimony from an unwilling witness who invokes the Fifth Amendment privilege against compulsory self-discrimination by conferring immunity from use of the compelled testimony and evidence derived therefrom in subsequent criminal proceedings. In any subsequent criminal prosecution of the witness, the prosecution has the burden of proving affirmatively that the evidence which it proposes to use is derived from a legitimate source wholly independent of the compelled testimony. See *Kastigar v. United States*, 406 U.S. 441 (1972); and *Zicarelli v. New Jersey*, 406 U.S. 472 (1972). The federal law has been copied by some states. In a previous case, the Supreme Court held that neither a state nor the federal government may use testimony given after immunity has been granted by either. *Murphy v. The Waterfront Commission of New York Harbor*, 378 U.S. 52, 84 S.Ct. 1594 (1964).

charge is to inform the jury of the legal aspects of the case and to indicate to them how they are to analyze the evidence in arriving at a verdict. The judge informs the jury that the presumption is that the defendant is innocent and that the burden is on the state to convince them "beyond a reasonable doubt"[24] that the defendant is guilty. In criminal cases, a verdict of guilty should not be based upon a mere "preponderance of evidence,"[25] although this is sufficient to justify a verdict in civil cases. In most states, the judge is not permitted to comment on the facts in such a way as to indicate his opinion regarding the weight of the evidence, the rule being that the law is for the judge and the facts are for the jury. In addition, the judge may agree to give to the jurors certain specific instructions suggested by the attorneys for the defense and the prosecution.

The jury is now ready to consider the facts and arrive at the verdict. Often in minor cases, they render it without leaving the jury box, but in more serious cases they retire to the jury room. When they have reached a decision, they return to the court room and the foreman announces the verdict. In certain cases in some states, the jury may make its recommendations regarding the sentence. A unanimous verdict[26] is usually required, and both the judge and the accused must be present when the verdict is announced. The accused has the right to have the jury polled, during which procedure each juror must state whether he concurs in the verdict. If a verdict, according to law, cannot be reached, the judge dismisses the jury without a verdict, but the defendant may be retried.

If the jury finds the defendant "guilty," he may make a motion for an arrest of judgment or ask for a new trial. The motion for an arrest of judgment is made by the defendant to contest matters appearing on

---

[24]In 1970, the Supreme Court ruled that the accused must be proved guilty "beyond a reasonable doubt" in all criminal cases in both state and federal courts. See In re Winship, 397 U.S. 358, 90 S.Ct. 1068 (1970). Proof "beyond a reasonable doubt" is not beyond all possible or imaginary doubt, but such proof as satisfies the judgment and conscience of upright men in an honest and diligent search for the truth. No person may be convicted of a crime unless each element of the crime is proved beyond a reasonable doubt.

[25]"Preponderance of evidence" means the greater weight of evidence that has convincing quality.

[26]Some states permit less than unanimous verdicts in criminal trials. Furthermore, the United States Supreme Court has held that less than unanimous verdicts are constitutionally sufficient to convict in state criminal trials. See Johnson v. Louisiana, 406 U.S. 356 (1972); Apodaca v. Oregon, 406 U.S. 404 (1972).

the face of the record which would render the judgment erroneous if it were given. It should be sustained, for example, if it appears that the court is without jurisdiction to try the case, or if the statute on which the indictment was framed is unconstitutional. If this motion is sustained, the defendant is discharged, but he may be prosecuted again for the same offense. A motion for a new trial is based upon some error committed during the course of the trial which deprived the defendant of some substantial right and thereby prevented him from receiving a fair and impartial trial. Thus, it may be based upon such grounds as the exclusion of proper evidence, the admission of improper evidence, the improper conduct of jurors, the prejudicial remarks of the prosecuting attorney or the judge, newly discovered evidence, and so on. In some jurisdictions, after a verdict of guilty but before judgment, the defendant may make a motion for a judgment of acquittal, notwithstanding the verdict, on the grounds that the evidence is not legally sufficient to justify a conviction. The granting of this judgment means that the defendant may not be retried.

If all motions by the defense have been denied, the defendant is brought before the court for sentence. The sentence is the penalty imposed by the court and consists of a fine or imprisonment, or both a fine and imprisonment, or execution. The penalties imposed for the various crimes are provided by state and federal statutes. In certain cases, however, the court may, at its discretion, suspend the sentence and place the convicted person on probation. In cases where the convicted person is committed to an institution, he is usually sent to a state or federal prison or reformatory if he is a felon, or to a jail or to a penal farm or camp if he is a misdemeanant, and his sentence may be for a definite or indeterminate length of time.[27]

In some cases, the convicted person may seek to correct the judgment of the court through a writ of error *coram nobis*. This writ is applied for in the trial court, and if it is issued, it has the effect of reopening the case. Thus, it may be used to show new facts which, if they had been known, would have resulted in a different judgment.

---

[27]In order to reduce the disparity in sentencing, the Model Penal Code, proposed by the American Law Institute, recommends that felonies be classified on the basis of their seriousness (as measured by the moral standards of society) into three degrees, and that an indeterminate sentence be provided for each of these degrees. *Model Penal Code, Proposed Official Draft* (Philadelphia: The American Law Institute, May 4, 1962).

APPEALS

The convicted person has still another step that he can take in his defense; he may appeal to a higher court. Although there is no guaranteed right to appeal in the United States Constitution, federal and state statutes provide for appeals in criminal cases and prescribe the method of procedure. The application for an appeal must usually be made within a few weeks after the final judgment of the trial court. The state also has a right of appeal under certain circumstances. In some states, for example, the prosecution may appeal from an order discharging the accused before trial or from a judgment quashing an indictment. However, because of the constitutional provision which gives the defendant the right to plead "double jeopardy," the general rule is that the state may not appeal from a verdict of acquittal. Nevertheless, some jurisdictions permit the state to appeal in cases resulting in an acquittal in order to obtain a clarification of the law, but, of course, even if legal error is found, the defendant may not be tried again for the same offense.

In cases where the defendant has been supplied with free counsel at the trial or where he cannot afford an appeal, the state must provide him with free counsel for this purpose when the appeal is a matter of right and must also furnish him with a transcript of the trial proceedings. However, when the appeal is not a matter of right but granted at the discretion of the court, failure to appoint counsel for the indigent defendant at the appeal level does not violate the Constitution.[28] When an appeal is allowed, it usually acts as a stay of the sentence until final disposition is made of the appeal.[29] The higher court may reverse the lower court and order the release of the defendant, reverse the conviction and remand the defendant for a new trial, affirm the conviction but with some modifications, or merely affirm the decision

---

[28]Although the Constitution does not guarantee the right to appeal, if the law provides for an appeal, the right to it must be equally available for both rich and poor. See *Griffin v. Illinois*, 351 U.S. 12, 76 S.Ct. 585 (1956); *Douglas v. California*, 372 U.S. 353, 83 S.Ct. 814 (1963); *Ross v. Moffitt*, 417 U.S. 600, 94 S.Ct. 2437 (1974).

[29]Many cases are heard in the United States Supreme Court on a *writ of certiorari*, by which a lower court is ordered to send up the record of a case for its review. This kind of hearing is not, strictly speaking, an appeal. An appeal lies as a matter of right, whereas the petition for the *writ of certiorari*, on the basis of which a review of a case can be obtained, may be granted or denied at the discretion of the Court. However, even on an appeal, the Court may refuse to grant a hearing if, in its judgment, the "federal question" in the case is not of a *substantial* nature.

of the lower court. If the higher court grants a new trial, the whole process of criminal prosecution from the arraignment onward must be repeated, but if it upholds the judgment of the lower court, the convicted person must submit to the penalty, unless he can take his case to a higher state court or to the United States Supreme Court.

THE RULES OF EVIDENCE

MEANING AND PURPOSE

The introduction of evidence during the trial is regulated by law.[30] Evidence is the means by which alleged facts are proved or disproved. Although the term "proof" is sometimes used as a synonym for the term "evidence," in the strict sense of the word, proof is the effect of evidence; that is, it is the establishment of fact by evidence. The law of evidence consists of rules regarding (1) the manner of presentation of evidence and (2) the exclusion of evidence.

Evidence may be classified as either direct or circumstantial. Direct evidence tends to show the existence of a fact in question without the intervention of the proof of any other fact—for example, an eyewitness account of an act. Circumstantial evidence provides inferential or indirect proof of the alleged facts. It establishes a condition of surrounding and limiting circumstances which point to the existence of the principal fact. Thus, testimony that the defendant was at the scene of the alleged crime when the victim was shot is circumstantial evidence. Evidence may be divided also into testimony, which is evidence given by a competent witness under oath or affirmation, and material or real evidence, which consists of tangible objects, such as weapons, articles of clothing, photographs, fingerprints, maps, documents, and so on.

BURDEN OF PROOF

The defendant is presumed to be innocent, and the prosecution

---

[30]Limitations of space permit only a brief presentation here of some of the basic rules of evidence. For a more complete treatment, see John C. Klotter and Carl L. Meier, *Criminal Evidence for Police* (Cincinnati: The W.H. Anderson Company, 1975); Gilbert B. Stuckey, *Evidence for the Law Enforcement Officer* (New York: McGraw-Hill Book Company, 1968); *McCormick's Handbook of the Law of Evidence*, ed. Edward W. Cleary (St. Paul, Minn.: West Publishing Co., 1972); David W. Louisell, John Kaplan, and Jon R. Waltz, *Principles of Evidence and Proof* (Mineola, N.Y.: The Foundation Press, Inc., 1972).

therefore has the burden of proving that he is guilty of the alleged crime beyond a reasonable doubt. To accomplish this, the prosecution must not only prove the *corpus delicti*,[31] or body of the crime, that is, all the essential elements that comprise the crime, but also prove beyond a reasonable doubt that the defendant committed each one of these elements. Not until this has been accomplished does the "alleged crime" become the "crime," and the "alleged criminal" the "criminal."

The burden of proof never shifts to the defendant during the trial, but the burden of going forward with the evidence does shift back and forth between the prosecution and the defense. So, when the prosecution shows that the defendant shot and killed another person and thus establishes a *prima facie* case[32] of murder, the burden of going forward with the evidence shifts to the defense. It must then introduce some contrary evidence, for example, evidence to the effect that the accused was justified in shooting the victim. Even though this evidence is slight, it may be sufficient to shift the burden of going forward with the evidence to the prosecution. However, regardless of the number of times this shift occurs, the burden of ultimately proving the guilt of the defendant remains with the prosecution.

SUBSTITUTES FOR EVIDENCE

These are used to save the time of the court and include (1) judicial notice, (2) stipulation, and (3) presumption of law.[33] Judicial notice is the recognition by the court of the existence of certain laws and geographical, historical, and scientific facts without the necessity of proof. A stipulation is an agreement by the prosecution and the defense that a certain fact, for example, the contents of a document, exists. It thus eliminates the need of introducing evidence regarding

---

[31]Although in popular language the term *"corpus delicti"* is used to describe the visible evidence of the crime, such as the dead body of a murdered person, it is properly applicable to any crime and relates particularly to the act element of criminality.

[32]A *prima facie* case exists when the evidence thus far introduced is sufficient to establish the alleged crime unless it is contradicted or overcome by other evidence.

[33] There are also presumptions of fact or inferences. For example, if the accused is caught with recently stolen property and offers no believable explanation, the inference is that such holding is guilty possession. Presumptions of fact are conclusions which common experience indicates can be drawn from certain circumstances. They are permissive, however, and may be accepted or rejected by the jury at its own discretion.

the fact. A presumption of law is a conclusion which the law says must be drawn from a certain set of facts. Presumptions of law are conclusive or rebuttable. A conclusive presumption (for example, everyone is presumed to know the law or a boy under fourteen years cannot commit rape) is final and cannot be overcome by contradictory evidence. However, a rebuttable presumption (for example, the accused is presumed to be innocent or every person is presumed to be same) can be overturned by contrary evidence.

ADMISSIBILITY OF EVIDENCE

To be admissible, evidence must be relevant, material, and competent. Relevant evidence is that which has some connection or relationship with the issues of the case. However, not all relevant evidence is admissible, for it may be too trivial or misleading, tending to waste the time of the court or to confuse it, or too prejudicial, tending, for example, to shock the jury unnecessarily. Material evidence, on the other hand, is not only relevant but also very important. It affects the issues of the case in a significant way and has great probative value. Therefore, it is always admissible if it is also competent. Competent evidence means evidence given by a competent witness.[34] The general test for the competency of a witness is: Can he communicate relevant material and understand his obligation to tell the truth? Thus, young children and persons of unsound mind may be held to be incompetent, but age by itself does not necessarily disqualify a child if he can pass the test of competency.

IMPEACHMENT OF A WITNESS

Impeachment is the discrediting of a witness. This may be done, for example, by showing bias or prejudice, a previous criminal record, prior inconsistent statements, limited ability to observe, remember, and recount facts, and so on. A witness, however, may be rehabilitated; that is, he may have his credibility restored by contrary evidence.

RULES OF EXCLUSION

Much of the law of evidence deals with the rules of exclusion.

---

[34]Evidence is sometimes said to be incompetent for reasons other than the incompetency of the witness. For example, some writers use the term "incompetent" in referring to evidence obtained in violation of some constitutional provision.

They are of basic importance and are designed to eliminate what is untrustworthy, misleading, or against public policy. Consequently, evidence may be relevant, material, and competent and still be excluded through the operation of these rules. Important among these rules are the following:

The Opinion Rule.   The general rule is that opinion evidence is not admissible and that witnesses must confine their statements to what they have learned through their senses—sight, hearing, touch, taste, and smell. The witnesses are to supply the facts; the jury is to weigh the facts and draw conclusions. However, necessity dictates that certain exceptions be made to the opinion rule, for sometimes it is impractical, perhaps even confusing, to limit the testimony to just the facts. Thus, the lay witness may give his opinion on matters of common observation, such as distance, time, speed, size, direction, general physical appearance of a person, and so on. For example, he may give his impression of a person's sobriety or his estimate of the speed of a moving vehicle. Furthermore, a witness who has been properly established as an expert may freely give his opinion, in the area of his specialty, in response to hypothetical questions or on facts already presented by other witnesses. So, a physician may give his opinion on medical questions; a toxicologist, on poisons; a phychiatrist, on mental diseases; a police authority, on fingerprints.

Privileged Communications.   The rule on privileged communications is designed to protect certain rights, interests, and relationships. Thus, public policy calls for the guarding of certain state and police secrets, such as grand jury deliberations, diplomatic correspondence, and so on, and of some personal communications, like those between husband and wife, attorney and client, doctor and patient, and clergyman and parishioner. In general, the privilege regarding communications is a personal one and must be claimed by the person who is protected—the client, the patient, the spouse, and so on. However, in some situations, this rule must give way before other considerations. Thus, it offers no shield to a client who has sought advice from his attorney on how to commit a crime in such a was as to avoid arrest, and physicians must report cases involving gunshot wounds, venereal diseases, child abuse, and so on. The modern rule, furthermore, is that either spouse may testify *for* the other but neither may do so *against* the other if either one objects when the testimony involves communications between husband and wife. The rule on communications between husband and wife, however, does not apply to communications (1) made in the presence of others, (2) made before or after a marriage terminated by divorce or death, or (3) when one spouse has injured the other or has committed a crime against the children of either.

Character and Reputation. Character may be defined as the aggregate of the qualities belonging to a person, whereas reputation is the sum of the opinions concerning him. In general, testimony about a person's character or reputation may not be introduced in order to raise an inference of his guilt. This rule is designed to guard against the possibility that the jury may be inclined to a verdict of guilty by evidence of the defendant's bad reputation or prior criminal record. The defendant, however, may introduce evidence of his own good character and reputation to indicate the probability of his innocence. The accepted way of proving character is to show that the defendant has a good reputation in the community with respect to specific character traits, like sobriety or chastity, that are related to the issue of his guilt or innocence. Thus, when the charge is assault and battery, the defense may introduce evidence showing that the community judges the defendant to be a peaceable man. Although the prosecution may not initiate this line of evidence, as soon as the defense has done so, the "door is open," and the state may then respond with countervailing evidence about the defendant's character and reputation.

Like other exclusionary rules, this one, too, has exceptions. Thus, evidence of a person's habit or custom is usually admissible to prove that his behavior on a certain occasion conformed to that habit or custom. Furthermore, evidence of the previous criminal behavior of the accused may be introduced, not to prove the criminal propensity of the defendant, but to show that the crime charged was one of a series of related crimes or part of a larger scheme, to prove that the method used in the crime charged was similar to the one employed in the commission of the defendant's previous crimes (*modus operandi*), to identify the defendant as the perpetrator of the crime charged, to reveal the state of mind of the defendant (his intent, motive, guilty knowledge, and so on), and to rebut a defense of ignorance or mistake.

The Hearsay Evidence Rule. Hearsay evidence is a written or oral statement made out of court by a person other than the witness but offered in court to prove the truth of the matters asserted in the statement. Its value, therefore, is based not on the credibility of the witness but rather on the veracity or competence of other persons. For example, if the witness says, "I know that the defendant stole the car because his sister told me so," this is hearsay evidence. Evidence is not hearsay, however, if it is presented only to prove that the statement was made and not to prove the truth of the statement.

Hearsay evidence is excluded for these reasons: (1) the person who is alleged to have made the statement is not present and under oath; (2) he cannot be cross-examined; (3) his demeanor cannot be observed by the court; (4) he cannot be confronted by the defendant; and (5) repeated tales tend to be unreliable. There are, however, many exceptions to the hearsay rule, although each of these exceptions to be admissible must meet the specific qualifications established for it. Nevertheless, when all these exceptions are examined, there will usually be found (1) some special necessity for the hearsay evidence, and (2) some guarantee of its reliability.

Some of the most common exceptions to the hearsay rule are:

1. Confessions and admissions. A confession is a complete acknowledgment of guilt by the defendant, whereas an admission is an act or statement which only partly incriminates him. Thus, when the accused stated that he was at the scene of the crime, he made an admission. Since confessions or admissions are so damaging, the likelihood of lying in such statements is greatly reduced. Furthermore, there is the necessity of admitting these statements as exceptions to the hearsay rule because the defendant cannot be compelled to testify.[35]

2. Dying declaration. A dying declaration is a statement concerning the cause and circumstances of a homicide made by the alleged victim who believed that he faced imminent death and who has since died. It must be shown, however, that he was competent at the time of the statement. Dying declarations are admissible because a solemnity equivalent to that produced by taking an oath is produced by the nearness of expected death and the victim is unavailable as a witness.

3. Spontaneous declarations (Res Gestae). A spontaneous declaration is an utterance about a startling event made by a person in a condition of excitement, shock, or surprise who was present at the event and able to observe it. To be admissible, however, such a declaration must be shown to have been actually spontaneous and so closely related in time to the event that it was not the product of deliberation or design. In other words, it must have been an integral part of the res gestae, or "the things done" or

---

[35]For additional discussion of confessions and admissions, see Chapter XI.

what happened. So if a wife, on seeing her husband shot, screams, "My God, Sam just killed my husband," her utterance is a spontaneous declaration.

4. Former testimony. Former testimony given in a prior trial by a witness who is not now available is admissible as an exception to the hearsay rule if the prior trial involved substantially the same parties and substantially the same issues. This exception is justified on the grounds that the unavailable witness who gave the former testimony was in court, under oath, and subject to cross-examination.

   In addition, in certain cases in some jurisdictions, the testimony of a witness who will not be available at the time of a trial may be taken in writing while he is under oath or affirmation and in response to interrogations by both the prosecution and the defense. This testimony is called a deposition and may later be admissible as an exception to the hearsay rule.

5. Documentary evidence. Certain documents may be introduced in evidence as an exception to the hearsay rule. Documentary evidence, however, is subject to the "best evidence" rule, which means that the best available evidence must be brought to court. Thus, the original of a document should be introduced whenever this is possible. But to insist that public reports and records in their original form be submitted to the court or to require all persons who had any part in the making of them to testify would seriously obstruct the machinery of government. Consequently, duly authenticated copies of public documents may be admissible in place of the testimonial evidence given by public officials.

   Business and hospital records of facts which are routinely made and kept and relied on in the daily work of a company, agency, department, or institution also are admissible. In support of this exception, it is reasoned that the entries made in this way are sufficiently credible to be admissible as evidence.

   Furthermore, when a witness has no present recollection of the facts in a writing but testifies that he does remember making the writing and that it was an accurate account of the facts, the writing is admissible as a substitute for his memory. When, however, a writing, like an investigator's notes, is used merely to refresh the memory of the witness, his testimony, and not the writing, is the evidence.

6. Pedigree or family history. Hearsay evidence pertaining to birth, marriage, divorce, death, race, ancestry, and other similar facts is

admissible if the original declarant is unavailable and the original statement was made by a member of the family or by one so intimately associated with it as to be likely to know the correct family history. So, writings in family Bibles, engravings on rings, and so on may be introduced to prove pedigree.

Evidence Unconstitutionally Obtained. Evidence may be excluded if it has been obtained in violation of some constitutional provision. Recent United States Supreme Court decisions on confessions, wire tapping, search and seizure, and the right to counsel have greatly enlarged the area in which this exclusionary rule applies.[36]

PUNISHMENT AND TREATMENT

Punishment is the penalty imposed by the state upon a person adjudged guilty of crime.[37] It has these two essential elements: (1) public condemnation of antisocial behavior, and (2) the imposition of unpleasant consequences by political authority. The infliction of punishment, therefore, always involves the intention to produce some kind of pain, which is justified in terms of its assumed values.

The principal purposes of punishment are retribution, deterrence, and reformation (or rehabilitation). Retribution is the pain which the offender is made to suffer because he has broken the law and which is proportioned according to the gravity of the offense. It helps to placate whatever passion for revenge the victim and his relatives and friends may have and so tends to regulate and control feelings that otherwise might be disruptive in organized society. But it does much more than this. It helps to unify society against crime and criminals, supports the moral code, and provides a basis for distinguishing one offense from other offenses according to the degree of seriousness attributed to them by the moral code. Thus, larceny, embezzlement, false pretense, and so on are not regarded with the same degree of seriousness as murder. Just as the rules in the game of football must be upheld and penalties must be imposed in accordance with gravity of the offense, so must it be with the law—the rules of a much more serious game—if the business of living is to go forward in peace and order. Retribution, therefore, must be viewed as

---

[36]Evidence that has been unconstitutionally obtained is sometimes called "incompetent evidence." For an extended dicussion of this kind of evidence, see Chapters X, XI.

[37]Caldwell, pp. 419-36.

constituting more than an "eye-for-an-eye" response to socially harmful conduct.

Deterrence is the use of punishment to prevent others from committing crimes. Thus, the offender is punished so that he will be held up as an example of what happens to those who violate the law. The fact that crime continues to exist does not mean that punishment is not efficacious as a deterrent, since there is no way to determine how much crime there would be if criminals were not punished. Furthermore, deterrence involves more than the instilling of fear in those who might be tempted to commit a crime. It involves also the positive moral influence which the law exerts in the educational and training processes. There, by stigmatizing certain acts in terms of prescribed penalties, it helps to engender attitudes of dislike, contempt, disgust, and even horror for these acts and thus contributes to the origin and development of personal forces hostile to crime. Thus, some persons abstain from murder because they fear the penalty, but many others do so because they regard murder with horror.

Some of those who believe that deterrence is important consciously or unconsciously base their belief on the doctrine of freedom of the will. According to this doctrine, a person is free, at least to some extent, to do as he likes, and society must in some way prevail upon him to bring his behavior into conformity with generally accepted standards. When a person violates the law, he is held not to have disciplined himself sufficiently, since he might have acted otherwise if he had so desired. Therefore, he must be punished so that he and others, taking this into consideration, will choose to obey the law. Those who argue in this way are called "libertarians." However, others, known as "determinists," reject the doctrine of freedom of will. They contend that human behavior is not an expression of free will but instead is the product of the hereditary and environmental forces that interact in the life of the individual. Therefore, since there is no freedom of will, it is both futile and unjust to punish the criminal so that he and others, impressed by his experience, will choose to obey the law.

The fact is that science can neither prove nor disprove that there is freedom of will. All that science thus far has been able to demonstrate is that the area in which determinism operates is greater than it was formerly believed to be. Yet it seems safe to conclude that the area of the unknown in human behavior is still so great that, as far as we know, there may well be an element of free will in every human act.

In any event, there has been some relenting on both sides of the freedom-of-will controversy. For example, many libertarians now speak of freedom of choice rather than freedom of will, thus conceding that the will is affected by previous experience and attendant circumstances and so not completely free. On the other side of the question, some determinists now use the term "soft determinism," thus indicating their admission that there may be elements of indeterminism in human behavior. Although these two views had their beginnings on opposite sides of the freedom-of-will controversy, each sees man as endowed with creative ability and capable of making choices.

Moreover, one may reject the doctrine of freedom of the will and still favor the punishment of criminals as a means of controlling human behavior through the development of law-abiding attitudes and the establishment of fear as causes of that behavior. Even the determinist, therefore, agrees that the criminal is responsible at least in the sense that he has in him the causes that produce criminality.

The third purpose of punishment is to reform, that is, to use pain and fear to direct the criminal away from crime and toward socially accepted forms of behavior. But every program of reformation must have positive as well as negative elements, and so at this point punishment comes into direct contact with treatment in the correction of offenders. Let us, then, examine the meaning of treatment.

Treatment is a process during which causes in the individual case are studied and the knowledge thus obtained is used to produce the desired effects in the individual's behavior. In this process, the experience of pain may be deliberately utilized, but more often no such pain is sought, or if it is caused it is merely incidental to action which is directed to other goals. Always, however, the emphasis in treatment is on the individual, his nature, his problems, and his interests. On the other hand, in the process of punishment, the emphasis is on the group and its interests. The crime is considered to be a threat to the group, and the individual must suffer so as to protect the group and the moral code. Even so, just as punishment cannot disregard the invididual, whose reformation is one of its goals, so treatment cannot ignore the group, to which the "treated" individual must be returned.

Furthermore, retribution, deterrence, and reformation should not be considered entirely separately and independently of one another. They must be seen in their interrelationship, for each affects and strengthens the others. Reformation must be conducted and deterrence exerted in terms of values—the values of organized society, whatever they may be—but these very values, which the offender must accept and for which he must develop a loyalty, are flouted and thereby weakened and perhaps destroyed if due recognition is not given to the importance of retribution, whose function is to support values. "Thus, reformation and deterrence to be effective need retribution, which in turn is facilitated when they are effective."[38]

However, the efficacy of the purposes and methods of punishment are affected by the values of the culture in which they are used. In many countries of Europe and the Western Hemisphere, including, of course, the United States, humanitarianism, increasing impersonality in social relationships,[39] and growing belief in the powers of science have significantly helped to give reformation, especially treatment, a prominent place in the field of corrections. At the same time, these same cultural features have tended to replace capital and corporal penalties with probation, imprisonment, and parole.

In fact, influenced by these developments, some writers have proposed that the term "punishment" be discarded, and that the entire program of corrections be called "treatment." However, such a proposal greatly oversimplifies the situation. The two processes of treatment and punishment must operate in terms of values—the values of organized society, which if it is to survive, must establish and preserve its norms. Therefore, although both the interests of the individual and the group must be considered in the handling of offenders, the interests of the group are always paramount, and both treatment and punishment must be administered within the limits imposed by the moral code, the values of which must be guarded by retribution.

Furthermore, it is highly dubious whether any interference with normal living, for whatever reasons, can ever be completely nonpunitive. Punishment and treatment are so integrated as to be inseparable; just as treatment is to some extent punitive, so punishment, if wisely administered, also rehabilitates. "Moreover, both the sensations of pain and pleasure can be utilized profitably during the process of rehabilitation." It is not, then, a question of whether there should be one or the other of these sensations, or whether there should be retribution, deterrence, or reformation, or whether there should be treatment or punishment, "but rather how both treatment *and*

---

[38]Ibid., p. 433.

[39]The increasing impersonality in social relationships contributes not only to widespread ignorance about the commission of crimes and the fate of these involved in them, but also to delay in the apprehension, prosecution, and conviction of criminals.

punishment can be most judiciously balanced to produce the best results in the control and modification of behavior." Courts and correctional institutions, therefore, "can never be just therapeutic agencies. They must be also moral agencies in the sense that they must express, protect, and strengthen the values of the organized society in which they function."[40]

Today, in Western civilization, the principal methods of punishment are the imposition of fines, the requirement of restitution, imprisonment, execution, probation, and parole. In the analysis of punishment, the methods of punishment should not be confused with the purposes of punishment. For example, the incapacitation of a criminal by his imprisonment—a method of punishment—should not be called a purpose of punishment. Why is it important not to confuse methods and purposes? The answer is that each method, whenever it is possible to do so, must seek to accomplish all three purposes of punishment—not one or two. Thus, if an inmate is pronounced "rehabilitated," he may have to remain institutionalized so that the moral code will be upheld by retribution and deterrence will be exerted. It should be clear, then, that the failure of prisons to rehabilitate most of their inmates does not in itself justify the elimination of prisons. They have additional functions to perform. They must also strive to deter and inflict retribution.

---

[40]Caldwell, pp. 434, 435.

CHAPTER XIII

THE JUVENILE COURT

ORIGIN AND DEVELOPMENT

The first juvenile court in the world began its legal existence in Chicago, Illinois, on July 1, 1899.[1] American ingenuity and enterprise contributed significantly to the establishment of this court, but it has legal roots that are deeply embedded in English jurisprudence.

One of these roots is the principle of equity or chancery[2] that originated to give greater flexibility to the law so that the interests of litigants might be balanced according to the merits of each case. Through equity, the king acted as *parens patriae*, or "father of his country," in exercising his power of guardianship over the persons and property of minors, who were considered wards of the state and as such entitled to special protection.

The other legal root is the presumption of innocence thrown about children by the common law. According to this doctrine, a child under the age of seven is conclusively presumed incapable of committing a crime. Between the ages of seven and fourteen, he may be held to be criminally responsible if he is shown to have enough intelligence to understand the nature of his act. After the age of fourteen, children, like adults, are presumed to be responsible for their acts. Thus, the creation of the juvenile court involved the extension of the common law doctrine that children below a certain age cannot be held criminally responsible.

In America, where English jurisprudence was introduced by the early colonists, such tendencies as the increase in the complexity of social relationships, the growth of humanitarianism, and the rise of the social sciences contributed to the expansion of the area in which

---

[1] For a more complete discussion of the origin and development of the juvenile court, see Robert G. Caldwell and James A. Black, *Juvenile Delinquency* (New York: The Ronald Press Company, 1971), pp. 186-95.

[2] Since equity was dispensed by the Council of Chancery, the terms "equity" and "chancery" came to be used interchangeably.

the child received differential treatment by law. Special institutions for juvenile offenders were established; agencies for free foster-home care were developed; the modification of court procedure in children's cases was effected in some states; probation was widely adopted; and public education was expanded. The establishment of the juvenile court, therefore, may well be considered a logical and exceedingly important step in a much broader movement for the expansion of the specialized treatment given to children in an increasingly complex society. Although the idea of the juvenile court combined already existing elements—institutional segregation, probation supervision, foster-home placement, separate judicial hearings, and an approach that emphasized the rehabilitation of the juvenile offender—it did constitute a significant achievement in judicial integration by providing for a more systematic and independent handling of children's cases.

However, in creating the juvenile court, the law made two fundamental changes in the handling of juvenile offenders that are especially noteworthy. First, it raised the age below which a child could not be considered a criminal from seven to sixteen and made the alleged delinquent subject to the jurisdiction of the juvenile court. Second, it placed the operation of the court under equity or chancery jurisdiction and thereby introduced into it an informal procedure and extended the application of the principle of guardianship to all children, including juvenile delinquents, who were in need of protection by the state. These two changes, in modified form, remain as essential characteristics of all juvenile court legislation.

TRENDS IN THE JUVENILE COURT MOVEMENT

Following the lead taken by Illinois, other states soon established juvenile courts. In fact, within ten years, twenty states and the District of Columbia enacted juvenile court laws, and by 1920, all except three states had done so. Finally, in 1945, when Wyoming took action, the list of states having juvenile court laws was complete. Today, all states, the District of Columbia, and Puerto Rico have some kind of juvenile court legislation, and the movement has had considerable success in other countries. However, there are no federal juvenile courts, and consequently, children under eighteen who violate federal laws are given a hearing in a state juvenile court or in a federal district court.

While the juvenile court movement was spreading, the jurisdiction of the court was being extended. In general, the definition of juvenile delinquency was broadened; the types of nondelinquency cases (such as those involving illegitimacy, mental and physical defectives, and so on) under the jurisdiction of the court were increased; the upper age level of the children subject to the authority of the court was raised from sixteen to seventeen or eighteen in many states and in a few states, to twenty-one; and the juvenile court was given jurisdiction over adults in certain cases involving children—for example, those in which an adult contributes to the delinquency of a juvenile.

Furthermore, the juvenile court has exerted an increasing influence on the principles and methods used in the adjustment of many other family problems and in the handling of adolescent and adult offenders. This influence, for example, can be seen in the establishment and operation of adolescent courts, family courts, and youth authorities and in the use of presentence investigation and probation in criminal courts.

The increasing complexity of American society has contributed significantly to these trends in the juvenile court movement. Such interrelated factors as industrialization, urbanization, the unprecedented movement of populations, the amazing utilization of the natural resources, the rapid accumulation of inventions and discoveries, and the acceleration of transportation and communication have tended to undermine the family and the neighborhood, and, forcing our communities to find additional means of social control, have given strong impetus to the establishment of juvenile courts and sent into them an increasing number and variety of cases.

In the meantime, other influences have more specifically affected the philosophy and methods of the juvenile court. Thus, the literature and various associations in the fields of social work, psychiatry, and psychology have widely, persistently, and effectively pictured juvenile delinquency as symptomatic of some underlying emotional condition which demands not punishment, but diagnosis and treatment by teams of specialists trained in these fields. Adding to this influence have been the many court decisions which have stressed the social service functions of the court and minimized its legal principles. The total effect of all this has been to put increasing emphasis on the treatment of the individual and to give decreasing attention to his legal rights and the security of the communtiy. Consequently, the balance between rights on one hand and duties and responsibilities on the other, which every court must endeavor to maintain, has been upset as the court has been pushed more and more into the role of a social work agency.

CHARACTERISTICS OF THE JUVENILE COURT

Although the juvenile court has had an uneven and diverse development, many of its supporters believe that a court must have at least the following characteristics or it cannot claim to be a juvenile court:

1. Separate hearings for children's cases.
2. Informal or chancery procedure.
3. Regular probation service.
4. Separate detention of children.
5. Special court and probation records.
6. Provision for mental and physical examinations.

Unfortunately, many so-called juvenile courts have few of these characteristics, and others possess them in varying degrees. Nevertheless, such organizations as the National Council on Crime and Delinquency and the United States Children's Bureau insist that the juvenile court, if it is to function effectively, must also have jurisdiction in all cases of children under eighteen, a specially trained judge, a well-qualified probation staff, with limitation of case loads and definite plans for constructive work in each case, availability of resources for individual and specialized treatment (such as medical, psychological, and psychiatric services, foster family and institutional care, and recreational services and facilities), and state supervision of probation work.

THE PRESENT STATUS OF THE COURT

The juvenile court in the United States varies greatly from one jurisdiction to another and at present manifests all stages of its complex development.[3] Only in a few cities is the court a distinct and highly specialized one, and in many rural areas it is largely of a rudimentary

---

[3]See Robert G. Caldwell, "The Juvenile Court: Its Development and Some Major Problems," *Journal of Criminal Law, Criminology, and Police Science* LI (January-February, 1961), 493-511, from which article parts of this section have been taken and used in modified form.

nature. Despite this diversity, however, it is possible to indicate in general terms the present status of the juvenile court with respect to certain important features.

PHILOSOPHY OF THE COURT

Generalizations about the juvenile court are difficult and hazardous, but the following appear to be important elements in its philosophy:

The Superior Rights of the State. The state is the "higher or ultimate parent" of all children within its borders and should intervene in the life of a child whenever the court deems such action necessary for his protection, care, and guidance, regardless of the wishes of his parents. This is an adaptation of the doctrine of *parens patriae*, which made all English children wards of the Crown.

Individualization of Justice. The court should seek to adapt its actions to the circumstances of the individual case by ascertaining the needs and potentialities of the child and coordinating the knowledge and the skills of law, science, and social work for the promotion of his welfare. This means that the court should balance interests in an equitable manner by administrative rather than adversary methods within a flexible procedure.

The Status of Delinquency. The state should protect the child from the stigma of criminality. To accomplish this, the law created the status of delinquency, to which the court assigns the child when it adjudges him an offender.

Noncriminal Procedure. By means of an informal procedure, the court should function in such a way as to give primary consideration to the interests of the child. Since its purpose is not to convict the child of a crime, but to protect, aid, and guide him, it does not violate the Constitution if it denies him certain rights which are guaranteed to an adult in a criminal trial.

Remedial, Preventive, and Nonpunitive Purpose. The court should act to save the child and to prevent him from becoming a criminal. Although the first juvenile court law did not stipulate that the child should not be punished, many court decisions and most of the literature on the subject insist that the substitution of treatment for punishment is an essential element in the philosophy of the juvenile court.

GEOGRAPHICAL AREA SERVED BY THE COURT

The county is the geographical area served by most juvenile courts in the United States, but for some the jurisdictional unit is the town, the city, the borough, or the judicial district. Since the county is the conventional unit of state government and of many private organizations, its use as the jurisdictional area for the court has obvious advantages in the coordination of its work with that of other agencies interested in child welfare. Most counties, however, cannot afford to maintain courts at modern standards, and even if they could, the volume of work would not justify the necessary expense. This problem could be solved in some states by making the area served by the juvenile court the same as the judicial district served by other courts in the state and thereby enable one juvenile court to handle the cases of two or more counties. Utah, Connecticut, and Rhode Island have pushed beyond this and, by establishing state systems of juvenile courts, have created larger jurisdictional districts within their borders.

TYPES OF JUVENILE COURTS

There are about 3,000 juvenile courts in the United States, although actually many are only slightly different from criminal courts. In fact, many observers have commented on the inferior performance of most of these courts, and in 1967, the President's Commission on Law Enforcement and Administration of Justice reported that the great hopes originally held for the juvenile court had not been fulfilled, and that it had not succeeded in rehabilitating delinquent youth, in reducing juvenile criminality, or in bringing justice and compassion to the child offender.[4]

The juvenile courts in the United States may be classified into these three types:

1. Designated courts, such as municipal, county, district, and circuit courts which have been selected or designated to hear children's cases and while so functioning are called juvenile courts.
2. Independent and separate courts whose administration is entirely divorced from other courts.

---

[4]The President's Commission on Law Enforcement and Administration of Justice, *Task Force Report: Juvenile Delinquency and Youth Crime* (Washington, D.C.: Government Printing Office, 1967), p. 7.

3. Coordinated courts, which are coordinated with other special courts, such as domestic relations or family courts.

The great majority of the juvenile courts are designated courts, and even some of the separate and independent ones are presided over by judges from other courts, so that their separateness and independence may be more nominal than real.

JURISDICTION OF THE COURT

All juvenile courts have jurisdiction in delinquency cases, and almost all of them have jurisdiction also in cases of dependency and neglect. In addition, some have authority to handle other problems, like feeblemindedness, adoption, illegitimacy, and guardianship. Although the definition of delinquency varies from state to state, in most states the violation of a state law or municipal ordinance (an act which in the case of an adult would be a crime) is the main category of delinquency. Yet in all states delinquency is more than this and includes such items as habitual truancy, incorrigibility, waywardness, and association with immoral persons.[5]

Juvenile court laws differ also with respect to the age of the children over whom the court has jurisdiction. The laws of most states do not specify any lower age limit, merely providing that children under a certain age are subject to the jurisdiction of the court. About two-thirds of the states make eighteen the upper age limit; some set it at sixteen or seventeen; and a few put it as high as twenty-one. In some states, the upper age limit differs according to the sex of the child. About forty states, however, provide for waiver or transfer by the juvenile court to the criminal court, thus giving the juvenile court some discretion and flexibility in exercising its jurisdiction. In addition, many states permit the juvenile court, after it has once acquired jurisdiction over the child, to retain it until he has reached the age of twenty-one.

In many states, however, the juvenile court does not have exclusive jurisdiction over all delinquency cases, but has only concurrent

---

[5]The New York Family Court Act provides that a child must be shown to be in need of supervision, treatment, or confinement before he can be adjudged a delinquent. This provision is intended to preclude court action in the cases of some children and thus prevent their acquiring delinquency records. However, this provision has been criticized on the ground that very few courts are equipped to determine which alleged delinquents are in need of the specified services.

jurisdiction with the criminal court, delinquency cases being handled by either court. But often such concurrent jurisdiction is limited by law to cases of children above a specified age, or to cases involving certain offenses, or to certain counties. Furthermore, in many states, certain serious offenses, for example, murder, manslaughter, and rape, are entirely excluded from the jurisdiction of the juvenile court, and in these states, children charged with such offenses are tried in the criminal court.

The jurisdiction of the court is affected in still another way by the provision in most states that it may exercise authority over adults in certain cases involving children. Thus, in many states, the juvenile court may require a parent to contribute to the support of his child, or it may try adults charged with contributing to the delinquency, neglect, or dependency of a child.

THE JUDGE AND THE PROBATION OFFICER.

Although the effectiveness of the juvenile court depends to a very large degree upon the efficiency of its personnel, relatively few courts have staffs that are especially qualified for their work. In most juvenile courts the judges have been appointed or elected on the basis of their general qualifications for judicial work, and they divide their time between adult and juvenile cases. Only in a very few courts has the judge been selected because he has some specialized training or experience in the handling of children's problems. Often, however, a referee is appointed to assist the judge in the performance of his juvenile court duties. Even though considerable progress has been made in improving the quality of probation in some parts of the country, the great majority of courts are still without the services of a sufficient number of well-qualified and adequately paid workers.

Some light was thrown on the inadequacy of the court's personnel in 1963, by a biographical survey of its judges, which was conducted under the sponsorship of the National Council of Juvenile Court Judges. This survey indicated that, in general, our juvenile courts were presided over by a group of part-time, inadequately compensated judges, many of whom had not had enough professional preparation or opportunity for in-service training, had excessive case loads, and did not have access to sufficient resources in the performance of their duties.[6]

---

[6]The President's Commission on Law Enforcement and Administration of Justice, pp. 6, 7.

PROCEDURE OF THE COURT

Police action initiates the procedure in most delinquency cases, but often it begins with action by a parent or by some other private person or with a referral by a social agency or another court. It is noteworthy that extensive screening and informal adjustment by the police on the street and in the police station significantly reduce the number of apprehended juveniles who are referred to court. The police favor this screening and informal adjustment on the grounds that it not only offers an opportunity for helping the child but also provides fertile soil for cultivating friendship and understanding between juveniles and the police. Many writers, however, believe that the police, in this exercise of their discretion—and they should have discretionary powers in dealing with juveniles—should be guided by a set of written rules and standards.[7]

Many juvenile court statutes provide that the court should make a preliminary inquiry into all complaints received by it to determine whether the interests of the child and the public require court action. This inquiry may vary from a cursory investigation to a full-fledged social study, involving a hearing and contact with numerous persons and agencies. In many juvenile courts, especially in those located in large metropolitan areas, this preliminary screening, known as "intake," is conducted by a special division of the probation department. As a result of the preliminary inquiry, the case may be dismissed, the filing of a petition may be authorized, or the case may be disposed of by some "informal adjustment," such as the referral of the case to another agency or the placing of the child on "informal probation." In recent years, about fifty percent of the delinquency cases have been handled informally or unofficially—that is, without an official record, or hearing. The judge or someone else, such as a probation officer, takes the necessary steps to dispose of the case. The types of cases handled in this way vary greatly from court to court, but the tendency seems to be to reserve official handling for older children and those brought before the court on serious charges.

When a case is not handled unofficially, a petition (which is merely a statement containing important facts of the case, such as the

---

[7]The importance of diverting as many children as possible from the criminal judicial system has been emphasized by both the National Advisory Commission on Criminal Justice Standards and Goals (see its *Task Force Report on Corrections* [Washington, D.C.: U.S. Government Printing Office, 1973], pp. 73-97) and the federal Juvenile Justice and Delinquency Prevention Act of 1974.

names and addresses of the child and his parents or guardians and the cause of the action) is filed in the court, and the case is then scheduled for a hearing. If the child is not being held in detention and his presence is required, a summons ordering him to appear, or in some cases a warrant for his arrest, is issued.

In the past, some jurisdictions required that the child be adjudged delinquent before his case was investigated, whereas many others conducted a prehearing investigation so that both the hearing and the disposition of the case could be based on the facts so obtained. However, under the impact of recent Supreme Court decisions, especially that in the Gault case,[8] the latter jurisdictions have had to modify their procedure. In the Gault case, the Supreme Court ruled that the proceedings to determine delinquency which may result in commitment to an institution must measure up to the essentials of due process and fair treatment. Consequently, unless the allegations in the petition are admitted, all cases that may result in commitment to an institution[9] must first have a fact-finding, or adjudicatory, hearing to determine whether the child is delinquent as charged before they receive a dispositional hearing. Furthermore, if an investigation of the case has been made prior to the fact-finding hearing, the report based on the investigation may not be used in this hearing. This precaution is taken because such a report normally contains much hearsay and other inadmissible evidence.

Juvenile court hearings are usually less formal than trials in the criminal court, but the procedure in the fact-finding hearing has some of the characteristics of such a trial. The child and his parents are present, and the hearing is held before a judge and, in some jurisdictions, a jury, although the United States Supreme Court has ruled that juveniles do not have a Constitutional right to trial by jury.[10] Wit-

---

[8]In re Gault, 387 U.S. 1, 87 S.Ct. 1428 (1967). Statutes seldom provide that the child must be represented by counsel at an intake hearing, and the Supreme Court has not held that he has the right to counsel prior to adjudication. However, many other courts hold the view that the juvenile has this right at the stage of police interrogation. See Sanford J. Fox, The Law of Juvenile Courts in a Nutshell (St. Paul, Minn.: West Publishing Co., 1971), pp. 148, 149.

[9]Since the need of an institutional commitment usually becomes apparent only after the fact-finding hearing has been held, in practice almost all delinquency cases and some cases that originally involve neglect charges fall within the scope of the Gault ruling.

[10]McKeiver v. Pennsylvania, 403 U.S. 528 (1971).

nesses testify under oath or affirmation and are subject to interrogation. The state is represented by an attorney, who examines and cross-examines witnesses. In accordance with the ruling in the *Gault* case, the child and his parents must be given sufficient notice of the charges, be advised of their right to counsel or, if they are unable to afford counsel, to have one appointed for them, be permitted to confront and cross-examine witnesses, and be protected against self-incrimination. In cases where the juvenile is charged with an act that would constitute a crime if committed by an adult, the adjudication of delinquency requires the same standards of proof as that used in the criminal court, that is, proof beyond a reasonable doubt.[11] In other kinds of delinquency cases, however, this standard varies, but almost always it is less than proof beyond a reasonable doubt.

However, despite these changes in the procedure of the juvenile court, privacy still characterizes most hearings, only persons who are definitely connected with the case being permitted to attend. When newspaper reporters are admitted, they are usually requested to refrain from using names or otherwise making the juvenile publicly identifiable. Few appeals are made from the decisions of the juvenile court, although the right of appeal in one form or another is available in most jurisdictions. The Supreme Court, however, in the *Gault* case, refused to include the right to appeal among the fundamental due process rights of juveniles.

DISPOSITION OF CASES

If a separate hearing is held for the disposition of a case, it is much more informal than the adjudicatory hearing. Although the Supreme Court has not extended the right to counsel to this stage of the juvenile court process, other courts have tended to do so.[12] When the defense attorney is present, he and the child's parents, along with the judge, the prosecutor, the probation officer, and any others who may be directly concerned in the case, enter into an informal discussion about its disposition. In arriving at his decision, the judge relies to a great extent on the social history, or predisposition, report, which the probation officer prepares after he has made a study of the physical

---

[11]*In re Winship*, 397 U.S. 358, 90 S.Ct. 1068 (1970).
[12]Fox, pp. 197, 198.

and mental conditions of the child and his social background and development.[13] Unfortunately, however, the inadequacy of personnel and excessive case loads often prevent this report from being more than a superficial inquiry.

Since most jurisdictions give the judge broad discretionary powers, usually he may hand down one of a variety of decisions. He may, for example, dismiss the case, warn the juvenile, fine him, place him on probation, arrange for restitution, refer him to a social agency, clinic, or hospital, put him in a foster or group home, commit him to an institution, or, perhaps, combine some of these possibilities. Nevertheless, despite some progress in the field of corrections, most juvenile courts are limited to only three realistic choices: outright dismissal, probation under perfunctory supervision, or commitment to an outmoded state institution. Usually, the length of institutional commitment is indefinite, but in most states it cannot extend beyond the juvenile's twenty-first birthday. Thus the period of institutionalization may be long, but in the opinion of many authorities, it should not be more than three years, unless a longer term is deemed necessary for the promotion of the child's welfare or the protection of the community's interests.

About ten states authorize their juvenile courts to commit juveniles directly to institutions for adult offenders. In addition, about a third of the states permit a child who has already been committed to an institution for juvenile delinquents by a juvenile court to be transferred administratively to an institution for adults who have been convicted of a crime. The United States Children's Bureau and other similar organizations, however, oppose the commitment or transfer of juveniles to adult correctional institutions. They contend that juvenile delinquency is legal status created by a juvenile court through the use of a noncriminal procedure, during which the child is denied certain legal rights guaranteed to the adult in a criminal trial. Therefore, they argue, the juvenile should not be

---

[13]Some authorities argue that the child and his counsel—and sometimes other interested persons—should have access to this report, explaining that this would act as a check on its accuracy and fairness and contribute to an understanding and acceptance of the disposition of the case. The majority of probation officers and legal experts, however, favor the confidentiality of the predisposition report, contending that the guarantees of due process end with the adjudication of the child as a delinquent, and that disclosure tends to dry up the sources of information and may unnecessarily disturb, confuse, and antagonize the child and thus hamper the treatment process.

treated as if he were an adult offender unless he is first given a trial in a criminal court.

The structure and function of the agencies which administer services and facilities for delinquent children vary as much as do those of the juvenile courts. This leads to much confusion, duplication, and ineffectiveness. One plan that has been developed to improve the situation—a plan already adopted by many states—vests the responsibility for the administration and expansion of a state's control and treatment program in a single state agency to which all children in need of care are committed.[14]

COOPERATION WITH OTHER AGENCIES

The success of the juvenile court depends in great part on the work of other agencies, such as the police, schools, clinics, churches, welfare organizations, and correctional institutions; in turn, it can contribute significantly to their success. Obviously, then, the court should play an important part in promoting greater coordination among the law enforcement and welfare agencies of the community and in the establishment of a delinquency prevention program. Some courts have taken steps to do this, coordinating their work with the efforts of other agencies, but many have done very little to foster this relationship.[15]

CRITICISMS OF THE JUVENILE COURT

Since the establishment of the juvenile court over seventy-five years ago, it has been severely criticized by both its friends and its enemies.[16] For example, in 1967, the President's Commission on Law Enforcement and Administration of Justice—certainly not an enemy of the court—felt compelled to conclude that juvenile courts had failed to achieve their goals. The following are three of the most important criticisms that have been directed against the court:

1. It does not deal effectively with juvenile delinquency. Various statistical attempts have been made to measure the effectiveness of the

---

[14]Caldwell and Black, pp. 209, 210.

[15]Ibid., p. 210.

[16]For a more complete analysis of these criticisms, see Caldwell and Black, pp. 211-20. See also The President's Commission on Law Enforcement and Administration of Justice, pp. 7-9.

court, but these have been inconclusive. Actually, nobody knows how effective the juvenile court has been, but even so, most observers continue to support it, and few of its enemies have the temerity to advocate its abolition. Furthermore, if we are to understand the problems of the court, we must remember (1) that it is only one part of a very complex culture, with which it is inextricably and functionally related; (2) that no systematic science of human behavior exists; (3) that there is no way of determining the extent to which influences other than that of the court affect the behavior of juveniles after they have been handled by it; (4) that even the "biggest" and "best" court could do little to change or control the conditions that are causing crime and delinquency; and (5) that the court is competing for appropriations that are urgently needed elsewhere.

2. Certain types of cases should not be handled by the court. As educational facilities and child welfare services have developed throughout the country, there has come an increasing demand that truancy, neglect, and dependency cases be taken from the court and placed under the jurisdiction of the schools and welfare agencies. Undoubtedly, some of the work of the court can be reduced in this way. However, since most schools and welfare agencies are already carrying heavy loads and since delinquency, neglect, and dependency are often closely interwoven, this change will have to be effected on a local basis through the development of greater cooperation among all agencies and institutions.

Other critics of the court have argued that the cases of older juveniles charged with serious crimes, such as murder, manslaughter, rape, and robbery should not be dealt with in the juvenile court but should be tried in the criminal court. In fact, many states now have laws giving the criminal court either original or exclusive jurisdiction over such cases. Opponents of this proposal have branded it as reactionary and in violation of the philosophy of the court. Nevertheless, no court can exist apart from the community in which it functions and to which it must look for support. Certainly, for the court to try to ignore the deep feelings and strong desires of the people, whose values it is called upon to enforce, would be highly unrealistic and arbitrary.

5. The court does not protect the rights of the child and his parents. On this point, criticism has been directed especially against (1) broad and vague definitions of delinquency, (2) unofficial handling of cases, (3) prehearing investigations, and (4) extreme informality of procedure. In general, these have been defended by the

claim that they facilitate preventive and nonpunitive action by the court. Opponents, however, have contended that they channel an increasing number of children who do not have serious problems into courts which, by general admission, are overloaded, understaffed, and inadequately equipped for preventive work. They have contended also that the rights of the child and his parents are endangered because often there is no attorney to guard against the abuse of authority, no rule to ward off hearsay and gossip, no way of breaking through the secrecy of the hearing, and no appeal from the court's decision.

Eventually, the controversy over the juvenile court reached the Supreme Court of the United States. That Court responded by handing down important decisions in the Kent,[17] Gault, and Winship cases, all of which were intended to provide greater protection for the rights of the child and his parents. The impact of these decisions on the operation of the juvenile court has considerably reduced the criticism that it does not protect the rights of those who appear before it, but the other two criticisms are still being strongly advanced.

PROPOSAL FOR STRENGTHENING THE COURT

There has been much debate about how the juvenile courts can improve their staffs, lower their case loads, and reduce their other operational problems, but most students of the court are in agreement on certain steps that can be taken to accomplish this. Thus, many communities can and should spend more money on their courts, and others should use their present expenditures more effectively. Many courts should have judges who are better trained in both the law and the social sciences, larger jurisdictional areas, and a stronger position in their state's judicial system so that their judgeships will enjoy a

---

[17]Kent v. United States, 383 U.S., 541, 86 S.Ct. 1045 (1966). The Supreme Court in the Kent case decided that the juvenile court of the District of Columbia, in waiving its jurisdiction and ordering Kent held for trial in the criminal court, had not measured up to the essentials of due process and fair treatment. In order to do so, the Court ruled, the juvenile court, as a condition to a valid waiver order, must grant the child these rights: (1) a full hearing on the issue of transfer to an adult court; (2) the assistance of counsel at such a hearing; (3) full access to social records used to determine whether transfer should be made; and (4) a statement of the reasons why the juvenile court judge has decided to waive jurisdiction. Although the Kent decision applied only to the District of Columbia, it called into question waiver procedures in juvenile courts everywhere in the United States.

higher status in the eyes of the bar. All courts should closely coordinate their operations with those of welfare and law enforcement agencies. And everywhere the public should be told more about the court and encouraged to support its work.

However, there are also major philosophical and legal problems that are troubling the juvenile court, and about the solution of these there is much less agreement. It is to these problems and some proposals regarding them that we now turn our attention.

PHILOSOPHY OF THE COURT

The juvenile court was established as a court, albeit a special one, and in nature, function, and procedure it remains essentially a court. Therefore, efforts should be made to strengthen its true, or judicial, nature and to retain and develop only that part of its social service function that is necessary for the administration of individualized justice. No court, not even the juvenile court, can be just a therapeutic agency. It is, and must be, a moral agency as well. Like all courts, it must try to balance the interests of the individual and society in the administration of its cases. And when a child is adjudicated a delinquent by the court, he is, and of necessity must be, stigmatized as a violator of the moral values of his society. In fact, the court must act in this way if it is to promote the rehabilitation of the child. If it did otherwise, it would flout the very values to which the child must learn to adjust and for which he must develop a loyalty. The action of the court involves both public condemnation of antisocial conduct and the imposition of unpleasant consequences by political authority— the two essential elements of punishment. It is, therefore, highly unrealistic to say that the juvenile court treats but does not punish. What it really does is to emphasize treatment in a correctional process which includes, and of necessity must include, both treatment and punishment.[18]

This view of the philosophy of the juvenile court is superior to that which is generally accepted for several important reasons. First, it clearly recognizes the necessity of balancing the interests of both the delinquent and the community in the process of "individualized

---

[18]The first juvenile court law did not stipulate that juvenile delinquents should be "treated" and not punished. It merely provided that the child should receive approximately the same care, custody, and discipline that his parents should give him.

justice." Second, it provides a practical basis of action which can be accepted without conflict by both law enforcement officers and court personnel. Third, by honestly admitting that the court must not only treat but also punish, it dispels the cloud of hypocrisy that envelopes the juvenile court and gives the court a position in society where it can be respected by all law-abiding citizens. Finally, by revealing the true nature of the court, it brings the possibility of the abuse of power out into the open where it can be clearly understood and effectively controlled.

JURISDICTION OF THE COURT

The jurisdiction of the juvenile court should be limited to (1) delinquency cases, and (2) those dependency and neglect cases in which a decision must be made affecting the legal status of the child, his custody, or the rights of his parents. All other dependency and neglect cases should be handled by administrative agencies without court action, and truancy should be dealt with by the schools. Juvenile delinquency should be defined as a violation of a state law or city or town ordinance by a child whose act would be a crime if committed by an adult.[19] This simple, specific definition eliminates all references to such vague conditions as "being ungovernable" or "growing up in idleness" which clutter up our statutes on delinquency and invite loose interpretation and abuse of authority, and it also prevents the court from moving into areas where other agencies can render more effective service.

The juvenile court should have original and exclusive jurisdiction over all children between the ages of seven and eighteen who are alleged to be delinquent, except in cases where a child is charged with a minor traffic offense or where a child of sixteen or over is charged with a serious felony, such as murder, armed robbery, or rape. In the cases involving minor traffic offenses, there is no need of special handling. They can be adequately dealt with by a police or traffic court, and thus the burden on the juvenile court can be reduced.

In cases where children sixteen or over are charged with serious felonies, the criminal court should have original jurisdiction but with

---

[19]In the first juvenile court law, a juvenile delinquent was simply defined as "any child under the age of 16 years who violates any law of this State or any city or village ordinance." It was not until later that this simple definition was modified to include other types of behavior which are illegal only for children.

authority to transfer such cases to the juvenile court if, in the opinion of the judge, this would be in the best interests of the child and the community. The criminal court should have the authority to act first in these cases, because it, more than the juvenile court, is held responsible for the security of society and the protection of the moral code and is organized and administered especially for this purpose. This point is particularly important, since a large and increasing percentage of serious crimes are being committed by young people. Thus, the handling of these young offenders in the juvenile court—a court which is not primarily concerned with the public sense of justice and security—will make the criminal law increasingly inoperative and cause additional confusion regarding our code of morality and the importance of rigorous law enforcement.

The case of an adult charged with an offense against a child should be handled not in the juvenile court but in the criminal court. This will place this type of case in a court better designed to assure protection of all fundamental rights in a criminal proceeding and will help the public to understand that the juvenile court is a special court for children and in no sense of the word a criminal court.

PROCEDURE OF THE COURT

Through its intake procedures, the juvenile court should carefully screen all cases brought to its attention so as to eliminate those that do not require the attention of the court or any other agency and to insure the referral of as many other cases as possible to agencies that are better equipped to provide curative and preventive treatment. The intake procedure is essentially an office, and not a field, procedure. It involves a review or evaluation of information which should be supplied by the person or agency seeking to file a petition, and thus should be distinguished from the investigation of the case, which seeks to discover the causative factors in the child's behavior and to develop a plan of correction. In order for a case to be accepted for action by the court, the intake procedure should show that the court has jurisdiction and that there is sufficient evidence to justify the filing of a petition, but it should not be used to dispose of cases unofficially.

The cases that are accepted by the court should receive official handling. If a case is not in need of official handling, it should not be handled by the court at all but should be referred to some other agency. Too often unofficial handling is merely the haphazard, ineffective disposition of cases by understaffed, overloaded courts, which is justified under the guise of avoiding the "delinquency tag."

The court should establish the fact of delinquency in a case before an investigation of the case is made. Prehearing investigations are not only an encroachment upon the rights of the child who has not yet been proved delinquent, but also costly in time, energy, and money in the cases of those who are discharged as not delinquent.

The procedure during the hearings of the court should be as informal as possible but based upon sufficient rules to insure justice and consistency. The child and his parents should be fully informed regarding their legal rights. These should include representation by their own or appointed counsel, adequate notification of the charges, confrontation and cross-examination of hostile witnesses, the summoning of witnesses in the child's defense, protection against irrelevant and hearsay testimony and compulsory self-incrimination,[20] a hearing before a jury if this is desired,[21] proof of delinquency beyond a reasonable doubt,[22] and access to a higher court for the purpose of an appeal.

DISPOSITION OF CASES

The disposition of the case should be made by the judge after a study of the predisposition report and consultation with the probation officer and other specialists who have worked on the case. However, simply because the judge must turn to specialists for assistance in his disposition of the case does not mean that it might be better to have the disposition made entirely by a panel of "experts." To do this would fragmentize the facts and dilute the sense of responsibility and

---

[20]The *Gault* decision already guarantees the child representation by counsel, adequate notification of the charges, confrontation and cross-examination of hostile witnesses, and protection against self-incrimination in all cases which may result in commitment to an institution.

[21]The first juvenile court law provided that any interested party might demand, or the judge might order, a jury of six to try the case.

[22]The *Winship* decision already requires that a juvenile must be found delinquent beyond a reasonable doubt if he is charged with an act which would constitute a crime if committed by an adult.

thus disrupt the process by which a creative and integrated decision in the case is achieved.[23]

These proposals seek to strip away the excrescenses that interfere with the expression of the true nature of the juvenile court, but they leave it with all the characteristics which are essential to its functioning and growth. It is recognized that not all of the proposals can immediately be put into effect everywhere. It is believed, however, that they do represent desirable goals toward which all juvenile courts should be directed so that they will become more effective agencies of social control.

ADOLESCENT AND FAMILY COURTS

Since the juvenile court was established in 1899, it has exerted an increasing influence on the principles and methods used in the handling of juvenile and adult offenders. Evidence of this influence, for example, is to be found in the movement to create special courts for adolescents, some of which have been established in such large cities as Chicago, Philadelphia, and New York. In general, the movement to establish such courts represents an attempt to combine some of the principles and methods of the juvenile court with certain features of the criminal court in proceedings against youthful offenders who are above the juvenile court age but below the age of twenty-one and who, it is claimed, are in need of specialized treatment, because they have the peculiar problems of adolescence.

The influence of the juvenile court has been shown also in the creation of special courts with jurisdiction over cases involving all kinds of family problems, such as delinquency, neglect, desertion, adoption, illegitimacy, nonsupport, alimony, divorce, separation, annulment, crimes by members of a family against one another, and commitment of an adult alleged to be mentally ill or defective. Thus, these courts, the first real one of which was established in Cincinnati in 1914, are really juvenile courts with extended jurisdiction, and where they are now operating, they are usually called family courts or courts of domestic relations.

---

[23]These proposals are adapted in part from Caldwell, "The Juvenile Court: Its Development and Some Major Problems."

CHAPTER XIV

THE SUPREME COURT
AND THE CONSTITUTION[1]

EXTENSION OF FEDERAL POWERS

The Constitution of the United States provides the political foundation for our form of government. Delegating certain powers to the federal government, it reserves many more to the states, including the police power for the protection of such matters as the health, morality, safety, and security of our communities. The growing tendency, however, has been to extend the powers of the federal government and to restrict those of the states, and the decisions of the Supreme Court have contributed significantly to this development.

Many years ago, a President of the United States, recognizing the great power that might be exerted by the Supreme Court in the operation of our government, made this searching statement: "The candid citizen must confess that if the policy of the government, upon vital questions affecting the whole people, is to be irrevocably fixed by decisions of the Supreme Court, the instant they are made, in ordinary litigation between parties in personal actions, the people will have ceased to be their own rulers, having to that extent practically resigned their government into the hands of that eminent tribunal."[2]

These words from President Lincoln's *First Inaugural Address* have been frequently quoted during the past few decades—and for good reason. The great expansion of the powers of the United States Supreme Court and its persistent intrusion into the affairs of the states and local communities have caused many citizens to have serious

---

[1]The material in this chapter and the next one is taken from the article "The Supreme Court and Law Enforcement," by Robert G. Caldwell, which appeared in the June, 1975, issue of the *Journal of Police Science and Administration*. It is published here in its present form with the permission of that journal.

[2]*The Speeches of Abraham Lincoln, Including Inaugurals and Proclamations* (New York: Lincoln Centenary Association, 1908). p. 316.

misgivings and, like Lincoln, to ponder on a proper role of the Court in the life of the nation.

Law enforcement is one of the important aspects of our national life that have been increasingly affected by the Supreme Court's interpretation of the Constitution. Therefore, it is easy to appreciate how important it is for the student of law enforcement to understand how and to what extent this has happened and to judge the effects in the light of the fundamental principles upon which our form of government was founded.

PRINCIPLES OF FEDERAL GOVERNMENT

Five of these principles are clearly evident in the work of the Founding Fathers. The *first* of these is that *the federal government is a creature of the states.* Evidence of this is not difficult to find. For example, turn to the concluding paragraph of the Declaration of Independence. You will see there these words: "That these United Colonies are, and of Right ought to be, Free and Independent States." Note, as Kilpatrick explains, the colonies were not to become one state or one nation but were to retain their identities as states; and, working together as separate and independent units, with sovereign rights and powers, they were in this way to form a union.[3]

Now look at the second article of the *Articles of Confederation* and read these words: "Each State retains its sovereignty, freedom and independence, and every power, jurisdiction and right, which is not by this confederation expressly delegated to the United States, in Congress assembled." Here again is evidence that the federal government, which was eventually established, was created by the sovereign states.

Finally, let us remember that the Constitution of the United States was ratified, not by a popular referendum submitted to all the people without regard to their state citizenship, but by the citizens of *each state* acting independently of what the citizens of the other states might do. Thus, they acted to form a more perfect *union of states*, not peoples. By June 21, 1788, the required nine out of the thirteen states

---

[3]James Jackson Kilpatrick, *The Sovereign States* (Chicago: Henry Regnery Company, 1957), p. 5. Some of the ideas on the fundamental principles of our form of government have been taken from this book, and full credit is here given to its author.

had ratified it,[4] and the new federal government was established at New York on April 30, 1789. If the other four states had decided not to accept the Constitution, they might possibly have continued their existence as separate and independent states down to the present day. In fact, Rhode Island did not ratify the Constitution until May 29, 1790, which was almost two years after the last of the required nine states had acted favorably—and then by the close vote of 34 to 32 in its state convention.

Thus, the evidence—only a portion of which has been mentioned here—conclusively shows that the federal government is a creature of the *states*, not of the people, and it was created by the states to enable them to work together *as states* in more effectively handling some of their problems. It is not surprising, then, that prominent public figures have repeatedly emphasized this fact since the very beginnings of the Republic.[5]

The *second* principle is that *the federal government is a government of delegated powers.* As we have already seen, the states, in creating the federal government, did not invest it with all powers but only those that were necessary for the functioning of the new union. Even John Marshall, who did so much to strengthen the powers of the federal government and weaken those of the states, clearly recognized the basic structure of divided powers.[6]

In the famous case of *McCulloch v. Maryland*,[7] Marshall stated: "No political dreamer was ever wild enough to think of breaking down the lines which separate the States, and of compounding the American people into one common mass. Of consequence, when they act, they act in their States."

And later in the same case, he said: "This government is acknowledged by all to be one of enumerated powers. The principle, that it can exercise only the powers granted to it, would seem too apparent to have required to be enforced by all those arguments which its enlightened friends, while it was depending before the people,

---

[4]The ratification of the conventions of nine states was sufficient for the establishment of the Constitution "between the States so ratifying the same." *The Constitution of the United States*, Article VII.

[5]See Kilpatrick, pp. 5,6.

[6]Ibid., pp. 32,33.

[7]This case involved the question of whether Maryland might levy a tax on the Baltimore branch of the Bank of the United States. See *McCulloch v. Maryland*, 4 Wheaton 316, 403 (1819).

found it necessary to urge. That principle is now universally admitted."

The principle of delegated powers in the field of criminal law was early recognized, and no act can be punished as a federal crime merely because it was a common-law crime. This was so held in 1812, by the United States Supreme Court in *United States v. Hudson and Goodwin*.[8] To be a federal crime, therefore, a misdeed must be so defined by an act of Congress. A state, on the other hand, has the power to punish a common-law crime even if it has no statute defining the act in question as a crime. Here, then, we have an example of the inherent powers of the states, as contrasted with the delegated powers of the federal government. Thus, the states, as administered by their citizens, were deemed to be *the real reservoirs of power in our republic*.

The *third* of the principles which we are examining is that *the federal government is a government of limited powers*. Every delegate in the Constitutional Convention of 1787 vividly remembered the grave abuses of political power which had led to the American Revolution and clearly recognized that *government from a distance* tended to separate itself from the people and to ignore or suppress their rights. Therefore, definite steps were taken to prevent such dangers from arising under the new federal system. Important among these was the adoption of the first ten amendments to the Constitution—the so-called Bill of Rights—which clearly impose specific limits upon the delegated powers of the federal government, in order to protect the rights of the people and the powers of the states.

These limits are firmly and finally fixed by the last two amendments of the Bill of Rights. Notice the wording of the Ninth: "The enumeration in the Constitution, of certain rights, shall not be construed to deny or disparage others retained by the people." Now add to this the stipulation of the Tenth: "The powers not delegated to the United States by the Constitution, nor prohibited by it to the States, are reserved to the States respectively, or to the people." Thus, it is clear that there was to be no doubt about the specific and binding nature of the limits imposed upon the federal government. It is clear, too, that the limits in the Bill of Rights were not intended in any way to apply to the states. Furthermore, the final power of constitutional amendment was lodged in the *states as states*—and not in a mere majority of the states but rather in no fewer than three-fourths of them.

However, despite the precautions taken by the Founding Fathers,

---

[8]See *United States v. Hudson and Goodwin*, 7 Cranch 32 (1812).

the Supreme Court, in recent years, has endeavored to repeal the Tenth Amendment by treating it as "a meaningless appendage to the Constitution—mere surplusage, a tautological expression of self-evident facts."[9] In 1931, for example, the Supreme Court asserted that the Tenth Amendment added nothing to the Constitution as originally ratified,[10] and ten years later, Chief Justice Stone said that the amendment "states but a truism."[11] But such statements by the Supreme Court cannot stand up in the face of the evidence. The states believed that the Tenth Amendment was vitally important, and that its addition to the Constitution was absolutely necessary in order to show that the delegated powers of the federal government were strictly limited and that the states intended to retain most of their inherent powers.

Furthermore, the Supreme Court does not have the authority to repeal any part of the Constitution. So eminent a member of the Supreme Court as Justice Frankfurter strongly emphasized this as recently as 1956, when he said: "Nothing new can be put into the Constitution except through the amendatory process. Nothing old can be taken out without the same process."[12] There can be no doubt, then, that as long as the Tenth Amendment, or any other provision of the Constitution, remains a part of that document, it must be given its full meaning, and the intentions of its authors must be granted proper respect.

The *fourth* principle is that *the federal government is a government of distributed powers.* With the establishment of this principle another step was taken to protect the rights of the people and the powers of the states. The totality of the federal power was distributed among the legislative, executive, and judicial branches of the government. Each received defined authority and functions, so that the power of any one branch would be checked and balanced by that of the other branches and prevented from becoming absolute and despotic. Moreover, this idea was introduced into the operation of each branch of government and even into that of each department and bureau. For example, the House was balanced against the Senate in the legislative branch, officials were chosen in different ways for

---

[9]Kilpatrick, p. 46.

[10]*United States v. Sprague*, 282 U.S. 716 (1931).

[11]*United States v. Darby*, 312 U.S. 100 (1941).

[12]*Ullmann v. United States*, 350 U.S. 428 (1955). This case was argued on December 6, 1955, and decided on March 26, 1956.

different terms, and often one official could not take action without the consent of two or more other officials. And each state likewise distributed its powers among the branches of its government and provided for strong local self-government.

In this way, there was created a comprehensive *system of checks and balances,* which was based on the belief that if each branch of government is given only a small part of governmental power, no one branch will become dangerous. This system and the limitation of federal powers—often referred to as the separation of powers and states' rights—became the two great principles of federalism. Indeed, they form an indispensable part of the very foundation of our constitutional government.

The *fifth* of the principles to which we have referred is that *the federal government is a republic.* This means that the people rule through their representatives—not directly as in a democracy. In fact, the word "democracy" is not even mentioned in the Constitution, and this was done deliberately, for the Founding Fathers recognized the instability of a democracy—especially one that was to operate on a large scale—and its tendency to degenerate into a dictatorship. Accordingly, suffrage was not to be granted by the federal government to all the people, but instead it was to be within the control of the states and regulated in terms of such criteria as age, sex, residence, literacy, and so on. Moreover, the President was not to be elected by popular vote but by electors chosen by the states, each state being entitled to as many electors as it had senators and representatives in the Congress, and each state, regardless of the size of its population, was to be represented in the Congress by two senators. In addition, the principle of republican government was extended to the states through Article IV of the Constitution, which declares, "The United States shall guarantee to every State in this Union a Republican Form of Government . . ."[13]

Thus, the fundamental principles of our form of government provide for a federal union of sovereign states organized into a republic, with the federal government having delegated, limited, and distributed powers.

---

[13]These provisions certainly provide no justification for the one-man-one-vote rule recently forced on the states by the United States Supreme Court.

Reasons for the Principles

You are probably saying to yourself, "Why were so much effort and ingenuity expended in creating such a complicated and finely balanced structure of government?" Two important reasons for this strongly motivated the leaders in American political life. In the first place, they remembered the tyrannical abuse of power by the kings of England, especially that by the Stuarts, and the more recent arrogance and arbitrary action of George III, which had shocked and angered them. They were determined, therefore, to do everything that they could to prevent accretion of excessive power in the hands of a central government. In fact, if there was one emotion that animated all the members of the Constitutional Convention of 1787, it was the fear of concentrated power. That their fear was well founded has been amply demonstrated by the events of recent history.

This, then, was one reason why the Founding Fathers built the way that they did. The second reason is to be found in their conviction that the country was too large to have all its affairs regulated and directed by one government. Believing that diversity of geographical, economic, religious, and political problems called for a variety of governments at the different levels of the political structure, they provided for strong state and local governments and in this way placed political power close to the people. This arrangement not only makes possible quick and effective consideration of the needs of the people, but also encourages the people to participate in public affairs and to engage in desirable testing, innovation, and refinement in the political processes. Thus, each state, in effect, becomes a separate laboratory for experimenting in self-government. To the extent that the states and the local communities are discouraged in the use of their powers in this regard, the vitality of the federal union as a whole is undermined, and the freedom and the sense of responsibility of the people are enfeebled.[14]

CHANGING THE PRINCIPLES

There are two general approaches to the interpretation of the Constitution of the United States. These are the strict constructionist

---

[14]Virginia Commission on Constitutional Government, We the States (Richmond, Va.: The William Byrd Press, Inc., 1964), pp. XXII-XXIX.

approach and the activist approach. The strict constructionist approach insists that there should be a strict adherence to the authoritatively established meanings that words had when they were written in the Constitution and the Amendments. The activist approach, on the other hand, contends that the spirit, and not the letter, of the Constitution and the Amendments should be emphasized. Therefore, assert the activists, the Constitution and the Amendments should be interpreted and reinterpreted so as to keep them continuously meaningful and adaptable with respect to changing social conditions and to give full recognition to what the Court determines to be the intent of those who drafted them. This should be done even if new meaning must be read into the words that the drafters used.

In the light of the principles that we have been discussing, let us now consider what the Supreme Court has done during the past few decades. In a series of landmark decisions—and in disregard of its own long-established precedents—it has used the Fourteenth Amendment, say the strict constructionists, to change the fundamental principles upon which our form of government was founded.[15] Pulling the provisions of the Bill of Rights through the "due-process clause" of that Amendment, it has applied them to the states and then declared—and this for the first time in its history—that its interpretation of the Fourteenth Amendment is the *supreme law of the land* instead of the *law of the case*, which has been the widely accepted view regarding the decisions of the Supreme Court.[16] According to the Court, therefore, any decision that it hands down is to be considered final and binding with respect to the provision of the Constitution in question, not only on the litigants in the case but also on the other branches of government and on all officials, at least until such time as the Court may change its view on the subject. In this work of the Court, protest the strict constructionists, each decision along a certain line has been used as a precedent for the next one that has come before it, and so the Court has moved our government farther

---

[15]Although this discussion will stress the past few decades and will refer especially to the field of law enforcement, the fundamental changing of the Constitution, which the strict constructionists allege has taken place, did not begin with the Warren Court. Previous Supreme Courts, by numerous decisions affecting many fields, had already prepared the way for the great changes wrought by the Warren Court.

Hereafter, those who advocate the strict constructionist approach will be referred to as strict constructionists, and those who support the activist approach will be called activists.

and farther away from the original principles of the Founding Fathers. Therefore, in our appraisal of the Court, assert the strict constructionists, we should *not* ask, "Is there a precedent?" but rather, "Are we going in the right direction?"

However, advocates of the expanding power of the Supreme Court, that is, the activists, have hailed its work as a great crusade to establish equal and uniform rights for the friendless, the poor, and the so-called minority groups throughout the United States. According to their view, the United States Supreme Court has a clear duty to keep the Constitution a viable and continuously meaningful instrument with respect to changing conditions, because that document not only created our form of government but also provides the basic law for the regulation of our governmental activities. But, declare the strict constructionists, such a view of the Court must be carefully examined. What the Court is really doing is contributing to the centralization of power in Washington to such an extent that it is jeopardizing the very rights that it contends it is protecting. In fact, the strict constructionists claim, we already have a federal government of *delegating* powers instead of *delegated* powers and are thus operating in violation of the original purpose of the Constitution. Does this dismay the activists? "Of courst not," they reply. Instead, they insist that the old concept of the Supreme Court as a tribunal to interpret the Constitution is old-fashioned, and that the Court must now be seen as an agency for the stimulation and guidance of social change.

In other words, contend the strict constructionists, what the Court has become in effect is a coterie of ideologists who are using the Constitution to reach their desired goals—the end justifying the means—and are thus imposing their philosophy upon millions of

---

[16]See *Cooper v. Aaron*, 358 U.S. 1, 18 (1958).

It is important to understand clearly the distinction between the statement that the Supreme Court's interpretation of the Constitution is the *supreme law of the land* and one that merely says that such an interpretation is the *law of the case.* Unlike the former, the latter means that the interpretation of the Constitution is the business of Congress, the President, and the states, no less than that of the Supreme Court, and that a challenged statute may be reenacted or even that a branch of the government or an official may act on the basis of a different opinion. For example, the President may instruct his Attorney General to prosecute under a statute which the Court has declared unconstitutional, although the Supreme Court may persist in its view and reverse later convictions and again strike down reenacted statutes. See L. Brent Bozell, *The Warren Revolution* (New Rochelle, N.Y.: Arlington House, 1966), pp. 115-20.

people, sometimes by a single vote. And all this, the Justices argue, is necessary to advance the interests of the "common man," but, continue the strict constructionists, as anyone who has read history knows, tyranny often rides to power on the back of the "common man."

If the Supreme Court, contend the strict constructionists, is no longer a court, then its members should not be granted the respect and security that judges enjoy and thereby be afforded the opportunity to legislate behind a judicial facade, but instead they should be compelled to step down sometimes from the bench and submit themselves to the people for election. Certainly a small group of appointed judges, who are not required by the Constitution, over which they now preside, to meet any qualifications for office, should not be endowed with plenary power and permitted to sit as a permanent constitutional convention for the rewriting of the Constitution, and, as some writers insist, all the while be free from criticism.

How has the Court been able to change the fundamental principles of our form of government despite the painstaking efforts of the Founding Fathers? According to the strict constructionists, three undermining methods used by the Court to accomplish this are especially worthy of our attention.[17] The first of these consists simply of lifting a clause or provision out of the Constitution and giving it an interpretation apart from its relationship to the rest of the document. The Court has repeatedly done this, even though any novice in the study of the law knows that one part of a document must be construed in connection with all the other parts of that document. The result, say the strict constructionists, has been that the "interstate-commerce clause," the "due-process clause," and other such parts of the Constitution have been stretched far beyond the intent of the Founding Fathers, the Ninth and Tenth Amendments have been virtually nullified, and the Constitution has been torn to pieces to suit the current philosophy of the justices.

Sometimes this twisting of words to suit the wishes of the Court and the piling of one distorting interpretation upon another have so shocked one of the Justices of the Court that he has spoken out in protest. So it happened in the 1970 case of *Coleman v. Alabama,* 399 U.S. 1 (1970), which held that a preliminary hearing may be a critical stage of the criminal proceeding at which the Sixth Amendment

---

[17]Usually two or more of the undermining methods have been used together by the Court in order to construct a decision in any one case.

requires counsel. In a dissenting opinion, Chief Justice Burger asserted that not a word in the Constitution itself either requires or contemplates the result reached. And then later in his opinion, one finds these very significant words: "By placing a premium on 'recent cases' rather than on the language of the Constitution, the Court makes it dangerously simple for future Courts, using the technique of interpretation, to operate as a 'continuing Constitutional Convention.' "

The second undermining method used by the Court, explain the strict constructionists, involves the disregard of the original meanings of the words and phrases of the Constitution and the substitution of other meanings more acceptable to the Justices. This, for example, has been done in the interpretation of the first section of the Fourteenth Amendment, which forbids a state to abridge a citizen's privileges or immunities, to deprive any person of due process of law, or to deny to any person the equal protection of the law.[18]

Although some of the fundamental ideas contained in the Bill of Rights were embodied in the first section of the Fourteenth Amendment, the Supreme Court, point out the strict constructionists, after decades of judicial review, failed to find any reason why it should use this amendment as a basis for applying the provisions of the Bill of Rights to the states.[19] In other words, the Court rejected what has become known as the "shorthand doctrine," which maintains that the Fourteenth Amendment is a shorthand summary of the first eight amendments, and that because of this, they are applicable to the states.

In fact, as recently as 1947, the Court, in its majority opinion in the *Adamson* case,[20] declared: "Nothing has been called to our attention that either the framers of the Fourteenth Amendment or the states that adopted it intended its due process clause to draw within its scope the earlier amendments to the Constitution." Justice Frankfurter wrote a concurring opinion in this case, and in explaining his rejection of the "shorthand doctrine," he said: "Between the incorpo-

---

[18]For a critical analysis of the use of this method in the so-called school segregation cases, see Virginia Commission on Constitutional Government, pp. 321-63.

[19]For a summary of the Supreme Court's interpretation of the first section of theFourteenth Amendment as of 1939, see Henry Rottschaefer, *Handbook of American Constitutional Law* (St. Paul,Minn.,: West Publishing Co., 1939), Chs. 14, 15.

[20]*Adamson v. California*, 332 U.S. 46 (1947).

ration of the Fourteenth Amendment into the Constitution and the beginning of the present membership of the Court—a period of 70 years—the scope of that Amendment was passed upon by 43 judges. Of all these judges only one, who may respectfully called an eccentric exception, ever indicated the belief that the Fourteenth Amendment was a shorthand summary of the first eight Amendments theretofore limiting only the Federal Government, and that due process incorporated those eight Amendments as restrictions upon the powers of the states."

On the other hand, in some cases the Court did apply certain provisions of the Bill of Rights to the states through the Fourteenth Amendment by using the "fundamental rights" theory. According to this theory, certain rights are protected against state invasion, because they are "fundamental rights" and not because they happen also to be contained in the Bill of Rights.[21] But it should not be assumed, warn the strict constructionists, that the "fundamental rights" theory necessarily imposes greater restrictions on the expansion of the powers of the Supreme Court than does the "shorthand doctrine." Although many of the proponents of the "fundamental rights" theory would exercise judicial restraint in its application, some would utilize it to destroy virtually all the powers of the states. Thus, explain the strict constructionists, the undermining methods may be used with either of these views regarding the meaning of the Fourteenth Amendment.[22]

During the past few decades, however, the Court has spurned any limited view of the Fourteenth Amendment. Abandoning the "fundamental rights" theory, it has applied most of the Bill of Rights to the States and infused the provisions of the Fourteenth Amendment with new meanings.[23] As a result, argue the strict constructionists, the

---

[21]John C. Klotter and Jacqueline R. Kanovitz, *Constitutional Law for Police* (Cincinnati: The W. W. Anderson Co., 1968), pp. 21, 22.

[22]For a brief discussion of some of the views regarding the meaning of the Fourteenth Amendment, see Jerold H. Israel and Wayne R. Lafave, *Criminal Procedure in a Nutshell* (St. Paul, Minn.: West Publishing Company, 1971), pp. 4-25.

[23]Justice Harlan, however, continued to disagree with the majority of the Court in their application of the Bill of Rights to the states through the Fourteenth Amendment. In 1968, he dissented in the case of *Duncan v. State of Louisiana* (88 S.Ct. 2145), that held that the Fourteenth Amendment guaranteed a right of jury trial in state criminal cases which were they to be tried in federal court, would come within the Sixth Amendment's guarantee.

powers of the states have been seriously eroded, and local self-government greatly weakened. And, continue the strict construc-tionists, now the Court has given new meaning to the words "cruel and unusual punishments" contained in the Eighth Amendment, and so, by a vote of five to four in a decision rendered on June 29, 1972, it practically abolished capital punishment in the United States.[24] But this decision was not a simple one, and its ultimate meaning was far from clear. In fact, each of the nine Justices wrote his own opinion on the key issue of "cruel and unusual punishment." Only two of them, however, declared that capital punishment, because of its very nature, was unconstitutional under any circumstances,[25] whereas the other three who joined in the majority opinion ruled against it because of the circumstances under which it was being administered in the United States. Apparently, therefore, Congress and the state legisla-tures could restore the death penalty if they provided that it was to be administered under conditions which would meet the approval of the

---

In criticizing the majority's interpretation of the "due-process clause," he stated: "I believe I am correct in saying that every member of the Court for at least the last 135 years has agreed that our Founders did not consider the requirements of the Bill of Rights so fundamental that they should operate directly against the states."

[24]See *Furman v. Georgia, Jackson v. Georgia, Branch v. Texas,* 408 U.S. 238 (1972).

[25]These two Justices (Justice Brennan and Justice Marshall) in their opinions left no doubt that they believed that the Court might exercise virtually unlimited powers as a policy-making agency.

For example, Justice Brennan, in his attempt to answer the contention that the "cruel-and-unusual-punishments clause" should be given the mean-ing that it had when the Eighth Amendment was adopted, argued, "Under this view, of course, any punishment that was in common use in 1791 is forever exempt from the Clause" (See Footnote 29 of his opinion). But in reply to this, one must call attention to the fact that the Ninth and Tenth Amend-ments reserve great powers to the states and the people so that they may regulate their own affairs, including the punishment of criminals, and that the final power of constitutional amendment is lodged in the states.

In his opinion, Justice Marshall assumed a posture similar to that of Justice Brennan regarding the powers of the Court. Thus, with respect to public opinion, he argued that the question with which the Court must deal was "not whether a substantial proportion of American citizens would today, if polled, opine that capital punishment is barbarously cruel, but whether they would find it to be so in the light of all information presently available." So, charge the strict constructionists, Justice Marshall, seeing the Court as a policy-making agency, believed that it should enlighten the people about capital punishment and tell them what was "good" for them.

majority of the Justices of the Supreme Court, and the federal government and some of states soon took steps to accomplish this.

The action of the Supreme Court against the death penalty was called a victory for the advocates of a more enlightened penology. Yet, warned some critics of the Court, in the long run, it might actually result in an increase in the use of this penalty. This might happen, they reasoned, for apparently the only way to gain the approval of the Court was to make the death sentence always mandatory, and never just discretionary, and thus overcome the objection, stressed by some of its members, that certain groups had been discriminated against in the imposition of capital punishment.

Although the decision against the death penalty did not directly affect law enforcement, state the strict constructionists, it so clearly illustrates how the Court has been undermining the Constitution that it is especially worthy of our attention. Thus, the majority of the Court ruled against capital punishment despite the fact that all the states and the federal government not only were using this penalty, but also were strongly in favor of it, at the time when the Eighth Amendment was ratified. Furthermore, far from being prohibited by the Constitution, capital punishment is explicitly recognized by it in both the Fifth and Fourteenth Amendments. The Fifth provides that "no person shall be held to answer for a capital . . . crime, unless on . . . indictment of a Grand Jury . . . ; nor shall any person . . . be twice put in jeopardy of life . . . ;" and the Fourteenth prohibits the deprivation "of life" without "due process of law." Since, according to the strict constructionists, any reasonable construction of the Constitution must harmonize the several parts and interpret each in the light of the others, it is clear that the Founders did not intend to recognize capital punishment in two provisions and to abolish it in another.

This decision also strikingly reveals the disarray of the Court. Splintered into nine separate opinions, the Justices expressed views that, in some instances, differed widely. However, all four of the dissenting Justices concurred in the view that the Court's majority had failed to exercise judicial restraint, that they had exceeded their judicial authority and trespassed upon the prerogatives of Congress and the legislatures of the states, and that the decision abolishing the death penalty was "not an act of judgement, but rather an act of will."[26]

---

[26]In his dissenting opinion, Justice Powell deplored the "shattering effect" that the Court's decision declaring capital punishment unconstitutional

Thus, say the strict constructionists, once more Justices on the Supreme Court twisted the meaning of words to suit their own moral principles, and abandoning their judicial role, they acted as policy makers, which is a legislative or executive function and not one for the judicial branch of government. But, as in so many other cases, while acting as policy makers, the Justices did not do their work well. Remiss in juristic clarity and negligent of social responsibility, they handed down an ambiguous and inconclusive decision and so caused uncertainty and confusion where certainty and order must prevail. According to Chief Justice Burger, the future of capital punishment in this country had been left in "an uncertain limbo."

But, aver the strict constructionists, far more important than the future of capital punishment is the proper interpretation of the Constitution. The words of any contractual instrument, such as a constitution, must be construed according to what they meant to the parties at the time when the instrument was agreed to by the parties. That is to say, their meaning is fixed as of that time, for the words are in fact the instrument itself, and to change them is to alter the instrument. So, when the Court changes the meanings of words in the Constitution to suit itself, it is, in effect, substituting judicial fiat for the amendatory process provided for in Article V and, to that extent, nullifying the Constitution. Instead of using such a method, what the Court must do is ask itself this question: "What did the words and phrases in question mean, as applied to particular situations, to the framers who

---

would have "on the root principles of *stare decisis,* federalism, judicial restraint and—most importantly—separation of powers." The fact is, say the strict constructionists, the strict observance of these principles in the past would have done much to prevent the undermining of the Constitution, which has already reached such serious proportions. Unfortunately, Justice Powell himself has not consistently supported what he has called the "root principles." See, for example, *Roe v. Wade* and *Doe v. Bolton,* 410 U.S. 113, and 179 (1973). On January 22, 1973, Justice Powell joined the majority on the Court in handing down decisions in these cases, which had the effect of making unconstitutional the state abortion laws of most states.

Justice Powell also attacked the discrimination argument against capital punishment, which was used by the majority opinion, and insisted that the same argument "could be made with equal force and logic with respect to those sentenced to prison terms." The basic problem, he explained, results "not from the penalties imposed for criminal conduct," but from social and economic factors that tend to cause more crime among the minorities and the poor than among the other groups in the population. And these factors, he argued, were "unrelated to the constitutional issues before the Court."

drafted the Constitution and its Amendments and to the states that ratified them?"[27]

It may seem strange, state the strict constructionists, but the twisting of the meaning of words in the Constitution by the Court recently distressed even Justice Black, who in the past had persistently employed it in his own interpretations of the Constitution. Here is what he said in his dissenting opinion in 1970, in the Winship case: "I believe that the Court has no power to add or subtract from the procedures set forth by the Founders. I realize that it is far easier to substitute individual judges' ideas of 'fairness' for the fairness prescribed by the Constitution, but I shall not at any time surrender my belief that that document itself should be our guide not our own concept of what is fair, decent, and right."[28]

On July 2, 1976, the United States Supreme Court again ruled on the death penalty, holding that it does not violate the cruel-and-unusual-punishments clause of the Eight Amendment if the law that imposes this penalty provides for standards of fairness acceptable to the Court. Such standards, explained the Court, should guard against arbitrary and capricious imposition of the penalty and furnish specific guidelines for an exercise of mercy by the judge and the jury.

In three seven-to-two decisions, the Justices upheld the death penalty laws in Florida, Georgia, and Texas, which provide for such standards. But by a five-to-four vote, the Court struck down the capital punishment laws of North Carolina and Louisiana, which failed to establish standards of fairness and made the death penalty mandatory. All the death penalty cases upheld by the Court involved convictions for murder. The Court left open the question whether the death penalty might be constitutionally applied to other crimes. In all these decisions, as in the one discussed above, only Justices Brennan and Marshall held that the death penalty because of its very nature was unconstitutional under any circumstances.[29]

The third of the undermining methods, assert the strict constructionists, is the deliberate selection of cases that are deemed appropri-

---

[27]Virginia Commission on Constitutional Government, pp. 323, 324.

[28]In re Winship, 397 U.S. 358, 90 S.Ct. 1068 (1970). In this case the Court ruled that proof of guilt beyond a reasonable doubt must be shown in all cases in the juvenile court when the youth is charged with an act that would constitute a crime if committed by an adult.

[29]See Gregg v. Georgia, 96 S. Ct. 2909 (1976); Proffitt v. Florida, 96 S. Ct.

ate by the Court for the recasting of the Constitution in the form of the Court's own philosophy. It is true that the Court cannot act in a case unless the case is before the Court for review. However, the Court does not have to accept every case that is brought to its attention, and it can wait until one comes along that suits its particular purpose and then utilize the case as a vehicle for making a fundamental change in the Constitution.

The Court is accused by one of its own members of having used this method in the controversial *Mapp* case,[30] which was decided by a five-to-three vote. In his dissent in this case, Justice Harlan, after denying that the principal issue in the appeal was whether illegally state-seized evidence was constitutionally admissible in state prosecution, said: "In this posture of things, I think it fair to say that five members of this Court have simply 'reached out' to overrule Wolf. With all respect for the views of the majority, . . . I can perceive no justification for regarding this case as an appropriate occasion for reexamining Wolf."

Those who have supported the Court in the use of these methods argue that it must find some way to take action, since the states have failed to do so. But, reply the strict constructionists, this is specious reasoning. The real question is: Does the Constitution give the Supreme Court the authority to act in a certain matter merely because the states have failed to act? The power of states to act embraces the power not to act. If the power to act is reserved to them by the Constitution, then any one of them has the right to act or not to act in a way that may seem wrong to another state or even to members of the Supreme Court. Such is the prerogative of the states, and part of the very essence of self-government in our federal system.[31]

Thomas Jefferson, with characteristic perspicacity, feared the enormous power that the Supreme Court might wield, and in 1825, about six months before his death, he warned against what he, even then, called the usurpations by the federal government. In a letter to William Branch Giles, he wrote:

2960 (1976); *Jurek v. Texas*, 96 S. Ct. 2950 (1976); *Woodson v. North Carolina*, 96 S. Ct. 2978 (1976); *Roberts v. Louisiana*, 96 S. Ct. 3001 (1976).

[30]*Mapp v. Ohio*, 367 U.S. 643, 81 S.Ct. 1684 (1961). In this case, the Supreme Court extended the "exclusionary rule" to the states and so made illegally seized evidence inadmissible in both state and federal courts. We shall return to this case later in our discussion.

[31]Virginia Commission on Constitutional Government, p. XXIX.

"I see, as you do, and with deepest affliction, the rapid strides with which the federal branch of our government is advancing towards the usurpation of all the rights reserved to the States, and the consolidation in itself of all powers, foreign and domestic; and that, too, by constructions which, if legitimate, leave no limits to their power. Take together the decisions of the federal court, the doctrines of the President, and the misconstructions of the constitutional compact acted on by the legislature of the federal branch, and it is but too evident, that the three ruling branches of that department are in combination to strip their colleagues, the State authorities, of the powers reserved by them, and to exercise themselves all functions foreign and domestic. Under the power to regulate commerce, they assume indefinitely that also over agriculture and manufactures, and call it regulation . . . the States should be watchful to note every material usurpation on their rights; to denounce them as they occur in the most peremptory terms; . . ."[32]

Unfortunately, protest the strict constructionists, the Supreme Court has continued its tendency to subvert the power of the states and to expand its role of policy-maker in the economic and social affairs of the nation. Alarmed by this tendency, the Chief Justices of the State Supreme Courts, in 1958, adopted a report that severely criticized the United States Supreme Court and urged its members to exercise greater judicial restraint.

Here are a few excerpts from the conclusions of this report:

"We believe that strong state and local governments are essential to the effective functioning of the American system of federal government; that they should not be sacrificed needlessly to leveling, and sometimes deadening, uniformity; and that in the interest of active, citizen participation in self-government—the foundation of our democracy—they should be sustained and strengthened . . .

"We are not alone in our view that the Court, in many cases arising under the Fourteenth Amendment, has assumed what seem to us primarily legislative powers. We do not believe that either the framers of the original Constitution or the possibly

---

[32]Ibid., pp. 272, 273.

somewhat less gifted draftsmen of the Fourteenth Amendment ever contemplated that the Supreme Court, would, or should, have the almost unlimited policy-making powers which it now exercises . . .

"It has long been an American boast that we have a government of laws and not of men. We believe that any study of recent decisions of the Supreme Court will raise at least considerable doubt as to the validity of that boast . . .

"It is our earnest hope, which we respectfully express, that that great Court exercise to the full its power of judicial self-restraint by adhering firmly to its tremendous, strictly judicial powers and by eschewing, as far as possible, the exercise of essentially legislative powers when it is called upon to decide questions involving the validity of state action, whether it deems such action wise or unwise . . ."[33]

---

[33]Ibid., 398-404. On August 23, 1958, at the close of the Conference of the Chief Justices of the State Supreme Courts, this report was adopted 36 to 8. Voting against adoption were the Chief Justices, or their representatives, from California, New Jersey, Pennsylvania, Rhode Island, Utah, Vermont, West Virginia, and Hawaii. Two states, Nevada and North Dakota, abstained. Three states, Connecticut, Indiana, and Arkansas, were not represented at the closing sessions. All other states voted in favor of the report. See also, Felix Morley, *Freedom and Federalism* (Chicago: Henry Regnery Company, 1959), pp. 226-40.

CHAPTER XV

THE SUPREME COURT
AND LAW ENFORCEMENT

THE REVOLUTION IN LAW ENFORCEMENT

The Supreme Court gave little heed to the report of the Chief Justices of the State Supreme Courts, and in a series of cases caused a revolution in law enforcement. Decision after decision was rendered until a high wall of so-called rights was built around the accused, and local law enforcement agencies were forced to submit to a kind of judicial control by the federal courts that was unprecedented in the history of the United States. Two decisions were especially important in the establishment of this judicial control. These were handed down in the *Mapp*[1] (1961) and the *Miranda*[2] (1966) cases.

MAPP V. OHIO

Consider these facts in the Mapp case. On May 23, 1957, three police officers arrived at the residence of Darlee Mapp, who lived on the top floor of a two-family dwelling in Cleveland, Ohio. These officers were acting upon information that a suspect in a bombing case was hiding in the Mapp home and that policy paraphernalia were concealed there. They knocked at the door and asked permission to make a search, but Miss Mapp, after telephoning her attorney, refused to admit them unless they had a search warrant. The officers left, but returning later, again sought entrance. When Miss Mapp failed to come to the door, the officers forced open the outer door, started up the stairs to the upper floor, and met her as she was coming down. She demanded to see the search warrant, and when one of the officers held

---

[1]*Mapp v. Ohio*, 367 U.S. 643, 81 S.Ct. 1684 (1961).
[2]*Miranda v. Arizona*, 384 U.S. 436, 86 S.Ct. 1602 (1966).

up a paper,[3] she grabbed it and a scuffle ensued. The paper was retrieved, a search of the home was made, and obscene material was discovered.

Subsequently, Darlee Mapp was convicted of knowingly having in her possession lewd and lascivious books, pictures, and photographs in violation of Ohio's criminal code. Upon appeal, her conviction was affirmed by the state supreme court, although that court found that her conviction was based primarily upon evidence secured by an unlawful search and seizure. (This the Ohio court was privileged to do because until then the "exclusionary rule" was a rule of evidence and not considered to be a constitutional mandate, in consequence of which the states could either follow or reject the "exclusionary rule."[4]) The United States Supreme Court, however, reversed the conviction and remanded, ruling that thereafter the "exclusionary rule" had to be applied by the states as a federal constitutional requirement; that is, evidence secured by a search and seizure would be inadmissible in state courts, just as it had been in federal courts by virtue of a federal rule of evidence. The Court's primary objective in its *Mapp* decision was to deter illegal police conduct; in other words, by forbidding any court, federal or state, from using illegally seized evidence, the police would be discouraged from searching or seizing evidence by illegal means.

However, Justice Harlan disagreed with the majority decision. In his dissent, in which he was joined by Justices Frankfurter and Whittaker, he declared that the Court had acted without judicial restraint and that the Court's action amounted to a summary reversal, without argument, of its prior holding that the "exclusionary rule" was not a part of the Fourth Amendment but instead a part of the federal rules of procedure. He also stated that the Court did not possess any general supervising power over the state courts and should not fetter them with an adamant rule which might thwart them in coping with their own peculiar problems in criminal law enforcement.

He concluded his dissent with these words: "But in the last analysis I think this Court can increase respect for the Constitution

---

[3]No search warrant was produced by the prosecution at the trial, nor was the failure to produce one explained. In fact, there is considerable doubt as to whether there ever was a warrant for the search of the defendant's home.

[4]At the time of the *Mapp* decision, illegally secured evidence was admissable in the courts of about one-half of the states.

only if it rigidly respects the limitations which the Constitution places upon it, and respects as well the principles inherent in its own processes. In the present case, I think we exceed both, and that our voice becomes only a voice of power, not of reason."

Before he was appointed to his present position, the Chief Justice of the United States Supreme Court, Warran E. Burger, expressed skepticism about the effectiveness of the "exclusionary rule" in deterring illegal police practices. In 1964 he wrote: "As I see it, a fair conclusion is that the record does not support a claim that police conduct has been substantially affected by the suppression of the prosecution's evidence."[5] After his appointment to the Supreme Court, Chief Justice Burger became much more explicit in his views about the "exclusionary rule." Thus, in the Coolidge case, he spoke of the "monstrous price" that we pay for this rule "in which we seem to have imprisoned ourselves."[6]

One of the most controversial cases involving the use of the "exclusionary rule" was that of Wayne D. Bumper.[7] Bumper was convicted in North Carolina on a rape charge and sentenced to life imprisonment. He raped a woman, tied her and her companion to a tree, shot them, and left them to die. The police went to the defendant's home, which was owned by his grandmother, and advised her that they had a search warrant. She let them in, and they found the rifle that had been used in the crime. It was later admitted as evidence in the trial.

In court, the grandmother testified: "I let them search and *it was all my own free will*.[8] Nobody forced me at all." The victims of Bumper's crime, having recovered, positively identified him as the person who had raped the girl and shot them. Furthermore, during the trial, there was no dispute about the facts, and it appeared that even without the rifle there was enough evidence to convict the accused.

Nevertheless, when the case reached the Supreme Court, the Court declared that since the police said that they had a warrant (the existence and validity of which had not been established in the state courts), they announced in effect that the grandmother had no right to resist the search. This, the court explained, amounted to coercion, and

---

[5]Fred E. Inbau, James R. Thompson, and Claude R. Sowle, *Cases and Comments on Criminal Justice* (Mineola, N.Y.: The Foundation Press, Inc., 1968), Vol. II, p. 73.

[6]*Coolidge v. New Hampshire*, 91 S.Ct. 2022, 2051 (1971).

[7]*Bumper v. North Carolina*, 391 U.S. 543, 88 S.Ct. 1788 (1968).

[8]The emphasis has been added.

therefore there was no lawful consent to the search. Thus, concluded the court, the search was unlawful, and the admission of the rifle in evidence was unconstitutional and not a harmless error. The Court therefore in its majority opinion, reversed the case and ordered a retrial.

Justice Black, however, strongly dissented. In his opinion, the search of the home was lawful, and the rifle therefore was admissible in evidence. Moreover, he added, "Whether one views the evidence of guilt with or without the rifle, the conclusion is inescapable that this defendant committed the crimes for which the jury convicted him. In these circumstances no State should be forced to give a new trial; justice does not require it."

Here, then, contend the strict constructionists, we have an excellent example of how the Court, absorbed in the juggling of abstractions and minimizing the fact that all the evidence pointed to the guilt of the accused, used a procedural technicality to impose its will upon a state court.

MIRANDA V. ARIZONA

Prior to the *Miranda* decision in 1966, a major step in the revolution in law enforcement occurred in the 1964 case of *Escobedo v. Illinois*,[9] the foundation for which had been laid only one week before when the Court, in a five-to-four decision, had applied the self-incrimination provision of the Fifth Amendment to the states through the Fourteenth Amendment.[10] Briefly here are the facts of the *Escobedo* case. Escobedo was arrested on a charge of having murdered his brother-in-law. At the police station, Escobedo requested permission to see his attorney, who was waiting in another room of the station, but this request, as well as the request of the attorney to see Escobedo, was denied. During the interrogation, Escobedo made some incriminating statements, and these were later used against him in his trial. He was convicted of murder, his conviction was upheld by the Illinois Supreme Court, and the case was appealed to the United States Supreme Court upon the contention that Escobedo had been denied "due process of law," because he had not been afforded the right to have counsel as provided by the Sixth Amendment. The state,

---

[9]*Escobedo v. Illinois*, 378 U.S. 478 (1964).
[10]*Malloy v. Hogan*, 84 S.Ct. 1489 (1964). Even before the *Malloy* case, and as a result of independent action, the right against compulsory self-incrimination had been recognized for a long time in all the states.

on the other hand, argued that this amendment granted the right to counsel at the time of the trial and not before.

However, the United States Supreme Court held that the adversary system begins when the criminal process shifts from investigatory to accusatory stage and that at this point the accused has the right to counsel. If the accused is denied the right to consult with his attorney after this point is reached, all statements made by him are inadmissible as evidence in court. On the basis of this reasoning, the Court, in another five-to-four decision, reversed the conviction of Escobedo and this created a new rule on the admissibility of confessions.

The Escobedo decision stirred up a storm of protest. It was certain that a confession in order to be judged voluntary could not be made in violation of the Escobedo ruling, but the complete meaning of this ruling was far from clear. In fact, many troublesome questions about it were raised. For example, just when does the case pass from the investigatory stage to the accusatory stage? And must the police furnish a person with legal assistance if he cannot afford counsel? In trying to answer such questions as these, the states went in different directions and gave conflicting interpretations. So, once again, assert the strict constructionists, the Supreme Court by meddling in matters that should be left to the states, created an intolerable situation.

Finally, on June 13, 1966, the Supreme Court, in its decision in the Miranda case, sought to dissipate some of the confusion caused by Escobedo. These are the essential facts of the Miranda case. On March 3, 1963, an 18-year-old girl was kidnapped and forcibly raped near Phoenix, Arizona. Ten days later, Miranda, an indigent, twenty-three-year-old man, who had less than a ninth-grade education, was arrested and taken to the police station. The victim picked Miranda out of a police lineup, and two officers then took him into a separate room, where, after less than two hours of interrogation, he confessed and signed a statement admitting and describing the crime. However, no force, threats, or promises were made to secure the confession, and it was made voluntarily by Miranda.

The confession was admitted into evidence, and Miranda was found guilty of kidnapping and rape. The Supreme Court of Arizona upheld the verdict, and the case was appealed to the United States Supreme Court. There it was reversed by a five-to-four decision. The Court held that for a confession to be admissible, officers must abide by a prescribed rule—now known as the "Miranda rule"—which was set forth in the Court's decision.

To bolster its decision in *Miranda*, the Court pictured the typical detained suspect as a forlorn, weak, intimidated, and frightened person subjected to unrelenting pressure and bewildering trickery by the police, inclined to confirm any statement made by his interrogators, and in great need of protection to insure his free choice and human dignity. Furthermore, the Court insisted, since the issues before it were of constitutional dimensions, it could not wait for the states to provide the necessary safeguards, and it had to make certain that the government itself did not become a lawbreaker in the treatment of the accused, even if this meant letting some guilty persons go free.

Four justices, however, strenuously dissented. Justice Clark said that he was proud of the work of police agencies, accused the majority on the Court of being unfair to the police and of having based their opinion of law enforcement practices on insufficient and inaccurate evidence, and stressed the importance and difficulty of custodial interrogation.

Justice Harlan, in his dissent, declared that the majority decision was poor constitutional law and entailed harmful consequences for the country at large, that the Fifth Amendment was not designed to eliminate all pressures on the accused, that the new rules would greatly reduce confessions,[11] thus making the solution of some crimes impossible, and that the social costs of crime were so great that the new rules had to be called a "hazardous experimentation."

Justice White asserted that the Court's decision in *Miranda* was based on a deep-seated distrust of all confessions. He contended that it virtually admonished the lawyer of the accused to advise his client to remain silent, that it erected a new constitutional barrier to the ascertainment of truth, and that it thus greatly reduced the effectiveness of the criminal law in the prevention of crime. Furthermore, he argued that there was a fundamental inconsistency in the majority's reasoning. Thus, he explained, they simultaneously claimed that an uncounseled defendant's decision to incriminate himself cannot be voluntary, because of the inherent pressures of custody, and that his

---

[11]Some recent studies purport to show that the police are now securing as many confessions as they did before *Miranda*. However, declare the strict constructionists, even if this were conclusively proved to be generally true—and as yet no such proof has been advanced—it would not in any way change the fact that *Miranda* is a serious usurpation of the powers reserved to the states by the Constitution, and for this reason, if for no other, it should be severely condemned and reversed.

decision to dispense with counsel, made under the same circumstances, can be voluntary.

SOME CONCLUDING REMARKS

This brief examination of a few cases indicates that the Supreme Court has used the same methods in the field of law enforcement that it has employed elsewhere. Casting aside judicial restraint and in the name of the Constitution, the Court, argue the strict constructionists, has seriously weakened the system of checks and balances and dangerously eroded the powers of the states. It has done so by imposing federal rules of procedure on state courts, thus pushing them toward the role of subsidiary federal courts, and by fastening rigid rules of operation on local law enforcement agencies. Furthermore, this was done at a time when the courts and law enforcement agencies were facing a crucial situation. Not only were they struggling to carry a load of crushing responsibilities, but they were also striving to professionalize their services and earnestly seeking assistance in their efforts to do so. In fact, at the time of the *Miranda* decision, important organizations, such as the American Bar Association, the American Law Institute, the Ford Foundation, and the President's Commission on Law Enforcement and Administration of Justice,[12] were engaged in studies of many aspects of law enforcement, and these studies would have inevitably provided a sound foundation for higher standards in the entire field of police work. But, declare the strict constructionists, the Court gave all of this scant attention. Without waiting for the result of these studies or making any independent investigations of actual conditions in the field, the Court, by a one-man majority, peremptorily imposed its own preconceived ideas on the courts and law enforcement agencies throughout the country.

What the Court has done in the law enforcement cases is to put the police on trial. In effect, explain the strict constructionists, it has said: "We do not trust you police, so we are going to set up a series of rules and you must measure up to them or, if necessary, we will let the defendant go free in order to teach you a lesson." In other words, as

---

[12]Inbau, Thompson, and Sowle, p. 137. See also Fred E. Inbau, " 'Playing God:' 5 to 4 (The Supreme Court and the Police)," *Journal of Criminal Law, Criminology, and Police Science,* LVII (December, 1966), 377,378.

Professor Inbau has argued, the Court was going to police the police.[13]

Not only have some members of the Court clearly evidenced a distrust of the police, but they have also indicated a lack of confidence in one another. In various opinions in the law enforcement cases, the Court stands condemned by some of its own members in the most scathing criticisms that one can find anywhere. For example, Justice Harlan, in his dissent in the *Mapp* case, rebuked the majority on the Court for not exercising judicial restraint and for breaking the Court's obligations to the states; and Justice Stewart, in the *Escobedo* case, accused the Court of perverting constitutional guarantees and of frustrating "the vital interests of society in preserving the legitimate and proper function of honest and purposeful police investigation." But even more revealing were the words of Justice White in the *Miranda* case when he condemned the majority of the Court for having erected a constitutional barrier behind which many criminals would escape from justice, and he emphasized his opposition by saying, "I have no desire whatsoever to share the responsibility for any such impact on the present criminal process."

In arriving at its decisions in the law enforcement cases, the Court has used its favorite device of applying various provisions of the Bill of Rights to the states through the Fourteenth Amendment. As we have already explained, the Supreme Court, during decades of judicial reviews, found no reason for using the Fourteenth Amendment to enforce provisions of the Bill of Rights against the states. Furthermore, insist the strict constructionists, if there were any reason for doing this, logic would call for the application of the entire contents of the Bill of Rights to the states by one Court and not through some long selective process, which enables a succession of Courts to pick and choose and to make the application in piecemeal fashion, as this or that moral consideration impels a majority of the justices to do so.

The strict constructionists contend that the United States Supreme Court should heed the advice of the Chief Justices of the State Supreme Courts, which was so wisely offered in 1958, and exercise judicial restraint, eschewing legislative functions and adhering strictly to judicial powers. It should interpret and not enact laws, and before it presumes to intrude into the lives of millions of Americans, it

---

[13]Fred E. Inbau, "Public Safety v. Individual Civil Liberties: The Prosecutor's Stand," *Journal of Criminal Law, Criminology, and Police Science*, LIII (March, 1962), 85-89.

should look beyond legal abstractions and ascertain what the facts of the situation are. The primary question before it should never be, "Is there a problem?" or "Do we like what is being done?" or even "Do we think that we can improve the situation?" Instead, it should be, "Does a strict interpretation of the Constitution give us the authority to act?" And if a return of the Court to its true role of interpreting and not enacting laws means the overturning of precedents, then, certainly, this should be done. But if the Constitution needs to be changed, this should be accomplished through the amendatory process provided for in the Constitution and not by a decree of the Supreme Court.

A departure from the strict interpretation of the Constitution sets us adrift in a sea of rationalization, tergiversation, and sophistry. One may argue that the end justifies the means and that the Constitution should be employed to promote this or that interest or to establish this or that set of principles, simply because some pressure group demands that this be done or some intellectual cabal believes it to be "right." But, protest the strict constructionists, if we use the Constitution in this way, it ceases to be a covenant for the best interest of all and becomes instead a club to be wielded first by one group and then by another to beat the opposition into submission—the beaters of today always facing the possibility that they will be the beaten tomorrow—and this in the name of justice. Thus, surely, government by law degenerates into government by men. It would be better to have no Constitution than to engage in such juggling and posturing to the ultimate detriment of all.

The fact is that the expansion of the Court's role as a policy-maker in the nation's economic and social affairs has not been accomplished without the payment of a high price. Each decision, explain the strict constructionists, has brought a new rule; and each new rule, a series of new interpretations, calling for a never-ending refinement of abstractions, until the Court has lost itself in a labyrinth of legal technicalities. Arrogating to itself powers that were wisely distributed among the three branches of government and usurping the powers of the states, the Court, to its consternation, now finds that its case load, and that of the lower courts as well, is so great that the machinery of justice is clogged and the rights of those that it claims to be protecting are jeopardized. Although much of the solution for its problems can be found in a return to constitutional government, the Court seems little inclined to do this.

Furthermore, continue the strict constructionists, the members of the Court have fallen into confusion over the question of how and in what direction they should expand their powers. Indeed, justices shift their positions from one decision to another; not one appears able to follow a consistent and logical course, and nearly every major case splinters the justices into a proliferation of concurring and dissenting opinions, in which they accuse one another of misunderstanding, perverting, or disregarding the Constitution, or even of injudiciously seizing power. And this disarray of the Court is rendered more conspicuous by poor craftmanship, which often leaves decisions obscure, incoherent, and almost incomprehensible.

The Founding Fathers, aver the strict constructionists, understood the importance of having a symmetrical political structure and of having not only a well-balanced distribution of powers, but also power commensurate with delegated responsibility. Today, the complexities of modern life force law enforcement officers to carry a heavy load of responsibilities. Charged with the prevention of crime, they must take and maintain the initiative and exercise a wide range of discretionary powers in handling a variety of changing and challenging situations. Civilians, furthermore, must expect to be inconvenienced and even subjected to hardship from time to time as the police perform their duties. This is the price that everyone must pay to insure the security and welfare of all. If the officer is encased in a box of complex rules, he ceases to be an alert and aggressive guardian of the law and becomes instead a mere puppet, the fruits of his initiative, imagination, and ingenuity being lost.

The real problem now before us is not the elimination of the discretionary powers of the officer, but rather his professionalization, so that he can wield these powers intelligently, competently, and effectively. Nevertheless, contend the strict constructionists, the officer, now ensnared in a tightening web of complex and obscure decisions, handed down by divided Supreme Courts, finds it increasingly difficult to make the split-second decisions so essential in good police work. One can readily understand why in desperation a police officer asks, "If the Court cannot give us a clear statement of what the rules are, how can we be expected to know what they are, especially since so often we have to act quickly to save lives and property?"

To improve the situation, assert the strict constructionists, the Supreme Court should stop trying to convert state courts into subsidiary federal courts and cease attempting to supervise the operation of local police departments. Certainly among the steps that it should take, say the strict constructionists, is the abandonment of the "exclusionary rule." There is no proof that this rule deters illegal police practices and thus accomplishes its alleged major purpose. Besides, it actually militates against the swift and sure enforcement of the law, and, by increasing the possibility that the criminal will go free, it discriminates against the law-abiding citizen and generates contempt for the courts.

Furthermore, add the strict constructionists, *Miranda* should be reversed. A confession should never become inadmissible solely because an officer has failed to follow a certain procedural rule, such as that prescribed in *Miranda*. On the contrary, the admissibility of a confession should be determined entirely on the basis of whether it was freely and voluntarily given. In this way, the accused, and not the officer, will be placed on trial. However, state the strict constructionists, they are not trying to minimize the importance of the rights of the people. Rather, they explain, they are making an effort to call attention to the dangers attendant upon the Supreme Court's usurpation of the powers of the states and its interference in the affairs of local governments.

In 1968, a reluctant Congress finally bestirred itself and passed the Omnibus Crime Control and Safe Streets Act. One of the aims of this law is to make inapplicable, in *federal* cases, the Supreme Court's decisions restricting in-custody interrogations *(Miranda v. Arizona)*, police line-up identifications *(United States v. Wade)*, and "unnecessary delay" between arrest and arraignment *(McNabb v. United States and Mallory v. United States)*, but its fate in the courts remains uncertain. In addition, a somewhat relenting Supreme Court has, by its own action in several recent cases, slightly weakened the "Miranda rule."[14]

But, insist the strict constructionists, these faltering steps are not enough. Pressure on the Supreme Court must be maintained; the controversy over the Court must not die, for there is too much at stake. Involved is not simply the establishment of a more effective law

---

[14]See, for example, *Harris v. New York*, 91 S.Ct. 643 (1971). In this case, the Supreme Court, in a five-to-four decision, held that a statement which is inadmissible as direct evidence at the trial of the accused, because the *"Miranda rule"* has not been followed, may be used to challenge his credibility if he takes the stand in his own defense and makes a statement contrary to the previous inadmissible one. Chief Justice Burger, who wrote the majority opinion, said, "The shield provided by *Miranda* cannot be perverted into a license to use perjury by way of a defense, free from the risk of confrontation with prior inconsistent utterances."

enforcement program, but rather the preservation of the very foundation of constitutional government in the United States.

Congress, argue the strict constructionists, must take much more decisive and fundamental action on the matter, and it has the power to do so. It appropriates the funds needed for the operation of the Court and has the authority to increase or decrease the Court's membership and to establish such inferior courts as it may deem necessary. Furthermore, although the Constitution specifies that the justices of the Supreme Court shall hold office during good behavior, it does not say that they shall be appointed for life. Consequently, Congress could provide that they be appointed for a term of years, at the end of which they would have to stand for reappointment. Thus, their performance in office should be periodically appraised, and their exercise of authority could be subjected to some restraining influence. Congress, moreover, could pass a law greatly reducing the appellate jurisdiction of the Court, eliminating, for example, the Court's judicial review of state court decisions, which has so seriously undermined the principles of constitutional government. In addition, it could, of course, initiate the move to modify or repeal the Fourteenth Amendment, the chink in the armor of our federal union through which the Court has forced most of its destructive influence. Thus, conclude the strict constructionists, only a moment's thought will show that Congress has the power to compel the Court to return to its proper role in the political life of America.

The ultimate source of all power under our form of government lies in the people. "All authority belongs to the people," said Jefferson, but he also fully realized that they would not exercise their authority unless they were kept well informed.[15] The people, therefore, argue the strict constructionists, must be reminded of their power and stimulated to exercise it. In every possible way, they must be taught the meaning and importance of constitutional government and urged to demand that their representatives in Congress work vigorously for its restoration in the United States.

---

[15]Virginia Commission on Constitutional Government, We the States (Richmond, Va.: The William Byrd Press, Inc., 1964), pp. XIX-XXII.

CHAPTER XVI

CORRECTIONAL INSTITUTIONS AND AGENCIES

CORRECTIONS AND THE CRIMINAL JUSTICE SYSTEM

The administration of criminal justice in the United States is comprised of three distinct and separately organized parts, which include the police, the courts, and corrections. The police are the first point of contact between the public and our system of criminal justice, and they activate the administration of the justice system when they arrest a person. The arrested person may then be confined to a police facility, jail, tried by a court, which represents the second phase of the system, and if he is found guilty he is placed on probation or committed to a jail or correctional institution.

We shall, in this chapter, discuss corrections, the third and final part of the criminal justice system.

THE NATURE AND PURPOSE OF CORRECTIONS

Corrections is considered to be that specialized aspect of government service which is responsible for the supervision, control, and correction of those adults or juveniles who have been arrested and found guilty of violating certain criminal or delinquency statutes. In the administration of this type of government service, several types of correctional programs and facilities have been established. These include probation, institutions, community correctional centers, and parole. Additionally, some authorities feel that correctional agencies should also be responsible for the untried offender confined in federal and local jails, and that the jails should be administered by trained correction staff rather than by the police.[1]

---

[1]National Advisory Commission on Criminal Justice Standards and Goals, *Task Force on Corrections* (Washington, D.C.: U.S. Government Printing Office, 1973), pp. 98-102, 273, 282.

Corrections, in this country, is administered by many different governmental units at the federal, state, and local levels. In this respect, it should be obvious that the administration of correction is no different from that of the police services, which also are essentially a local government responsibility.

The American correctional system, including jails, handles nearly 1.3 million offenders on an average day, and it has 2.5 million admissions in a given year. Some of these agencies have developed excellent programs for the control and rehabilitation of offenders, but most are unable to deal with the problems of preventing the criminal from committing further offenses.

In 1966, a national survey of corrections was completed in the United States, and it concluded that there are many distinct and separate correctional systems and programs which operate independently not only of the police and the courts but also of one another. The survey further noted the following important characteristics of correction in the United States:[2]

1. Alaska is the only state in which all correctional services are organized in a single state department of correction.
2. In most states, some correctional programs are administered by state and local agencies which are also responsible for such other services as mental health, welfare, hospitals, and so forth.
3. Institutions for state adult felons are administered only by the states. They are more commonly known as prisons, penitentiaries, reformatories, prison farms, and forestry and conservation camps.
4. Jails, which detain those awaiting trial or serving sentences of a year or less, are the responsibility of county sheriffs in 73 percent of the cases, and a city police function in 22 percent of the cases. The remaining jails are usually operated jointly by the county and the city, or by the state.
5. In forty-six states, institutions for juvenile delinquents are administered by a parent agency, which in twenty-one of these states has only correctional responsibilities. Other common administrative arrangements place these institutions under a state department of welfare or under a state board of institutions.

---

[2]The President's Commission on Law Enforcement and the Administration of Justice, *Task Force Report: Corrections* (Washington, D.C.: U.S. Government Printing Office, 1967), pp. 199-202.

6. Only one-third of all convicted offenders in the United States are imprisoned in institutions, while two-thirds are under probation or parole supervision in the community.

7. Probation and parole services for adult offenders are administered by a single state agency in all but fourteen states, where probation is a responsibility of the county trial court.

Probation is always granted only by the court, and parole by either a state board or institutional board. However, in most states the supervision of adult probationers and parolees is done by non-judicial agencies.

8. Juvenile probation is administered by juvenile or county courts in thirty-two states and by a central state agency in the other states. That is, juveniles are put on probation by the juvenile court only, but they may be supervised by a non-judicial state agency.

9. Juvenile parole, or "aftercare," as it is commonly known, is administered by the individual training schools from which the juvenile is released in thirty-four states, and by separate institutional or youth parole boards in the other sixteen jurisdictions and the District of Columbia.

10. Probation programs for misdemeanant offenders are practically non-existent in most jurisdictions, because of the large volume of these cases, the relatively short sentences of the offenders, and the lack of personnel to supervise and administer such programs. However, where misdemeanant probation programs exist, they are usually the responsibility of either a state correctional system or some court.

In summation, it should be obvious that corrections in this country is administered at different levels of government and by different agencies. However, the current trend is to establish single state departments of correction, which will include all correctional programs for adults and juveniles. The American Correctional Association and the National Council on Crime and Delinquency have recommended this type of administration through the publication of a Standard Act for State Correctional Services.[3]

---

[3]National Council on Crime and Delinquency, *Standard Act for State Correctional Services* (New York: National Council on Crime and Delinquency, 1966).

PROBATION

Probation is that part of corrections in which the sentence of an offender is suspended while he is permitted to remain in the community, subject to the control of the court and under the supervision of a probation officer.[4] The offender is thus permitted to live with his family, in the community, under certain conditions ordered by the court. For example, the adult probationer is expected to support his family, maintain lawful employment, behave properly and not violate any laws, and report regularly to his probation officer. Of course, if the probationer does not comply with the conditions of his probation, the court may impose another type of sentence, which could include a revocation of his probation and commitment to a correctional institution.

The purpose of probation is to correct the unlawful behavior of the offender, and it is one technique available to the court for use in appropriate cases. Not all offenders should be granted probation. Where it is granted, it should be in the best interest of the community and in cases where it will most likely assist the offender in leading a law-abiding life. The decision to grant probation should be based upon a presentence investigation, which should include sufficient background information about the offender to assist the judge in imposing the best possible sentence. Judges generally may grant probation at their discretion except in those types of cases where probation is prohibited by statute. For example, most states prohibit probation for those who have committed murder, but fifteen states have no statutory restrictions on granting probation, regardless of the type of crime committed. A few states prohibit probation by law if an offender has had previous convictions or if he might receive a prison sentence of five years or more.[5] However, except in such cases as those noted above, all fifty states and the federal government authorize probation by statute.

ADVANTAGES AND OBJECTIONS TO PROBATION

If probation is used in appropriate cases, and if there is a sufficient number of well-trained probation officers to supervise and

---

[4]Robert G. Caldwell, *Criminology* (New York: The Ronald Press Co., 1965), p. 462.

[5]The President's Commission on Law Enforcement and the Administration of Justice, pp. 170-71.

counsel the offender, probation has many advantages for the public and the criminal. Some of the more positive aspects of probation are as follows:

1. The offender remains in the community to lead a normal life and learns to assume the responsibilities of a law-abiding member of society.
2. The probationer can support himself and his family and make restitution to the victim of his crime.
3. The offender is not exposed to the negative influences of prison life and thus left embittered and stigmatized as a convict and more deeply schooled in criminality.
4. It costs much less to keep a man on probation than to maintain him in an institution.

On the other hand, a number of objections have been raised against probation, and although they are valid, they deal with the improper administration or supervision of probation and not with probation as such. Some of the criticisms of probation are:

1. Probation pampers the offender and allows him to avoid punishment, and thus does not deter the offender or others from committing new or additional crimes; however, this is true only if an offender is not well supervised. Furthermore, his probation can be revoked, and he does suffer some humiliation and disgrace by being convicted and under supervision.
2. Probation provides an opportunity for those with influence to "fix" a case and thus avoid commitment to an institution. This may happen, but there is no evidence that it happens very often.
3. Probation does not protect the community, since the offender is still at large and may repeat his crimes. This, however, will rarely occur if offenders are carefully selected for probation, and properly supervised.
4. Probation is impractical because many jurisdictions do not have the personnel for the proper investigation and supervision of probationers. This is so in many instances, but the solution is to provide adequate staff and resources and not to eliminate probation.[6]

---

[6]The reader is referred to the following texts for a further discussion of probation and parole: Caldwell, Chapters 19 and 28; Reed K. Clegg, *Probation and Parole* (Springfield, Ill.: Charles C. Thomas, 1964); David Dressler, *Probation and Parole* (New York: Columbia University Press, 1959); Robert M. Carter and Leslie T. Wilkins, *Probation and Parole* (New York: John Wiley & Sons, Inc., 1969).

INSTITUTIONS FOR DETENTION
AND SHORT-TERM OFFENDERS

As was stated earlier, the correctional process should include the detention of offenders and their commitment to various types of institutions, currently referred to as correctional institutions. In the United States, there are, of course, many different kinds of correctional institutions which have been established to confine, discipline, and correct diverse types of offenders.

Available information indicates that there are about 4,037 local institutions for misdemeanants, best known as county and city jails, and more than thirty-seven federal and 350 major state institutions for adult felons.[7] Additionally, there are some 200 major institutions for juvenile delinquents. These institutional facilities are prisons or penitentiaries, reformatories, workhouses, training schools, or farms, ranches, and camps. The prison or penitentiary provides maximum or medium custody for older felons, usually over thirty years of age. Reformatories are designed to provide for the maximum or medium security of youthful felons between the ages of sixteen and thirty, and prison farms, camps, and ranches are usually used for felons of all ages who require only minimum custody. Training schools are operated for housing and rehabilitating juvenile delinquents, and such schools provide for the confinement of all types of delinquents from the most sophisticated and recalcitrant to the first offender with minimal problems. Finally, jails and workhouses are used to confine misdemeanants.

Of all the correctional institutions in the United States, the ones with which the police have the most contact are the city and county jails. These facilities are used:

1. To detain persons who have been arrested by the police and are awaiting trial but who have not been released on bail or their own recognizance.
2. To detain important witnesses who might otherwise disappear before being called to testify.
3. To detain the mentally ill, the feeble-minded, and others who are suffering from various mental or physical conditions, and who,

---

[7]National Advisory Commission on Criminal Justice Standards and Goals, pp. 274, 341-343.

although they are not charged with any offense, are being detained for their own protection until some other arrangements can be made for their care.

4. To house misdemeanants serving a sentence of one year or less. Of the 3,500 local jails in the United States, 73 percent are county jails and 22 percent are city jails; the remainder are joint city-county facilities.

The county jail is usually administered by the sheriff and is used to confine those awaiting trial or sentencing, as well as convicted offenders serving sentences for one year or less. The city lockup, which is usually operated under the control of the city police department, is often located in the district police station and is used primarily to confine persons for short periods of time. The small town lockup, also, is operated by the local police in much the same way as the city lockup. It has been estimated that more than a million persons are confined in our jails each year.

Although the police are primarily responsible for administering jails, it is the feeling of many authorities that jails should be a correctional responsibility, and, as such, should be administered by professionally trained corrections personnel. This would free police personnel to perform those police duties for which they were trained. Unfortunately, the condition of many jails is appalling; they are often inadequate and archaic, with poor lighting, ventilation, and heating, and inadequate space. Physical examinations are seldom given to incoming prisoners, and the well and the sick, the clean and the infected are confined in close association in crowded quarters. Perhaps the worst feature of our jails is the confining together of a highly heterogeneous group of offenders, that is, the old, the young, and the first offender with the sophisticated criminal. Furthermore, most jails do not provide programs of employment, education, recreation, and rehabilitation.

In conclusion, it can be said that the jails are the most important of all correctional institutions, for two-thirds of all convicted offenders serve out their sentence in jails. They are the place for detaining the untried offender, and they are the first contact the offender has with the institutional phase of the criminal justice process. Jails are also the reception centers for all other institutions, as convicted offenders are first detained in jails before being sentenced to a prison, reformatory, or training school. Unfortunately, jails too often corrupt rather than correct the offender.

INSTITUTIONS FOR ADULT FELONS

The correctional institutions for adult felons convicted of state crimes are administered by the states, and those for adult felons convicted of federal crimes are administered by the federal government. Today, the typical state institution for adult felons is a walled fortress of stone and steel. Within the walls is a total community of felons who work, eat, sleep, and attend religious, educational, and recreational services and programs. Outside the prison walls are the principal administrative offices, houses for the warden and his deputies, and often one or more prison farms. The normal capacity of a prison ranges from a few hundred to several thousand inmates. Most institutions house from 1,000 to 3,000 felons; a few from 3,000 to 4,000; and one or two confine some 5,000 inmates.

Most of the institutions for felons are old, difficult to maintain, and not suited to correct or rehabilitate offenders. Such institutions are too large and often over-crowded, and the imprisoned are idle much of the time due to a lack of programs and personnel. Furthermore, many diverse types of criminals are confined together, as in the case of the jails. Because of such difficult conditions, a current trend is to establish small community correctional centers and community-based programs.

COMMUNITY-BASED CORRECTIONS

Community-based corrections has been receiving widespread attention as a promising method for accomplishing the changes in offender behavior which the public expects. It includes all types of correctional programs that take place in the community, such as: (1) nonresidential programs requiring supervision as probation and parole; supervision by a private citizen or citizen group such as an employer, a relative, a "big brother," or a local social service agency or neighborhood center, or other nonresidential programs of counseling, education, or training, and (2) residential alternatives to imprisonment such as foster and group home arrangements, halfway houses, residential educational programs on campuses, and community-based correctional centers.[8]

---

[8]National Advisory Commission on Criminal Justice Standards and Goals, p. 238.

Such programs and facilities are located in or near the high crime and delinquency areas from which most offenders come. The purpose for establishing small community correctional facilities is to treat the offender in the community from which he comes and to which he will return after he finishes his sentence or is released on parole. Additionally, such programs and facilities will influence the community to help the offender become a law-abiding member and to develop community attitudes which will assist in producing fewer criminals in the future. The hope is that community resources will be used in correctional programs in such a was as to prepare the offender for a law-abiding life in the community in which he will live. Of course, maximum security institutions will be necessary for those who cannot function in the less secure community institution.

There are many types of community correctional programs which include: (1) prerelease centers—a program designed to prepare prisoners for release after they have been granted parole or are nearing the expiration of their sentences; (2) work-release programs which involve offenders who work in the community at regular jobs during the day and return to a center at night and on weekends; they are required to pay for their keep and to support their families; and (3) short-term intensive treatment programs for selected juveniles and youthful felons sentenced directly by the courts to a community center. In the third type of program listed above, the offender is kept under close supervision for the first thirty days or so and then allowed to work in the community. Finally, he will receive intensive counseling and guidance until he is released to live and work in the community, returning only weekly to the institution until the expiration of his sentence.[9]

INDIANA COMMUNITY-BASED CORRECTIONS

In 1971, the Indiana State Legislature passed into law an act entitled "Community Correctional Centers" which enables the Indiana Department of Correction to "establish, maintain and operate commu-

---

[9]For a discussion of community correctional programs, the reader is referred to the following: Vernon Fox, *Introduction to Corrections* (Prentice-Hall, 1972), pp. 215-36; American Correctional Association, *Manual of Correctional Standards* (College Park, Md.: The American Correctional Association, 1971), pp. 43-78; *The Institute for the Study of Crime and Delinquency, The Non-Prison* (New York: Bruce Publishing Co., 1970).

nity correctional centers and programs . . . which may be used for the detention, treatment, diagnosis, and rehabilitation of adult and juvenile offenders either before or after conviction and adjudication of any offense."[10] In addition to this, Indiana legislators passed a work-release law in 1967 including a later revision which allows inmates sentenced to institutions to return to the community near the end of their sentence for the purpose of educational or vocational training. Finally, on October 15, 1973, the Indiana Board of Correction passed a motion to support the development of a multi-purpose regional community correctional center for adults to be located in Fort Wayne, Indiana. The result of these actions has been the completion of two final plans to implement the new law entitled "Region II Community Corrections Program" and the "Ten-Year Master Plan for a Community-Based Correction Program for the Indiana Department of Correction."[11]

The first plan, the Indiana ten-year plan, calls for the establishment of alternatives to the traditional institutionalization of sentenced offenders to include (1) community-based work release centers where offenders will demonstrate an ability to adjust to community living and prepare themselves to assume a socially useful and law-abiding life in the community after release; (2) community-based prerelease programs which will provide for vocational and supportive counseling in a minimum security and small group living facility; (3) parole programs that will provide for close supervision and counseling for parolees who violate technical parole regulations when these violations are not serious enough to return the violator to a correctional institution; (4) residential treatment programs for offenders who do not require the close custody and confinement of a prison, including work release, educational release, vocational training, counseling, and the use of other available community resources to assist in the rehabilitation of the offender; and (5) drug and alcohol treatment programs for appropriate offenders which will be integrated with the other programs listed above.[12]

---

[10]General Assembly of the State of Indiana. *Public Law No. 154: Community Correctional Centers* (Indianapolis, Ind.: March 29, 1971), Chapter 5.

[11]See the excellent report of the Governor's Region Two Community Corrections Committee, City-County Building, Fort Wayne, Indiana, October 15, 1973.

[12]Indiana Department of Correction, *Ten-Year Master Plan for a Community Based Program* (Indianapolis, Ind.: October, 1973), pp. 4-5.

The second plan is a project to implement the above plan on an experimental basis and is exemplified in the establishment of a Regional Community Correctional Center to serve nine counties in northeastern Indiana with a total citizen population of almost 500,000 people. This center will have multiple purposes, including: (1) maximum security detention of male and female offenders awaiting trial; (2) medium-to-minimum security housing and programs for sentenced male and female adult offenders commited directly by the court or transferred there from state correctional institutions; (3) diagnosis and classification of adjudicated offenders, utilizing the combined resources of community mental health and other social services; (4) research and evaluation of correctional activities; and (5) training and education of criminal justice personnel and interested citizens regarding the correctional process.[13]

The Indiana plan is an outstanding example of the development of new and sensible correctional programs for the protection of society and the rehabilitation of offenders and is a far-reaching program for dealing with the crime problem.

PAROLE AND OTHER RELEASE PROCEDURES

After a person is arrested by the police, found guilty of a crime, and is sentenced to a correctional institution, he is released in one of the following four ways: (1) parole, (2) pardon, (3) mandatory (conditional) release, and (4) expiration of sentence (discharge).

Parole is a method by which a prisoner serves a part of his sentence in an institution and the remainder of his sentence in the free community. The prisoner does not have a right to parole, but for the protection of the community and the rehabilitation of the offender, all prisoners should be released under some kind of supervision prior to the expiration of their sentence. Under such an arrangement, the offender is helped by a parole officer to reenter society and is supervised to determine whether he is ready for release and how he can be assisted in his efforts to lead an accepted life.

Conditional pardon is a form of executive clemency granting release on the condition that the offender comply with certain rules or

---

[13]Governor's Region Two Community Corrections Committee, *Region II Community Corrections Program* (Indianapolis, Ind.: Office of the Governor, October 15, 1973).

requirements. For example, a conditional pardon may require a person to leave the country; if he fails to do so, his pardon becomes void and he is returned to prison. A pardon may also be absolute or unconditional, that is, one that frees an offender without any restrictions whatsoever.

Mandatory release is a type of conditional release in which a prisoner must be released by law when he has accumulated sufficient good time received for proper behavior while in the institution. Such good time diminishes the time spent in the institution, but not the actual length of his sentence. Thus a prisoner may have received six months of good time, and thereby be eligible for release from the institution six months prior to the end of his sentence. He is also subject to revocation of parole and return to the institution for violation of parole regulations while under mandatory release.

Discharge from prison is another method by which a prisoner is released. As the term implies, it occurs when the prisoner has completed the maximum term of his sentence, and he must be released by law. In this type of release, the offender receives little or no help from prison or parole officers and must make his own way after release.

Two-thirds of all prisoners are released by way of parole or conditional release, and one third at the expiration of their sentence.[14] It has been established that approximately 65 percent of all adult felons are released on parole, and the national average parole period is about twenty-nine months.[15] Juvenile parole is often referred to as "aftercare," to differentiate it from adult parole. Most delinquents are released on parole from training schools when the staff feel they are ready for release; they usually remain under parole supervision for less than one year. There are usually no statutory prohibitions preventing the release of juveniles on parole, but such is not the case with adults. For example, in forty-two of the states, by statute, an adult offender must serve a minimum period of time in prison before he can be released on parole. Additionally, the laws in twenty-seven states prohibit the parole of adult prisoners who have committed certain types of crimes, such as treason, murder, or rape, or who have become habitual offenders.

It is important to realize that while parole has been referred to as "leniency," if properly administered it is basically a means of public

---

[14]President's Commission on Law Enforcement and the Administration of Justice, pp. 186-87.

[15]Ibid.

protection. About 98 percent of all adult sentenced prisoners return to the community, most of them after a few years of imprisonment. Given this fact, it is better to release offenders under the supervision of the state, in order to expedite their rehabilitation and to protect the community for the remainder of their sentence, than it is to release them with no help or supervision at the end of their sentences.

In conclusion it should be noted that most offenders who have gone through this nation's correctional system have had previous arrests and will continue to commit crimes in the future. We cannot hold the correctional agencies solely responsible because we do not have valid data and criteria by which to increase the effectiveness of corrections. Many offenders have set attitudes and habits before they are committed to a correctional agency, and the influence of even the most modern program is only one of many that enter into the offender's life. However, in the final analysis, a well-managed and adequately programmed correctional agency will be more likely to rehabilitate an offender. Then it is up to the community to accept the ex-offender and give him the necessary help to lead a law-abiding life.

CHAPTER XVII

PREVENTION AND WORK
WITH JUVENILES

PREVENTION

A BASIC OBJECTIVE

The prevention of crime and delinquency is one of the basic objectives of law enforcement in the United States. The reason for this can be readily understood when one considers what these problems cost this country each year. For example, in 1931, the National Commission on Law Observance and Enforcement estimated this cost at about $900 million, and in 1954, J. Edgar Hoover, Director of the Federal Bureau of Investigation, placed it at about $20 billion. In 1967, the President's Commission on Law Enforcement and Administration of Justice estimated that police work alone cost more than $2.5 billion a year and that the annual cost of operating the nation's state and local correctional services probably approached one billion dollars. These estimates, however, refer only to the economic costs of crime and delinquency. While economic costs are important, of far greater significance are the costs that cannot be estimated in dollars and cents—such costs as the death, disease, insanity, pain, anguish, misery, impoverishment, disruption of families, corruption of government, and disorganization of community life resulting from the growth and persistence of these problems.

It is true that our knowledge regarding the nature and causes of human behavior is meager and that the available methods and techniques used in the application of this knowledge are crude and largely unproductive. Yet it is also clear that it is far better to do what we can to prevent crime and delinquency than it is merely to struggle with these problems as they appear and to endure passively the increasing burden they impose.

Furthermore, law enforcement agencies are in a favorable position to play a major role in the prevention of crime and delinquency. Of all the agencies that are directly concerned with the control of these problems, the police[1] have the most specific and binding orders to prevent them and the greatest familiarity with the conditions in the community that contribute to their causation. They also have the most clearly defined legal authority to act, the strongest organization for quick and decisive action, the best local, state, and national records on offenders and their methods and offenses, and the most adequately trained, equipped, and deployed personnel.[2] Thus, it can be said that the police are on the "front line." Their competence, vigor, and efficiency largely determine society's reaction to violations of the law and may significantly affect the possibility of the offender's rehabilitation.

However, what the police can accomplish in the prevention of crime and delinquency can easily be exaggerated. In the first place, one must clearly recognize that the police did not create, nor do they have any control over, most of the basic conditions that are contributing to crime and delinquency. They did not start, nor can they stop, industrialization, urbanization, mobility of population, and other such convulsive changes that are transforming and disorganizing America—and along with it, the police themselves—and overwhelming towns and cities with an avalanche of social problems. They do not enact the laws that they are under oath to enforce. They do not prosecute the alleged criminals whom they arrest, determine the disposition of their cases in the courts, or administer their correction in the agencies and institutions to which they are committed. In short, the police are only part of the system of law enforcement and the administration of justice, and, of course, only a small part of society. The prevention of crime and delinquency, therefore, is not their sole responsibility. Rather, it is the responsibility of all parts of society—indeed, of every citizen.[3]

The police, moreover, in all their work, including their efforts in the field of prevention, are confronted with serious difficulties. Public apathy often permits corrupt political machines to dominate and sap the vitality of police departments. The public does not understand the

---

[1]The word "police" is used here in its broadest sense to include all law enforcement agencies.

[2]Robert G. Caldwell and James A. Black, *Juvenile Delinquency* (New York: The Ronald Press Co., 1971), p. 330.

[3]The President's Commission on Law Enforcement and Administration of Justice, *Task Force Report: The Police* (Washington, D.C.: Government Printing Office, 1967), pp. 1-3.

problems of modern police work, frequently fails to provide adequate cooperation in the apprehension and prosecution of alleged criminals, tends to expect impossible results from the police, and neglects to give sufficient recognition to policemen who day after day render efficient and conscientious service, often at the risk of their lives. And while modern society imposes enormous duties and responsibilities upon law enforcement agencies, it fails to provide them with a sufficient number of well-trained, properly equipped, and adequately paid personnel. These and other such matters must be taken into account if a realistic appraisal is to be made of the prevention work of police.

THE PREVENTION PROGRAM

A law enforcement agency that vigorously and efficiently enforces the law operates as a definite deterrent to the commission of crime and delinquency and, therefore, contributes in a significant way to the prevention of these problems.[4] Indeed, the preventive role of the individual patrolman is a fundamental part of modern police service, the mere presence of a well-organized and competent patrol force being generally considered one of the most effective deterrents of crime and delinquency in contemporary society.[5] Nevertheless, authorities agree that the police should go beyond this and set up a special program for prevention, although they differ regarding the extent to which this should be done. However, the establishment of this kind of program does not necessarily require the assignment of a special group of police to prevention work. Often it involves merely the expansion and intensification of the work already being performed by the regular patrol, and, of course, the needs and resources of a law enforcement agency will affect the nature and size of its program. But, even so, it is desirable that the prevention program include at least these elements: (1) patrol and observation, (2) supervision of public gatherings, (3) inspection, (4) investigation, (5) public education, and (6) participation in the broader community prevention program.

The principal purposes of *patrol and observation* are: (1) to

---

[4]Robert G. Caldwell, *Criminology* (New York: The Ronald Press Co., 1965), p. 720.

[5]V. A. Leonard and Harry W. More, *Police Organization and Management* (Mineola, N.Y.: The Foundation Press, Inc., 1971), p. 315.

eradicate unwholesome influences, lessen opportunities for misconduct, enforce regulations, and apprehend persons contributing to the
delinquency of juveniles; (2) to discover persons in need of correction; (3) to assist in the supervision of children being dealt with by the
police and other agencies; and (4) to discover the need of prevention
activities. Consequently, patrol and observation activities are directed especially against taverns, dance halls, poolrooms, bowling
alleys, swimming pools, skating rinks, bus and railroad terminals,
airports, parks, playgrounds, theaters, moving picture houses, vacant
lots, and other such places where persons may become subject to
exploitation and corrupting influences.[6]

The primary mission of the police in the *supervision of public
gatherings*, such as meetings, assemblies, and the spontaneous
crowds at fires and accidents, is to maintain order and prevent violence. However, they must also guard against the obstruction of traffic, trespassing on private property, vandalism, picking of pockets,
molestation of women, and other such illegal activities that crowds
tend to generate. In this supervision, the constitutional rights of
persons must be respected, and great tact must be used in the exercise
of authority, so that the public relations of the police will not be
undermined; but on the other hand the police must be firm, vigorous,
and courageous in their enforcement of the law.

The police should also conduct an *inspection* of schools, court-
houses, and other public buildings, business establishments that
tend to attract burglars and robbers, temporarily vacant homes, and
empty buildings. When the policeman discovers conditions which
tend to invite criminal activities, he should inform the building custodian or the proprietor and urge him to strengthen the existing
security measures.

Investigation should be carried on to obtain additional facts
about certain conditions and activities in the community. Some of
these may grow out of patrol observations, supervisory missions, and
inspections; others may result from "tips" and complaints. Investigation should also include such activities as gathering evidence on vice
activities, questioning of door-to-door canvassers, and checking vehicles with defaced or missing license plates.

However, as we have indicated, the prevention of crime and
delinquency is not, and cannot be, the business of the police alone.

---

[6]O. W. Wilson, *Police Administration* (New York: McGraw-Hill Book
Co., Inc., 1963), pp. 338-40.

This has been emphasized over and over again by many writers. Commenting on this question in 1967, the President's Commission on Law Enforcement and Administration of Justice succinctly observed: "On an average night in a city of half a million population, 65 police officers will be on patrol duty. No matter how well trained, well organized, and well equipped they are, they cannot be at the scene of every crime when it is committed, and this would be true if they numbered 65 or 650."[7] Obviously, then, the police need help from individual citizens, from private organizations, from other public agencies, and from the courts and legislatures.

Some of this help springs spontaneously from concerned individuals and groups. Much of it, however, has to be created, nurtured, and sustained, especially through the initiative and enterprise of the police themselves, and in this endeavor, *public education* is essential to overcome the ignorance, apathy, and sometimes the hostility of the community. In many cases, public educational campaigns are undertaken by the police alone; in others—and these are often the best—in cooperation with interested citizens, civic organizations, and businessmen's groups. In all educational campaigns, every medium of communication should be utilized, including circulars, pamphlets, books, journals, magazines, newspapers, motion pictures, radio, television, lectures, exhibits, and citizen visitations and conducted tours in law enforcement agency buildings.

Furthermore, all aspects of prevention should be covered. Obviously, citizens should be given advice about how they can reduce the threat of crime to their persons and property. For example, they can be urged to take such commonsense precautions as the following:

1. When you leave your home or place of business, be sure to lock all doors and windows.
2. During lengthy absences from your property, leave automatically activated night lights burning, cancel milk and newspaper deliveries, and notify neighbors and the police of your departure.
3. Maintain an alertness in encounters with strangers at the door of your home or on the street and, without frightening your children, tell them about the possible dangers of advances from strangers.

---

[7] The President's Commission on Law Enforcement and Administration of Justice, p. 221.

4. When you leave your garage or car, lock all doors and remove the keys from the locks or ignition.
5. Keep a minimum amount of cash on hand in your place of business, vary the routine of taking money to the bank, balance cash registers away from checkout counters, locate safes in well-lighted spots highly visible from the outside of the building, and use two-man teams to open and close your stores.
6. Obtain advice from the police about the possible installation of a burglar alarm and the delivery to them of a floor plan, so that they will know how to make a strategic entry in case of an attempted burglary.
7. Place lights near high walls and in dead-end driveways and trim hedges and shubbery to give nearby areas as much visibility as is consistent with usefulness and aesthetics.[8]

In addition, one or more police officers may be charged with special prevention duties, such as giving personal instructions to citizens about security measures, rendering follow-up services to the victims of crimes, distributing prevention literature, teaching prevention courses, and conducting prevention clinics. Furthermore, citizens should be urged to report promptly all relevant information about crimes and suspicious incidents, given instructions about the gathering, preservation, and presentation of evidence, and encouraged to organize in various ways so as to furnish effective assistance to the police. For example, citizens can be organized to assist in finding stolen cars, runaways, and escapees, in patroling beaches, parks, and playgrounds, and in keeping empty buildings and the homes of absent families under observation.

Increasingly, moreover, the police must *participate in the broader community prevention program;* that is, they must extend their efforts beyond the activities that are directly related to their own duties and assist in the planning and administration of programs that are not so closely connected with law enforcement and that may not be immediately productive in the reduction of crime and delinquency. Thus, the police should encourage the creation of groups like the following and support them in their work:

1. Parents' and teachers' associations that can provide volunteer

---

[8]Ibid., pp. 221, 222.

parents, foster homes, remedial tutoring, and supervised daytime activities.

2. Organizations, such as the "Big Brothers," "Big Sisters," Boys Clubs, Boy Scouts, Girl Scouts, Camp Fire Girls, Y.M.C.A., Y.W.C.A., and so on, that can work with young people and direct them into constructive and law-abiding activities.

3. Prisoners' aid societies and other such groups that can assist released prisoners to reestablish themselves in community life.

4. Groups of businessmen and representatives of labor unions that can participate in the prerelease programs of correctional institutions, giving advice and guidance to inmates who are preparing for life on the "outside."

5. Citizen crime commissions that can help to coordinate the efforts of other private groups, promote public education in prevention, secure the enactment of better laws, and improve the administration of justice.

Finally, some of the prevention effort of the police can be more effective if it is exerted through a coordinating council or some similar organization in which law enforcement officials can work with other officials representing the administration of justice, corrections, medicine, education, religion, welfare, recreation, and industry, in a concerted attack on crime and delinquency. And this point should not be forgotten: The efforts of the police to prevent these problems go hand in hand with the building of better public relations, each affecting and strengthening the other.[9]

WORK WITH JUVENILES

THE PROBLEM OF DELINQUENCY

In the United States, one out of every nine children—one out of every six male children—will be referred to the juvenile court in connection with some delinquent act (other than a traffic offense) before his eighteenth birthday. Furthermore, of all the persons arrested in the United States during 1975 (not including traffic offenders), 42 percent were under 21 and 26 percent under 18.

The number of arrests (except for traffic offenses) of persons

---

[9]Ibid., pp. 223-28.

under 18 for 1975 represented an increase of two percent over that for 1974, but during the five-year period 1970-1975, these arrests went up 13 percent. And there is additional evidence that the problem of delinquency is becoming more serious. In fact, the number of juveniles who have been arrested has been sharply increasing during recent years, and more and more young people are committing serious crimes. Thus, from 1970 to 1975 the number of arrests of persons under 18 years of age for serious crimes[10] rose 27 percent. Moreover, studies have shown that juvenile delinquency is important as a forerunner of adult crime and that the recidivism rates for young offenders are higher than those of any other age group. One must conclude, therefore, that the best hope for reducing America's crime problem lies in the lowering of its juvenile delinquency and youth crime.[11]

The authority and organization of the police place them in a strategic position not only to detect crime and delinquency, but also to initiate preventive action. That this is so is attested to by the estimate that about 75 percent of the delinquency cases that appear before the juvenile court are brought there by police agencies. And what may be even more significant is the estimate that about three-fourths of the total number of children dealt with by the police are not referred to the juvenile court but are handled in some other way. Thus, the police act as an important screening agency in their work with juveniles.[12] In effect, each time a police officer has to deal with a child, he "holds court," and he may dispose of the "case" in a number of different ways. For example, he may let the child go after a word of

---

[10]The term "serious crimes" here includes murder, non-negligent manslaughter, forcible rape, aggravated assault, robbery, burglary, larceny, and auto theft.

[11]The statistics on arrests quoted above have been drawn from the *Uniform Crime Reports*. As these reports explain, arrests are primarily a measure of police activity, which varies from place to place and within a community from time to time, but they do provide "a useful index to indicate involvement in criminal acts by the age, sex, and race of the perpetrators, particularly for those crimes which have a high solution rate." Federal Bureau of Investigation, *Uniform Crime Reports, 1974* (Washington, D.C.: Government Printing Office, 1975), pp. 37, 41, 184 (Table 32), 186 (Table 34); The President's Commission on Law Enforcement and Administration of Justice. *The Challenge of Crime in a Free Society* (Washington, D.C.: Government Printing Office, 1967), pp. 46, 55, 56.

[12]Caldwell and Black, pp. 161, 162.

warning. He may conduct him to the police station, where he may be turned over to a juvenile officer or to the juvenile bureau or reprimanded and released. He may take him home and have a talk with his parents. He may escort him back to school. He may refer his case to a clinic, a family society, a welfare agency, or the juvenile court, or he may initiate some other similar action.

The police need these discretionary powers in order to give maximum protection to both the juvenile and the community. Thus, the police officer determines to a considerable extent what action society will take regarding the child's behavior and often takes the first basic step in a corrective program which may eventually involve many agencies and professions. Clearly, then, the way in which the officer handles his "case" may have a great effect on the child's ultimate chances for success and happiness. It is for this reason that some authorities believe that guidelines should be established to help the police in their work with juveniles.

LEGAL BASIS FOR POLICE ACTION

The criminal law provides for action against all persons—not just adults—who violate its provisions. The police, therefore, have the authority to arrest juveniles who allegedly have committed acts which would have been crimes if they had been committed by adults, and the police operation is the same for both juveniles and adults in cases of this kind.[13] Thus, if the delinquent conduct is in progress, the officer must first stop the conduct and then decide what he should do with the juvenile. In this situation, if some provision of a local, state, or federal criminal law or ordinance has been violated, the officer, as in the case of an adult, has the authority to take the child into immediate custody. If the delinquent conduct is not in progress, the officer, again as in the case of an adult, must have reasonable grounds to believe that the person committed an act which the law defines as a felony before he makes an arrest. When this is not so, police action may have to wait until sufficient evidence is available to support a referral to the court. In minor cases, however, the juvenile is rarely referred to court and almost never taken into custody. Usually, in such cases, he is left with his family or referred to some social service or welfare agency.

On the other hand, in many cases the police can proceed in an

---

[13]See Chapter X for the law on arrest.

investigation without getting a search warrant or without making an arrest, because the person involved consents to waive his constitutional rights. In their efforts to determine whether the consent of a juvenile is truly voluntary when he makes such a waiver, the courts have considered his immaturity as one of the factors that must be weighed, but the overall test is whether the young person has been treated with fundamental fairness.[14] This means that in each case, the police have to decide whether the child is sufficiently mature and sophisticated to know what he is doing when he consents to be searched or to be taken to the police station to be questioned, without first being taken into custody or arrested on the basis of probable cause. If the officer decides that he can accept the child's consent, then he must explain to the child what this consent means, that he has the right to remain silent, that anything he says can be used against him in court, and that he has the right to get in touch with his parents and to have legal counsel.

Sometimes, however, the circumstances are such that the officer must take the juvenile into custody. When he does this, he has the same right to secure, search, and question a juvenile taken into custody as he has in the case of an arrested adult, but he also has the same responsibilities.[15] He must, therefore, inform the juvenile about his legal rights, permit him to contact parents, friends, relatives, or counsel, insure his having a hearing before some judicial officer within a specified period of time, and abide by the general standards of fair treatment accorded to all citizens. If the case is referred to the juvenile court on an allegation that the juvenile has committed an act that would be criminal if it were committed by an adult, the police should understand that there must be proof *beyond a reasonable doubt* of every element of the alleged offense.

However, it must be remembered that the juvenile court laws of all states provide that certain types of behavior, such as truancy, incorrigibility, and so on, constitute delinquency, although they are not covered by the criminal law and so are not crimes. It is in this area of possible police action that there may be some uncertainty regarding

---

[14]The law is not entirely clear on the meaning of the test of fundamental fairness, and future decisions may change the interpretation that is offered here.

[15]Here again the law is not entirely clear, for there have been no specific Supreme Court rulings on the question, but the interpretation given above seems to be a reasonable one in the light of the *Gault* decision, which indicated that the Bill of Rights is not for adults alone. See Chapter XIII.

police authority. The juvenile court laws of some states specifically grant authority to the police to act in cases involving such behavior, but in states where this has not been done, police authority must be inferred from the general provisions of the law through the use of the doctrine called "protective custody." This causes no difficulty when the juvenile agrees to cooperate, but the authority of the police is not clear when he objects to having the "benevolent assistance" of the state. It appears, therefore, that those states that have not yet specifically given the police adequate authority to act in cases of this kind should do so.

In abuse and neglect cases, the officer has the authority to take the juvenile into protective custody immediately and later have the case referred to the juvenile court or to some welfare or social service agency. Such action should be taken by the officer whenever he believes that this is necessary to protect the child. Furthermore, the parents may be subjected to criminal prosecution if it appears that the child has been harmed or exposed to acute danger by them.[16]

ORGANIZATION FOR JUVENILE WORK

The work of police with juveniles has been greatly expanded in order to cope with the increasing problem of juvenile delinquency. However, as in other areas of law enforcement, the effectiveness of this police work is significantly affected by the kind of organization within which it must be done. Since juveniles cannot be handled in the same way as adults, some degree of specialization in juvenile work is advisable except in the smallest law enforcement agency. In fact, even when a police department has only a few members, some specialization may be effected by arranging for one officer to devote part of his time to juvenile cases. A department, furthermore, does not have to become very large before one officer will have to spend all of his time in work with juveniles, and so the need of some kind of organization is soon felt. Naturally, the degree of specialization and the extent of organization will vary from one department to another, and decisions regarding these matters will have to take into consideration such factors as the size of the force, the quality of personnel, the amount of work involved, the pressure of other duties, and so forth.

For example, rural police units are usually limited to one or two men, which means that the rural officer handles all kinds of police

---

[16]Caldwell and Black, pp. 163-65.

work and has little or no staff, inadequate crime detection equipment, and relatively meager detention facilities. Furthermore, the independent and self-sufficient mode of life of most rural peoples prevents the officer from getting very close to family problems. Nevertheless, even in this simple situation, the officer's effectiveness in dealing with juveniles may be strengthened by some organization and specialization through the creation of a community council or similar coordinating device, which can assume responsibility in planning and developing ways of providing needed services for young people. In addition, farm organizations, schools, churches, parent-teacher associations, and service clubs can be used for the building of public opinion in support of the improvement of rural law enforcement agencies.[17]

As police work with juveniles has progressed, women have been brought in to assist in the handling of some of the peculiar problems that have emerged. Apparently, the first woman to work with police in the prevention of juvenile delinquency was Mrs. Lola Baldwin. She was appointed in 1905 to provide protection for girls at the Lewis and Clark Centennial Exposition in Portland, Oregon, but since she was not called a policewoman, the claim has been made that the first woman in the world to have that title was Alice Stebbins Wells, of Los Angeles, who was appointed to her position in 1910.

A few years later, another important step was taken in the development of police work with juveniles. This happened when Portland, Oregon, created the first juvenile bureau in America.[18] Today, many police departments have bureaus of this kind, staffed by both men and women who have received special training in juvenile work. A study that was made a few years ago estimated that 552 police departments in cities having a population of more than 10,000 had specialized juvenile officers or juvenile units.[19] In smaller departments, the head of the juvenile bureau may report directly to the chief of police, but in the larger ones, in order to avoid having too many

---

[17]Caldwell, pp. 722, 723.

[18]Edward Eldefonso, *Law Enforcement and the Youthful Offender: Juvenile Procedures* (New York: John Wiley and Sons, Inc., 1967), pp. 108, 109. The juvenile unit is sometimes given another name, such as juvenile aid bureau, crime prevention bureau, youth division, and so on, but in this text it will be called the juvenile bureau.

[19]Richard A. Myren and Lynn D. Swanson, *Police Work with Children,* U.S. Children's Bureau Publication, No. 399 (Washington, D.C.: Government Printing Office, 1962), p. 22.

persons reporting to the chief, some other arrangement may be used. For example, the heads of the juvenile bureau and the detective bureau may report to an assistant or deputy chief, who in turn reports to the chief of police.

The number of persons assigned to the juvenile bureau varies from department to department. According to one rough rule that has been used, this number should be 5 percent of the total force, but the question of proper staffing can be answered only by sound planning and an adequate review of the bureau's effectiveness. However, it must not be forgotten that work with juveniles is not limited to that done by officers in the juvenile bureau. In fact, every police officer, regardless of his specific duties, has contacts with persons of all ages in many different situations, and so all officers should receive some training in the proper techniques and procedures to be used in dealing with children.[20]

SELECTION AND TRAINING OF PERSONNEL

The success of the juvenile bureau depends largely on the competence of its personnel. Therefore, they should be carefully selected through the use of written examinations, background and character investigations, and thorough interviews. Policemen for the juvenile bureau are usually selected from the patrol division in accordance with the promotion policies of the department, but policewomen must almost always be found through outside sources. If they are available, college graduates who have had courses in the social and behavioral sciences and some experience in such fields as education, recreation, and welfare should be given preference.[21] However, if any candidate for a position in the juvenile bureau has not had any police experience, he should first receive regular police training and serve a probationary period of six months in general police work before his assignment to the juvenile bureau. In this way, he will become familiar with general police problems, the organization, operation, and procedures of the department, and have enough training for work in

---

[20]Caldwell and Black, p. 166.

[21]The Institute for Training in Municipal Administration, *Municipal Police Administration* (Washington, D.C.: The International City Management Association, 1971), pp. 152-54; The Institute for Training in Municipal Administration, *Municipal Police Administration* (Ann Arbor, Mich.: Lithoprinted by Cushing-Malloy, Inc., 1961), pp. 213-18.

other branches of the service to make possible his reassignment if this becomes necessary.

Juvenile officers should have all the qualifications that are required to make a good police officer. They should be in excellent physical condition and above the average in character, intelligence, personality, and appearance. In addition, they should have a special interest in juveniles and an eager desire and an unusual ability to work with them.

After their selection, juvenile officers should receive special training, both on the job and in classes conducted by the department or the police academy, or by colleges and universities, some of which offer short courses in juvenile work. Included in their program of training should be such subjects as these: the philosophy of police work with children, with its emphasis on protection, guidance, and education; the laws regarding juveniles; the causation of crime and delinquency; the functions, procedures, and techniques of the juvenile bureau and its relationship with other parts of the department; the principles of investigation in juvenile cases; interviewing; community organization and resources; public relations; and prevention of crime and delinquency.

OPERATION OF THE JUVENILE BUREAU

The juvenile bureau should have attractive quarters in the building that houses the police department. It should have at least two rooms—one for office space and one for interrogation—and an informal and noninstitutional appearance, so that it does not make the child feel that he is a condemned felon on his way to prison. Furthermore, since relatives, witnesses, and others who have little knowledge of police work and often wish to remain as inconspicuous as possible will have to go to the bureau, it should be so situated that it can be easily found with a minimum of public attention.

Policewomen assigned to the bureau usually specialize in the handling of young women, girls, and young boys, whereas policemen work with young men and older boys. In every case, the officer should treat the child or young person with consideration and try to gain his confidence and respect and discover and understand his problems. He should never be ingratiating or coaxing but always firm, positive, and definite, so that the person in custody will clearly understand that he must behave himself and obey the law. Nevertheless, the officer should never resort to profanity, vulgarity, or obscenity and should avoid harsh and loud language and excessive force. In many cases, the child is afraid, antagonistic, suspicious, and resentful. Consequently, clumsy, inept, or cruel treatment may drive him beyond the reach of guidance and counseling and even solidify the hostile feelings that he has for the police and the law.

The juvenile bureau has the following five basic functions:

1. The discovery of delinquents, potential delinquents, and the conditions contributing to delinquency.
2. The investigation of cases of juveniles who are delinquents or involved as accessories or victims of adults.
3. The protection of juveniles.
4. The disposition of juvenile cases.
5. The prevention of juvenile delinquency.

The *discovery* of delinquency or conditions contributing to it may be made as a result of a complaint lodged by such persons as parents, neighbors, teachers, and social workers, or as a result of information supplied by cab drivers, waitresses, bartenders, bellhops, theater doormen, and so forth. Many discoveries, however, are made through patrolling and inspection, both by juvenile officers and other police officers, especially of places where juveniles may be exposed to harmful conditions, such as dance halls, poolrooms, playgrounds, penny arcades, skating rinks, bus stations, railroad depots, cheap hotels, all-night restaurants, taverns, bars, drive-ins, motels, and theaters.

The *investigation* of juvenile cases is often more difficult than that of adult cases, for it requires special techniques to deal with the mental and emotional immaturity of children and their changing relationships with various gangs and other groups. In addition—and this is important—it should be based on carefully planned and generally understood policies, so as to avoid friction and conflicts with detectives who also may be involved in certain aspects of juvenile cases. During the investigation in a juvenile case, the child may be held by the police or he may be released to his parents.

Interviewing is the most important method that the officer can use in the investigation of juvenile cases. It is desirable to conduct at least part of the interview with the juvenile when he is alone, so that others will not interfere and influence the outcome, but this may not be possible in some cases. All kinds of children, including the frightened, the confused, the bewildered, the hardened, and the arrogant, as well as many adults, such as parents, teachers, employers, and so on, must be questioned. The interview, therefore, has to be adjusted to fit the individual case, but a realistic balance between the rights of the individual and those of the community must always be maintained. During the interview, the officer should be tactful, considerate, and patient but at all times firm and positive. Using every skill at his command, he should try to gain the confidence and respect of the child and in simple, definite language encourage him to tell his own story. Although the purpose of the interview is to learn as much as possible about the child, prolonged questioning should be avoided. Usually the interview of juveniles is more fruitful than that of adults, and often it reduces the fears, tensions, and hostilities of the child and helps to lay the foundation for later treatment in his case.

The police frequently find children who are in need of *protection*. Many of these children are neglected or even abused by their parents and may be inadequately clothed and nourished. Others are runaways or are exploited, or in danger of being exploited, by adults. Sometimes the police find it necessary to take immediate action to help these children, obtaining food, clothing, and shelter for them, or returning them to their homes. Usually, however, they initiate action for sending children who need protection to schools, churches, welfare departments, and other such agencies and institutions, or to the juvenile court. Nevertheless, if the police are not careful, they will become more and more involved in welfare service. They should try to prevent such a development, for welfare work is not a legitimate police function and it can drain off money and personnel that are urgently needed in the performance of basic police duties.

Various procedures are used by the police in the *disposition* of juvenile cases. They include, for example, referring the child to a school, church, welfare agency, or probation department, releasing the child to his parents, dropping the charges because of insufficient evidence or exoneration of the child, or sending the case to the juvenile court or, if certain offenses are involved, to the criminal court. There is, of course, no hard and fast rule by which the officer can decide whether a case should go to the juvenile court. However, the presence of certain conditions, such as any of the following, usually indicates that this should be done.

1.   The alleged offense is a serious one.
2.   The alleged act is not intrinsically serious but the facts point to the need of protective action.

3. The child has a record of numerous delinquencies.
4. The child and his parents have been unable or unwilling to cooperate with other agencies.
5. Casework with the child by other agencies has failed.
6. The services needed by the child can be obtained most adequately through the court and its probation department.
7. The child denies the offense, but sufficient evidence exists to warrant referral and judicial determination is called for.
8. The child is to be placed in detention.

The juvenile court, however, does not always take jurisdiction in a case just because the case has been referred to it by the police, but instead, through its intake process, it may send the case to some other agency.

When the police refer a case to the juvenile court, they should provide the court with the following: (1) the alleged facts that give the court jurisdiction over the case and the pertinent personal data about the child; (2) information about any co-delinquent; (3) information about the complainant or the victim, including a statement regarding injuries or damages; (4) an explanation of the request for juvenile court action, other than the present alleged offense, such as previous police contacts with the child that did not result in a court referral; and (5) a brief summary of any significant factors revealed in the investigation, such as court records of parents, that point to the need of action by the juvenile court.

In 1967, the President's Commission on Law Enforcement and Administration of Justice recommended the establishment of Youth Services Bureaus. These were to be community-based centers to which juveniles could be referred by the police, the courts, parents, schools, and social agencies for counseling, education, work or recreation programs, and job placement. The commisson believed that such bureaus were needed partly because society had "failed to give the juvenile court the resources that would allow it to function as its founders hoped it would."[22] By 1972, more than one hundred cities had created bureaus of this kind. Their goal is to divert children and youth from the justice system and to help solve their home, school,

---

[22]The President's Commission on Law Enforcement and Administration of Justice, *The Challenge of Crime in a Free Society* (Washington, D.C.: Government Printing Office, 1967), p. VII; The Institute for Training in Municipal Administration, *Municipal Policy Administration* (Ann Arbor, Mich.: Lithoprinted by Cushing-Malloy, Inc., 1961), pp. 218-24.

and community problems. In their efforts to do this, they rely heavily on neighborhood volunteers but also enlist the assistance of other social and welfare organizations.

The juvenile bureau should also play an important part in the general *prevention* program of the police department, which has already been presented. The juvenile officers, of course, would devote their time primarily to the prevention of juvenile delinquency. In some large cities, a special youth council has been established to coordinate the efforts of schools, the juvenile court, the welfare department, the family agencies, the police, and other agencies concerned with delinquency problems. In some other communities, the council of social agencies or some other existing organization includes the coordination of youth services in its program of activities. Many authorities believe that where no such community organization exists, the police should take the initiative in creating one. In the meetings of these coordinating councils, the juvenile bureau can not only call the attention of other agencies to the needs of youth in various neighborhoods, but also receive from them information which will be quite helpful to the police in the discharge of their duties.

In fact, police agencies may miss many opportunities to influence their communities and promote better understanding of law enforcement problems if they do not cooperate with local organizations and institutions. For example, close cooperation between police and schools will facilitate the identification of potential delinquents and the solution of their problems. In some cities, this cooperation has led to the assignment of police officers to troublesome schools in an effort to create the image of the modern policeman as a "friend" to youth rather than as an "adversary." These "juvenile specialists" patrol the schools and surrounding areas, teach safety education, and participate in various other school activities. However, this program has drawn considerable adverse criticism, especially on the grounds that police departments, already suffering from manpower shortage, cannot spare men for school assignments, and that the "juvenile specialist" faces the real possibility of becoming the school's disciplinary officer instead of the students' "friend," and so the policeman's "image" may actually deteriorate.

ADMINISTRATIVE QUESTIONS

FINGERPRINTING AND PHOTOGRAPHING

The police must establish definite policies with respect to certain administrative questions involved in the handling of juvenile cases. One of these is the fingerprinting and photographing of children, which, in general, the police favor. However, some persons have advanced arguments against the practice, except in extreme cases. They contend that it is a stigma that affects both the attitude of the juvenile and that of others toward him, sometimes giving him the impression that he has become a "tough guy" and so must measure up to his new label. They say also that it is contrary to the philosophy of the juvenile court, since it treats the juvenile as a criminal, and that it is a threat to his future, since, even after many years, it may interfere with employment or security clearance. On the other hand, the police argue that it is the best method of identification, that it is no longer a criminal stigma, since it is now so widely used for noncriminal purposes, and that it is not any more objectionable than the practice of asking for the child's name, age, place of birth, and so on, which is now generally accepted. They believe also that it is a good method not only of protecting the child against unjust accusations when fingerprints are found at the scene of the alleged act, but also of identifying him in case of injuries that produce unconsciousness or amnesia, and that it is a deterrent, since many children are afraid to take chances when their fingerprints are on file. Although the controversy over the photographing of children is not so intense, the arguments for and against it are about the same as those that have been used about the fingerprinting of juveniles.

The agitation over these questions continues, but many authorities in the field of law enforcement believe that the police should have the power to formulate their own policy regarding the identification of juveniles, and that, without first receiving permission of any other agency, like the juvenile court, they should fingerprint and photograph the juvenile when he is suspected of having committed a felony or has admitted that he has done so, when he has a long history of delinquencies and will probably continue to be a "repeater," and when identification is specifically needed, as, for example, when his fingerprints might be compared with those of a known offender or when he is unable or unwilling to identify himself. Some other authorities, however, insist that the fingerprinting and photographing of juveniles by police should occur only when the juvenile court specifically gives its consent, and that after the fingerprints and photographs have served their immediate purpose, they should be destroyed.[23]

USE OF THE TERM "ARREST"

Some critics of police practices also oppose the use of the term "arrest" in connection with juveniles, claiming that this term clashes with the principles of the program of treatment which should be used in dealing with children, and that therefore the term "taken into custody" should be used instead.[24] In reply, police explain that the term "arrest" is universally employed to refer to the taking into custody of a person on a charge of violation of a law or ordinance, that it will continue to be so used, and that the mere changing of the term would not alter in any way what happens when an arrest is made or reduce the responsibilities of those who are involved. In fact, they argue, this change in terms would cause a great deal of confusion in police reports and records, and they must follow the instructions of the Federal Bureau of Investigation in the preparation of records for the Uniform Crime Reports, so that the data received from all agencies will remain comparable.

RELATIONS WITH PARENTS

Some police officials advocate the punishment of parents for the delinquent acts of their children. This, they argue, would force parents to assume greater responsibility in the training and supervision of their children and enable the victims of delinquency to collect restitution. In opposition to this proposal, it has been explained that often parents are not entirely responsible for the delinquency of their children, that in many cases punitive action would be ineffective, that many parents could be more influenced through education and counseling than through punishment, that many families do not have enough money to make restitution payments, and that the punish-

[23]See, for example, Advisory Council of Judges of the National Probation and Parole Association in cooperation with the National Council of Juvenile Court Judges, Guides for Juvenile Court Judges (New York: National Probation and Parole Association, 1957), pp. 32, 33.

[24]See, for example, the Standard Juvenile Court Act (New York: National Council on Crime and Delinquency, 1959), p. 37.

ment of parents might destroy the home and cause the family to become a public charge. There does not appear to be any sound reason for the adoption of a general policy for the punishment of parents in delinquency cases. Of course, sometimes parents should be punished, but a decision to do this should be based on the facts of the individual case.

PLAIN-CLOTHES OFFICERS

There is, however, considerable agreement on another question, the use of "plain-clothes officers" and unmarked cars in juvenile work. In general this appears to be a wise policy, for a uniform or a marked car may give warning to those who are being observed, inspected, or investigated and, indeed, may cause antagonism or hostility if the officer has to talk to the juvenile in his home or at a play ground or school. There are exceptions, of course, and in some situations a uniform or a marked car may be needed so that there will be no mistake about the identity of the officer or his authority.

CURFEW

The use of the curfew is another favorite proposal of some law enforcement officials, who contend that it provides both parents and the police with a clear and uniform basis for dealing with juveniles after a certain time in the evening. Undoubtedly, the curfew has been helpful in some communities, but its opponents insist that it suffers from many limitations. Thus, they argue that the police are faced with the problem of ascertaining whether the juvenile is above or below the age set by the curfew law, that many parents resent having their children stopped and questioned by the police, that it does little to remove the causes of delinquency, and that it is most effective in the regulation of the juveniles who are carefully supervised by their parents and so the least likely to become delinquent.

SCHOOL SAFETY PATROLS

Less controversial is the proposal that the police establish school safety patrols, which utilize boys and girls for full traffic control at most intersections near schools. This type of patrol enjoys strong support among both educators and police, since it provides an opportunity for the development of an extensive safety education program in the schools and the promotion of good relations between juveniles and the police.

PUBLIC IDENTIFICATION OF DELINQUENTS

Another administrative question that has attracted widespread attention is that concerning the release of the names and photographs of juvenile offenders to the news media. Some states have laws which forbid this, and many news services have voluntarily adopted a policy against publishing the names of juveniles. Even so, some writers believe that the press should be free to publish the names of all offenders and that the public is entitled to know about them. The general view appears to be that usually the names of juvenile offenders or of juvenile victims of adult acts should not be publicized, since the resulting notoriety might unnecessarily complicate or even ruin their lives. However, it is generally agreed that the name of the juvenile should be released when he is charged with a serious offense or is judged to be highly dangerous and the publication of his name, description, and photograph will assist in his apprehension.

DETENTION OF THE JUVENILE

Two other questions have generated some controversy. These are: When should the juvenile be detained? and When he is detained, how long should he be held? Obviously, few investigations can be completed immediately, and often the juvenile must be held until some progress has been made in an examination of his case. It is equally clear, however, that detention should not be used as a form of punishment and that the child should not be detained just because detention will enable officers to investigate his case at their convenience. Still, the child should be detained in cases in which (1) his presence will greatly facilitate the completion of the investigation, (2) he is so incorrigible that he is beyond the control of his parents, (3) his parents cannot be located or probably will not assume responsibility for him, (4) he has no home or his home cannot be located, and (5) his previous record indicates that he should be kept in custody. Moreover, the juvenile may have to be detained for a short time at the station house, instead of being sent to a regular detention facility when, for example, the investigation is moving so fast that it would be highly inconvenient to go back and forth to the detention facility in order to question the juvenile or confront him with witnesses or accomplices.

The length of time that the child will have to be detained will, of course, depend upon the nature of the case. One procedure for the police to follow when they must detain a child for more than a few hours is to hold him in a proper place until the juvenile court judge (or someone who is authorized to act for him) is available and can be properly informed of the facts of the case. The judge can then give his decision regarding the detention of the juvenile.

The National Council on Crime and Delinquency has recommended that children who are apprehended for delinquency should be detained for the juvenile court when, after proper intake interviews, it appears that casework by a probation officer will not enable the child to control his own behavior. Such children, according to the National Council, fall into the following groups:

1. Those who are almost certain to run away during the period when the court is studying their cases, or during the period between the disposition and the transfer to an institution or another jurisdiction.
2. Those who are almost certain to commit an offense dangerous to themselves or to the community before court disposition or between disposition and transfer to an institution or another jurisdiction.
3. Those who must be held for another jurisdiction—for example, parole violators, runaways from institutions to which they were committed by a court, or certain material witnesses.[25]

WELFARE OR CORRECTIONAL WORK

Should the police do welfare or correctional work with juveniles? Although police generally support programs of rehabilitation for juveniles, they tend to resist efforts to force them into correctional or welfare work. In this resistance, the police are justified, for correctional and welfare work is not a police function and the police are not selected or trained to do it. Even so, sometimes the police are tempted to act as "unofficial probation officers" or as recreational workers in

---

[25]*Standards and Guides for the Detention of Children and Youth* (New York: National Council on Crime and Delinquency, 1961), p. 15.

order to reduce or prevent delinquency and to improve the attitude of the public toward law enforcement. Nevertheless, they should not succumb to this temptation, for it will soon carry them beyond their official duties. Furthermore, if they do begin this work, they may find that they are expected to continue, even though their new responsibilities become an increasing load on an already overburdened budget. The proper solution is the employment of more probation officers and recreational workers.

JUVENILE RECORDS

One more question should be examined here. This has to do with the keeping of juvenile records. These records must be kept because (1) they assist in the investigation of cases, (2) they help to locate conditions that contribute to delinquency and thus facilitate its prevention, (3) they provide a basis for the evaluation of police work with juveniles, and (4) they furnish information that the police must have if they are to dispose of juvenile cases in the proper way. The police, however, should limit juvenile records to those that are necessary for law enforcement purposes and should not expand them merely for the convenience of other agencies. Moreover, juvenile records should be kept in the regular centralized record system of the department, and not in a separate unit like the juvenile bureau. Also, although they should be segregated from adult records, access to them should be open to police officers on a "need-to-know" basis through the same procedures that are followed in the use of other records. Nevertheless, a definite policy should be established to protect juvenile records from indiscriminate and harmful use by others. On this point, the United States Children's Bureau recommends that juvenile records should be kept at an absolute minimum, that the files containing them should be purged at regular intervals, and that they should be closely guarded against unauthorized access. When the files are purged, records of defined categories of juveniles should be removed and destroyed, the Children's Bureau explains, so that the files will not become overloaded with outdated and useless information and young persons can begin their adult lives with a clean slate.[26]

---

[26]Caldwell and Black, pp. 170-74, 331, 332; The Institute for Training in Municipal Administration, *Municipal Police Administration* (Washington, D.C.: The International City Management Association, 1971), pp. 147-52; Eldefonso, pp. 112-17; Myren and Swanson, pp. 77-94; John F. Kenney and Dan G. Pursuit, *Police Work with Juveniles* (Springfield, Ill.: Charles C. Thomas, 1965), pp. 91-121.

CHAPTER XVIII

POLICE-COMMUNITY RELATIONS

MEANING AND IMPORTANCE

One important area of police administration which until very recently has received little attention is that dealing with the relationship between the police and the citizen. Police-community relations is that aspect of police administration which actively seeks to establish positive interpersonal relationships between the police and the citizenry so that the police may perform their required services in accordance with the law and with the support and respect of the community. Police-community relations is not, ". . . a public relations program to sell the police image to the people. It is not a set of expedients whose purpose is to tranquilize for a time an angry neighborhood by, for example, suddenly promoting a few Negro officers in the wake of a racial disturbance. It is a long-range full-scale effort to acquaint the police and the community with each other's problems and to stimulate action to solve these problems."[1]

It is important to remember that America is a vast land inhabited by many diverse ethnic groups—a nation that in a short time has transformed itself into the most technologically advanced country in the world. The results have been a rapid rate of social change, including mass migrations of different ethnic groups into the large cities, and a significant disorganization of all of the nation's basic institutions, including the police and the administration of justice systems. These results, in turn, have increased the complexity of police work and required the police to have an understanding of complex social problems over which they have little or no control but which are directly related to crime and delinquency. Adequate police-community relations can be achieved only when there is mutual respect, cooperation, and the adequate performance of duties and

---

[1]The President's Commission on Law Enforcement and Administration of Justice, *The Challenge of Crime in a Free Society* (Washington, D.C.: U.S. Government Printing Office, 1967), p. 100.

responsibilities by both the police and the citizen. It should be obvious that both the police and the community need each other, for without the police there would be lawlessness, and without citizen support the police would be unable to adequately enforce the law.[2]

THE POLICE ROLE IN COMMUNITY RELATIONS

The police are not, and should not be, professional social workers. A social worker is professionally educated and trained to deal entirely with problems of welfare, standards of living, and social relationships. He is not a law enforcement officer who patrols the streets, interrogates suspects, and makes arrests. However, an understanding of the community the police serve and of how best to interact with its citizens is essential. To achieve this, there must be good police-community relations. As a basic principle, all police personnel should be selected without regard to race, color, or creed, and should be required to meet high standards of fitness. After all, good personnel are the first prerequisite to good police work.

The police must perform a major role in establishing sound public relations. This can be accomplished by ensuring that the police treat all citizens equally under the law, by performing their duties in a courteous, efficient, and economical manner, and by educating the public regarding the work and the problems of the police.[3] The individual police officer is the first point of contact between the citizen and the administration of justice system. In fact, for most people, he is

---

[2]The reader is referred to the following texts on police-community relations: A. F. Brandstatter and Louis A. Radelet, *Police and Community Relations: A Source Book* (Beverly Hills, Cal.: The Glence Press, 1968); The President's Commission on Law Enforcement and Administration of Justice, *The Challenge of Crime in a Free Society* (Washington, D.C.: U.S. Government Printing Office, 1967), pp. 99-103; Institute for Training in Municipal Administration, *Municipal Police Administration* (Washington, D.C.: International City Management Association, 1971), Chapter 13; Victor G. Strecher, *The Environment of Law Enforcement* (Englewood Cliffs, N.J.: Prentice-Hall, Inc., 1971); Alan Coffey, Edward Eldefonso, and Walter Hartinger, *Police-Community Relations* (Englewood Cliffs, N.J.: Prentice-Hall, Inc., 1971); National Advisory Commission on Criminal Justice Standards and Goals, *Task Force on Police* (Washington, D.C.: U.S. Government Printing Office, 1973), pp. 29-44.

[3]Robert G. Caldwell, *Criminology* (New York: The Ronald Press, 1965), p. 315.

the police department, and it will be judged largely by his appearance, his attitude, his conversations, and his actions. A police officer should always be neat, clean, alert, dignified, courteous, and efficient. When called upon to serve, he should listen courteously to complaints and move quickly to the assistance of those in trouble. When dealing with an offender, the officer should act with firmness and decisiveness but should avoid abuse, lecturing, and scolding.

In addition to performing routine police work, the police should establish programs to build public good will, and such programs should include the following: (1) establishing mutual understanding and harmonious relations with the press, radio, and television; (2) giving public lectures, talks, and demonstrations by members of the department on various aspects of police work; (3) providing special services for those in distress, underprivileged children, and visitors to the city; (4) giving public awards to officers who render outstanding services; (5) publishing annual reports to inform the public of police problems, accomplishments, and plans; (6) allowing the public to tour police facilities, and give demonstrations of police methods; (7) exhibiting police displays of the crime problem, police equipment, and methods of law enforcement; (8) initiating a regular and constructive dialogue with the public regarding police-citizen problems; and (9) participation by the police in community planning projects affecting the health, morals, and safety of the public.[4] This type of program will greatly assist in the establishment of good police-community relations, and will be of tremendous assistance in developing a professional and effective police department.

THE ROLE OF THE COMMUNITY

The previous discussion has essentially dealt with the steps the police must take to judiciously and professionally enforce the law. However, as earlier stated, the police need the help and understanding of citizens to prevent crime and to rehabilitate the offender. Therefore, private citizens have an equally important responsibility in law enforcement.

First, and most important, every citizen should obey the law and assist the police in their enforcement responsibilities by identifying

---

[4]O. W. Wilson and Roy C. McLaren, Police Administration (New York: McGraw-Hill Book Co., 1972), pp. 216-44.

criminals, giving information about offenders and their crimes, testifying as witnesses, and taking all necessary precautions to reduce the threat of crime. This latter citizen responsibility can be accomplished by: (1) locking doors and windows of residences and businesses when absent from such dwellings; (2) leaving automatically activated night lights during lengthy or overnight absences from residences and business establishments; (3) alerting the police or neighbors during absences and discontinuing home delivery services during such times; (4) instructing children not to ride with strangers and to refrain from loitering in inappropriate places, especially late at night; (5) removing keys from parked cars and locking them securely; (6) adequately lighting the inside and outside of business premises; and (7) refraining from leaving large quantities of cash in dwellings overnight. These and many more such simple measures can be taken by the public to lessen its chances of being victimized.

However, the community must do much more to prevent crime and to assist the police in their law enforcement responsibilities. A given community will have the kind of police services it deserves. To make certain that the best possible policing exists, the citizenry must be interested and concerned and must demand such services. It can do this by insisting that the police be paid adequate salaries, that professional standards be utilized in selecting police personnel, and that the police be provided with the necessary equipment and public support to enforce all laws and treat all citizens equally under the law.

An alert, responsible, interested, and active public is most important in bringing about effective law enforcement. Crime is not the exclusive responsibility of the police. The prevention of crime is everybody's business and should be a routine part of community planning. Citizens should insist that all agencies of government work together in the prevention of crime. For instance, the police should be aware of public transportation developments as they relate to crime at terminals or on public transit facilities. Public works departments should adopt building designs and lighting provisions that minimize crime hazards. Parks and recreation agencies need advice on the location, lighting, and supervision of playgrounds and recreation areas. Schools should provide better perimeter lighting for schoolyards and other structures after hours, and public utilities should provide adequate street lighting.[5] Finally, and most impor-

---

[5]The President's Commission on Law Enforcement and Administration of Justice, pp. 100-101.

tantly, the public must see to it that politics is eliminated from the enforcement function and that the many causes of crime and delinquency are reduced or eradicated.

POLICE-COMMUNITY RELATIONS PROGRAMS

It should be obvious from the preceding discussion that all police agencies must have active police-community relations programs. This type of program includes a specially structured unit in the department, methods for permitting citizen participation, and internal and external police review procedures.

POLICE-COMMUNITY RELATION UNITS

The President's Commission on Law Enforcement and Administration of Justice recommended that community relations machinery should be both a line and staff function and that such a unit should be allocated sufficient personnel and accorded the appropriate status and authority to become effective. Community relations units should be supervised by a high-ranking officer at the central office level, and personnel should be assigned in the precincts in the larger cities where regular contacts should be maintained with the citizen. In essence, the President's Commission on Law Enforcement and Administration of Justice, recommended the following additional programs:

1. In smaller police departments, the Chief of Police himself should directly supervise community relations, or at the least, assign this responsibility to a top assistant.
2. The community relations unit must have the full support, status, and respect of the entire department, and it is the responsibility of the Chief of Police and his assistants to make certain that this becomes a reality.
3. The community relations unit should participate fully with all other units of the department in formulating policies carried out by the police in their daily services to the public.
4. Personnel of this unit should participate in the selection, recruitment, training, and promotion of all police personnel to make certain that only those men will be appointed and pro-

moted who will know how to serve the community and thus avert police-community conflicts and tensions.

5. A sufficient quality and quantity of personnel must be selected for the community relations unit to ensure its effectiveness.[6]

Even though a community relations unit is established, all personnel must still remember that each individual officer is a community relations officer. Therefore, in the normal course of his work with the public he must be neat, courteous, and respectful to all citizens and must treat all of the public equally under the law.

CITIZEN PARTICIPATION

One of the most effective ways for citizen involvement in law enforcement is through the creation of citizen advisory committees. These committees should meet regularly with the police to work out solutions to problems that exist between the police and the community. Furthermore, a citizens' advisory committee should be composed of representatives of all segments of the community, including those who have grievances as well as those who do not. It is only through such communication that the police and the citizen will come to know one another and learn of the problems that must be solved. After all, in America the police, as is the case with all government officials elected or appointed, are servants of the people. However, the citizens' advisory committee is advisory only and should have no authority over police operations, for such authority is the legal responsibility of the chief of police.

One of the first citizens' advisory committees was established in St. Louis in 1955. Its purpose was to "promote increased cooperation between the police department and other community agencies" and to "educate private citizens to their responsibilities in the preservation of law and order."[7] Under the St. Louis plan, three district committees were established under a citywide committee representing high crime areas populated by Negroes and poor whites. The committees were composed largely of clergymen, social workers, and other responsible citizens who met regularly with police officials. At the present time, there are nine district committees, which elect their

---

[6]Ibid.

[7]Curtis Bronston, "Police Planning Operations and Techniques," *The Police Chief*, June, 1963, p. 38.

own officers and meet as a total city-wide committee on a regular basis with the chief of police. Other cities followed the St. Louis plan and, starting in 1962, citizen advisory committees were established in San Francisco, Cincinnati, and New York City. Citizens' advisory committees can serve a worthwhile purpose if they are representative of the community and if their members will pursue the goal of better police-community relations.

INTERNAL AND EXTERNAL REVIEW PROCEDURES

The President's Commission on Law Enforcement and Administration of Justice does not recommend the establishment of civilian review boards, in jurisdictions where they do not exist, for the purpose of reviewing police conduct.[8] The establishment of such a board would usurp the legal authority and responsibility of the chief of police and other elected public officials, especially the mayor and the governor. A civilian review board usually means that the citizens have authority to censure or discipline police officers or to change existing police procedures. This would be a most unwise and inappropriate use of power which could result in having the chief of police being held legally responsible for decisions made by a board of citizens not responsible for the administration of police services. Many other governmental agencies do not permit this, and the police should not be singled out for such purposes. If legitimate citizens' grievances against the police, or any other government agency, are not properly handled, the citizen has other avenues of appeal, such as the prosecutor, the courts, the mayor, the governor, legislators, the U.S. Department of Justice, and the civil rights commissions.

On the other hand, every police department must have formal procedures for properly investigating and resolving complaints against police personnel. These procedures should provide for a full and fair processing of all citizen grievances and complaints regarding the conduct of any police officer. Generally speaking, internal review procedures usually include the establishment of a board of high-ranking officers which investigates charges of misconduct by police personnel and submits its findings and recommendations to the chief of police.

---

[8]President's Commission on Law Enforcement and Administration of Justice, p. 102.

Charges of police misconduct may originate from within the police agency—that is, may be brought by another officer or employee—or complaints may be initiated by citizens who feel aggrieved. Once complaints or charges of police misconduct are made, a thorough and impartial investigation must be conducted and proper discipline administered against the guilty officer. There should be no "whitewash" or "cover-up" of proven cases of police misconduct, for to allow such incidents to occur will only result in negative police-community relations, a loss of public confidence, and thus ineffective police service to the community. O. W. Wilson, a noted police authority, has made this point clear: "If the police do not take a vigorous stand on the matter of internal investigation, outside groups—such as review boards—will step into the void."[9]

If a charge of police misconduct is established, various disciplinary actions are taken, depending upon the seriousness of the act. These include an oral reprimand, written reprimand, suspension from the force for a specified number of days, and dismissal from the police department. Of course, any police officer who violates the law should be prosecuted and dealt with in court as any other citizen would be under similar circumstances.

POLICE BRUTALITY

In recent years, there have been highly vocal complaints by some citizens alleging police brutality. These have been used as the basis for demanding the establishment of civilian review boards to supervise police agencies, but they have also been largely responsible for the initiation of extensive police-community relations programs. Some charges of police brutality have been justified, others have not.

What is police brutality? In 1966 Albert J. Reiss, Jr., a well-known and respected sociologist, conducted an extensive study of police-citizen encounters in the cities of Boston, Chicago, and Washington, D.C. to determine, among other things, the extent of police mistreatment of citizens, whether or not police mistreat Negroes more than whites, and what citizens mean by police brutality.[10] Reiss found that by police brutality citizens mostly refer to the following police practices:

---

[9]Wilson and McLaren, p. 208.

[10]Albert J. Reiss, Jr., *Police Brutality—Answers to Key Questions* (New York: Warner Modular Publications, Inc., 1973), Reprint 46, pp. 1-10.

1.   The use of undignified, profane, or foul language.
2.   Police orders to citizens to move on or return to their homes.
3.   The stopping and questioning of people and the search of their persons or cars.
4.   Threats to use physical force if people did not heed police orders.
5.   The use of physical force against citizens.[11]

During a seven-week period, the Reiss study group made these findings: (1) force was used improperly in 37 cases; (2) in all, 44 citizens had been assaulted, but in 15 of these cases no one was arrested; (3) of those 15, eight had not resisted the police verbally or physically and seven had resisted; (4) an arrest was made in 22 cases; (5) force was used against 13 persons in the police station when other police were present; (6) force was applied in two cases when there was no verbal or physical resistance to the arrest; (7) in two other cases the police applied force to a handcuffed offender in the field, and (8) in five cases the offender did resist arrest, but the police continued to use force even after he had been subdued.[12] However, the Reiss study further concluded that of the 44 cases of assaults on citizens, about one-half of the individuals appeared to be little more than physically bruised, and in three cases the use of police force was great enough to require the citizen to be hospitalized.

As to the police mistreatment of Negroes and whites, Reiss concluded, "The fact is that the rate of excessive force for all white citizens in encounters with the police is twice that for Negro citizens."[13] In fact, it was generally concluded that at the most white suspects are more likely to be improperly treated by the police than Negro suspects are, and at the least the rates of police mistreatment of Negroes and whites are comparable.

There is no question that police brutality or misconduct exists, just as inappropriate behavior occurs in many other professions. Of course, what is important is that all improper or brutal conduct be eliminated in all professions, including the police. The careful selection, training, education, discipline, and supervision of the police, as well as citizen interest in good police work, are the best antidote to police misconduct. Therefore, the development of sound police-community relations programs is an important part of police work,

---

[11]Ibid., p. 2.
[12]Ibid., pp. 3-4.
[13]Ibid., p. 7.

and it can contribute immeasurably to the eradication of needless police-citizen conflicts.

POLICE ETHICS

The police are entrusted with enforcement of the criminal law, and therefore high ethical standards are more essential for the police than for many other groups in society. If a policeman violates the law or fails to enforce it, he dishonors the law and the authority he represents. Dishonesty within a police agency will quickly undermine public confidence in the police and the administration of justice process, for the policeman is the law to most citizens.[14]

It is also important to remember that the dishonest policeman is usually influenced by dishonest politicians, businessmen, and private citizens. Police are subjected to many conflicting pressures, for they are often required to enforce laws, such as those regarding traffic and gambling, which are unpopular with many members of the community. When the public objects to the enforcement of such laws, the policeman is often tempted to accept bribes and favors or to ignore violations. Dishonest policemen make the "headlines," and they negatively affect the morale of thousands of honest policemen and certainly undermine public confidence and support for the police.

Goldstein listed some of the most common types of corrupt practices by the police. These include: (1) failing to arrest and prosecute persons whom the police know have violated the laws involving traffic violators, gamblers, homosexuals, prostitutes, narcotics users, and those engaged in organized crime; (2) agreeing not to pursue an investigation when such would produce evidence leading to a criminal charge; (3) agreeing not to inspect premises where illegal activity is known to occur; (4) reducing the seriousness of a charge against an offender; (5) agreeing to alter testimony at a trial or the failure to provide all evidence at trial; and (6) influencing departmental recommendations regarding the granting of liquor or amusement licenses by not submitting derogatory information.[15]

What is the extent of police dishonesty or corruption in the

---

[14]The reader is referred to the following recent study on police corruption: Herbert Goldstein, *Police Corruption* (Washington, D.C.: The Police Foundation, 1975).

[15]Herman Goldstein, pp. 16-19.

United States? Field studies completed by the President's Commission on Law Enforcement and Administration of Justice revealed that, at least in some cities, a significant number of officers engaged in varying forms of criminal and unethical conduct.[16] A 1970 investigation of corruption in the New York City Police Department, mandated by the mayor of that city, was initiated because of newspaper reports that charged widespread police corruption and official laxity in dealing with such corruption.[17] The Knapp Commission, so named in recognition of its chairman Whitman Knapp, did find corruption to be widespread in the New York City Police Department.[18] The Commission concluded that corruption took various forms, but its most sophisticated form involved plainclothesmen assigned to enforce gambling laws. Both plainclothes officers and their supervisors were involved, as well as some uniformed personnel. The nature of police corruption in the New York City Police Department included gambling and narcotics payoffs, fixing court cases, shaking down a tow-truck operator, accepting bribes, receiving stolen merchandise from drug addicts, extortion, and the "fixing" of traffic tickets or, because of a payoff, allowing motorists to park illegally.[19] A number of plainclothesmen and uniformed police officers were indicted as a result of the Knapp Commission investigation.

The Chicago Police Department was hit by allegations of corruption and brutality in 1973, and a police captain and 18 other policemen were found guilty by a federal jury of extorting money from tavern owners; 21 more policemen have been convicted since then and 13 more are still under indictment.[20]

The above are specific examples of police corruption in the nation's two largest urban city police departments. There is no question that unethical or illegal police conduct occurs in some police agencies in the United States. The extent and nature of such conduct varies from department to department. What is equally important to remember is that most policemen are *not* corrupt.

---

[16]President's Commission on Law Enforcement and the Administration of Justice, p. 208.

[17]Commission to Investigate Allegations of Police Corruption and the City's Anti-Corruption Procedures, *The Knapp Commission Report on Police Corruption* (New York: George Braziller, 1973).

[18]Ibid., p. 1 of the Summary.

[19]Ibid., pp. 1-11.

[20]Monty Hoyt, "Top Chicago Police Charting Reforms," *Christian Science Monitor* [Boston], November 21, 1973.

CAUSES OF POLICE CORRUPTION

Many factors contribute to police dishonesty. They include negative political control, dishonest police supervisors and fellow officers, poor recruitment, training, and salaries, and the isolation of the police from the community.[21]

Improper political influence or dominance of police prevents the police from adequately discharging their responsibilities. When political "pull" and preference are introduced, the welfare of the political party, rather than that of the people, is given primary consideration. Once a political machine control is established over a police department, votes can be won and campaign contributions can be obtained by granting favors to those who come into conflict with the law, seek relief from bothersome civic duties, or want to avoid exacting legal regulations. Traffic violation summonses can be "fixed"; criminal charges can be "adjusted" or not prosecuted; police officers can be "persuaded" not to appear as witnesses; evidence can be "lost"; investigations can be "bogged down"; juries can be controlled.[22]

Another major reason why police dishonesty occurs is because many private citizens contribute to it or excuse it. Some citizens use their positions of authority to give small gifts or gratuities with the expectation that the police will overlook their minor law violations. Businessmen and private citizens often want to bribe policemen to ignore illegal parking or traffic violations.

Finally, the police must attract, and retain, persons of high character. This is only possible through a non-political merit system which will recruit and appoint new police officers on the basis of their intellectual and emotional fitness and not on the basis of political influence. Furthermore, the police must be adequately compensated for their work, and they must be regularly and professionally educated and trained.

PREVENTING POLICE CORRUPTION

There are many ways in which police corruption can be prevented, or eliminated if it exists. As earlier mentioned, negative political control of the police must be removed, and a good civil

---

[21]President's Commission on Law Enforcement and Administration of Justice, pp. 210-12.

[22]Robert G. Caldwell, p. 283.

service system initiated to allow for the professional recruitment, appointment, training, and promotion of personnel. However, of great importance is the requirement that all citizens demand ethical and professional police services by pressuring their political leaders to implement such services in their respective communities.

Police agencies themselves should insist that all their administrators should be responsible for rooting out corruption in their areas of responsibility and should be held accountable for doing so. An internal Investigation and Inspection Division should be established, and this unit should be directly responsible to the Chief of Police. Its principal responsibility is to investigate specific cases of police misconduct or corruption and to assist in the prosecution of officers and citizens involved in illegal activity. If a policeman knows that participation in corrupt activities will result in his being detected, apprehended, and convicted, the deterrent affect will greatly reduce such behavior. Finally, every officer must be taught the importance of ethics in law enforcement. Through training, each officer should be taught the types of actions he should take when he witnesses or learns of dishonest acts on the part of another officer, and all officers should understand their obligation to rid the profession of the unethical.

Many police departments require their members to sign a code of ethics similar to the following one adopted by the International Association of Chiefs of Police:

LAW ENFORCEMENT CODE OF ETHICS

AS A LAW ENFORCEMENT OFFICER, my fundamental duty is to serve mankind; to safeguard lives and property; to protect the innocent against deception, the weak against oppression or intimidation, and the peaceful against violence or disorder; and to respect the Constitutional rights of all men to liberty, equality and justice.

I WILL keep my private life unsullied as an example to all; maintain courageous calm in the face of danger, scorn, or ridicule; develop self-restraint; and be constantly mindful of the welfare of others. Honest in thought and deed in both my personal and official life, I will be exemplary in obeying the laws of the land and the regulations of my department. Whatever I see or hear of a confidential nature or that is confided to me in my official capacity will be kept ever secret unless revelation is necessary in the performance of my duty.

I WILL never act officiously or permit personal feelings, prejudices, animosities or friendships to influence my decisions. With no compromise for crime and with relentless prosecution of criminals, I will enforce the law courteously and appropriately without fear or favor, malice or ill will, never employing unnecessary force or violence and never accepting gratuities.

I RECOGNIZE the badge of my office as a symbol of public faith, and I accept it as a public trust to be held so long as I am true to the ethics of the police service. I will constantly strive to achieve these objectives and ideals, dedicating myself·before God to my chosen profession . . . law enforcement.

APPENDIX A

SELECTED PROVISIONS OF THE
UNITED STATES CONSTITUTION

ARTICLE I

Sect. 1. All legislative powers herein granted shall be vested in a Congress of the United States, which shall consist of a Senate and House of Representatives.

Sect. 2. The House of Representatives shall choose their Speaker and other officers; and shall have the sole power of impeachment.

Sect. 3. The Senate shall have the sole power to try all impeachments. When sitting for that purpose, they shall be on oath or affirmation. When the President of the United States is tried, the Chief Justice shall preside: and no person shall be convicted without the concurrence of two-thirds of the members present.

Judgment in cases of impeachment shall not extend further than to removal from office, and disqualification to hold and enjoy any office of honor, trust or profit under the United States; but the party convicted shall nevertheless be liable and subject to indictment, trial, judgment and punishment, according to law.

Sect. 8. The Congress shall have power:

To lay and collect taxes, duties, imposts and excises, to pay the debts and provide for the common defense and general welfare of the United States; but all duties, imposts and excises shall be uniform throughout the United States;

To borrow money on the credit of the United States;

To regulate commerce with foreign nations, and among the several states, and with the Indian tribes;

To establish an uniform rule of naturalization, and uniform laws on the subject of bankruptcies throughout the United States;

To coin money, regulate the value thereof, and of foreign coin, and fix the standard of weights and measures;

To provide for the punishment of counterfeiting the securities and current coin of the United States;

To establish post-offices and post-roads;

To promote the progress of science and useful arts, by securing for limited times to authors and inventors the exclusive right to their respective writings and discoveries;

To constitute tribunals inferior to the Supreme Court;

To define. and punish piracies and felonies committed on the high seas, and offenses against the law of nations;

To declare war, grant letters of marque and reprisal, and make rules concerning captures on land and water;

To raise and support armies, but no appropriation of money to that use shall be for a longer term than two years;

To provide and maintain a navy;

To make rules for the government and regulation of the land and naval forces;

To provide for calling forth the militia to execute the laws of the union, suppress insurrections and repel invasions;

To provide for organizing, arming, and disciplining the militia, and for governing such part of them as may be employed in the service of the United States, reserving to the States respectively, the appointment of the officers, and the authority of training the militia according to the discipline prescribed by Congress;

To exercise exclusive legislation in all cases whatsoever, over such district (not exceeding ten miles square) as may by cession of particular states, and the acceptance of Congress, become the seat of the government of the United States, and to exercise like authority over all places purchased by the consent of the legislature of the state in which the same shall be, for the erection of forts, magazines, arsenals, dock-yards, and other needful buildings;—And

To make all laws which shall be necessary and proper for carrying into execution the foregoing powers, and all other powers vested by this Constitution in the government of the United States, or in any department or office thereof.

Sect. 9.   The privilege of the writ of *habeas corpus* shall not be suspended, unless when in cases of rebellion or invasion the public safety may require it.

No bill of attainder or *ex post facto* law shall be passed.

Sect. 10.   No state shall enter into any treaty, alliance, or confederation; grant letters of marque and reprisal; coin money; emit bills of credit; make any thing but gold and silver coin a tender in payment of debts; pass any bill of attainder, *ex post facto* law, or law impairing the obligation of contracts, or grant any title of nobility.

ARTICLE II

Sect. 1.   The executive power shall be vested in a President of the United States of America.

Sect. 2.   The President shall be commander in chief of the army and navy of the United States, and of the militia of the several states, when called into the actual service of the United States; he may require the opinion, in writing, of the principal officer in each of the executive departments, upon any subject relating to the duties of their respective offices, and he shall have power to grant reprieves and pardons for offenses against the United States, except in cases of impeachment.

ARTICLE III

Sect. 1.   The judicial power of the United States, shall be vested in one Supreme Court, and in such inferior courts as the Congress may from time to time ordain and establish. The judges, both of the Supreme and inferior Court, shall hold their offices during good behavior, and shall, at stated times, receive for their services, a compensation, which shall not be diminished during their continuance in office.

Sect. 2.   The judicial power shall extend to all cases, in law and equity, arising under this Constitution, the laws of the United States, and treaties made, or which shall be made, under their authority; to all cases affecting ambassadors, other public ministers, and consuls; to all cases of admiralty and maritime jurisdiction; to controversies to which the United States shall be a party; to controversies between two or more States, between a state and citizens of another state, between citizens of different states, between citizens of the same state claiming lands under grants of different states, and between a state, or the citizens thereof, and foreign states, citizens or subjects.

In all cases affecting ambassadors, other public ministers and consuls, and those in which a state shall be a party, the Supreme Court shall have original jurisdiction. In all the other cases before mentioned, the Supreme Court shall have appellate jurisdiction, both as to law and fact, with such exceptions, and under such regulations as the Congress shall make.

The trial of all crimes, except in cases of impeachment, shall be by jury; and such trial shall be held in the state where the said crimes shall have been committed; but when not committed within any state, the trial shall be at such place or places as the Congress may by law have directed.

Sect. 3.   Treason against the United States, shall consist only in levying war against them, or in adhering to their enemies, giving them aid and comfort. No person shall be convicted of treason unless on the testimony of two witnesses to the same overt act, or on confession in open court.

The Congress shall have power to declare the punishment of treason, but no attainder of treason shall work corruption of blood, or forfeiture, except during the life of the person attainted.

ARTICLE IV

Sect. 1.   Full faith and credit shall be given in each state to the public acts, records and judicial proceedings of every other state. And the Congress may by general laws prescribe the manner in which such acts, records and proceedings shall be proved, and the effect thereof.

Sect. 2.   The citizens of each state shall be entitled to all privileges and immunities of citizens in the several states.

A person charged in any state with treason, felony, or other crime, who shall flee from justice, and be found in another state, shall, on demand of the executive authority of the state from which he fled, be delivered up, to be removed to the state having jurisdiction of the crime.

Sect. 4.   The United States shall guarantee to every state in this Union a republican form of government, and shall protect each of them against invasion; and on application of the legislature, or of the executive (when the legislature, cannot be convened) against domestic violence.

ARTICLE VI

This constitution, and the laws of the United States which shall be made in pursuance thereof; and all treaties made, or which shall be made, under the authority of the United States, shall be the supreme law of the land; and the judges in every state shall be bound thereby, any thing in the constitution or laws of any state to the contrary notwithstanding.

The senators and representatives before mentioned, and the members of the several state legislatures, and all executive and judicial officers, both of the United States and of the several states, shall be bound by oath or affirmation, to support this constitution; but no religious test shall ever be required as a qualification to any office or public trust under the United States.

AMENDMENTS

AMENDMENT I. (1791)

Congress shall make no law respecting an establishment of religion, or prohibiting the free exercise thereof; or abridging the freedom of speech, or of the press; or of the right of the people peaceably to assemble, and to petition the Government for a redress of grievances.

AMENDMENT II. (1791)

A well regulated Militia, being necessary to the security of a free State, the right of the people to keep and bear Arms shall not be infringed.

AMENDMENT III. (1791)

No Soldier shall, in time of peace be quartered in any house, without the consent of the Owner, nor in time of war, but in a manner to be prescribed by law.

AMENDMENT IV. (1791)

The right of the people to be secure in their persons, houses, papers, and effects, against unreasonable searches and seizures, shall not be violated, and no Warrants shall issue, but upon probable cause, supported by Oath or affirmation, and particularly describing the place to be searched, and the persons or things to be seized.

AMENDMENT V. (1791)

No person shall be held to answer for a capital, or otherwise infamous crime, unless on a presentment or indictment of a Grand Jury, except in cases arising in the land or naval forces, or in the Militia, when in actual service in time of War or public danger; nor shall any person be subject for the same offense to be twice put in jeopardy of life or limb; nor shall be compelled in any criminal case to be a witness against himself, nor be deprived of life, liberty, or property, without due process of law; nor shall private property be taken for public use, without just compensation.

AMENDMENT VI. (1791)

In all criminal prosecutions, the accused shall enjoy the right to a speedy and public trial, by an impartial jury of the State and district wherein the crime shall have been committed, which district shall have been previously ascertained by law, and to be informed of the nature and cause of the accusation; to be confronted with the witnesses against him; to have compulsory process for obtaining witnesses in his favor, and to have the Assistance of Counsel for his defense.

AMENDMENT VII. (1791)

In Suits at common law, where the value in controversy shall exceed twenty dollars, the right of trial by jury shall be preserved, and no fact tried by a jury, shall be otherwise reexamined in any Court of the United States, than according to the rules of the common law.

AMENDMENT VIII. (1791)

Excessive bail shall not be required, nor excessive fines imposed, nor cruel and unusual punishments inflicted.

AMENDMENT IX. (1791)

The enumeration in the Constitution, of certain rights, shall not be construed to deny or disparage others retained by the people.

AMENDMENT X. (1791)

The powers not delegated to the United States by the Constitution, nor prohibited by it to the States, are reserved to the States respectively, or to the people.

AMENDMENT XIII. (1865)

Sect. 1. Neither slavery nor involuntary servitude, except as a punishment for crime whereof the party shall have been duly convicted, shall exist within the United States, or any place subject to their jurisdiction.

Sect. 2.   Congress shall have power to enforce this article by appropriate legislation.

AMENDMENT XIV. (1868)

Sect. 1.   All persons born or naturalized in the United States, and subject to the jurisdiction thereof, are citizens of the United States and of the State wherein they reside. No State shall make or enforce any law which shall abridge the privileges or immunities of citizens of the United States; nor shall any State deprive any person of life, liberty, or property, without due process of law; nor deny to any person within its jurisdiction the equal protection of the laws.

Sect. 5.   The Congress shall have power to enforce, by appropriate legislation, the provisions of this article.

AMENDMENT XV. (1870)

Sect. 1.   The right of citizens of the United States to vote shall not be denied or abridged by the United States or by any State on account of race, color, or previous condition of servitude.

Sect. 2.   The Congress shall have power to enforce this article by appropriate legislation.

APPENDIX B

CHART NO. 1.   **VERY SMALL DEPARTMENT
UP TO 25 PERSONNEL**

Suggested Organizational Structures

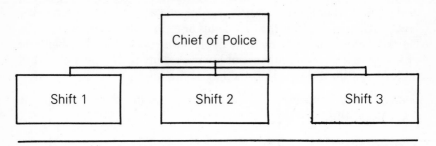

CHART NO. 2.   **SMALL DEPARTMENT
20 TO 100 PERSONNEL**

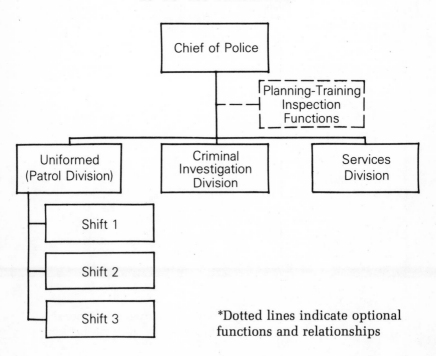

*Dotted lines indicate optional
functions and relationships

CHART NO. 3.   **MEDIUM DEPARTMENT
80 TO 250 PERSONNEL**

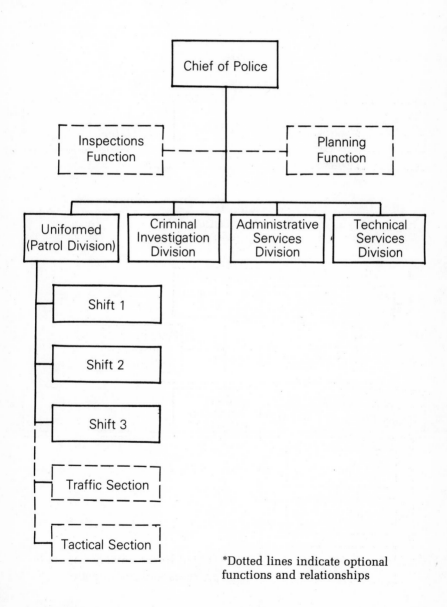

*Dotted lines indicate optional
functions and relationships

CHART NO. 4.   **LARGE DEPARTMENT
200 TO 1,200 PERSONNEL**

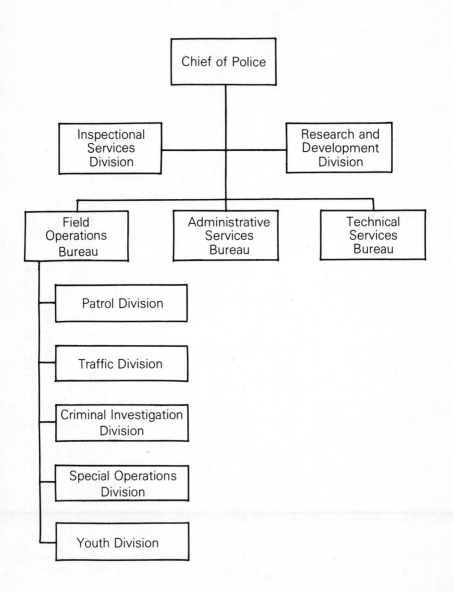

CHART NO. 5.

VERY LARGE DEPARTMENT OVER 1,200 PERSONNEL

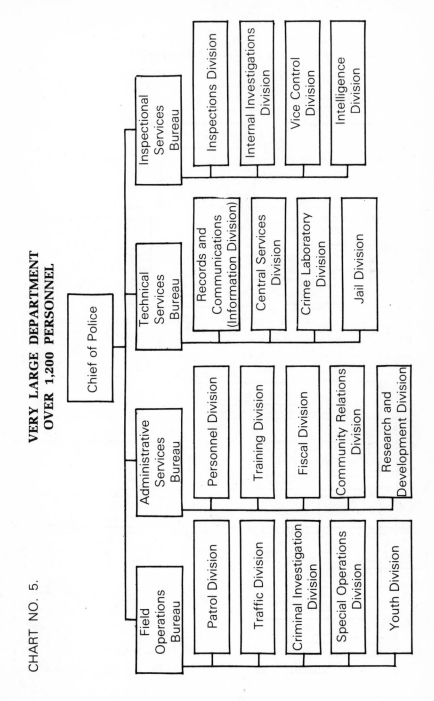

CHART NO. 6.   **STEPS IN CRIMINAL PROSECUTION**

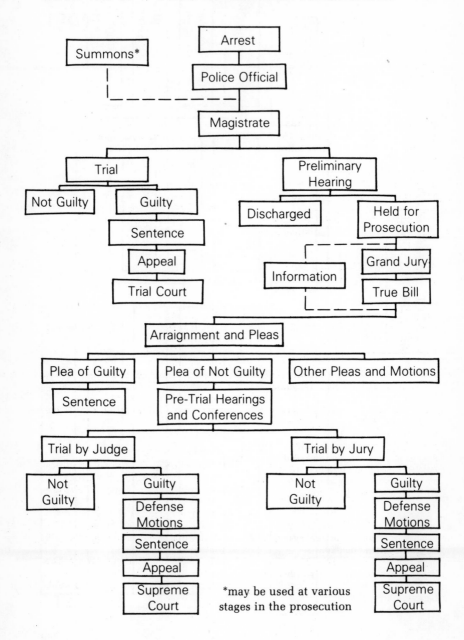

Summons*

Arrest

Police Official

Magistrate

Trial

Not Guilty

Guilty

Sentence

Appeal

Trial Court

Preliminary Hearing

Discharged

Held for Prosecution

Information

Grand Jury

True Bill

Arraignment and Pleas

Plea of Guilty

Sentence

Plea of Not Guilty

Pre-Trial Hearings and Conferences

Other Pleas and Motions

Trial by Judge

Not Guilty

Guilty

Defense Motions

Sentence

Appeal

Supreme Court

Trial by Jury

Not Guilty

Guilty

Defense Motions

Sentence

Appeal

Supreme Court

*may be used at various stages in the prosecution

INDEX

vestigation of, 330; role in crime prevention, 299-301, 301-303; salaries in
early America, 10. See also city police;
law enforcement; metropolitan police,
reform of police; state police.
police-community relations, 323-329;
role in crime prevention, 303-305
police force, development of paid, 7
Police Foundation, 69-70
police services (field): criminal investigation, 55; juvenile work, 309-312, 318-
320; patrol, 54; traffic control, 55; vice
control, 55-56
police services (technical): administration, 52-53; budget and property management, 52; criminalistics, 53; internal
inspection, 50; jail administration,
52-53; legal services, 53-54; planning
and recordkeeping, 50; public education, 51-52; training, 51
police system, development of in early
England, 5
police work: as a profession, 74; benefits
of, 76; eligibility requirements for,
77-80, 83-84
political influence on police, 14, 15; and
police corruption, 334; in early
America, 10, 11
political structure and vice, 136
polygraph, 125-127
pornography, 137
portrait parle, 122
posse comitatus, defined, 175-176
Postal Service, 16, 17
Postmaster General, Assistant, office of,
49-50
Powell, Justice, 268-269n
preliminary hearing, function of, 210-
211; in criminal proceedings, 264
President's Commission on Law Enforcement and Administration of Justice, 1, 79n, 89, 138, 280, 299, 315, 327,
329, 333
pretrial hearings, use of, 216
principals in crime, defined, 164-165
prison conditions, 293
prison farms, 291
prisoners' aid groups, 305
prisoners, disposition of, 179
prisons, services offered in, 293. See also
corrections.
probable cause, 180, 181; as requirement
for surveillance, 190; for arrest, 171,
172, 175; search based on, 185
probation: definition and purpose, 289;

advantages and disadvantages of, 289-
290; for misdemeanants, 288; programs, 288. See also detention centers.
probation officers, need for in juvenile
work, 322
private detective agencies, 3
private police, 3
privacy, right to, 189; limits on, 191
professionalization of the police, 12, 74,
89-90
prosecution, steps in criminal, 208-223
prostitution, 137
protection of home, right to use force in,
170
protective custody, 309; use of by police,
179
proximate cause, defined, 163-164
psychological theory on criminal behavior, 25-29
public attitudes toward police, in early
America, 11. See also police-
community relations.
punishment: cruel and unusual, 267,
267n; purposes of, 230-234. See also
corrections.

qualifications for police work, 74-75

racism, charges of police, 330-331
racketeering, 134
Radio Communications Systems, 71-73
rape, defined, 160
"rattlewatch," 9
reasonable grounds, defined, 175
recidivism rates among juveniles, 306
recordkeeping by police departments,
63-66
recreation and criminal behavior, 35-36
recruitment of police, 75-76
reform of police: in early America, 11, 12;
in early England, 8
reformatories, 287
regional police concept, 18
rehabilitation, 298; as a purpose of
punishment, 230; of juvenile delinquents, 321
Reiss, Albert J., 330
religion, and criminal behavior, 34-35
research, defined, 66; uses of in law enforcement, 67-68
Reserve Aero Squadron, 97
Revenue Cutter Service, 16
right to bail, 209
right to counsel, 209, 210, 213n, 214,
217-218, 222, 264-265; in Escobedo
case, 277

LAW ENFORCEMENT CODE OF ETHICS

AS A LAW ENFORCEMENT OFFICER, my fundamental duty is to serve mankind; to safeguard lives and property; to protect the innocent against deception, the peaceful against violence or disorder; and to respect the Constitutional rights of all men to liberty, equality and justice.

I WILL keep my private life unsullied as an example to all; maintain courageous calm in the face of danger, scorn, or ridicule; develop self-restraint; and be constantly mindful of the welfare of others. Honest in thought and deed in both my personal and official life, I will be exemplary in obeying the laws of the land and the regulations of my department. Whatever I see or hear of a confidential nature or that is confided to me in my official capacity will be kept ever secret unless revelation is necessary in the performance of my duty.

I WILL never act officiously or permit personal feelings, prejudices, animosities or friendships to influence my decisions. With no compromise for crime and with relentless prosecution of criminals, I will enforce the law courteously and appropriately without fear or favor, malice or ill will, never employing unnecessary force or violence and never accepting gratuities.

I RECOGNIZE the badge of my office as a symbol of public faith, and I accept it as a public trust to be held so long as I am true to the ethics of the police service. I will constantly strive to achieve these objectives and ideals, dedicating myself before God to my chosen profession . . . law enforcement.